PRINCIPLES
AND PRACTICES
OF
RESIDENTIAL
CONSTRUCTION

PRINCIPLES AND PRACTICES OF RESIDENTIAL CONSTRUCTION

JOSEPH D. FALCONE

PRENTICE-HALL, INC., Englewood Cliffs, New Jersey 07632

Library of Congress Cataloging-in-Publication Data

Falcone, Joseph D.
    Principles and practices of residential
construction.

    Bibliography: p.
    Includes index.
    1. Dwellings—Design and construction.
2. Building.   I. Title.
TH4811.F36 1987   690'.837   86-25423
ISBN 0-13-702002-3

Editorial/production supervision
  and interior design: *Mary Carnis*
Cover design: *20/20 Services, Inc.*
Manufacturing buyer: *John Hall*
Page layout: *Peggy Finnerty*

Portions of all chapters are taken from *How to Design, Build, Remodel and Maintain Your Home*
by Joseph D. Falcone, © 1978, John Wiley & Sons, Inc., New York, N.Y.,
reprinted by permission of the publisher.

Printed in the United States of America

10 9 8 7 6 5 4 3 2 1

ISBN 0-13-702002-3 025

Prentice-Hall International (UK) Limited, *London*
Prentice-Hall of Australia Pty. Limited, *Sydney*
Prentice-Hall Canada Inc., *Toronto*
Prentice-Hall Hispanoamericana, S.A., *Mexico*
Prentice-Hall of India Private Limited, *New Delhi*
Prentice-Hall of Japan, Inc., *Tokyo*
Prentice-Hall of Southeast Asia Pte. Ltd., *Singapore*
Editora Prentice-Hall do Brasil, Ltda., *Rio de Janeiro*

To my wife, *Flora*
and to my daughters, *Nancy* and *Elena*

Contents

Preface

"Be it ever so humble, there is no place like home." These historical words symbolize people's feelings about their homes. Considerable time, effort, energy, and money are necessary to make homes comfortable, secure, attractive, and as maintenance-free as possible. The selection of location, type of construction, and design is of prime importance. People must "live with" the building material selected for home building.

This book has been written for the student who considers light-frame construction a mystery. When more than one person knows a fact, it is no longer a secret or a mystery. That is the purpose of this book—to reveal that so-called "mystery" in residential construction. Anything we do not understand is a mystery. This book will unravel that mystery.

It begins at the beginning, site selection, and continues in sequential order to completion. Each chapter is self-explanatory in detail, using simple terms and explanations. The many illustrations strengthen the text and lead to a better and easier understanding.

The book has been written especially for students in secondary, college, university, trade, technical, and vocational schools who are concentrating their studies on architecture and construction. The book presents acceptable, sound construction principles for light-frame construction of a house. The three essentials for successful completion of a house are: an efficient plan; proper use of materials; and good, sound, acceptable construction practices. It also deals with the mechanical part of the house, such as plumbing, heating, electricity, air conditioning, and ventilation, for no house is complete without these elements. In short, this book deals with the "whole house," not simply with its parts.

The latest developments and trends are presented to inform the student of up-to-date advances in construction techniques. The entire process, from site selection to moving in, is included for a complete, thorough, easy-to-understand review of house construction.

Joseph D. Falcone

ACKNOWLEDGMENTS

Portions of the text are taken from *How to Design, Build, Remodel and Maintain Your Home*, by Joseph D. Falcone, copyright 1978, John Wiley & Sons, Inc., New York, N.Y., reprinted by permission of the publisher. The following figures and tables are also from this source and are reprinted with permission: Figures: 3-1, 4-2, 8-19, 8-22, 8-23, 9-5a and b, 9-6, 9-7, 9-11b, 9-12b, 9-13 to 9-16, 9-17c, 9-18, 9-19, 9-21 to 9-27, part of 9-28, 10-1, 10-6, 10-13b and c, 10-14 to 10-17, 10-19, 10-22, 11-2, 11-5, 11-6, 11-8, 11-9, 12-1, 12-3, 12-4, 12-9 to 12-11, 16-2c and d, 16-8 to 16-11, 16-14, 16-15, 16-20, 16-21, 16-22b, 17-2, 17-6a, 17-8, 17-10, 17-11, 18-11 to 18-13, 18-16 to 18-18, 19-2, 19-19, 19-25, 19-28, 19-31, 19-32, 19-35b, 20-1, 20-2, 20-3, 21-6, 21-7, 21-9 to 21-12, 22-1 to 22-9, 23-1 to 23-4, 23-8 to 23-18; and Tables: 9-1, 9-2, 11-1, 12-1, 19-2.

1

The Construction Industry

INTRODUCTION

By providing houses for people, the construction industry contributes to human security, comfort, and relaxation. There are many jobs in construction that are open to beginners, ranging from laborer to company owner. The financial rewards are satisfying, and the sense of creativity and accomplishment is not equaled in any other job. The construction worker can choose either inside or outside work, and the opportunity of constantly moving about provides an ongoing, built-in physical exercise routine.

Construction workers are offered the opportunity to work with many people and learn to get along with co-workers. Not only does the industry offer a chance for gainful employment, but it also gives one the opportunity and "know-how" to perform the many jobs required around the house in which the construction worker lives. With this background, construction workers can also perform small jobs around the house for other people, thus obtaining additional income. There will be a need for construction workers as long as there are people.

OVERVIEW OF TIMBER

The sixteenth-century Spanish explorers Ponce de León and de Soto were the first white men to penetrate the forests of North America. Little did they realize the great value and future economic importance of the vast areas of virgin timber.

From early colonial days, the history of the United States has been closely associated with our forest wealth. To some of the pioneers, the forest was an enemy, to be fought and conquered to make room for the planting

1

of crops. To all, it offered a fine, versatile building material with which to build homes, forts, stockades, boats, and ships.

The development of the English colonies in the seventeenth century marked the beginning of the commercial use of timber. There is on record a sawmill at Jamestown, Virginia, as early as 1625, believed to be the first commercial sawmill in the United States. Early mills were powered by water and often doubled as gristmills. Such a mill was operated by George Washington at his Mount Vernon estate. The sawmill soon became an essential factor in almost every colony, supplying its lumber requirements and often providing a surplus for exporting.

In 1803, at New Orleans, a man built a new type of mill. This new mill had a circular saw and was operated by steam power. The rapid increase in the population of the country toward the end of the nineteenth century resulted in a tremendous demand for construction lumber. The pioneers quickly learned of the unusual strength and versatility of wood, and as the century developed, numerous buildings, many of which are still standing today and some of which are historically famous, were constructed of wood.

Not long ago, many people believed that the lumber industry could not continue without eventually exhausting the forests. But lumberpersons, in cooperation with federal and state forestry agencies, have adapted forestry practices involving fire prevention and control, selective logging, and reforestation. More and more manufacturers of lumber are placing their operations on a sustained-yield basis, which means planting a tree for every one cut. Such a practice will make the forest industry permanent.

WOODWORKING

The facets of woodworking and construction are vast and varied, providing an opportunity for many types of jobs. In addition, woodworking is one of the most popular leisure-time activities in the United States. Millions of people earn their living by working in some field of the wood-related industries. There are unlimited opportunities for skilled, semiskilled, limited-skilled, and unskilled woodworking trade occupations. In addition, there are many jobs related to or directly associated with the industry.

Unskilled and limited-skilled people begin as helpers in the industry and progress to higher-paying jobs as their skill increases. This is usually done through on-the-job training. Most employers prefer their workers to have at least a high school education. Those who wish to enter the industry without a high school education can attend classes in the evening while working during the day.

Generally, a limited-skilled worker or helper will go through several steps to become a master craftsperson or skilled worker. A good source of training besides on-the-job training is education in a public or private trade, vocational, or technical school, with concentration in a particular work area. The major subjects needed for advancement are: reading of plans, mathematics (including shop math and geometry), and English.

The order of advancement begins with the helper or apprentice, advances to the semiskilled, and ends at the master craftsperson or skilled level. The time required to advance depends on the individual, but generally it will take about three years to reach a craftsperson level of proficiency.

CARPENTRY

The craft or skill of shaping, cutting, fitting, and assembling wood is called carpentry and is performed by a carpenter. The carpenter is the backbone of the construction industry, and the position is considered one of importance and prominence.

The carpenter is involved in most of the construction of a home. He or she builds foundation forms, floors, walls, ceilings, roofs, and interior finishes. He or she knows how different woods will react and what tool to use for a specific job. The carpenter must know the various construction techniques and must be able to read and interpret plans. There are many levels of carpenter from carpenter's helper to skilled carpenter.

JOB SATISFACTION

People in construction must be all-around workers with many skills and a thorough knowledge of building construction. They are important craftspeople on the construction team. The income earned by construction workers is above average and provides a good living. The satisfaction and pride that results in good craftsmanship is an experience that is not enjoyed in many other occupations. The successful worker must have the ability to cooperate and get along with other workers, and to show courtesy, respect, loyalty, and honesty.

GROSS NATIONAL PRODUCT

The goods and services required in the field of construction are greater in number and variety that in any other occupation. More people are employed directly in the construction industry or related fields than in any other field of employment. Generally, there is no season of employment; construction workers are needed at all times of the year. Job selection in the construction field is almost unlimited. Construction has become more than a job requiring working with tools. It cannot be defined that simply; it would take many books to describe all the construction-related jobs. For those who have the abilities or are willing to learn, the field of construction is one of enormous opportunity.

LABOR UNIONS

A "closed shop" company is one in which the workers are represented by a labor union. An "open shop" is nonunion.

In a closed-shop company, all workers must be members of the same union. All members must pay union dues, which are generally deducted from wages. These dues are used for administration costs and to pay benefits to union members. Closed-shop companies must pay the workers a wage arbitrated with the union. Open-shop companies pay their workers at rates agreeable to both workers and owners, with or without benefits.

EQUIPMENT

Construction companies supply their workers with material and special tools or heavy equipment, but each worker must have personal general-purpose hand tools.

CAREERS

The following are some of the positions in the construction industry.

Apprentice

This is the beginning of all trades (see the sample application for an apprenticeship shown in Fig. 1-1). The construction industry is in the forefront in apprentice activities. Apprentices, who are paid while learning their trade, start producing almost immediately, and each job they do is carefully supervised and inspected. The quality of their work is tested as they advance from one stage of training to another (Fig. 1-2). In addition, the care with which applicants are selected, and the entrance tests required, assure, to a large extent, that the apprentice will make a good craftsperson. In 1937, Congress passed the National Apprenticeship Law, better known as the Fitzgerald Act, "to promote the furtherance of labor standards of apprenticeship. . . ." As a result of this act, the Bureau of Apprenticeship and Training was established as the national administrative agency in the Labor Department to carry out the law's objectives. Employers and vocational schools have set up and conducted apprenticeship programs throughout the country.

The following are the basic standards of apprenticeship:

1. To provide the most efficient way to train craftspeople to meet present and future needs
2. To assure an adequate supply of skilled tradespeople in relation to employment opportunities
3. To assure the community of competent craftspeople, skilled in all branches of their trades
4. To assure the consuming public of the high-quality products and services that only trained hands and minds can produce
5. To increase the individual worker's productivity
6. To give the individual worker a greater sense of security
7. To improve employer–employee relations
8. To eliminate close supervision; craftspeople are trained to use initiative, imagination, and ability in planning and performing their work
9. To provide a source of future supervisors
10. To provide the versatility to meet changing conditions
11. To attract capable young people into the industry
12. To raise general skill levels in the industry

For the young worker entering employment, apprenticeship holds these important values:

1. The opportunity to develop skills, creating greater economic security and a higher standard of living

No. _ _ _ _ _ _ _ _ _ _ _

APPLICATION FOR APPRENTICESHIP IN CARPENTRY

Desiring to become an apprentice in the Carpentry Trade, I hereby make application for an Apprenticeship to the

_ Date _
(Indenturing Agent)

Name (Please Print) _
(Last Name)   (First Name)   (Middle Name)

Address _ _ _ _ _ _ _ _ _ _ _ _ _ _ _ _ _ City _ _ _ _ _ _ _ _ _ _ _ _ _ _ _ _ _ _ _ Soc. Sec. No. _ _ _ _ _ _ _ _ _ _ _ _ _ _

Phone _ _ _ _ _ _ _ _ _ _ _ _ _ _ _ _ _ _ _

Date of Birth _ Age last Birthday _ _ _ _ _ _ _ _ _ _ _ _ _
(Month)   (Day)   (Year)

Height _ _ _ _ _ _ _ _ _ _ _ _ _ _ Weight _ _ _ _ _ _ _ _ _ _ _ _ _

Grade completed in school _ _ _ _ _ _ _ _ _ _ _ Date _ _ _ _ _ _ _ _ _ _ _ _ _ Married ( )   Single ( )
(Year)

General physical condition _

Note any physical handicaps _

_ _

Father or Guardian's Name _

Address _

His occupation _

Were you in the Armed Forces _ _ _ _ _ _ _ _ _ _ _ _ _ _ _ _ How Long? _

Have you ever worked at the Carpentry Trade? _ _ _ _ _ _ _ _ _ If so, what type of construction? _ _ _ _ _ _ _ _ _ _ _ _

_ _

Do you understand that you will be on _ _ _ _ _ _ _ _ _ _ _ days trial, if your application is approved? _ _ _ _ _ _ _ _ _

Are you willing to work for the established wage scale for Carpenter Apprentices throughtout your indenture-

ship? _

Have you read and do you understand the Apprenticeship Standards?_ _ _ _ _ _ _ _ _ _ _ _ _ _ _ _ _ _

Will you obey all rules and instructions of the Apprentice Committee? _ _ _ _ _ _ _ _ _ _ _ _ _ _ _ _ _ _

Are you willing to serve an apprenticeship of four years? _

Will you place yourself under the jurisdiction of the Apprentice Committee? _ _ _ _ _ _ _ _ _ _ _ _ _ _ _ _ _ _

Do you understand that it is compulsory for you to attend the apprentice school during the hours designated

by the apprentice committee, and that you will be accountable to the school during that time? _ _ _ _ _ _ _ _ _ _ _ _

REFERENCE OTHER THAN RELATIVES

I have known _ for two years or more, and certify that he is of good character and habits.

Personal Signatures of Vouchers

Name	Address	Business
_ _ _ _ _ _ _ _ _ _ _ _ _ _	_ _ _ _ _ _ _ _ _ _ _ _ _ _ _ _ _ _ _	_ _ _ _ _ _ _ _ _
_ _ _ _ _ _ _ _ _ _ _ _ _ _	_ _ _ _ _ _ _ _ _ _ _ _ _ _ _ _ _ _ _	_ _ _ _ _ _ _ _ _
_ _ _ _ _ _ _ _ _ _ _ _ _ _	_ _ _ _ _ _ _ _ _ _ _ _ _ _ _ _ _ _ _	_ _ _ _ _ _ _ _ _

(a)

Figure 1-1 Application for apprenticeship in carpentry. (Courtesy of Carpenters' District Council.)

ADDITIONAL INFORMATION CONCERNING YOUR FITNESS FOR AN

APPRENTICESHIP ---

CASE HISTORY

RECOMMENDATIONS OF APPRENTICESHIP COMMITTEE

On Probation Period, From_____ To_____

Qualifying Examination given------------------------------, 19------. Grade------------.
                                    (date)

We have investigated the qualifications of this applicant and recommend:

Date---------------------

Approved for apprenticeship_____Place on waiting list_____

Not approved for apprenticeship_____

Remarks: _____

	Trade Experience Period and Wage Rate		
	Period	Rate	Starting Date
	1st 6 months	_____	_____
	2nd 6 months	_____	_____
------------------------------	3rd 6 months	_____	_____
	4th 6 months	_____	_____
------------------------------	5th 6 months	_____	_____
	6th 6 months	_____	_____
------------------------------	7th 6 months	_____	_____
	8th 6 months	_____	_____

(b)

Figure 1-1 (continued)

RATING FORM FOR APPRENTICESHIP ENTRY
RECOMMENDED BY
NATIONAL JOINT CARPENTRY APPRENTICESHIP AND
TRAINING COMMITTEE

-- Joint Apprentice Committee

Name --- Social Security No. ----------------------

Address --- Phone No. ----------------------------------

City -- State ---------------------------- Zip --------------

	Yes	No
1. Minimal age requirement reflective of local standards and state statutes--------------	--------	--------
2. Minimal formal education requirement reflective of local standards-------------------	--------	--------
3. A score of 70% correct response on the "Qualifying Test for Apprenticeship and Trainee Applicant" ---	--------	--------
4. Physical qualifications, reflective of local standards and/or state statutes--------------	--------	--------

NOTE: All of the above criteria must be answered in the affirmative for an applicant to be accepted into training.

Applicant has validated experience as follows:	Points
1. Carpentry craft experience, civilian or military, _____ years, 5 points per year, 3 year maximum--	--------
2. Construction work experience (non-Carpentry), 2 points per year, 3 year maximum---------------	--------
3. Approved pre-apprenticeship experience, 5 points °--	--------
4. Approved vocational-education experience, 5 points °°-------------------------------------	--------
5. Work experience (non-construction), 1 point per year, 3 year maximum------------------------	--------
6. Experience in the regular military establishment, with honorable discharge, 2 points per year, 3 year maximum--	--------
Total------	--------

(a)

Figure 1-2   Rating form for apprenticeship entry. (Courtesy of Carpenters' District Council.)

Optional personal interview may be given with point credit from 0 - 4 points.

Four (4) points are the maximum number of points allowed for the personal interview. Each of the criteria is valenced at five-tenths (½) of a point value.

The interview should be conducted to draw from the applicant evidence of:

Points

1. Interest in the carpentry craft, .5 maximum _____ _____

2. Positive attitude towards physical labor, .5 maximum _____ _____

3. Ability to accept direction/supervision, .5 maximum _____ _____

4. Ability to work with others, .5 maximum _____ _____

5. Knowledge of the trade, .5 maximum _____ _____

6. Positive attitude towards related instruction, .5 maximum _____ _____

7. Understanding of the obligations of an apprenticeship, .5 maximum _____ _____

8. Maturation, .5 maximum _____ _____

Total_____ _____

Total from page one_____ _____

Grand Total_____ _____

°Approved pre-apprenticeship experiences are those structured and implemented by member organizations of the National Joint Carpentry Apprenticeship and Training Committee such as, but not limited to, Project Transition and Job Corps.

°°Approved vocational-education experiences are those institutionalized vocational carpentry programs utilizing the local joint carpentry apprenticeship and training committee as the technical committee advisory to the program.

(b)

Figure 1-2 (continued)

2. Further training and education, with pay
3. Assurance of a wage, with regular increases, while serving the apprenticeship
4. Opportunities for employment and advancement
5. Recognition as a skilled craftsperson in a chosen trade

Rough Carpenter

The work of the rough carpenter is generally restricted to the wood framework of a building, which includes foundation forms, floor framing, wall framing, ceiling framing, and roof framing (Fig. 1-3). The rough carpenter must learn the skill required to join the component parts of a frame building together to form a tight fit. Being a rough carpenter does not mean doing work that is a rough fit or that is less than acceptable. Careful cutting of each member is vital to the safety of the building because each member depends on the other in framing a building, and all work must be joined together properly. If the fitting or joining is not done properly, the building may suffer or fail in one or more areas. Generally, the rough carpenter works mostly outdoors.

Finish Carpenter

Once the rough carpenter has completed the framework of a building, the finish carpenter is required to install the finish work, such as doors, siding, windows, and floors. This phase of the industry is extremely important be-

Figure 1-3 Rough carpentry. (Courtesy of National Forest Products Association.)

cause the joints must be tight and carefully assembled. No hammer marks are tolerated on the finish wood. This job requires a little more skill than that of the rough carpenter.

Carpenter-in-Charge or Foreman

When carpenters become good at their jobs, they can be promoted to the position of carpenter-in-charge. The carpenter-in-charge, who may have several carpenters working for him or her, is responsible for progress, scheduling, and quality of the work and for all people working under his or her supervision. The carpenter-in-charge may or may not have the responsibility to hire or fire but is responsible for any mistakes made by carpenters working under him or her.

Superintendent

This is a position of responsibility second only to that of the owner. The superintendent is responsible for the entire project, including all workers, even the carpenter-in-charge. Generally, the superintendent does not work with tools, but acts as an administrator and may be responsible for more than one project at a time. The superintendent will assign projects to the carpenter-in-charge, maintain close supervision over all workers, and be responsible for the entire project. Part of the job is to make sure that material is available when needed, to avoid delays in the progress of the building. As a rule, the superintendent will have the responsibility to hire and fire.

Cabinetmaker

Of all the wood-related jobs, that of cabinetmaker requires the greatest amount of skill. Cabinetmakers construct and build furniture, cabinets, office equipment, and so on, using electric and hand tools. Generally, they work from a set of design drawings made by architects. The cabinetmaker must be skilled in being able to identify different wood species, often choosing wood for color, matching of grain, texture, and general appearance of the finished product. The cabinetmaker-in-charge is responsible for the finished product.

Pattern Maker

The job of the pattern maker, building models of machinery and other objects from wood to be used for production into metal, requires great skill. The skill required in reading plans is high because of the complicated product being worked on. Pattern makers must not only be skilled in woodworking, but must have knowledge of metals and alloys which will be made into molds from the wooden pattern. The model being worked on must account for the expansion and contraction of metals and must allow for how the various parts of the wooden model will be cast from metal by the foundry. An exact pattern or model must be made from wood before any casting is done.

Millworker

Basically, a millworker is a good "jack of all trades" and may be called on to repair furniture; set up furniture; do general maintenance; work with wood, metals, paints, and stains; install hardware; and even repair electrical work, plumbing, or roofing leaks.

Millwright

The person who keeps machinery in working order and sharpens knives, blades, and other cutting tools is called a millwright. Millwrights must have a thorough knowledge of the various machines used in the woodworking industry. Some mathematics is required to work with the angles and pitches of various cutting tools. The work must be accurate and exact.

Model Maker

Similar to the pattern maker, the model maker builds models of automobiles, airplanes, buildings, and furniture and of scenes and settings used in stage plays, moviemaking, and television. Model makers must be highly skilled at their trade and have a thorough knowledge of wood and the woodworking trade. They may build scaled-down or full-size models.

Forester

There are a variety of jobs related to the forest industry, some of which are the following:

> *Lumberjack:* cuts the tops of tall trees
> *Faller:* cuts down the trees (Fig. 1-4)

Figure 1-4 Tree fallers. (Courtesy of National Forest Products Association.)

Swamper or limber: trims off the branches of trees

Log bucker: cuts the trees into standard lengths

Equipment operator: operates various motorized equipment in forest or mill

Scaler: measures logs to determine the number of board feet

Grader: selects the quality of lumber after milling

Cruiser: selects trees for cutting (Fig. 1-5)

Research scientist: studies tree growth characteristics (Fig. 1-6)

Tree farmer: grows trees for profit (Fig. 1-7)

Professional and Semiprofessional Personnel

There are many people who may not work with wood but who are associated with the wood industry. Some are employed in creative activities, designing but not producing wood products. Others sell, manage, own, teach, or do research in the wood industry.

Figure 1-5 Tree cruiser. (Courtesy of National Forest Products Association.)

Figure 1-6 Research. (Courtesy of American Forest Institute.)

(a)

(b)

Figure 1-7 Tree farming. [(a) Courtesy of American Forest Institute; (b) courtesy of Boise Cascade Corporation.]

SAFETY

One of the most frequent causes of injury to workers in the carpentry field is the power saw. The reason is improper use—not following manufacturers' safety recommendations for adequate blade shielding. Most power saw users are under the misconception that the blade shield gets in the way and interferes with use of the saw; this is not true. Of the injuries reported, the most frequent are amputations, caused by workers falling into or onto moving blades. Other injuries are caused by loose clothing getting caught in moving parts, improper electrical grounding of power tools, unsharpened blades, improperly mounted blades, and not following manufacturers' instructions.

Hand tools also cause serious injuries when improperly used. When using sharp tools, always cut away from the body and always use the right tool for the right job.

Safety glasses should be worn when working with power tools. Safety helmets could prevent serious head injuries. Poor housekeeping is another cause of injury: failing to pick up and properly store tools, or leaving lumber around that has protruding nails. Tools dropping on people who are working at a lower level results in a high injury rate.

More accidents occur with dull tools than with sharp tools. All tools with handles, such as hammers, planes, chisels, files, and saws, should be checked to see that the handles are firmly attached to the tool.

All sharp tools should be used by cutting away from the body, never toward the body. All loose clothing such as ties should be removed, and if wearing long sleeves, be sure the buttons are fastened or roll up the sleeves. Do not wear sneakers or sandals. Jewelry can also cause serious accidents. A ring could catch under a splinter of wood or a hanging pendant could get caught in moving parts of machinery or tools. When carrying long pieces of building material, give warning to others.

Safety precautions mean that your safety is of prime importance. Do not get into the habit of thinking that you will be wasting time by reading instructions. They have been written to save time and to help you. For your safety, it is best to develop a strong feeling for and habit of safety, which can be accomplished by giving your job time and attention and by following the rules.

Trousers should not have cuffs. Shoes should have thick soles with reinforced toes to prevent injury from loads up to 2500 lbs. Safety glasses should be of sufficiently high quality that a $\frac{1}{8}$-in. steel ball dropping from a height of 50 in. should not break the glasses' lens.

Keep hands free of grease and oil. Wear gloves that do not restrict the use of hands and fingers. When working in a dusty area, wear a face mask. When carrying tools, keep the sharp edges pointed down and do not swing arms over your head with tools in hands. Do not carry sharp tools in pockets, and carry only what is needed. If you use fingers as a guide in cutting material, be very careful. Avoid hitting fingernails with a hammer, as this can be very painful. Do not use a finger to test the sharpness of a tool.

Rushing will generally not produce more work but, in fact, may well cause the loss of time involved in reworking. Work at a good steady pace without hurrying. Remember that overconfidence could be a sign of danger.

Do not alter factory-made electric plugs. Grounded plugs have three prongs, one of which is a ground. Without that third prong, electricity could pass through your body should there be an electrical problem with the power tool. Do not remove the third prong. If it does not have three prongs, use a three-prong adapter.

Place all building material in a neat pile until ready for use and do not pile it in a passage or aisle. Stand on a firm, solid base when using power tools. Do not reach beyond stretch length, and stay well away from the edge of walls, excavations, scaffolding, and ladders. If liquid is spilled, wipe it up immediately. Do not use a ladder for a scaffold or as a horizontal working platform.

HEAVY LOADS

When carrying heavy loads, do not twist the body. Change positions by shifting feet. If the load is heavy and bulky, do not lift or carry it alone; seek help. Never underestimate the weight to be lifted or overestimate strength. When lifting heavy objects, use leg and arm muscles, not back muscles. If the object is too heavy, seek help.

FIRE PROTECTION

Many fires of different causes and classes can occur on any building site. Class A fires are those that involve burning wood and debris. Class B fires arise from burning of gasoline, oil, paints, and oil-soaked rags. Class C fires are caused by faulty electrical equipment, such as extension cords and power tools. Each class of fire requires a specific fire extinguisher designed to extinguish that class of fire (Table 1-1).

TABLE 1-1

Portable and Wheeled Fire Extinguishers

type of agent	regular dry chemical	tri-class dry chemical	pressurized water	Halon 1211	carbon dioxide
Class A fire Paper, wood, cloth etc., where quenching by water or insulating by Tri-Class general purpose dry chemical is effective.	not recommended	yes/excellent Fire-retardant blanket to prevent reflash.	yes/excellent Water saturates material and prevents rekindling.	not recommended	not recommended
Class B fire Gasoline, oils, paints burning liquids, cooking fats, etc., where smothering action is required.	yes/excellent Chemical powder smothers fire. Screen of dry chemical shields operator from heat.	yes/excellent Chemical powder smothers fire. Screen of dry chemical shields operator from heat.	no Water will spread fire, not put it out.	yes/excellent Halon 1211 snuffs out fire, doesn't effect equipment or foodstuffs	yes/excellent Carbon dioxide leaves no residue, does not affect equipment or foodstuffs.
Class C fire Live electrical equipment Fire in motors, switches, appliances, etc. where a nonconducting extinguishing agent is required.	yes/excellent Chemical is a non-conductor; screen of dry chemical shields operator from heat.	yes/excellent Chemical is a non-conductor; screen of dry chemical shields operator from heat.	no Water, a conductor should not be used on live electrical equipment.	yes/excellent Halon 1211 is a non-conductor, leaves no residue, will not damage equipment.	yes/excellent Carbon dioxide is a non-conductor, leaves no residue, will not damage equipment.
How to choose your Extinguishers Determine what type of hazard (class of fire) or hazards you need to protect. Determine the degree of hazard—light, medium heavy, select the extinguisher with appropriate extinguishing agent and rating.					

Source: Walter Kidde, Division of Kidde, Inc.

Always check electrical cords and cables on power tools for worn insulation, splices, or broken wire. Keep oil- and grease-soaked rags in a covered container. Fire extinguishers should be easily available and ready for use. Check the charge in all fire extinguishers at least once a year.

OSHA

The Occupational Safety and Health Act, passed by Congress in 1970, is administered by the federal government under the Secretary of Labor. It requires all owners and other administrators in business and industry to provide safe and healthful working conditions for all employees. The only people not covered by these laws are those working for federal and state governments, but there are special provisions for these workers.

Enforcement

The Labor Department enforces the law by making unannounced visits to work sites. If the inspectors find violations or dangerous conditions, the area will be closed until the standards are met.

Penalties

When violations are discovered, the penalties to owners or inspectors are as follows:

1. For wilfully or repeatedly violating standards under the law, an employer is fined not more than $10,000 for each violation.
2. For the citation of a serious violation, an employer is fined up to $1000 for each violation.
3. For failing to correct a violation within the time allowed, a fine of not more than $1000 is levied for each day that the violation continues.
4. For the death of an employee because of wilfully violating the law, the employer may be jailed for not more than six months and fined not more than $10,000.
5. For giving advance notice of an inspection, the penalty is a fine of not more than $1000 or jail for not more than six months or both.
6. For making false statements in any application or record, the penalty is a fine of not more than $10,000 or jail for not more than six months, or both.
7. For causing a person's death while making an inspection, the penalty is life imprisonment.

Records

Every employer must keep accurate records, which must be available to the inspectors. They include the following:

1. Records necessary or appropriate for enforcement of the law
2. Records necessary or appropriate for research

3. Records reporting death and injury related to the job
4. Records showing employee exposure to possibly harmful materials or conditions.

Inspection

An OSHA inspector has the right to enter any workplace without notice to inspect conditions and may question any worker or owner. Inspections are made during regular working hours and when the inspector arrives, he or she will state the reason for the visit and the type of inspection to be made. Usually, a member of the company will follow the inspector around while the inspection is being made.

Cooperation

The proper attitude is important during an OSHA inspection. When the inspector arrives, he or she should not be kept waiting for any length of time. Do not try to prevent the inspector from making the inspection or ask him or her to come back another time. If any violation is reported, it must be posted near the site where the violation occurred.

Disagreement

If the owner disagrees with the citation, he or she may appeal in writing by asking for a hearing within 15 working days.

Standards

OSHA safety requirements are contained in five volumes, available from the Superintendent of Documents, U.S. Government Printing Office, Washington, D.C. 20402.

The construction industry regulations are found in Volume III, under the following categories:

A. General
B. General Interpretations
C. General Safety and Health Provisions
D. Occupational Health and Environmental Controls
E. Personal Protection and Life Saving Equipment
F. Fire Protection and Prevention
G. Signs, Signals, and Barricades
H. Materials Handling, Storage, Use, and Disposal
I. Tools: Hand and Power
J. Welding and Cutting
K. Electrical
L. Ladders and Scaffolding
M. Floors and Wall Openings and Stairways
N. Cranes, Derricks, Hoists, Elevators, and Conveyors
O. Motor Vehicles and Mechanical Equipment
P. Excavation, Trenching, and Shoring

Q. Concrete, Concrete Forms, and Shoring
R. Steel Erection
S. Tunnels, Shafts, Caissons and Cofferdams, and Compressed Air
T. Demolition
U. Blasting and Use of Explosives
V. Power Transmission and Distribution
W. Rollover Protection Structures and Overhead Protection
X. Effective Dates

Safety Practices

Following are some of the OSHA provisions to ensure safety habits for workers:

1. All employees shall follow safe practices, use personal protection equipment as required, render every possible aid to safe operations, and report all unsafe conditions or practices.
2. Work shall be well planned and supervised to prevent injuries.
3. All employees shall be given frequent accident prevention instructions.
4. Supervisors shall insist that employees observe and obey every rule, regulation, and order necessary for the safe conduct of the work.
5. All unsafe, unhealthy, or hazardous conditions or places shall be immediately placed off limits, out of order, out of bounds, and so on, then promptly removed or corrected.
6. No one shall knowingly be permitted or required to work with impaired ability or alterness caused by fatigue, illness, or other factors such that employees or others may be exposed to accidents or injury.
7. No one will be allowed on the job while under the influence of intoxicating liquor or drugs.
8. Horseplay, scuffling, and other acts that have or tend to have an adverse influence on the safety or well-being of employees are prohibited.
9. Crowding or pushing when boarding or leaving any vehicle or other conveyance is prohibited.
10. Employees shall be alert to see that all guards and other protective devices are in their proper places and adjusted prior to equipment operation and report deficiencies promptly.
11. Workers shall not handle or tamper with any tools, equipment, machinery, or facilities not within the scope of their duties, unless they are thoroughly qualified and have received instruction from their supervisors.
12. All injuries shall be reported promptly so that arrangements can be made for medical or first-aid treatment.
13. When lifting heavy objects, use the large muscles of the legs instead of the smaller muscles of the back.
14. Protect the eyes at all times through the proper use of goggles, hoods, and so on.

15. Know where you are going and how you are going to get there. Look before you move.

16. Watch out for others; they may not be aware of what you are doing or where you are going.

17. Wash thoroughly after handling injuries or poisonous substances, and follow all special instructions from authorized sources. Hands should be thoroughly cleaned just prior to eating.

18. Loose or frayed clothing, dangling ties, finger rings, and so on, should not be worn near moving machinery or other sources of entanglement.

19. Apparatus, tools, equipment, and machinery shall not be repaired or adjusted while in operation, nor shall oiling of moving parts be attempted except on equipment that is designed or fitted with safeguards to protect the person who is performing the work.

20. Use common sense; if you do not know, don't do it. The following checklist will serve as a reminder of the items that need regular attention in order to establish safety:
   a. Housekeeping:
      (1) Workplaces—clean and orderly.
      (2) Floors—clean and dry.
      (3) Floors in good repair.
      (4) Aisles and passageways clear.
      (5) Aisles and passageways marked.
      (6) Covers and guardrails in place.
      (7) Floor loading plates in place.
      (8) Safe floor and roof loading.
   b. Means of egress:
      (1) Adequate emergency exits.
      (2) Exits clear and unlocked.
      (3) Exits clearly marked.
      (4) Exits lighted.
   c. Stairways:
      (1) Stair railings.
      (2) Stair strength.
      (3) Stair steepness.
      (4) Stair length.
      (5) Tread gripping.
      (6) Overhead clearance.
   d. Fire protection:
      (1) Fire extinguishers charged.
      (2) Number of fire extinguishers.
      (3) Extinguisher location.
      (4) Location marking of extinguishers.
      (5) Extinguisher mountings.
      (6) Special-purpose extinguishers.
      (7) Automatic sprinklers.
      (8) Water supply.
      (9) Fire department connection.
     (10) Sprinkler system maintenance.
     (11) Fire alarm boxes.
     (12) Fire alarm testing.
   e. Employee facilities:
      (1) Drinking and washing water available.

          (2) Men's and women's toilets.
          (3) Toilet room construction.

f. Medical and first-aid provisions:
          (1) Hospital or medical facilities.
          (2) First-aid trained personnel.
          (3) Medical personnel available.
          (4) Eye-wash emergency facilities.

g. Storage of materials:
          (1) Safe clearances.
          (2) Stacked materials.
          (3) Storage area kept free.
          (4) Drainage system.
          (5) Warning signs.

h. Machine guarding:
          (1) Are machines guarded?
          (2) Additional hazards.
          (3) Guard locations.
          (4) Machinery anchored.

i. Floor and wall openings:
          (1) Floor holes guarded.
          (2) Pits and trapdoors guarded.
          (3) Toe boards on ladderway or platform.
          (4) Skylight protection.
          (5) Temporary floors protection.
          (6) Wall openings guarded.
          (7) Open-sided floors and platforms.

j. Personal protection equipment:
          (1) Protective equipment used and maintained.
          (2) Reliability ratings.
          (3) Employee-provided equipment.
          (4) Eye protection use.
          (5) Eye protection construction.
          (6) Respirators provided and used.
          (7) Respirator use training.
          (8) Respirator check.
          (9) Respirator cleanliness.
        (10) Hard hats: use and construction.
        (11) Safety glasses.

FIRST AID

A knowledge of first aid and sound judgment are very important for treating injuries. Knowing what not to do, and doing nothing except calling for help, are as important as knowing what to do properly. An accident victim may be injured more if treated by an unqualified person than if untreated. First-aid treatment information and instructions are available from any Red Cross office. A first-aid kit should be handy for treatment of even the slightest injuries, cuts, or scratches, to prevent possible infection (Fig. 1-8). Nothing is more important than your safety and the safety of others. Any injury may cause a physical handicap or cause time lost from the job and consequent loss of money. Many accidents can be avoided by using common sense and not taking dangerous shortcuts. The quickest way is not always the best or safest way.

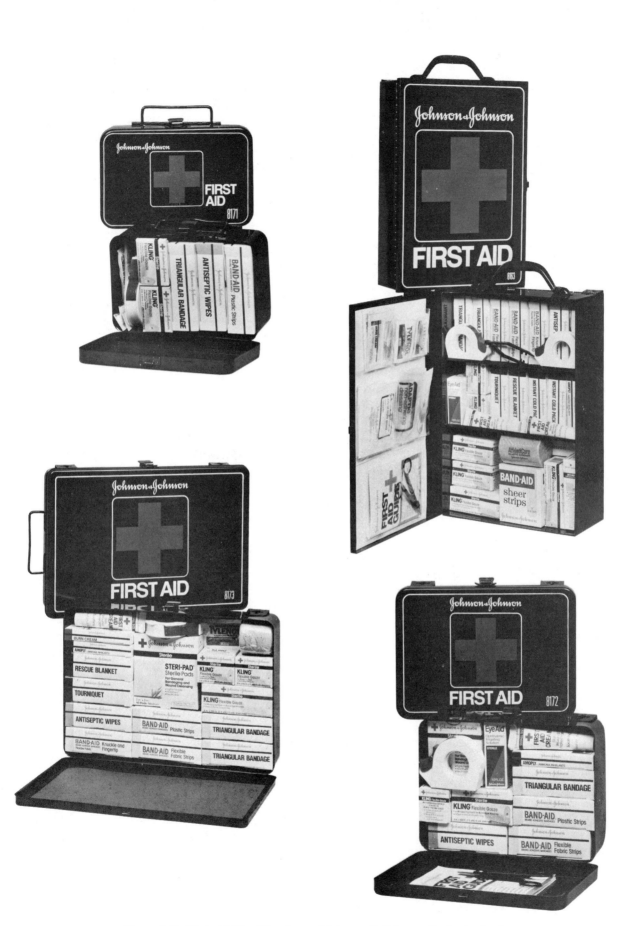

Figure 1-8   First-aid kits. (Courtesy of Johnson & Johnson Products, Inc.)

Other reasons for injury on the job are lack of interest, inattention, tiredness, careless and sloppy methods, overconfidence, and not following safety rules. Construction work is one of the most prone to dangerous accidents because of the use of sharp tools, heavy material, and scaffolding. The hazards in construction require the development of good safety practices and learning to use proper tools for a specific task.

QUESTIONS

1. What type of training is used to teach unskilled people? _____
   _____

2. (a) What is a closed shop? _____
   _____

   (b) What is an open shop? _____
   _____

3. Most construction workers are union workers.   True or False

4. "Rough" carpentry means which of the following?
   A. Measurements need not be exact
   B. Building framework
   C. Semiskilled worker

5. "Finish carpentry" means which of the following?
   A. Fired carpenter
   B. Doors, windows, trim
   C. Formwork

6. A pattern maker makes clothes.   True or False

7. Define *millworker:* _____
   _____

8. Construction companies supply workers with all necessary tools.
       True or False

9. Name two jobs related to forestry:
   1. _____
   2. _____

10. A superintendent can hire and fire.   True or False

2

Building and Zoning Laws

INTRODUCTION

Before building plans are developed, local building and zoning laws must be studied. These laws are designed to protect life, property, health, safety, and the general welfare of people. The building laws pertain to the actual construction of the building, and the zoning laws pertain to use of the land. These laws are updated from time to time to reflect the trend or change in the area.

Minimum construction requirements are specified in the building laws, which are under the jurisdiction of the local building inspector. All plans must comply with these laws before a building permit is issued. During the construction stage, the local building inspector will make periodic visits to the construction site unannounced, and if any code violations are found, the building inspector can halt construction until the violation is corrected.

Building codes or laws control the quality of material; indicate how much weight a floor, ceiling, or roof will support; and control egress, fire safety, plumbing, heating, and electrical work, air conditioning, ventilation, and a host of other details. These laws control not only new construction but also alterations, reconstruction, repair, remodeling, additions, demolition, and the inspection of buildings for safety purposes. Building laws have been developed through trial and error, and by standards developed through testing of building materials by builders, material manufacturers, building trade associations, architects, engineers, government agencies, and tradespeople. All have a desire to establish levels of quality for common benefit. The intent of the building laws is to effect the establishment of uniform standards and requirements for construction and construction materials.

Not only are local building laws established, but some communities may adapt parts or all of the following codes:

1. Uniform Building Code
2. Building Officials and Code Administrators International (BOCA)
3. National Building Code
4. Standard Building Code
5. Basic Building Code
6. Basic Fire Prevention Code
7. Basic Housing Code

Should more than one code be used in a community, the most severe code prevails.

ZONING LAWS

The use of buildings, and their height and density, are controlled by zoning laws (Tables 2-1 and 2-2). To regulate a city or town, sections are divided into various areas of usage called zones or districts (Fig. 2-1). Districts serve the purpose of promoting health, safety, and the general welfare of the community. They are designed to lessen congestion in the streets; to secure

TABLE 2-1

Zoning Districts

Districts	Intended Primarily for the Use of
Residential A-80	Single-family dwellings on lots not served by public water and of minimum areas of 80,000 square feet
Residential A-20	Single-family dwellings on lots of minimum areas of 20,000 square feet
Residential A-12	Single-family dwellings on lots of minimum areas of 12,000 square feet
Residential A-8	Single-family dwellings on lots of minimum areas of 8,000 square feet
Residential A-6	Single-family dwellings on lots of minimum areas of 6,000 square feet
Residential B-1	Single-family and two-family dwellings
Residential B-2	Single-, two- and multi-family dwellings
Commercial C-1	Office business
Commercial C-2	Neighborhood business
Commercial C-3	General business
Commercial C-4	Highway business
Commercial C-5	Heavy business, industry
Industrial M-1	Restricted industry
Industrial M-2	General industry
Open Space S-1	Uses containing high proportion of open space or natural character
Planned districts	Uses in buildings arranged in an efficient, harmonious and convenient manner on sites

Source: City of Cranston, R.I.

TABLE 2-2

Intensity Regulations

District	Minimum Lot Area (sq. ft.)	Minimum Lot Width and Frontage (ft.)	Minimum Yards (ft.)			Maximum Lot Coverage (%)	Maximum Building Height (ft.)
			Front	Rear	Side		
S-1, A-80	20,000	200	40	100	20	10	35
A-20	20,000	125	30	30	15	20	35
A-12	12,000	100	25	20	10	30	35
A-8	8,000	80	25	20	10	30	35
A-6	6,000	60	25	20	8	30	35
B-1	6,000	60	25	20	8	35	35
B-2	6,000	60	25	20	8	50	- -
C-1	6,000	60	25	20	8	60	- -
C-2	6,000	60	25	20	8	60	30
C-3	6,000	60	0	20	0	100	35
C-4	12,000	120	60	20	8	50	35
C-5	10,000	80	30	20	8	60	35
M-1	30,000	150	40	30	20	60	- -
M-2	60,000	200	40	30	25	60	- -

Source: City of Cranston, R.I.

safety from fire, panic, and other dangers; to provide adequate light and air; to prevent overcrowding of land; to avoid undue concentration of population; to facilitate adequate provisions for transportation, water, sewerage, schools, parks, open spaces, and other public requirements; and to secure a reasonable balance of industrial, commercial, manufacturing, and residential land use throughout the community. Zoning laws are drawn with reasoned consideration of the character of each district and its particular suitability for a specific use. They are made with a view to conserving the value of buildings and land, both private and public, and to encourage the most appropriate use of land throughout the community. Examples of districts utilized in zoning laws to regulate the type of building use are as follows:

1. Single-family dwelling
2. Two-family dwelling
3. Multifamily dwelling
4. Commercial
5. Industrial
6. Manufacturing
7. Open space

Zoning laws also regulate the amount of land area to be used (Table 2-2); minimum side-yard, front-yard, and rear-yard dimensions; and number of off-street parking places required.

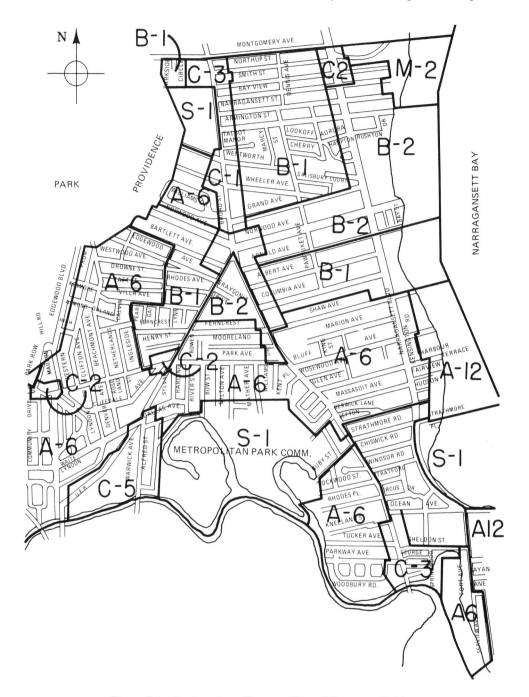

Figure 2-1 Zoning plan. (Source: City of Cranston, R.I.)

Residential: A-80, A-20, A-12, A-8, A-6, B-1, B-2
Commercial: C-1 to C-5
Industrial: M-1, M-2
Open space: S-1

It is also the purpose of zoning laws to preserve, for public purposes,
structures of historic and architectural value. The laws safeguard the heritage
of a community by preserving districts that reflect elements of cultural, social, economic, political, and architectural history. Zoning laws also stabilize
and improve property values, foster civic beauty, strengthen the local econ-

Land Use

• = special permit X = Permitted — = prohibited Principal Use		Districts										
A-80	A-20 A-12 A-8 A-6	B-1	B-2	C-1	C-2	C-3	C-4	C-5	M-1	M-2	S-1
Food stores, delicatessen	—	—	—	—	—	X	X	X	—	—	—	—
Bakery, provided all baked goods sold on premises	—	—	—	—	—	X	X	X	—	—	—	—
Drug store, newstand, variety and notice stores	—	—	—	—	—	X	X	X	—	—	—	—
Book, stationery, and gift shops	—	—	—	—	—	X	X	X	—	—	—	—
Florist shops 1. excluding greenhouse	—	—	—	—	—	X	X	—	—	—	—	—
2. including greenhouse	—	—	—	—	—	—	—	X	X	—	—	—
Hardware stores	—	—	—	—	—	X	X	X	X	—	—	—
Banks and financial institutions	—	—	—	—	X	X	X	X	X	•	•	—
Barber shops and beauty parlors; tailor and custom dressmaking shops	—	—	—	—	—	X	X	X	—	—	—	—
Laundry, dry cleaning, and pressing establishments 1. 5 employees or less working at any one time within the establishment	—	—	—	—	—	X	X	X	X	—	—	—
2. 6 employees or more working at any one time within the establishment	—	—	—	—	—	—	—	—	X	X	X	—

Source: City of Cranston, R.I.

Figure 2-1 (continued)

omy, and promote the use of historic districts for the education, pleasure, and welfare of the people of a community.

If a building's use does not conform to the zoning law for its district, a petition may be filed with the zoning board of review. This is a somewhat involved procedure. The documents necessary are the building plans, including the plot plan; the application for petition; a plan showing all the property surrounding the lot in question, with the names and addresses of all the property owners; and a list of all the buildings on the surrounding property. Registered letters are mailed to the surrounding property owners, inviting them to a public hearing. The date and time of the hearing are published in the local newspaper for the information of the general public. All who have an interest in the case will attend the public hearing to speak for or against the petition.

Testimony collected by the zoning board of review secretary will be studied by the board members in making their decision for or against the petition. If the petition is granted, the building may be constructed; the building site thus becomes a "nonconforming" lot. If the petition is denied, no building may be constructed on that particular lot. The decision can be appealed to the civil courts.

Zoning laws are changed from time to time to reflect changes in the community. Before any change is made, the public is informed, through newspaper notices, of the time and place of the meeting. The changes are discussed at the meeting and approved or disapproved by the people. If a zoning law is violated, the violator can receive a fine or imprisonment, or both.

Zoning laws cover a wide range of circumstances. They prohibit a gasoline station from being built in the middle of a residential neighborhood. They may not allow trailers or mobile homes to be parked in a yard. They prevent buildings from being built too close together and control the height of buildings. They state the maximum amount of land a building can cover, and control the dimensions for the front, side, and rear yards. In nonresidential buildings, zoning laws control traffic by indicating how many off-street parking spaces must be allowed.

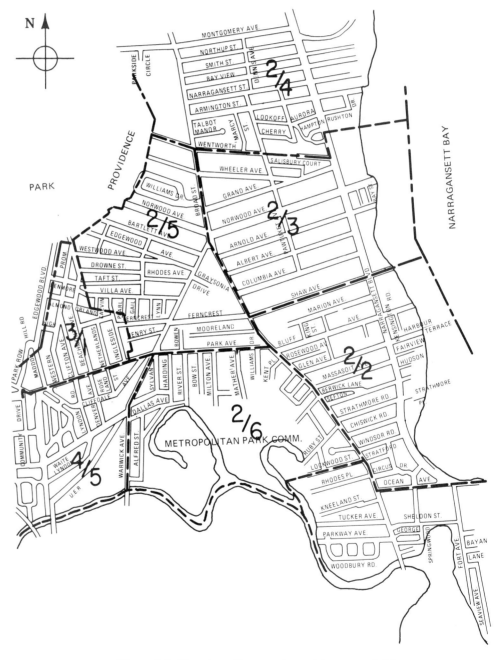

Figure 2-2 Plat plan. (Source: City of Cranston, R.I.)

The use of the land is controlled as to the construction of one-family houses, two-family houses, and multifamily houses. This means that if a building lot is zoned for single-family houses, a two-family house cannot be constructed on that lot. It must be constructed in an area where two-family houses are allowed. The zoning board also controls public land use, such as playgrounds, cemeteries, and parks.

PLATS

Segments of the community are divided into sections called plats (Fig. 2-2). Within these plats are lots (sometimes called "plots") (Fig. 2-3). Plots and lots are numbered to identify a particular lot within a particular plat. The size and use of lots are regulated by zoning laws. This information is a matter of permanent record at the local town hall and is available to the public. The records will also show who owned the lots, together with dates of purchase and sales from the time the local record office began keeping records. Occasionally, the zoning of a lot may change, and this change is reflected on the record. Also on record will be all utilities serving the lot, such as sewer, water, and gas; curbing; sidewalk width; street width; and the depth below the street level of all utilities and the size of pipes and wires. Sometimes streets are indicated on the plat plans but have not been built. These, called "paper streets," indicate that space has been reserved for street construction for building at a future date. Easements and rights-of-way are also shown in plat plans. These are land areas set aside for public use, such as public beaches and parks; railroads; underground water, sewer, and gas serving the community; and for overhead electric wires crossing property. Any utility line crossing private property for public use constitutes an easement. Easements or rights-of-way are not used for buildings of any type. It is possible for any local, state, or federal government to take, from any land owner, property that is needed for public services, such as roads, schools, fire stations, police stations, post offices, and court houses; this is called the right of eminent domain. Any land taken under eminent domain must be for public use.

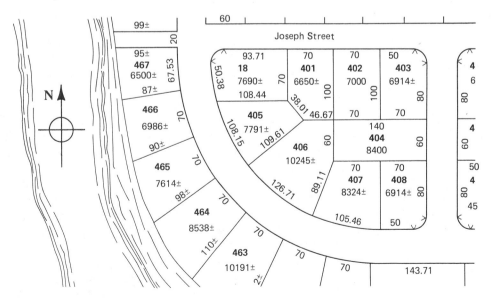

Figure 2-3   Plot plan. (Source: City of Cranston, R.I.)

PLAT RESTRICTIONS

In addition to building and zoning laws, other rules, called plat restrictions, may have been established. These rules may have been established by the land developer to help control the type of development and building for high-quality, desirable home sites. Although these restrictions may not be part of the law, they are part of an agreement between the land seller and the land buyer, and any land buyer agrees to follow these restrictions.

The restrictions may call for no house to be built below a minimum cost; no animals, such as horses, cows, or sheep, to be housed on these properties; no fence to be installed or a fence not to exceed 3 ft in height; no boats, trailers, or mobile homes to be parked in the area; only a building of a particular style of architecture may be built in the area; front, side, and rear yard dimensions set by the developer (these dimensions may not be less than allowed by the zoning laws, but can be greater); the house size may have a minimum number of square feet; as part of the restrictions, no accessory building, such as a workshop, toolroom, or storage shed may be allowed; no fence may be erected in front of the house; if the lot sizes are large, such as 2 or more acres, the restriction may not allow subdividing the property into two or more lots; the restrictions may control the type of landscaping allowed on the land; there may be a time restriction required for completing the house from the day construction is begun; or one-and-one-half story, raised ranch, bilevel, and split-foyer houses may not be allowed. All of these plat restrictions are designed to establish and maintain a high-standard, high-quality neighborhood and to protect each homeowner from having someone develop a neighboring home site that would have the effect of lowering the standard of the area.

LOCAL BUILDING CODES

Before any building permit is issued (see the sample application shown in Fig. 2-4), building plans and specifications must comply with the local building laws. The latest addition must be used because from time to time the rules will change to reflect the latest developments and techniques. The same set of plans and specifications may not be legal in another community because the laws may be different.

The first record of a building code goes back to 2100 B.C. in the Code of Hammurabi, the King of Babylonia. One of the more interesting regulations was the following: "In the case of collapse of a defective building, the Architect is to be put to death if the Owner is killed, and the Architect's son, if the Owner's son is killed."

The ancient Romans were the first to introduce formal laws governing building construction. When houses were built in Rome during the time of Julius Caesar, they sometimes collapsed, so the Romans introduced a code or law that limited the height of a building to 7 ft.

It has been proven many times that building laws or codes are necessary to protect lives, and the courts have ruled in favor of codes to protect people from harm, injury, or death from unsafe buildings. The building code derives its justification from municipalities' police power, the power of governments to protect people from harm on matters of safety and health when using buildings. Each city or town may have a different building code, or the code may apply to the entire state. It is the responsibility of the building inspector to review plans and specifications before issuing a building permit to make certain that they conform to the laws of the area. The building inspec-

BUILDING PERMIT APPLICATION   OFFICE FILE (LOCATION)

MUNICIPALITY _____ NUMERICAL CODE _____ PERMIT NO. _____

APPLICATION DATE _____ CENSUS TRACT _____ FEE RECEIVED: $ _____ BY _____

I.   IMPORTANT: PLEASE PRINT - APPLICANT TO COMPLETE ALL ITEMS

1. STREET LOCATION _____ 2. ZONING DISTRICT _____

3. PLAT _____ 4. LOT _____ 5. FILE _____ 6. AREA _____ 7. FIRE DISTRICT NO. (0 or 1) _____

8. USE OF STRUCTURE: PREVIOUS _____ PROPOSED _____

9. OWNER _____ ADDRESS _____ TEL. NO. _____

10. CONTRACTOR (0 or 1 *) _____ ADDRESS _____ TEL. NO. _____

11. ARCH. OR ENG. _____ ADDRESS _____ TEL. NO. _____

12. RHODE ISLAND REG. NO. _____ 13. Stamped Prints (Circle one) Yes No   14. Certificate of Occupancy Required Yes No

15. DESCRIPTION OF WORK TO BE PERFORMED. _____

	16. USE OF EACH FLOOR
	BSMT.
	1st
	2nd
	3rd
	Other

II.   TYPE AND COST OF BUILDING · PLEASE CHECK APPROPRIATE ITEMS AND ENTER REQUESTED DATA

A. TYPE OF IMPROVEMENT

1. _____ NEW STRUCTURE
2. _____ ADDITION TO STRUCTURE
3. _____ INSTALLATION
4. _____ RECONSTRUCTION
5. _____ REPLACEMENT
6. _____ FOUNDATION ONLY

B. OWNERSHIP

PUBLIC

1. _____ STATE
2. _____ CITY OR TOWN
3. _____ OTHER, SPECIFY
_____

PRIVATE

4. _____ TAXABLE
5. _____ TAX EXEMPT

C. ESTIMATED COST MATERIAL AND LABOR

1. STRUCTURAL $ _____ .00
TO BE INSTALLED BUT NOT INCLUDED IN THE ABOVE COST
2. ELECTRICAL $ _____ .00
3. PLUMBING OR PIPING $ _____ .00
4. HEATING, AIR COND. $ _____ .00
5. OTHER, ELEVATOR, ETC. $ _____ .00
    TOTAL COST $ _____ .00

D. PROPOSED USE RESIDENTIAL

1. _____ R-1 MOTEL, HOTEL
2. _____ R-2 MULTI-FAMILY
3. _____ R-3 One and Two Family Attached
4. _____ R-4 One and Two Family Detached
5. _____ GARAGE
6. _____ CARPORT
7. _____ MOBILE HOME
8. _____ SWIMMING POOL
9. _____ FENCES
10. _____ SIGNS
11. _____ FIREPLACE
12. _____ OTHER, SPECIFY _____

E. PROPOSED USE NON-RESIDENTIAL

1. _____ A-1-A THEATRES W/STAGE
2. _____ A-1-B THEATRES W/O STAGE
3. _____ A-2 NIGHT CLUBS
4. _____ A-3 RESTAURANTS
5. _____ A-4 SCHOOLS.
6. _____ B BUSINESS.
7. _____ F FACTORY.
8. _____ H HIGH HAZARD
9. _____ I-1 INSTITUTIONAL, RESTRAINED.
10. _____ I-2 INSTITUTIONAL, INCAPACITATED
11. _____ M MERCHANTILE
12. _____ S-1 STORAGE, MODERATE.

13. _____ S-2 STORAGE, LOW
14. _____ T TEMPORARY
15. _____ MIXED USE
SPECIFY _____
16. _____ TANKS, TOWERS
17. _____ SWIMMING POOL
18. _____ FENCES
19. _____ SIGNS
20. _____ OTHER
SPECIFY _____

F. RESIDENTIAL
(COMPLETE FOR NEW BUILDINGS. AND RECONSTRUCTION)

SINGLE FAMILY
1. _____ TOTAL SINGLE FAMILY UNITS
2. _____ TOTAL NO. OF BEDROOMS
TOTAL NO. OF BATHROOMS 3. _____ Full 4. _____ Half

MULTI-FAMILY
5. _____ TOTAL NO. OF KITCHENS
TOTAL NO. OF BATHROOMS 6. _____ Full 7. _____ Half

TOTAL NO. OF APARTMENTS BY NO. OF BEDROOMS
8. Effic. _____   9. 1 _____   10. 2 _____
11. 3 _____   12. 4 _____   13. 5 _____
14. _____ MORE, Please Specify _____
15. _____ TOTAL NUMBER OF BUILDINGS IN PROJECT.

G. FOUNDATION SET BACKS FROM PROPERTY LINES

1. FRONT _____ ft., _____ in.
2. REAR _____ ft., _____ in.
3. LEFT SIDE _____ ft., _____ in.
4. RIGHT SIDE _____ ft., _____ in.

H. DIMENSIONS

1. No. of Stories _____ 2. Basement: Yes __ No __
3. Height of Construction Ft. _____ MAX. WIDTH _____ MAX. DEPTH _____
4. Total Floor Area Sq. Ft. w/o Basement _____

I. PRINCIPAL TYPE OF CONSTRUCTION
(CCNSTRUCTION CLASS (Check one))

1. 1A _____   5. 2C _____   9. 4A _____
2. 1B _____   6. 3A _____   10. 4B _____
3. 2A _____   7. 3B _____
4. 2B _____   8. 3C _____

J. FLOOD HAZARD AREA - 1. YES 2. NO

1. Elev. (MSL) of lowest floor incl. basement _____
2. Elev. (MSL) of 100 year flood _____

K. TYPES OF SEWAGE DISPOSAL

1. _____ PUBLIC   2. _____ PRIVATE SYSTEM*
3. ISDS NO. _____ DATE _____

L. PRINCIPAL TYPE OF HEATING FUEL

1. _____ GAS   2. _____ ELECTRICITY
3. _____ OIL   4. _____ COAL
5. _____ SOLAR   6. _____ OTHER _____

M. NUMBER OF OFF-STREET PARKING SPACES

1. ENCLOSED _____
2. OUTDOORS _____

N. TYPE OF WATER SUPPLY

1. _____ PUBLIC
2. _____ PRIVATE SYSTEM
3. _____ INDIVIDUAL, WELL,

O. EQUIPMENT*

1. INCINERATOR _____
2. ELEVATOR _____
(Enter Number)

P. TYPE OF MECHANICAL AND AIR CONDITIONING

1. _____ Central-Electric   5. _____ Heat Pump
2. _____ Central-Gas   6. _____ Solar Hot Water
3. _____ Individual RM. A/C   7. _____ Solar Heat
4. _____ Oil   8. _____ Other

I hereby certify that I have the authority to make the foregoing application, that the application is correct, and that the owner of this building and the undersigned agree to conform to all applicable codes and ordinances of this jurisdiction.

* IN-STATE CONTRACTOR = 0   TEL. NO. _____ APPLICANTS SIGNATURE _____
OUT-OF-STATE CONTRACTOR = 1
*STATE APPROVAL REQUIRED   FOR _____
SEE BACK OF FORM FOR
INFORMATION

Figure 2-4 Application for a building permit. (Source: City of Cranston, R.I.)

tor will make periodic site inspections to ensure that builders conform to the laws. The laws also control the plumbing, heating, ventilation, air-conditioning, and electrical portions of the building.

Building codes state rules in terms of measured performance, not as rigid specifications of materials. This makes it possible to accept new materials and methods of construction that have been tested and found to be acceptable. The building code allows designers the widest possible freedom and does not restrict or hamper their plans. The codes accept nationally recognized standards as the basis for evaluation of minimum safe construction practices.

Building codes are changed and kept up to date through review of revisions proposed by code enforcement officials, industry and design professionals, and other interested persons and organizations. Changes are discussed in a public hearing, carefully reviewed by committees, and acted on by code enforcement officials in an open meeting. The changes are then published as amendments to the building code. About every three years a new code is printed that incorporates all the changes that have been made since the last published edition.

The people who make changes in the building code are not only code officials but also architects, engineers, technicians, builders, contractors, material producers, trade associations, and many more, all working toward the common goal of making buildings safe for the people who live or work in them.

Another area that building codes cover relates to the amount of load the floor, ceilings, and roof will support. Codes specify where the exits in the house will be and what areas are to be treated for fire protection. They discuss chimneys, flues, and vents. Codes also cover how much electric power is required, the location of smoke and fire detectors, and the minimum size of electric wire. The depth below ground of foundations is included in the building code.

Before any planning is done, thorough knowledge of the applicable building codes is necessary. In addition to local building codes, the federal government has a minimum standard building code. Its standards apply only to buildings financed in part or completely by federal funds. The plans are reviewed by federal inspectors and if found not in compliance with federal building laws, the government will not release funds for construction. Federal inspectors also visit the construction site unannounced to make sure that the building contractor is complying with the rules. When the building is completed, a final inspection will be made; if there are any violations, they must be corrected. The building inspector has the right to order the contractor to remove any work that is in violation of the building code.

If any of the laws governing building present a hardship in construction, a petition or application may be submitted to the building board of review as an exception to the law, stating the reasons why an exception should be granted. The board of review will study the evidence presented and make a decision for or against the petition. If a situation is presented that is not covered by the building law, the building inspector has the right to render a decision.

Building laws apply not only to new buildings, but also to buildings that are altered, rebuilt, or remodeled. In the case of a building that is to be rebuilt or reconstructed following damage by fire, some building codes may require a permit for the work to be done only if the damage is 50% or more of the physical value of the building.

If there is a single building code for the entire state, each city and large town within the state will have a building inspector, who is an agent of the state. Although a building is considered private property, the building inspector or his or her agent has the legal right to enter the property without permission for the purpose of inspection.

A building permit (Fig. 2-5) must be displayed at the construction site, and when the electrical or plumbing inspector makes an inspection, a stamp of approval is usually posted on the building site. A copy of the plans are kept on file in the office of the building inspector. If any changes are made during construction, the changes may require the approval of the building inspector. The cost of the building permit is generally based on the total cost of construction, although this rule varies in some communities.

BUILDING PERMIT

FEE PAID $ ....

Received By ....

Date Granted ....19........

Numerical Code ....

THIS CERTIFIES THAT ....

has permission to ....

....

....

Located at .... Plat .... Lot ....

provided that the person accepting this Permit shall in every respect conform to the terms of the application on file in this office and to the provisions of the Statutes and Ordinances relating to Zoning, Construction, Alteration and Maintenance of Buildings in the municipality and shall begin work on said building within SIX MONTHS from the date hereof and prosecute the work thereon to a speedy Completion.

Any person who shall violate any of the Statutes and Ordinances relating to Zoning, Construction, Alteration and Maintenance in the municipality shall be punished by penalties imposed by the State Building Code and Local Zoning Ordinances.

....

Building Official

BUILDING INSPECTION APPROVALS: WORK SHALL NOT PROCEED UNTIL THE INSPECTOR HAS APPROVED THE VARIOUS STAGES OF CONSTRUCTION.

STAGE OF CONSTRUCTION	SIGNATURE	STAGE OF CONSTRUCTION	SIGNATURE
1.		5.	
2.		6.	
3.		7.	
4.		8.	

This Permit must be returned for Certificate of Occupancy.

On remote sites this card may be kept within the contractor's vehicle, readily available for inspection.

Figure 2-5   Building permit. (Source: City of Cranston, R.I.)

QUESTIONS

1. Zoning laws control the use of the land.   True or False

2. A commercial building may be built in a residential area provided that
   A. A building permit is issued.
   B. A variance has been issued by the zoning board.
   C. The price is right.

3. Define *plat*. _____
   _____

4. An easement makes it easier to construct a building.   True or False

5. Plat restrictions are not as important as zoning laws, and may be ignored.   True or False

6. Building laws are designed to discourage building construction.
   True or False

7. Who were the first people to introduce building laws? _____
   _____

8. The building laws in one state will apply to all states.   True or False

9. The building inspector has the right to stop construction.
   True or False

10. Building codes are permanent and never need to be changed.
    True or False

3

Site Utilities

INTRODUCTION

For a building to be livable, it must be connected to water, gas, electricity, and sewer services; these are called utilities. They are usually supplied by local utility companies and all that is necessary is to make a connection from the street to the house. If the local community does not supply utilities, they must be provided privately. This is done by means of wells for water and septic tanks with a leach field for the sewer. Electricity is usually provided by the local electric company, but if not, an electric generator must be installed to supply electricity. Gas is not a necessity but if desired and not available, it can be provided in the form of bottled gas.

WATER

One of two systems of domestic water supply will be connected to a residence: a private water supply such as a well, or public water (Fig. 3-1). If a public water supply is available close by, a record will be found at the local town hall. It will show the size of the pipe, depth below the street, location of the pipe, and the pipe fitting needed to make a connection. Usually, the local water supply authorities will connect the water from the street to the sidewalk or property line. Making the connection from there to the house is the responsibility of the owner. A shutoff valve will be installed at the sidewalk by the local water authority. This valve is controlled by the water authority and is called a curb cock (Fig. 3-2). If public water is not available on the lot, it may be close enough that it will be less expensive to extend the public water line to the lot instead of putting in a well.

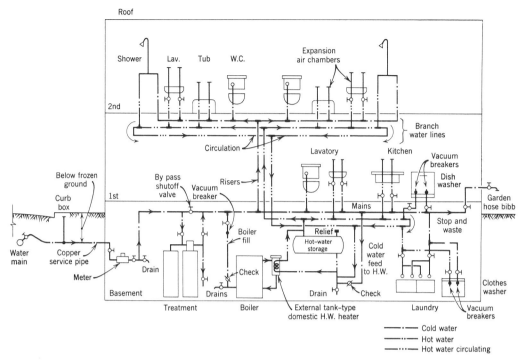

Figure 3-1   Public water supply.

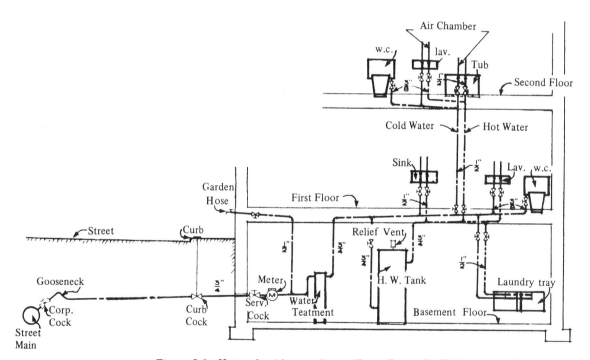

Figure 3-2   Hot and cold water lines. (From Ernest R. Weidhaas, *Architectural Drafting and Construction*, 2nd ed. Copyright © 1981 by Allyn and Bacon, Inc. Reprinted with permission.)

A second type of domestic water supply is a private well. This can be a surface well or an artesian well. Simply stated, a surface well is a hole in the ground with stone walls. The hole fills up with water. An artesian well is a pipe driven into the ground as deep as required to get enough water.

This pipe is driven to one or more water veins in the ground, which supply the water (Fig. 3-3). The location of water veins will determine the depth of the well and how much water will be available. Water supply from a private well, measured by time and gallons, is called a yield.

The minimum amount of water required for a household will be about 4 gal/minute yield from the well. Another important factor to consider is the depth of the well and the level of the underground water table. Water will be contained in the well pipe, which is a reserve. The deeper the well pipe, and the higher the water table, the greater amount of water will be in the reserve. As water is drawn from the well, it is replaced by the underground supply. The well maintains a constant level of water in the well, provided that no more water is drawn from the well than the well will supply or yield.

In either case the water needs to be piped and pumped into the house. Two types of electric pumps are available for a well, one pushing the water from the well to the house, the other pulling the water from the well to the house. The pump can be located in the well or in the house. A storage water tank is necessary in either case. Once the private domestic water supply is available, the water must be tested by the local department of health to determine if the water is safe for drinking.

Recommendations will be made by the health department as to how the water should be treated. Occasionally, a high iron deposit will produce hard water, which makes soap sudsing difficult or impossible. This can be corrected by a water softener, which is a small mechanical unit attached to the water supply.

Occasionally, a private water supply or well will have a chemical in the water that needs to be neutralized. This is accomplished by the water treat-

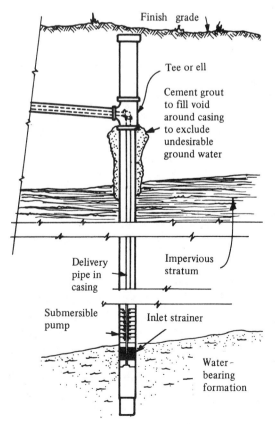

Figure 3-3 Artesian well water system. (Courtesy of U.S. Department of Housing and Urban Development.)

ment system. Such a system simply filters out the harsh chemicals. A water treatment system has a filter type of screen which traps the impurities, passing only treated water. The filter needs to be replaced periodically.

If a public water supply system is used, a water meter is installed at the beginning of the cold water line before pipe is connected to the plumbing fixtures. This meter measures the amount of water used, for the purpose of billing. Water travels through the pipes under pressure, which pushes the water through the pipe. No electricity is required for public water.

From the cold water main pipe inside the building, pipes are connected to all plumbing fixtures (see Figs. 3-1 and 3-2). If a hot water heating system is used, cold water must be connected to the boiler. Every plumbing fixture must have a means of shutting off the hot and cold water in the pipe. This is done by a valve. The purpose of the valve is to make it possible to carry out necessary repairs at the plumbing fixture without shutting the water off in the rest of the house. There is also a valve at the cold water pipe as it enters the building. This valve will shut off the water in the entire building. A valve is also installed on the hot water or main line.

HOT WATER

The cold water entering the house from the outside is connected to a water heater, called a hot water tank. From the hot water tank, pipes are installed to all plumbing fixtures that supply hot water (Figs. 3-1 and 3-2).

GAS

Although gas is not a necessity in a residence, it is sometimes used for heating the house, for cooking, and/or for heating water. If a public gas line is available, all that is required is a pipe of a size recommended by the local gas company from the main line in the street to the house.

If gas is chosen and public gas is not available, a private gas service system must be installed. This is commonly known as bottled gas. The gas is stored in a tank, which must be refilled as the gas is consumed. Most gas-burning appliances are convertible from bottled gas to natural or public gas. Since gas is highly dangerous, all joints must be leakproof. The utility company is responsible for the piping to the building, including the gas meter. From that point it becomes the responsibility of the owner to run the gas piping to the appliance or fixture. If gas is supplied at high pressure, a pressure-regulating valve is furnished and installed by the utility company. A shutoff valve is placed on the main line to shut off the entire system; in addition, each fixture has a valve.

Gas piping should be of best-quality, standard, black wrought-iron or steel pipe. The fittings should be of galvanized iron with brass valves. A certain amount of moisture is contained in gas, so all pipes should be straight, without sags, and pitched back so that condensation will flow back into the service pipe, or the piping should be dropped. Gas piping should not be bent; changes in directions are made with screw couplings and changes in pipe size with reducing fittings. Connections at fixtures should be made with flexible pipe to allow for positioning the fixture or appliance.

PUBLIC SEWER

There are two types of sewer systems: public and private. A public system involves only connecting the house sewer pipe to the main line already installed in the street. Generally, when a public sewer system is installed, a connection is put into the main line at each building lot, ready to tie in from the house sewer line. The size of pipe used from the house to the sewer main is generally 4 in. (Fig. 3-4).

Waste Lines

All plumbing fixtures in a house require drainage of waste. Connected to each plumbing fixture is a pipe; each such pipe eventually joins a single pipe leading through the wall of the house underground and connected to a sewer line. The waste travels through the pipe by gravity. If plumbing fixtures are installed in the basement of the house, the sewer pipe must be lower than the lowest plumbing fixture in the basement, because the system works on gravity. If this is not possible and plumbing fixtures in the basement are still desirable, a pump must be installed to eject the waste up and

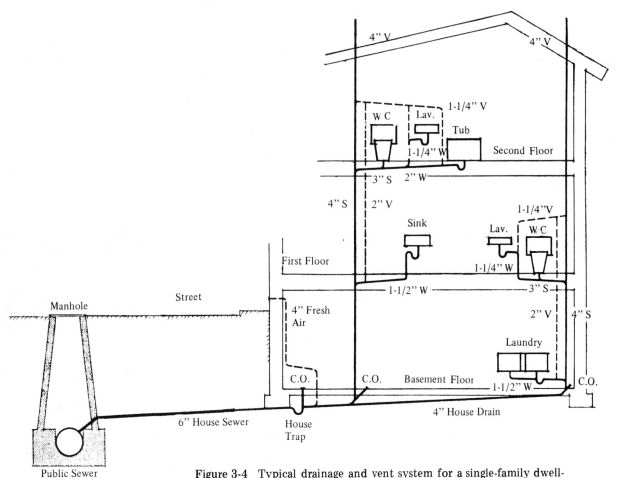

Figure 3-4 Typical drainage and vent system for a single-family dwelling. (From Ernest R. Weidhaas, *Architectural Drafting and Construction*, 2nd ed. Copyright © 1981 by Allen and Bacon, Inc. Reprinted with permission.)

into the higher waste pipe. Each fixture must have another pipe connected to allow air to circulate in the pipe to allow gravity to work; otherwise, a vacuum will prevent the waste from flowing. The air pipe is called a vent and leads up and through the roof. The location of vents is determined by building laws.

Pipes carrying waste are not under pressure and depend on gravity for removing waste. The minimum pitch or slope of pipe is $1/8$ in./ft, to facilitate even flow. To prevent decomposition of waste in the pipe, air circulation must be provided through the waste piping. The air circulation dilutes poisonous gases, retards pipe corrosion, and maintains balanced atmospheric pressure in the system. This is accomplished by extending air or vent stacks up through the roof.

Local codes for plumbing may require a minimum distance for vents from doors or windows and minimum pipe size and height above roof. Cleanouts are provided in waste lines to clean out the line if blockage should occur. These are located at the foot of each rise and at changes of pipe direction. In horizontal lines the maximum distance between cleanouts is about 50 ft. A cleanout is a threaded plug that is removable for pipe access, to release any blockage.

For a distance of 5 ft away from the house outside the building, cast-iron pipe or PVC must be used. From that point on, the sewage piping may be vitrified clay, concrete, or fiber piping; where there are trees, cast-iron pipe should be used to prevent tree roots from blocking the lines. All waste drainage lines should be as straight and direct as possible, to minimize friction. Changes in direction of drains should be made with easy bends so as not to restrict flow. Standard plumbing fittings used are: T or 90° bend, Y or 45° bend, TY, $1/6$ bend, $1/8$ bend, $1/16$ bend, and $1/4$ bend. T fittings should not be used for waste lines but can be used for vent lines. Pipes of different sizes are connected by a reducer or increaser fitting.

Plumbing Traps

The gases generated in a sewer can be dangerous to health. These gases are prevented from entering the house from the waste pipe by installing a trap on all plumbing fixtures. Occasionally, blockage occurs in the pipe, which must be removed. This is done by means of a threaded connection on the waste line called a cleanout. Once the threaded connection is removed, the blockage is released and the nut is reinstalled on the pipe (Fig. 3-5). Traps

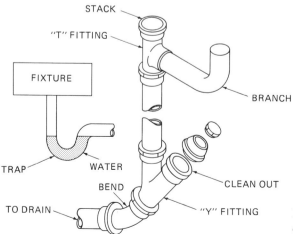

Figure 3-5 Plumbing fittings, cleanout, and trap.

are nothing more than an offset in the waste pipe designed to retain water, which then forms a seal. Traps must be installed under all plumbing fixtures except the water closet; the water in the bowl acts as a built-in trap. Vent stacks through the roof discharge gases to the outside.

PRIVATE SEWER

In a private sewer system, all parts of the system must be sited within the confines of the property on which the house is built. In designing the system, the two main considerations are the condition of the ground and the number of occupants for which the house is designed (usually based on the number of bedrooms). A test of the ground must be taken to determine how much water the ground will hold. This test, called a percolation test or a "perc test," is a simple procedure that involves digging a hole of a specified size and pouring a specific amount of water in the hole. The time it takes for the ground to absorb the water determines how much water the ground will hold (Table 3-1). This test is usually controlled by local laws, and if the ground will not support the number of people rated as living in the house, a building permit for constructing the house may not be granted. If this is the case, the ground or earth will have to be changed to support the system. This is accomplished by removing the existing earth and replacing it with a more water-absorbing earth, such as gravel.

Once the perc test has been approved, the system constructed consists of a 4-in. waste pipe from the house to a septic tank. The size of the tank is determined in gallons based on the number of people rated as living in the house (Table 3-2). The tank has a connection on top for cleaning and emptying the tank when necessary. The pipe leading to the tank from the house, called an inlet, is connected close to the top of the tank; another pipe, called an outlet, is connected to the opposite side of the tank, just a little lower than the inlet pipe. From the outlet, the pipe is connected to a distribution box, which is about 18 in. square and made of concrete or fiberglass. The distribution box has a series of knockouts which are removed where other pipes are installed to the leach field or absorption field. This field consists

TABLE 3-1

Data for Determining Field Requirement from Percolation Tests

Average time required for water to fall one inch in minutes	Effective absorption area (in bottom of disposal trench) in sq. ft. per bedroom
2 or less	50
3	60
4	70
5	80
10	100
15	120
30	180
60	240
Over 60 unsuitable except for special design with seepage pits	

TABLE 3-2

Minimum Capacities for Septic Tanks

Number of Bedrooms	Min. Liquid Capacity of Tank in Gallons*†
2 or less	500
3	600
4	750
5	900
6	1100
7	1300
8	1500
12	2000

*† Increase minimum liquid capacity by 50% when household garbage grinder discharges into system.

of a series of pipes with holes facing the bottom of the pipe to allow the waste to be absorbed into the ground (Fig. 3-6). The leach field piping is laid over a bed of crushed stone about 12 in. deep so that the earth will not block the holes; another piping method is to use pipe with open joints. The leach piping is about 18 in. below the ground. The number of feet of leach

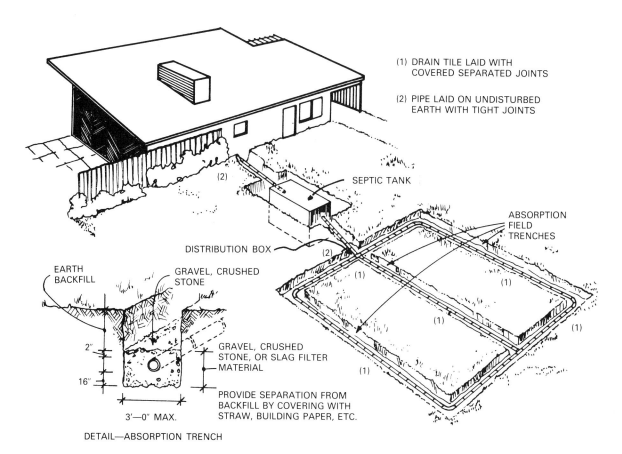

(1) DRAIN TILE LAID WITH COVERED SEPARATED JOINTS

(2) PIPE LAID ON UNDISTURBED EARTH WITH TIGHT JOINTS

SEPTIC TANK

ABSORPTION FIELD TRENCHES

DISTRIBUTION BOX

EARTH BACKFILL

GRAVEL, CRUSHED STONE

GRAVEL, CRUSHED STONE, OR SLAG FILTER MATERIAL

PROVIDE SEPARATION FROM BACKFILL BY COVERING WITH STRAW, BUILDING PAPER, ETC.

2"

16"

3'—0" MAX.

DETAIL—ABSORPTION TRENCH

Figure 3-6 Absorption field installation. (Courtesy of U.S. Department of Housing and Urban Development.)

piping is determined by the amount of water the ground will support and the number of people rated as living in the house.

Septic Tank

When the liquid and solid waste from a house goes into a septic tank, the solid settles to the bottom of the tank and the liquid goes on to the distribution box and into the leach field. The solids in the bottom of the tank are broken down by bacterial action into sludge, which is carried away by the liquid to the leach field. Sometimes the sludge in the septic tank builds up faster than the liquid will carry it away and the septic tank becomes too full to function properly. When this happens, the septic tank must be emptied. No matter what type of earth is used to support the system, eventually the ground becomes saturated and will no longer hold or support any more waste. This generally takes about 10 years of constant use, after which the system has to be rebuilt by removing the dirt from the leach and filling in with clean, fresh dirt, to start the cycle again. The sun also plays an important part in the operation of a leach field, through evaporation. It is wise to construct the leach system on the street side of the house for possible future connection to a public sewer.

The operation of the system is simple. Waste from the house is directed to a septic tank, which is built of concrete or fiberglass. This tank converts waste solids into liquid through bacterial action. The liquid flows into a distribution system, which distributes the liquid into a wide underground area. Between the sun evaporating the liquid and the ground absorbing the liquid, the system is very functional. The depth of the tank depends on the inlet grade level from the house. The grade should be 1 in. for every 4 ft of pitch. The minimum tank size for any house should be 500 gal. The larger the tank, the more efficient it is. A tank 50% larger than minimum will double the time between cleanouts. The depth should be at least 5 ft, regardless of other dimensions. If a garbage disposal system is used, the tank should be 50% larger than minimum, because grease interferes with tank operation.

The size of the system depends on local codes and the number of people the system is designed to serve. It also depends on the condition of the soil, which is determined by a percolation test. The procedure is to separate the solids from the liquids by sedimentation. The natural disintegration of sewage is divided into two stages, putrefaction and oxidation. The first stage produces ammonia, carbon dioxide gas, and hydrogen sulfide, which causes dark discolorations. As the process continues, methane gas is produced and the solids change to humus and decompose no further. A lack of oxygen causes a slow but continuous decay through the action of anaerobic bacteria. The ammonia is oxidized to nitrates and the sulfur compounds to sulfate. The process then consists of removing the solids to a receptacle (septic tank), where they putrefy and then leading the liquid into the soil or drain field, where it oxidizes without odor or danger to health. Later, bacteria act to break down the solids, resulting in sludge, which needs to be removed from the tank about every 3 or more years.

The tile lines in the distribution system are placed on a gravel and crushed stone bed and are about $1/4$ in. apart with open joints. These are placed about 16 in. below the surface of the ground and are sloped about $1/2$ in./ft. The length and size of tiles are determined by local code, based on the number of occupants and the absorption rate of the soil. From 100 to 300 ft of tile is usually required for the average residence.

Detergents interfere with the bacterial action in septic tanks. Waste from washing machines should empty into a separate drainage system. Watertight or sealed wells should be at least 100 ft away from a sewage drainage system. No structure of any type is allowed over a disposal system. When locating disposal systems, swampy land, muck soil, flower beds, vegetable gardens, roadways, and pavements should be avoided. Porous soil, in a location where the disposal field will not be disturbed, yet may easily be inspected, is most suitable. The system should run in as straight a line as possible in the same direction as that in which the sewer pipe leaves the house. The exception to this is on slopes, where it is necessary to run the disposal field across the slope to slow the flow and allow absorption. When laying out the system, it is wise to plan for later extension of the disposal field. If the system is not properly designed or built, it will become a health hazard, and could cause typhoid fever, dysentary, cholera, or other diseases. It is poor practice and illegal to discharge wastes into streams, oceans, or any body of water. Drainage fields must be located where there are no trees; otherwise, the roots will interfere with the system. When inspecting septic tanks for repair or emptying, do not use an open flame because the gases produced by decomposing sewage may explode and cause serious injury.

ELECTRICITY

The electric wire from the local electric company lines is for public use. From these lines, an electric wire is brought to the house and connected to an electric meter, which measures the amount of electricity that is used. The size of this wire will determine how much electricity is carried to the house. The unit of measurement used is the ampere. The minimum number of amperes for residential use should be 100 A. If electric heat is used, the minimum should be 200 A. From the meter, the service goes to an electric distribution panel.

Distribution Panel

The distribution panel can be either a fused panel or a circuit breaker panel (Fig. 3-7). The fused type has removable screw-in fuses which can be replaced when blown. The circuit breaker type has switch-like fuses. Both types of panel serve the same function. The purpose of the fuse and the circuit breaker is for safety. If more electricity is called for than the wires will carry, the wires get overheated, causing a possible fire. A fuse or circuit breaker interrupts the flow of electricity when a wire gets too hot, resulting in a blown fuse or a tripped circuit breaker. In the fuse type, a new fuse is installed; in the case of a circuit breaker, the circuit can be reactivated by flipping the switch.

The number of circuits in the house is determined by the number of fuses or circuit breakers. From the circuit, the wires are distributed to various parts of the house for plugs or lights.

Junction Box

It is impossible to have one endless continuous electric wire in the house. Many wires must be used, spliced together. The splicing is contained in a junction box with a cover (Fig. 3-8). This box is a safety precaution and is required by law.

Figure 3-7   Electric panel. (Courtesy of Square D Company.)

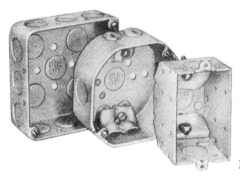

Figure 3-8   Electric outlet boxes.

Service Line

The main electric wire from the street to the house can be overhead or underground. In either case, the local electric company will connect the wire from the street to the house. Once connected to the house the owner is responsible for all electric wiring from the electric meter to the inside of the house.

Electric Poles

If the house is set back several hundred feet from the street and if the service is overhead, several electric poles may be needed. These poles are spaced about 100 ft apart and must be paid for by the owner. If the service is underground, no poles are needed.

QUESTIONS

1. Name two types of water supply systems.
   1. _____
   2. _____

2. Domestic water is always heated by a hot water heating system.
   True or False

3. All plumbing fixtures require hot water connections.   True or False

4. Which of the following is the purpose of a water valve?
   A. To slow down the water flow
   B. To speed up the water flow
   C. To allow more water in the pipe
   D. To shut off the water.

5. Gas piping is always required in a house.   True or False

6. Name the two types of available gas service.
   1. _____
   2. _____

7. Name two types of sewage systems.
   1. _____
   2. _____

8. All plumbing fixtures require a _____ to prevent harmful gases from entering the house.

9. Name the two factors that determine the design of a private sewage system.
   1. _____
   2. _____

10. Two types of electric panels are circuit breakers and volts.
    True or False

Wood Specie and Use

INTRODUCTION

The basic raw material for lumber is trees. There are many species of trees, each with a particular characteristic for a special purpose. Trees are classified into two types: hardwood and softwood. Softwood trees are evergreens; hardwood trees shed their leaves every season. The growth and strength of trees is controlled by soil condition, water, sun, and disease. Damaged or diseased trees will affect the quality of lumber cut from the trees.

In today's technology there is no wasted lumber from trees. The parts of the tree that are not suitable for use as building lumber are used in packing boxes and shipping crates. The waste and sawdust are used to manufacture building panels. The small branches are ground into ground cover or mulch used in landscaping. Trees are used to heat homes by converting them to firewood.

It takes many years for a tree to grow large enough to be harvested. When the tree is ready for harvesting, another tree is planted, making the supply of lumber endless; wood is a truly renewable natural resource.

Time and tests have distinguished tree species for maximum use. The weight that wood will support is determined in part by the closeness of its grain. Another factor that affects the use of wood is the condition of the tree. Damage to a tree affects the structural integrity of the lumber. Rules have been established by professional organizations to control the manufacture of lumber to provide safety in buildings. Lumber sizes have been established to standardize the industry. Smaller pieces of lumber are glued together to provide materials that carry heavy loads with wide spans.

Lumber is invaluable to the construction industry because wood is one of the easiest materials to cut, assemble, bend, and shape without losing its strength or beauty. In addition, wood is an excellent insulator.

The abundance of trees in most areas makes wood readily available for use in buildings. This building product is easy to work with, strong, and light. It is used for both interior and exterior structural framing.

Wood growth takes place during the spring of the year. There are two types of wood in a tree: the heartwood, the center of the tree, which is dense and strong, and the sapwood, the outer area of the tree, which is lighter and more porous.

The grain characteristics of wood are determined by the growth or width of the annual rings. A ring develops for each year the tree grows. It is the grain and species of wood that determines its strength.

Lumber freshly cut from a tree, called green lumber, cannot be used for construction. The moisture and sap from greenwood must be removed; otherwise, it will check and crack while drying and will have an ill effect on the building. It therefore becomes essential to treat the wood. This treatment, which consists of heating the greenwood in an oven called a kiln, is called seasoning and reduces the moisture content to between 12 and 20% (Fig. 4-1). When the wood is treated, it shrinks in width by about ½ in. What was a 2 in. × 4 in. board (a 2 × 4) when it went into the kiln comes out 1½ in. × 3½ in. (Table 4-1).

TREE STRUCTURE

There are three main parts to a tree: the roots, the trunk, and the crown (Fig. 4-2). The active part of the tree, which provides food, consists of the root tips and the leaves. The food and water are absorbed by the roots of the tree, and through a process called osmosis, the water is absorbed by the leaves through the sapwood. The food in the leaves produces chlorophyll, which gives leaves their green coloring. The life processes of the leaves are assisted by the sun and by carbon dioxide from the air and water. All of this produces carbohydrates which are carried to other parts of the tree by the inner bark. This process is repeated over and over, causing the tree to grow.

Figure 4-1 Kiln-drying of wood. (Courtesy of U.S. Department of Commerce.)

TABLE 4-1
Softwood Lumber Sizes for Finish Lumber and Boards

	Thickness (in.)			Thickness (in.)	
	Nominal	Dressed		Nominal	Dressed
Finish	$3/8$	$5/16$	Boards	6	$5^1/2$
	$1/2$	$7/16$		7	$6^1/2$
	$5/8$	$9/16$		8	$7^1/4$
	$3/4$	$5/8$		9	$8^1/4$
	1	$3/4$		10	$9^1/4$
	$1^1/4$	1		11	$10^1/4$
	$1^1/2$	$1^1/4$		12	$11^1/4$
	$1^3/4$	$1^3/8$		14	$13^1/4$
	2	$1^1/2$		16	$15^1/4$
	$2^1/2$	2		2	$1^1/2$
	3	$2^1/2$		3	$2^1/2$
	$3^1/2$	3		4	$3^1/2$
	4	$3^1/2$		5	$4^1/2$
Boards	1	$3/4$		6	$5^1/2$
	$1^1/4$	1		7	$6^1/2$
	$1^1/2$	$1^1/4$		8	$7^1/4$
	2	$1^1/2$		9	$8^1/4$
	3	$2^1/2$		10	$9^1/4$
	4	$3^1/2$		11	$10^1/4$
	5	$4^1/2$		12	$11^1/4$
				Over 12	Off $3/4$

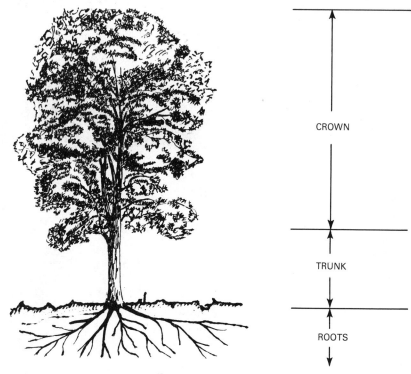

Figure 4-2 Tree parts.

A tree grows fastest in the spring; growth begins to slow down in the summer. The age of a tree can be determined by counting the rings of a cut tree, each ring representing one year of growth (Fig. 4-3).

The outer layer of a tree is called the bark. It is a layer of dead material and acts as a protectant, much like the skin of a person. The layer directly

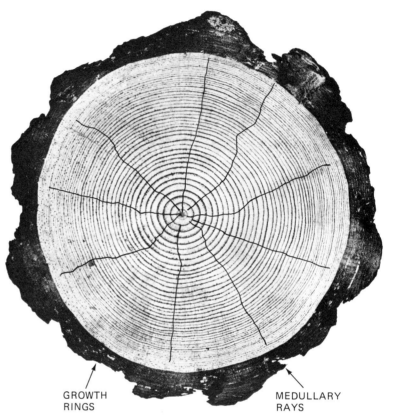

GROWTH
RINGS

MEDULLARY
RAYS

Figure 4-3   Tree growth rings. (Courtesy of Forest Products Laboratory, Forest Service, USDA.)

Figure 4-4   Tree parts. (Courtesy of Champion International.)

behind the bark, called the inner bark, carries food from the leaves to the growing part of the tree. Next is the cambium layer, which is responsible for new growth. Next to the cambium is the sapwood, which carries the food from the roots to the leaves; it is also a growing part of the tree. The sapwood later turns into heartwood, which is no longer growing but determines the color of the wood. In the very center of the tree is the pith, which is the soft center (Fig. 4-4). Through all of these parts of the tree run the medullary rays, which connect to all the tree parts. The medullary rays carry food across the various sections of the tree (Fig. 4-3).

TREE GROWTH

Of all the trees in the forest, only about one-fourth are harvested for lumber. Three-fourths are lost to forest fires, insects, storms, improper grazing, and other destructive forces.

Forest fires destroy millions of acres of woodland each year, but the greatest timber loss is caused by insects and disease, which cause about 10 times more loss than fire. Most forest fires are caused by careless smokers, campers, and hunters. There are three types of forest fires: surface fire, ground fire, and crown fire. A surface fire burns young trees and seedlings. A ground fire is usually without flame; instead, it smolders in humus and soil deep in the ground and burns for long periods. A crown fire causes most of its damage by burning the tops of trees. This happens most often with cone-bearing trees, whose gums and resins are highly flammable. The wind can easily spread a crown fire, causing total destruction.

LUMBER MANUFACTURE

When logs reach the lumbermill they are passed through a giant circular saw and cut into lumber. How the log is cut determines the quality and appearance of the lumber. Two methods are used to cut logs: one is called plain-saw and the other is called quarter-saw (Fig. 4-5).

In plain-sawing the log is squared and the boards are cut tangentially to the growth rings. This type of sawed lumber is cheaper to buy than quarter-sawed lumber. The boards are wider, which makes them warp and shrink more. They are also easier to dry. In quarter-sawed lumber, the log is first cut into four quarters and then each quarter is cut into boards. Quarter-sawed lumber will wear longer and resist warping, twisting, and shrinking because the growth rings are exposed, which forms a 45 to 90° angle with the cut.

LUMBER GRADING

To ensure good-quality, structurally sound lumber, grading rules have been established by lumber associations, such as the National Lumber Manufacturers' Association, Southern Pine Association, West Coast Lumberman's Association, and U.S. Department of Agriculture. During the growth process of trees, defects caused by disease, fires, and weather have an effect on the

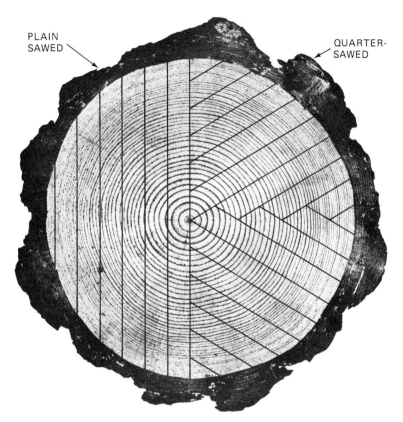

Figure 4-5 Lumber sawing diagram: left, plain sawing; right, quarter-sawing. (Courtesy of Forest Products Laboratory, Forest Service, USDA.)

growth of the trees, which will affect the quality of the wood. Some of these defects are: decay (checks caused by seasoning), shakes (cracks), knots (grain running at right angles), pitch pockets (openings between growth rings), wanelack (bark on the edge of a corner of a piece, caused by the lumber-mill), knot holes (voids caused by knots dropping from the wood), pitch streaks (well-defined accumulations of pitch), warp (bow, crook, cup, or twist), bow (bend from end to end on the flat side), crook (bend on the edge side), cup (twist across the narrow side of lumber), and split (grain separation). Specifications and rules have been established to control the quality of lumber for strength and density. This is important because wood varies according to its species and density and freedom from defects. The grades are determined by the working strength of the lumber, that is, how many pounds it will safely support. Lumber is graded as to whether it is hardwood or softwood (Fig. 4-6).

1. *Softwood.* Needle-leafed trees, usually called evergreens, are softwood trees (Fig. 4-7). Species include pine, spruce, hemlock, cedar, fir, juniper, cypress, Douglas fir, and redwood.
2. *Hardwoods.* Broad-leaved trees which shed their leaves every season are called hardwood trees (Fig. 4-8). Species include oak, ash, maple, beech, birch, cherry, elm, sycamore, and walnut.

Through laboratory tests, it has been determined that certain trees are best suited for certain jobs.

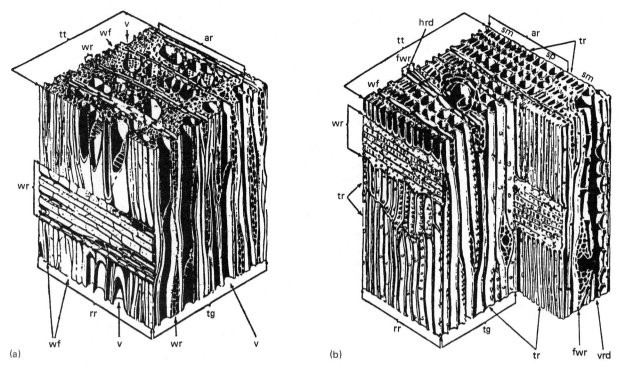

Figure 4-6 Structure of (a) hardwood, and (b) softwood. (Courtesy of U.S. Department of Agriculture.)

ar	Annual ring	tg	Tangential surface
fwr	Fusiform wood	tr	Tracheids or fibers
hrd	Horizontal resin duct	tt	Transverse surface
rr	Radial surface	v	Vessel or pore
sm	Summer wood	wf	Wood fibers
sp	Spring wood	wr	Wood rays

Figure 4-7 Softwood trees: (a) redwood; (b) Douglas fir. (Courtesy of The American Forestry Association, 1319 18th Street NW, Washington, DC 20036.)

53

Figure 4-8 Hardwood trees: (a) white ash; (b) American sycamore; (c) beech. (Courtesy of The American Forestry Association, 1319 18th Street, NW, Washington, DC 20036.)

Softwood Grading

The U.S. Department of Commerce has developed a standard called the American Softwood Lumber Standard. This standard provides minimum bases for species and sizes (Table 4-2).

TABLE 4-2

Softwood Lumber Grades

Product	Grade	Character of grade and typical uses
Finish	B&B	Highest recognized grade of finish. Generally clear, although a limited number of pin knots permitted. Finest quality for natural or stain finish.
	C	Excellent for painted or natural finish where requirements are less exacting. Reasonably clear but permits limited number of surface checks and small tight knots.
	C&Btr	Combination of B&B and C grades; satisfies requirements for high-quality finish.
	D	Economical, serviceable grade for natural or painted finish.
Boards S4S	No. 1	High quality with good appearance characteristics. Generally sound and tight-knotted. Largest hole permitted is $1/16$ in. A superior product suitable for wide range of uses, including shelving, form, and crating lumber.
	No. 2	High-quality sheathing material, characterized by tight knots. Generally free of holes.
	No. 3	Good, serviceable sheathing, usable for many applications without waste.
	No. 4	Admit pieces below No. 3 which can be used without waste or contain usable portions at least 24 in. in length.
Dimension: Structural light framing 2 to 4 in. thick 2 to 4 in. wide	Select Structural Dense Select Structural	High quality, relatively free of characteristics that impair strength or stiffness. Recommended for uses where high strength, stiffness, and good appearance are required.
	No. 1 No. 1 Dense	Provide high strength; recommended for general utility and construction purposes. Good appearance, especially suitable where exposed because of the knot limitations.
	No. 2 No. 2 Dense	Although less restricted than No. 1, suitable for all types of construction. Tight knots.
	No. 3 No. 3 Dense	Assigned design values meet wide range of design requirements. Recommended for general construction purposes where appearance is not a controlling factor. Many pieces included in this grade would qualify as No. 2 except for single limiting characteristic. Provides high-quality, low-cost construction.
Studs 2 to 4 in. thick 2 to 6 in. wide 10 ft and shorter	Stud	Stringent requirements as to straightness, strength, and stiffness adapt this grade to all stud uses, including load-bearing walls. Crook restricted to 2 in. $\times$ 4-8 ft to $1/4$ in., with wane restricted to one-third of thickness.
Structural joists and planks 2 to 4 in. thick 5 in. and wider	Select Structural Dense Select Structural	High quality, relatively free of characteristics that impair strength or stiffness. Recommended for uses where high strength, stiffness, and good appearance are required.
	No. 1 No. 1 Dense	Provide high strength; recommended for general utility and construction purposes. Good appearance; especially suitable where exposed because of the knot limitations.
	No. 2 No. 2 Dense	Although less restricted than No. 1, suitable for all types of construction. Tight knots.

TABLE 4-2 (cont.)

Product	Grade	Character of grade and typical uses
	No. 3 No. 3 Dense	Assigned stress values meet wide range of design requirements. Recommended for general construction purposes where appearance is not a controlling factor. Many pieces included in this grade would qualify as No. 2 except for single limiting characteristic. Provides high-quality, low-cost construction.
Light framing 2 to 4 in. thick 2 to 4 in. wide	Construction	Recommended for general framing purposes. Good appearance, strong, and serviceable.
	Standard	Recommended for same uses as Construction grade, but allows larger defects.
	Utility	Recommended where combination of strength and economy is desired. Excellent for blocking, plates, and bracing.
	Economy	Usable lengths suitable for bracing, blocking, bulkheading, and other utility purposes where strength and appearance not controlling factors.
Appearance framing 2 to 4 in. thick 2 in. and wider	Appearance	Designed for uses such as exposed-beam roof systems. Combines strength characteristics of No. 1 with appearance of C&Btr.
Timbers: 5 in. X 5 in. and larger	No. 1 SR No. 1 Dense SR No. 2 SR No. 2 Dense SR	No. 1 and No. 2 are similar in appearance to corresponding grades of 2 in. dimension. Recommended for general construction uses. SR in grade name indicates Stress Rated.

Source: Southern Forest Products Association.

The classification is broken down as follows:

Finish lumber: first-quality lumber, with no defects, that can be natural-finished or stained

Board grade: used for sheathing, subflooring, shelves, boxes, crates, and packing units

Dimension lumber: used for joists, rafters, studs, and small timbers

Structural light framing: used for high strength and to support heavy loads

Light framing: framing of good appearance and low design level

Studs: used for outside and inside framing of walls

Structural joists and planks: members used to carry heavier loads

Appearance framing: used for framework that will be exposed to view

Timbers: larger than 5 in. X 5 in.

The lumber classifications above are broken down into grades, from the highest finish grade to the most economical grade. The grade selection is based on where the lumber is being used. If it will be covered, an economical grade will be used. If the wood is to be exposed, the highest quality will probably be used. Each piece of lumber has the grade stamped on it for proper identification (Fig. 4-9).

Hardwood Grading

Rules for grading hardwood lumber are set by the National Hardwood Lumber Association, and several professional groups or associations concern themselves only with specific species of hardwood.

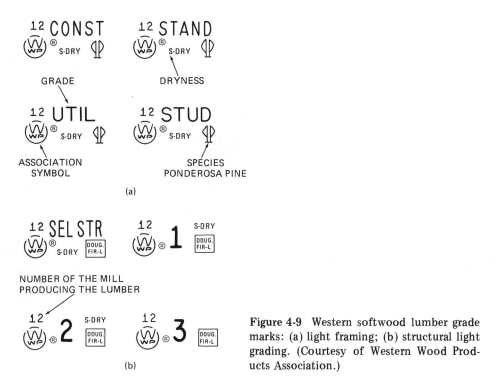

Figure 4-9 Western softwood lumber grade marks: (a) light framing; (b) structural light grading. (Courtesy of Western Wood Products Association.)

The basic grades are: Firsts and Seconds (FAS), select No. 1 common, No. 2 common, and No. 3 common. Firsts and Seconds are the best grade of hardwood boards. The three numbered grades are boards of lower quality and are graded by the number of defects in the wood such as checks, knots, worm holes, bird pecks, stains or sound knots ¾ in. or less.

The differences in hardwood grading have to do with how much of a piece is usable. Hardwood is cut in lengths from 4 to 16 ft in 2-ft increments. These are called standard lengths. The thickness of hardwood lumber is expressed in quarter inches. A piece of hardwood 1¼ in. thick is expressed as ⁵⁄₄ thick.

Knot Grading

There are many qualities of knots (Fig. 4-10):

> *Sound knot:* solid with no decay; firm
> *Firm knot:* solid but signs of decay
> *Encased knot:* growth rings not the same as surrounding area
> *Single knot:* by itself
> *Corner knot:* intersection of adjacent faces
> *Fixed knot:* holds its place but can be moved under pressure
> *Pin knot:* not over ½ in. in diameter
> *Small knot:* over ½ in. but not more than ¾ in. in diameter
> *Medium knot:* over ¾ in. but not more than 1½ in. in diameter
> *Large knot:* over 1½ in. in diameter
> *Knot occurrence:* branch knots
> *Watertight knot:* growth rings intergrown with surrounding wood

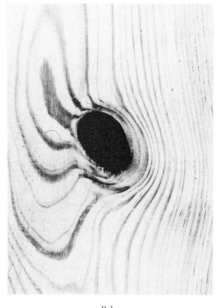

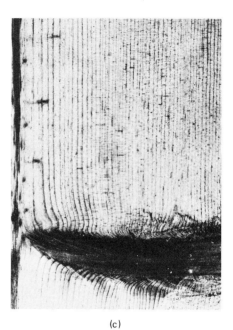

(a)   (b)   (c)

Figure 4-10 Most common types of knots: (a) spike; (b) intergrown (usually solid); (c) encased (often loose). (Courtesy of Forest Products Laboratory, Forest Service, USDA.)

Hollow knot: sound but contains hole over ¼ in. in diameter
Tight knot: fixed and retains position
Intergrown knot: partially or completely intergrown with the rings
Decayed knot: softer than surrounding wood, with advanced decay
Loose knot: may not remain in place
Star-checked knot: radial checks
Knot cluster: more than one knot grouped together

LUMBER CLASSIFICATION

Lumber (Fig. 4-11) is divided into three classes:

1. *Yard lumber:* available from retail lumberyards for general-purpose use. Includes boards and siding less than 2 in. thick, and finished lumber used for flooring and shingles. Also includes planks and joists less than 4 in. thick such as 2 × 4's, 2 × 6's, 3 × 4's, 3 × 6's, and 4 × 4's. Yard lumber is graded in six categories: A, B, and C, which include lumber for interior work, either painted or stained, and No. 1 common, No. 2 common, and No. 3 common, grades for use where appearance is not important.

2. *Structural grades:* used for load-bearing construction, such as beams, girders, posts, sills, and heavy plank flooring. Divided according to density, strength, and stiffness.

3. *Factory or shop lumber:* graded by appearance; for such uses as the manufacture of doors, windows, molding, patterns, and toys.

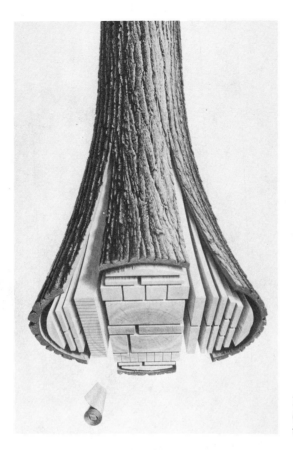

Figure 4-11 Lumber cut from tree. (Courtesy of Champion International.)

BOARD MEASURE

All lumber is sold by the board foot. One board foot is a piece of lumber 1 in. thick, 12 in. wide, and 12 in. long. In the formula used to determine the number of board feet, called the board foot measure (BFM), the thickness is multiplied by the width by the length (if more than one piece is involved, the total length of all the pieces is used), all in feet, divided by 12. The dimensions used are full dimensions. Example: A 2 × 4 does not actually measure 2 in. by 4 in. but measures 1½ in. by 3½ in. A 1-in-thick board measures only ¾ in. thick. Thus, one 2 × 4, 8 ft long contains 5⅓ BFM: (2 × 4 × 8)/12 = 5⅓ BFM. A 6 × 10, 16 ft long contains (6 × 10 × 16)/12 = 80 BFM. A 1 × 10, 12 ft long contains (1 × 10 × 12)/12 = 10 BFM.

WOOD STRENGTH

The strength of wood is determined by the characteristic of the grain. The closer the grain, the stronger the wood. The species of wood has a great deal to do with the loads that it will support (Fig. 4-12). The load that lumber will support is determined by the distance of support, what it is being used for, the species of the wood, and the size of the wood. For example, pine, fir, oak, and spruce are used for but not restricted to posts, girders, trusses, and heavy framing. Birch, pine, hemlock, and spruce are used for light fram-

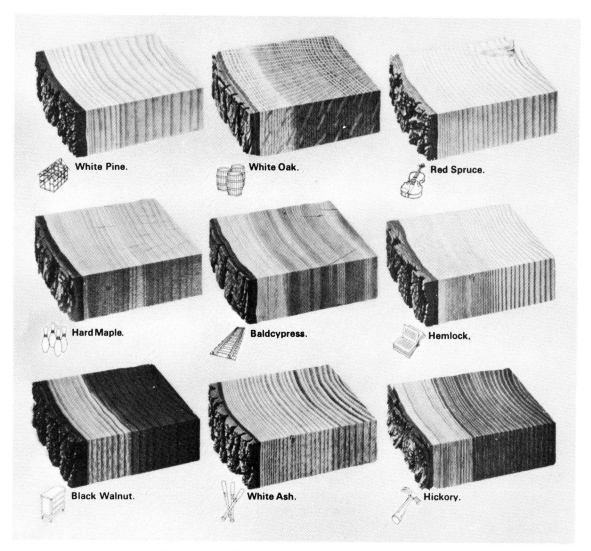

Figure 4-12 Uses for various woods. (Courtesy of Champion International.)

ing, such as studs, joists, and rafters; for outside finish, pine, cypress, red-wood, poplar, and spruce; for shingles, cedar, cypress, and redwood; for doors, windows, and frames, pine and fir; for floors, oak, maple, pine, birch, and beech; for interior painted finish, pine, birch gum, redwood, and poplar; for natural finish, oak, chestnut, mahogany, pine, birch, redwood, and cedar.

COMPOSITION LUMBER

Man-made wood-based building panels can be called composition lumber. These are generally made from wood waste products, such as sawdust and wood chips, processed and mixed with a composition of glue into the shape of panels (Fig. 4-13). The thickness will vary from ⅛ in. in 1⅛-in. incre-ments and 4 ft wide by 8, 10, and 12 ft long. These units are used for sheath-ing and subflooring. Also, man-made units are manufactured for exterior finish siding and interior prefinished paneling. Man-made units should not be used where structural support is required.

Figure 4-13 Composition panel. (Courtesy of Blandin Wood Products Co.)

PLYWOOD

Panels made from real wood are called plywood. This is a broad term with many meanings and many uses. Thin sheets of wood are peeled from a log by a giant lathe. These thin sheets of wood are glued together, alternating the grain of each layer (Fig. 4-14). This has a tendency to reduce shrinkage, warping, and splitting of the wood. Total thickness will vary from $\frac{1}{8}$ to $1\frac{1}{8}$ in. and 4 ft wide by 8, 9, 10, and 12 ft long. The reason a module of 4 ft has been selected in the size of plywood and composition panels is because studs, rafters, and joists are generally spaced 16 in. apart, and there

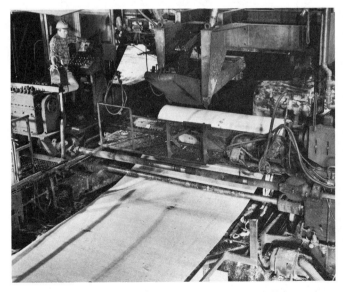

(a) At the lathe

(b) At the drier

Figure 4-14 Plywood manufacturing and quality control program. (Courtesy of American Plywood Association.)

(c) At veneer grading belt

(d) At the glue spreader

(e) At the press

(f) During final grading

Figure 4-14 (continued)

are an even number of multiples of 16 in. in a 4-ft module. Plywood is manufactured for both interior and exterior use in many grades, qualities, thicknesses, and finishes (Fig. 4-15). It is used for subflooring, wall and roof sheathing, specially built trusses, beams, and girders, and concrete formwork. It is also used for wall paneling, cabinets, counters and marine use, roof decking, cabinets, and as finish exterior siding.

The outer layers of plywood are called the face and the back. The face of the plywood is visible and a high-quality wood species is used. Some plywood, such as that used for cabinet doors, has two faces. The inner layers of the plywood are called crossbands. Crossbands are cut to about $\frac{1}{10}$ to $\frac{5}{16}$ in. thick and are glued together with alternate graining.

Plywood is classified by hardwood and softwood. The hardwood grades are usually for finish or decorative purpose. The quality of the hardwood grading of the plywood is classified as follows:

Premium grade A: best grade, used for staining or natural finish; has a carefully matched veneer or face; matched for color and wood grain, making several pieces look like one

Good grade 1: good face but not carefully matched; used for staining or natural finish

Sound grade 2: open defects on the face of the plywood; used for painted surfaces

Utility grade 3: cracks or knot holes on the face; used for sheathing, backing, or formwork

Backing grade 4: knots and splits on the face wood, grain matching or unselected grain; used for making boxes, crates, foundation forms, and for temporary use

Specialty grade (SP): special-order plywood for jobs where a specific wood species is needed; matched grain; used in banks, executive offices, and corporate offices.

All hardwood grading plywood has a hardwood face.

Softwood plywood is made up of softwood plies. The inner plies are made from a variety of softwoods. The hidden side of the panel is called back veneer. Grades are classified as N, A, B, C, and D from highest to lowest. Softwood plywood can be ordered face sanded or unsanded (Tables 4-3 to 4-5, pages 64–68).

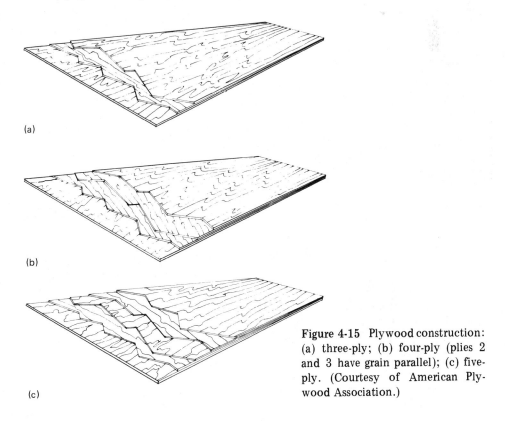

(a)

(b)

(c)

Figure 4-15 Plywood construction: (a) three-ply; (b) four-ply (plies 2 and 3 have grain parallel); (c) five-ply. (Courtesy of American Plywood Association.)

TABLE 4-3

Guide to APA Performance-Rated Panels

	Grade Designation	Description & Common Uses	Typical Trademarks	Most Common Thicknesses (in.)				
				5/16	3/8	1/2	5/8	3/4
PROTECTED OR INTERIOR USE	APA RATED SHEATHING EXP 1 or 2	Specially designed for subflooring and wall and roof sheathing, but can also be used for a broad range of other construction and industrial applications. Can be manufactured as conventional veneered plywood, as a composite, or as a nonveneered panel. For special engineered applications, including high load requirements and certain industrial uses, veneered panels conforming to PS 1 may be required. Specify Exposure 1 when construction delays are anticipated.	APA RATED SHEATHING 32/16 1/2 INCH SIZED FOR SPACING EXPOSURE 1 000 PS 1-74 C-D INT/EXT GLUE NRB-108	●	●	●	●	●
	APA STRUCTURAL I & II RATED SHEATHING EXP 1	Unsanded all-veneer PS 1 plywood grades for use where strength properties are of maximum importance: structural diaphragms, box beams, gusset plates, stressed-skin panels, containers, pallet bins. Made only with exterior glue (Exposure 1). STRUCTURAL I more commonly available.	APA RATED SHEATHING STRUCTURAL I 24/0 3/8 INCH SIZED FOR SPACING EXPOSURE 1 000 PS 1-74 C-D INT/EXT GLUE NRB-108	●	●		●	●
	APA RATED STURD-I-FLOOR EXP 1 or 2	For combination subfloor-underlayment. Provides smooth surface for application of resilient floor covering and possesses high concentrated and impact load resistance. Can be manufactured as conventional veneered plywood, as a composite, or as a nonveneered panel. Available square edge or tongue-and-groove. Specify Exposure 1 when construction delays are anticipated.	APA RATED STURD-I-FLOOR 24 oc 23/32 INCH SIZED FOR SPACING T&G NET WIDTH 47-1/2 EXPOSURE 1 000 INT/EXT GLUE NRB-108 FHA-UM-66				● 19/32	● 23/32
	APA RATED STURD-I-FLOOR 48 oc (2-4-1) EXP 1	For combination subfloor-underlayment on 32- and 48-inch spans and for heavy timber roof construction. Provides smooth surface for application of resilient floor coverings and possesses high concentrated and impact load resistance. Manufactured only as conventional veneered plywood and only with exterior glue (Exposure 1). Available square edge or tongue-and-groove.	APA RATED STURD-I-FLOOR 48 oc 1-1/8 INCH 2-4-1 SIZED FOR SPACING EXPOSURE 1 T&G 000 INT/EXT GLUE NRB-108 FHA-UM-66			1-1/8		
EXTERIOR USE	APA RATED SHEATHING EXT	Exterior sheathing panel for subflooring and wall and roof sheathing, siding on service and farm buildings, crating, pallets, pallet bins, cable reels, etc. Manufactured as conventional veneered plywood.	APA RATED SHEATHING 48/24 3/4 INCH SIZED FOR SPACING EXTERIOR 000 PS 1-74 C-C NRB-108	●	●	●	●	●
	APA STRUCTURAL I & II RATED SHEATHING EXT	For engineered applications in construction and industry where fully waterproof panels are required. Manufactured only as conventional veneered PS 1 plywood. Unsanded. STRUCTURAL I more commonly available.	APA RATED SHEATHING STRUCTURAL I 24/0 3/8 INCH SIZED FOR SPACING EXTERIOR 000 PS 1-74 C-C NRB-108	●	●		●	●
	APA RATED STURD-I-FLOOR EXT	For combination subfloor-underlayment under resilient floor coverings where severe moisture conditions may be present, as in balcony decks. Possesses high concentrated and impact load resistance. Manufactured only as conventional veneered plywood. Available square edge or tongue-and-groove.	APA RATED STURD-I-FLOOR 20 oc 19/32 INCH SIZED FOR SPACING EXTERIOR 000 NRB-108 FHA-UM-66				● 19/32	● 23/32

Source: American Plywood Association.

TABLE 4-3 (continued)
Protected or Interior Use

Grade Designation	Description & Common Uses	Typical Trademarks	Veneer Grade			Most Common Thicknesses (in.)					
			Face	Inner Plies	Back	1/4	5/16	3/8	1/2	5/8	3/4
APA N-N, N-A, N-B INT	Cabinet quality. For natural finish furniture, cabinet doors, built-ins, etc. Special order items.	N-N G-1 INT-APA PS1-74 000	N	C	N, A, or B						●
APA N-D INT	For natural finish paneling. Special order item.	N-D G-2 INT-APA PS1-74 000	N	D	D	●					
APA A-A INT	For applications with both sides on view: built-ins, cabinets, furniture, partitions. Smooth face, suitable for painting.	A-A G-1 INT-APA PS1-74 000	A	D	A	●		●	●	●	●
APA A-B INT	Use where appearance of one side is less important but where two solid surfaces are necessary.	A-B G-1 INT-APA PS1-74 000	A	D	B	●		●	●	●	●
APA A-D INT	Use where appearance of only one side is important: paneling, built-ins, shelving, partitions, flow racks.	APA A-D GROUP 1 INTERIOR 000 PS 1 74 EXTERIOR GLUE	A	D	D	●		●	●	●	●
APA B-B INT	Utility panel with two solid sides. Permits circular plugs.	B-B G-2 INT-APA PS1-74 000	B	D	B	●		●	●	●	●
APA B-D INT	Utility panel with one solid side. Good for backing, sides of built-ins, industry shelving, slip sheets, separator boards, bins.	APA B-D GROUP 2 INTERIOR 000 PS 1 74 EXTERIOR GLUE	B	D	D	●		●	●	●	●
APA UNDERLAYMENT INT	For application over structural subfloor. Provides smooth surface for application of resilient floor coverings. Touch-sanded. Also available with exterior glue.	APA UNDERLAYMENT GROUP 1 INTERIOR 000 PS 1 74 EXTERIOR GLUE	C Plgd.	C & D	D			●	●	● 19/32	● 23/32
APA C-D PLUGGED INT	For built-ins, wall and ceiling tile backing, cable reels, walkways, separator boards. Not a substitute for UNDERLAYMENT or STURD-I-FLOOR as it lacks their indentation resistance. Touch-sanded. Also made with exterior glue.	APA C-D PLUGGED GROUP 2 INTERIOR 000 PS 1 74 EXTERIOR GLUE	C Plgd.	D	D			●	●	● 19/32	● 23/32
APA DECORATIVE INT	Rough-sawn, brushed, grooved, or striated faces. For paneling, interior accent walls, built-ins, counter facing, display exhibits.	APA DECORATIVE GROUP 4 INTERIOR 000	C or btr.	D	D		●	●	●	●	
APA PLYRON INT	Hardboard face on both sides. For countertops, shelving, cabinet doors, flooring. Faces tempered, untempered, smooth or screened.	PLYRON -INT-APA 000		C & D					●	●	●

TABLE 4-3 (continued)

Exterior Use

Grade Designation	Description & Common Uses	Typical Trademarks	Veneer Grade			Most Common Thicknesses (in.)					
			Face	Inner Plies	Back	1/4	5/16	3/8	1/2	5/8	3/4
APA A-A EXT	Use where appearance of both sides is important: fences, built-ins, signs, boats, cabinets, commercial refrigerators, shipping containers, tote boxes, tanks, ducts.	A-A G-1 EXT-APA PS1-74 000	A	C	A	•		•	•	•	•
APA A-B EXT	Use where the appearance of one side is less important.	A-B G-1 EXT-APA PS1-74 000	A	C	B	•		•	•	•	•
APA A-C EXT	Use where the appearance of only side is important: soffits, fences, structural uses, boxcar and truck linings, farm buildings, tanks, trays, commercial refrigerators.	APA A-C GROUP 1 EXTERIOR 000 PS 1-74	A	C	C	•		•	•	•	•
APA B-B EXT	Utility panel with solid faces.	B-B G-2 EXT-APA PS1-74 000	B	C	B	•		•	•	•	•
APA B-C EXT	Utility panel for farm service and work buildings, boxcar and truck linings, containers, tanks, agricultural equipment. Also as a base for exterior coatings for walls, roofs.	APA B-C GROUP 1 EXTERIOR 000 PS 1-74	B	C	C	•		•	•	•	•
APA UNDERLAYMENT C-C PLUGGED EXT	For application over structural subfloor. Provides smooth surface for application of resilient floor coverings where severe moisture conditions may be present. Touch-sanded.	APA UNDERLAYMENT C-C PLUGGED GROUP 2 EXTERIOR 000 PS 1-74	C Plgd.	C	C			•	•	19/32	23/32
APA C-C PLUGGED EXT	For use as tile backing where severe moisture conditions exist. For refrigerated or controlled atmosphere rooms, pallet fruit bins, tanks, boxcar and truck floors and linings, open soffits. Touch-sanded.	APA C-C PLUGGED GROUP 2 EXTERIOR 000 PS 1-74	C Plgd.	C	C			•	•	19/32	23/32
APA HDO EXT	High Density Overlay. Has a hard semi-opaque resin-fiber overlay both faces. Abrasion resistant. For concrete forms, cabinets, countertops, signs, tanks. Also available with skid-resistant screen-grid surface.	HDO A-A G-1 EXT-APA PS1-74 000	A or B	C or C Plgd	A or B			•	•	•	•
APA MDO EXT	Medium Density Overlay. Smooth, opaque, resin-fiber overlay one or both faces. Ideal base for paint, both indoors and outdoors. Also available as a 303 Siding.	MDO B-B G-2 EXT-APA PS1-74 000	B	C	B or C			•	•	•	•
APA MARINE EXT	Ideal for boat hulls. Made only with Douglas fir or western larch. Special solid jointed core construction. Subject to special limitations on core gaps and number of face repairs. Also available with HDO or MDO faces.	MARINE A-A EXT-APA PS1-74 000	A or B	B	A or B	•		•	•	•	•
APA PLYRON EXT	Hardboard faces both sides, tempered, smooth or screened.	PLYRON EXT-APA 000		C					•	•	•
APA 303 SIDING EXT	Proprietary plywood products for exterior siding, fencing, etc. Special surface treatment such as V-groove, channel groove, striated, brushed, rough-sawn and texture-embossed (MDO). Stud spacing (Span Rating) and face grade classification indicated in trademark.	APA 303 SIDING 18-S/W 24 OC 23/32 INCH GROUP 1 EXTERIOR 000 PS 1-74 FHA UM 64		C	C			11/32	15/32	19/32	
APA T 1-11 EXT	Special 303 panel having grooves 1/4" deep, 3/8" wide, spaced 4" or 8" o.c. Other spacing optional. Edges shiplapped. Available unsanded, textured and MDO.	APA 303 SIDING 6-S/W 16 OC 19/32 INCH GROUP 2 EXTERIOR 000 T1-11 PS 1-74 FHA UM 64	C or btr.	C	C					19/32	
APA B-B PLYFORM CLASS I and CLASS II EXT	Concrete form grades with high reuse factor. Sanded both sides and mill-oiled unless otherwise specified. Special restrictions on species. Class I panels are stiffest, strongest and most commonly available. Also available in HDO for very smooth concrete finish, in STRUCTURAL I (all plies limited to Group 1 species) and with special overlays.	APA PLYFORM B-B CLASS I EXTERIOR 000 PS 1-74	B	C	B					•	•

TABLE 4-4

Classification of Species

Group 1		
Apitong	Keruing	Pine, Southern
Beech, American	Larch, Western	Loblolly
Birch	Maple, Sugar	Longleaf
Sweet	Pine	Shortleaf
Yellow	Caribbean	Slash
Douglas Fir 1	Ocote	Tanoak
Kapur[a]		

Group 2		
Cedar, Port Orford	Lauan	Pine
Cypress	Almon	Pond
Douglas Fir 2	Bagtikan	Red
Fir	Mayapis	Virginia
Balsam	Red Lauan	Western White
California Red	Tangile	Spruce
Grand	White Lauan	Black
Noble	Maple, Black	Red
Pacific Silver	Mengkulang	Sitka
White	Meranti, Red	Sweetgum
Hemlock, Western	Mersawa	Tamarack
		Yellow-Poplar

Group 3		
Alder, Red	Red	Redwood
Birch, Paper	Jack	Spruce
Cedar, Alaska	Lodgepole	Engelmann
Fir, Subalpine	Ponderosa	White
Hemlock, Eastern	Spruce	
Maple, Bigleaf		

Group 4	
Aspen	Cottonwood
Bigtooth	Eastern
Quaking	Black (Western
Cativo	Poplar)
Cedar	Pine
Incense	Eastern White
Western Red	Sugar

Group 5
Basswood
Poplar, Balsam

Source: American Plywood Association.

Exterior and Interior Plywood

The principal difference between exterior and interior plywood is in the quality of glue used to fuse the wood plies together. Interior glue or adhesive is used for interior use only. Intermediate adhesive is intended for use in an area that is protected, where moderate delays in providing protection for the plywood might be expected or where high humidity or some water leakage is expected. Waterproof exterior adhesive is used where protection against moisture is delayed for long periods but where protection eventually will be provided.

Plywood for exterior permanent use is bonded together with an adhesive that will hold when repeatedly wet or dry, such as marine plywood.

TABLE 4-5

Veneer Grades

The veneer used for PS 1 plywood **face, back** and **inner plies** is graded during manufacture on the basis of wood characteristics, such as knots, knotholes, splits, etc. There are six veneer grades designated by letters. These, in descending order of quality, are **N, A, B, C Plugged, C,** and **D.** N, for example, is the most nearly perfect (and for that reason a special-order item), while D is the lowest allowable veneer grade.

Most veneer can be repaired to raise its quality to the next higher grade. C Plugged, for example, is an improved C-grade veneer. Veneer is repaired by machining out knots or other defects and then filling the holes with **wood** or **synthetic patches** of the same thickness. The patches may be any of several shapes — oval, round, or long and narrow. **Stitching** is a nonstructural method of temporarily sewing thin strips of C- or D-grade veneer together into sheets before lamination. Veneer grading specifications are detailed in PS 1. The table below summarizes those specifications.

Grade of veneer on panel face — **A-C GROUP 1**
Grade of veneer on panel back —

APA

EXTERIOR

000

PS 1-83

N	Smooth surface "natural finish" veneer. Select, all heartwood or all sapwood. Free of open defects. Allows not more than 6 repairs, wood only, per 4x8 panel, made parallel to grain and well matched for grain and color.
A	Smooth, paintable. Not more than 18 neatly made repairs, boat, sled, or router type, and parallel to grain, permitted. May be used for natural finish in less demanding applications.
B	Solid surface. Shims, circular repair plugs and tight knots to 1 inch across grain permitted. Some minor splits permitted.
C Plugged	Improved C veneer with splits limited to 1/8 inch width and knotholes and borer holes limited to 1/4 x 1/2 inch. Allows some broken grain. Synthetic repairs permitted.
C	Tight knots to 1-1/2 inch. Knotholes to 1 inch across grain and some to 1-1/2 inch if total width of knots and knotholes is within specified limits. Synthetic or wood repairs. Discoloration and sanding defects that do not impair strength permitted. Limited splits allowed. Stitching permitted.
D	Knots and knotholes to 2-1/2 inch width across grain and 1/2 inch larger within specified limits. Limited splits are permitted. Stitching permitted. Limited to Exposure 1 or 2 or Interior panels.

Source: American Plywood Association.

One other type of plywood is called structural plywood. This is designed for carrying heavier loads or load-carrying structural members. These plywood panels have special requirements as to wood grade, species, and glue.

LAMINATED LUMBER

Small high-strength structural lumber pieces are glued together to make laminated lumber (Fig. 4-16). Laminated members are structurally designed into beams, girders, and trusses. The small pieces are bent over a form and se-

Precise finger joint cutter insures tight fit for maximum strength after gluing.

This glue extruder gives complete coverage across the face of the lam stock.

Workmen inspect a massive curved beam as it comes from planer.

Figure 4-16 Manufacturing of laminating beams. (Courtesy of American Institute of Timber Construction.)

Figure 4-17 Bowstring trusses. (Courtesy of American Institute of Timber Construction.)

cured. Glue is applied and pieces are clamped and placed in position. This process is repeated until the desired shape and size is obtained. The lamination is controlled by pressure and temperature. Almost any curve can be achieved with lamination. Bowstring trusses spanning 300 ft can be built with laminated lumber (Fig. 4-17).

QUESTIONS

1. Wood growth in trees takes place in which of the following seasons?
   A. Summer
   B. Spring
   C. Fall
2. The grain of wood is determined by _____.
3. Lumber cut from trees can be used without further treatment.
   True or False
4. Name three defects in trees.
   1. _____
   2. _____
   3. _____
5. Wood classification includes:
   A. Yard lumber
   B. Structural
   C. Factory
   D. None of the above
   E. All of the above
6. How many board feet are in eight pieces of 2 X 4, 12 ft long?
   _____
7. Name three species of softwood.
   1. _____
   2. _____
   3. _____
8. Composition lumber is made from wood waste.   True or False
9. Define *plywood.* _____
   _____
10. Laminated lumber will not span more than 150 ft.   True or False

5

Soil Investigation

INTRODUCTION

All buildings depend on soil for their ultimate support. For proper design of the foundation of a building, the type of soil must be known. This will vary from beach sand to solid rock, with many characteristics in between. Investigating the soil on the surface of the ground will offer little help in designing a building because the foundations will be supported below the ground surface. This is the soil we must investigate to learn its characteristics and how much weight it will support. Our concern is how much bearing capacity, in pounds per square foot, the soil will support.

If the ground condition will not support a building's weight, undue and dangerous movement of the building will occur, possibly endangering the lives of the people occupying the building. Once an examination and study of the subsoil is completed, this information will be translated into proper safe building design.

Soils have been separated into classifications ranging from soft clay to rock. Each soil classification has been analyzed as to its ability to support a safe load. The soil classification is the key to proper support of a building.

TEST BORING

One method of determining the condition of the earth below the ground surface is by a system called test boring. It involves a pipe attached to a machine which drills or pounds into the ground, collecting soil in the hollow pipe as it penetrates the ground. The soil is collected and analyzed in the laboratory to determine the safe loads that it will support. Test borings can be made to great depths. These tests will also determine the amount of water in the ground or underground water table, which will also have an effect on the building structural design.

71

The test samples should be taken undisturbed, in their natural state, and intact. The soils collected must be carefully controlled at various depths. The tip of the drill rod is replaced to force the undisturbed soil into the rod. This test boring technique permits drilling through rock.

SOIL TYPE

Bedrock is a formation of the earth's surface. It is solid rock and through time, weather, erosion, wind, and water, it is broken down into outcroppings. The outcroppings, in turn, are broken down into residual soil. The residual soil is relocated and redeposited by water at other sites. This re-deposit soil is called alluvial soil. The size of the alluvial soil particles depend on how far the water carried them and how fast. This is what causes the different strata of deposits.

Another type of soil is called loess. This is a very fine-grained sand, blown by the wind, much like desert sand.

When fine particles are separated from bedrock through chemical action, the resulting soil is called rock flour. All soils are formed by the breaking down or disintegration of rock.

Soil is divided into two general types based on the size of the grain. Coarse-grained soils are called gravel and sand; fine-grained soils are called silt and clay. The shape of the grains varies from round to oblong. The grains are made up of hydrous aluminum, silicate, quartz, and iron oxide.

SOIL COMPOSITION

How a grain of soil moves and comes to rest is related to its makeup. Grains of sand that are deposited in water move close together to form a dense deposit. Fine clay particles stick to each other, but are not dense. Clay has water in the spaces between the particles; these spaces are called voids or pores. The voids are filled not only with water, but may also be filled with air or gas.

The most important element affecting the strength of soil is water. Too much water will weaken the soil. The ideal amount of water in soil is when the particles of soil give the most density when compacted.

VISUAL INSPECTION

In residential construction, it may be cost-prohibitive to take test borings. Visual inspection of the soil can be made by excavating a test hole anywhere within the area of the foundation. This will reveal the characteristics of the subsurface soil. If different soil strata and color are encountered, or if parts of plastic, metal, brick, or any waste product is seen, it may mean that the ground has been filled or may have been used as a dumping site. Care should be taken to design the proper foundation.

If the soil proves to be firm and of uniform color and strata, chances are that the soil has not been disturbed; this is called virgin soil. If water fills in the test hole, it could indicate a wet area with a high underground water table.

Frequently, when excavating for a foundation, rock or ledge may be encountered. Rock can be removed by machine, but ledge, which is a form of rock covering a large area, cannot be removed without blasting. If ledge is encountered, it may not be necessary to remove it if it does not interfere with the function of the building. No harm will come to the building if a portion of the ledge is visible in the basement. Any foundation resting on ledge does not require a special study, because the ledge itself is sufficient bearing. Following is a breakdown of soil types.

Gravel: particles over 2 mm in diameter

Sand: gritty; finest particles visible to the naked eye: 0.5 to 2 mm

Silt: invisible to the eye but can be felt: 0.002 to 0.05 mm

Clay: smooth and flour-like consistency, or crumpy when dry, plastic and sticky when wet: 0.002 mm or smaller

Organic matter: decomposed vegetation

Simple field tests can be made to identify soil type. This unofficial test may be used for simple, uncomplicated buildings. This test is divided into mixtures of gravel, sands, silts, and clays.

1. Clean gravel contains less than 10% silt and clay and is predominantly gravel.
2. Most gravel will have more than 10% silt and clay and is called silty and clay-like gravel.
3. Clean sand has less than 15% silt and clay.
4. Sand with more than 10 to 15% silt or clay is called silty or clay-like sand.
5. A very fine sand with less than 50% water or soil which flows like mud is called nonplastic silt.
6. Very fine sand with more than 50% water is called plastic silt.
7. Silt with less than a 5% water content and with organic material is called organic silt.
8. Very fine clay with less than a 50% water content is called nonplastic clay.
9. Clay with a water content of 50% or higher and no organic material is called plastic clay.

To field test the soil, take a handful of soil and spread it out. If you can see the particles, chances are that it is a sand or gravel. If more than half of the particles are over ¼ in. in size, it is gravel; if less than ¼ in. in size, it is sand.

To test the dryness of the soil, take a handful, wet it, and mold it into a cube. Try breaking it with only the pressure of your fingers. If it cannot be broken easily, or makes a sound when it breaks, the soil is a plastic-clay. If it can be broken easily, the soil is an organic or nonplastic clay. If after it breaks, it crumbles, it is plastic silt, organic silt, or a nonplastic silt.

Another field test is called a thread test. With a handful of soil, add just enough water to pat the soil so that it will not stick to your hands. Roll the soil on a hard surface into a thread about ⅛ in. in diameter, then shape it into a ball. If this can be done several times without cracking, the soil is a plastic clay. If it cracks, the soil is a nonplastic clay. If it cannot be molded into a ball, it is a plastic silt. If it cannot be rolled into a thread, it is a nonplastic silt. If it feels spongy to the fingers, chances are that it is an organic soil.

TABLE 5-1

Allowable Pressures on Soil and Rock

Material	Tons/ft^2
Soft clay	1
Firm clay, fine sand, wet	2
Clay or fine sand, dry	3
Hard clay, coarse sand, dry	4
Gravel	6
Hardpan	8–15
Rock	15–75

One of the best soils for building is gravel. It is stable and has good bearing qualities. Loose sand may shift when loaded, but if well drained, will make a good foundation. Gravel is also good for seepage disposal systems. Care should be exercised when silt is found on a site because it will erode and it expands when frozen. It can be very unstable when wet.

Clay can be a good bearing soil if kept dry. When wet, it is loose and soft, but it is also less resistant to frost.

A poor soil for building is peat, because it is spongy, weak, and the particles have little ability to stick together. Allowable pressures on a variety of soils and rock are given in Table 5-1.

FILL

Filled land does not have the same load-bearing capacity as that of virgin soil. If a building excavation indicates previously filled land, precautions must be taken to support the building properly by continuing the excavation until solid virgin soil has been reached. This means a greater foundation depth. A second alternative is to remove the unwanted fill area to virgin soil and replace with gravel in layers 6 in. thick, compacting each layer until the desired height is reached.

SOIL ANALYSIS

Things to look for to determine the soil conditions for a building:

1. Will the soil support the building without settling or cracking?
2. Will the basement area remain dry?
3. Will the soil support a septic system?
4. Is the lot subject to flooding from nearby rivers, streams, brooks, ocean, or heavy rains?
5. Does the lot shape and soil condition make it subject to erosion?
6. Will the soil grow grass and plants?

In general, the ideal soil for most uses is one that is moderately permeable to water, free from flooding or high water tables, and level to gently sloping. Such soils will generally support both buildings and growing plants.

With the abundance of good soils it is obviously better to select a site with minimum building disadvantages than to try to correct troublesome and costly soil problems after construction has begun or been completed. However, some soils can be changed if for some reason a poor site must be

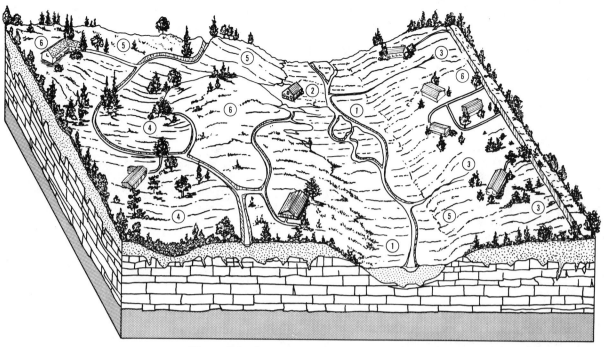

Figure 5-1 Common topographic positions. (Courtesy of U.S. Department of Agriculture.)

Area 1 is a floodplain. It is subject to flooding during heavy storms. Ask yourself: If it should rain hard, where would the water flow in relation to the proposed house and site?

Area 2 is an alluvial fan. The soil has been forming over the years as a result of water eroding material from the watershed above and depositing it near the mouth of the waterway. An alluvial fan can be hard hit by flash floods after heavy rains unless an adequate water-disposal system has been provided to control the runoff from the watershed above.

Area 3 is an upland waterway where water flowing from the higher surrounding land will concentrate. Natural waterways should not be used unless an adequate ditch or diversion terrace has been constructed to divert water from the site.

Area 4 is a low depressed area where water accumulates from higher surrounding areas. These soils remain wet and spongy for long periods.

Area 5 is a steep hillside. Many soils on steep slopes are shallow to rock. Some are subject to severe slippage. On all slopes, one must be careful of soil movement through gravity or by water erosion. Yet some steep hillsides can be used safely as building sites. The problem can be solved by studying the soils and avoiding the bad ones.

Area 6 is a deep, well-drained soil found on ridgetops and gently sloping hillsides. Generally, these areas have the smallest water-management problems. They are the best building sites, other things being equal.

used. Soil poorly suited for growing most plants or for supporting foundations can be replaced with other soil material. Plants can be found that will grow in almost any soil. Foundations can be designed to withstand the stresses. Problems caused by wetness can be overcome through drainage if there is some place to discharge the water. Slow soil permeability can be corrected for some uses by removing or altering the soil. But these changes can be costly; they can cost more than the original site.

A good, hard scientific look at the soil before developing, buying, or building may save a great deal of grief and money. How can one choose good soils and a good location for a building? The most important rule might be: Read the clues written on the landscape itself.

Consider the topographic position of the prospective building area in relation to its surrounding landscape (Fig. 5-1). Figure 5-2 shows examples of some soil problems.

(a)

(b)

(c)

Figure 5-2   Soil problems. (Courtesy of U.S. Department of Agriculture.)

(a) These houses were built on a floodplain. It is subject to periodic flooding. More than 10% of the land in the United States is subject to flooding, and millions of dollars worth of damage is done by floods every year. Much of this is along our thousands of small streams, not just near the large ones. Protective measures are costly and usually require community action.

(b) These floodplain soils are always adjacent to a stream, ditch, or drainageway and are nearly level. Water may or may not be present in the waterway. You can judge the size of the floodplain by standing on a streambank and noting the width of the level area adjacent to the stream. If you dig in the soil, you usually find a dark surface layer but no naturally developed subsoil layers. Floodplain soil is often uniform in texture (sand, silt, and clay content) down to 4 feet or so. In some places there are layers of coarse and fine materials.

(c) Soil with a high clay content often swells when wet and shrinks when dry, thus cracking foundations unless special provisions are made during construction. This soil can expand up to 50% between wet and dry conditions. In addition, it may have some of the other undesirable features described elsewhere.

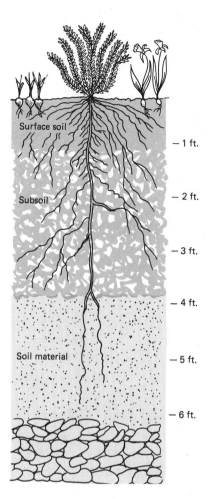

Figure 5-3 Contrasting layers (horizons) of soil. (Courtesy of U.S. Department of Agriculture.)

This country has numerous types of soil, more than 70,000, varying widely in their uses and characteristics (Fig. 5-3). It is a major function of soil scientists in the Soil Conservation Service, U.S. Department of Agriculture (USDA), and cooperating agencies to classify, map, and describe soils so that they may be used for their best purposes.

USDA soil scientists, in cooperation with State Agriculture Experiment Stations and other agencies, have been at work since 1899. Their soil surveys contain valuable information, in the beginning intended mainly for farmers. Now these experts are widely used by developers, contractors, government planners, highway engineers, and individual homeowners as well. Most soil users will be interested in the same soil properties. About 45% of all privately owned land in the United States has been surveyed. Many of these surveys are modern and up to date; many of those more than 25 years old are still useful for general land-use planning but do not have all the detailed information needed for current interpretations. It is entirely possible that a soil survey is available for any land being considered for development. If so, it may be seen in the office of the local soil conservation district or county extension service.

Soil scientists are experts with years of experience in studying soils and interpreting soil properties for many uses. They walk over the land and using various tools, stop frequently to dig into the soil and study its properties. They describe, name, and classify the soils according to a national classification system. Their field work is supported by laboratory examinations of samples of the soil layers. Soil boundaries and symbols are plotted

Figure 5-4 Soil map. (Courtesy of U.S. Department of Agriculture.)

The symbols indicate the different soils and the solid lines show the extent of each. WhA is a floodplain soil and presents the type of problem shown in Fig. 5-2a. WoA, a wet soil in upland drainageways, is similar to those shown in Fig. 5-2b, areas 2 and 3; water from higher surrounding areas runs off and concentrates in the natural drainage courses, resulting in frequent flooding. IdB2, because of a dense layer of clay that is very slowly permeable to water and has a high shrink-swell potential. LeB2, LeB3, LeC2, and LeC3 are shallow to rock and some have lost all original surface soil.

Soil and water conservation practices to control erosion and reduce runoff are needed on all the steeper slopes, shown by C and D on the map. They also require more excavation for construction and great care in installing filter fields for the effluent from septic tanks. The severely eroded areas, shown by a 3 on the map, may need topsoil for good lawns and gardens.

on high-quality aerial photos (Fig. 5-4). The lines and symbols show the location and extent of various soils. Soil descriptions and their interpretations are prepared to accompany the soil map. Soil scientists and other specialists use this information to advise on safe uses of soil.

Traditionally, soil surveys have been used to identify farmland and to match suitable land areas with suitable crops, vegetation, and soil and water conservation practices. But it was soon learned that the basic principles of soil behavior the farmer needs to know are also useful to many others. Soil surveys are now extensively used by both rural and urban people. In fact, soil maps are especially important for urban users. If farmers use a soil in the wrong way, they may suffer losses that year but can adjust the next year. But urban users can hardly do that if their "crop" is a cracking super-highway or a sinking house. These types of "crop failures" are followed by years of unusable or damaged roads and buildings and high costs for maintenance.

Soil surveys show soil wetness, overflow hazards, depth to rock, hardpan, tight layers, erodibility, clay layers that crack when dry and swell when wet, and the hazard of slippage on slopes. They show the location and extent of different soils and provide information about their properties to a depth of about 6 ft.

For good living without excessive costs and taxes, advanced community planning is becoming more and more necessary. Such planning requires accurate knowledge of the available soils and their alternative potentials.

Estimates by community planners of the value of soil surveys for site selections run as high as $2 million per year per county for counties with rapid increases in population. Some communities report savings of $250,000 by choosing the right site for a school building. Specifically:

1. A developer in southeastern Wisconsin bought 80 acres which he divided into 60 lots. The local board of health, using a soil survey, inspected the site and rejected 58 to 60 lots because of poor soil conditions. The estimated saving to the community was about $1 million.

2. The planning board of Millis, Massachusetts, has estimated that soil-survey information will save the community about $500,000 in its home-building program. Soil surveys provide an inventory of suitable sites prior to purchase. This can save costs for land preparation and building foundations. Substantial savings are anticipated for other uses of the soil survey.

3. San Antonio, Texas, has many soils that are poor for building purposes. It costs between $1000 and $1500 more to put down a minimum house foundation in some San Antonio soils than it does in soils with good bearing strength. They shrink when dry and swell when wet, and this makes it difficult to build and maintain good roads and underground utilities. Using a soil map, contractors and builders can either avoid these high shrink-swell areas or design their structures with the extra strength needed. This has saved many thousands of dollars annually.

4. The Southeastern Wisconsin Regional Planning Commission estimates savings to local citizens of more than $300 million on housing alone in southeastern Wisconsin during the next 25 years through the use of soil surveys. Additional savings in other land uses are also expected.

The more soil surveys and soil interpretations are used by builders and construction companies, the less will be the chance that any future house will be destroyed through flooding or cracking.

An individual home buyer or builder may spend months checking and considering the design, materials, and construction of a new home. One should be equally concerned about the soil underneath. The soil on which a house is built can seriously affect the stability of the home, repair bills, comfort, and the resale value of the property. Soil maps made by soil scientists do not eliminate the need for on-site sampling and testing of soils for design or construction of specific engineering works.

Uncontrolled runoff and accelerated erosion often occur when land is developed, especially during the construction stage. This runoff can cause rills and gullies, washed-out roads, and scour, cut, and fill areas. The resulting sediment fills road ditches, storm drains, and lakes and streams, limiting land use. These sediment deposits also destroy vegetation and the aesthetic quality of the land. Damages are costly to the developer and those using land below the affected site. Careful application of proven conservation practices can prevent much of this damage.

Soil erosion occurs when particles from bare soil are loosened by the impact of falling rain or by scouring action. These soil particles are transported by flowing water and are deposited at a location downstream. The transported soil is called sediment.

Sheet erosion is the removal by water of fairly uniform layers of soil from the land surface. This type of erosion is difficult to detect, as it removes one thin layer of soil at a time. Rill erosion results when runoff water moves quickly enough to scour out small channels in the soil. As these channels become larger (approximately 6 in. deep), gully erosion occurs.

Streambank and shore erosion are other types of erosion caused by development. Fast-flowing stream and channel water causes the streambank to erode when it dislodges the soil along its banks. Shore erosion is caused by the impact of waves and currents.

Fortunately, however, most soil is held in place naturally by vegetation and other materials. When grasses, shrubs, and trees remain undisturbed, runoff does not deposit sediment in rivers and other desirable places.

Factors involved in erosion control by vegetation can be illustrated by this simple experiment. Two boxes contain the same type of soil, one protected by grass, the other bare. As shown in Fig. 5-5, when water is sprayed on the bare soil, it rushes off into the jar, taking soil with it. The flow soon stops, but the jar contains muddy water.

Water flow from the box protected by the grass will take longer to start and will continue longer. A smaller amount of water will reach the jar, and it will be reasonably clear. The amount of water in the two samples of soil before the experiment begins may affect the results.

This experiment illustrates one of the most fundamental principles of soil and water conservation. Grass and other vegetation protect soil against the action of raindrops and the movement of running water. The grass breaks the force of the raindrops so that the soil is not pounded and broken apart by the impact (Fig. 5-6). Grass roots provide channels to let water get into the soil. Organic matter furnished by decayed grass crops also lets water enter the soil more readily. As the water runs off, the stems of grass slow it down so that it does not have enough speed to disturb the soil. Established grasses reduce soil losses by approximately 90% compared to losses from bare soil.

The need for conservation measures at a particular site depends in part on determining the amount of erosion that will occur. It is also necessary to predict the quantity of sediment that will be produced in order to design

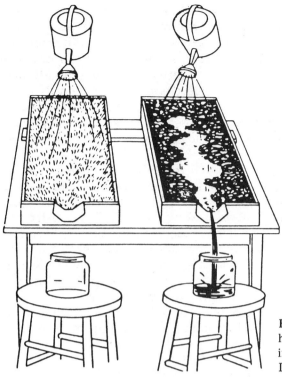

Figure 5-5 Experiment showing how grass prevents soil from washing downstream. (Courtesy of U.S. Department of Agriculture.)

(a)   (b)

Figure 5-6 (a) Falling raindrop. (b) Impact of a raindrop on bare soil. (Courtesy of U.S. Department of Agriculture.)

adequate conservation measures. Calculating potential soil loss during area development is helpful in making wise land-use decisions.

Soil erosion is caused primarily by runoff from rainfall and melted snow. Much of the soil loss is from erosion at disturbed areas such as construction sites. Factors that influence the amount of soil loss include: climate, vegetation, soil characteristics, slope, and degree of development. Temperature and the amount, intensity, and frequency of rainfall are climatic factors of importance.

Vegetation reduces erosion by holding the soil in place mechanically. It also increases infiltration into the soil and dissipates the energy of raindrops before they hit the soil. Soil characteristics affect the amount of runoff and mechanical displacement of the soil. These characteristics include: permeability, infiltration, texture, and structure.

The length and degree of slope influence the volume and velocity of water flow and the removal of soil. Developing areas with more extensive paved and roofed sections decrease infiltration and increase the amount and rate of runoff. Soil survey information is necessary to identify soils for the general area and to furnish other helpful information.

Loss of soil at development sites is costly to developers and may affect land and water users downstream from the sites. Washed-out roads, undercut pavements, and loss of fertile topsoil are samples of erosion problems that increase construction and maintenance costs and cause delays in work schedules.

As much as 600 to 1040 tons (600 to 800 yds^3) of soil may be lost in one year from a 15-acre construction site that is left in a disturbed condition. These quantities are based on the USDA Universal Soil-Loss Equation with site location in West Warwick, Rhode Island (average 8% slope, 250 ft slope length, Charlton loam soil with exposed subsoil).

This soil loss does not include large quantities of soil material that may be lost by rill and gully erosion. It is not difficult to visualize the cost to a developer in replacing lost soil, especially if it is topsoil. Time and energy must be expended to alleviate an erosion problem, much of which could be saved by the application of conservation practices. Good management and vegetative and structural conservation measures can reduce soil loss to an acceptable level.

QUESTIONS

1. (a) What are test borings? _____

   _____

   (b) What do they reveal? _____

   _____

2. How many tons per square foot will gravel support?
   A. 3 tons
   B. 8 tons
   C. 6 tons

3. How can a visual examination of soil be made? _____

   _____

4. How is ledge removed from the site? _____

   _____

5. A building can be constructed over ledge without removal of ledge.
      True or False

6. A spread footing is required over a ledge.   True or False

7. Filled land has the same load-bearing capacities as virgin soil.
      True or False

8. A building can be supported on filled land.   True or False

9. How should filled land be treated? _____

   _____

10. How should layers of gravel be filled? _____

   _____

Staking Out

INTRODUCTION

Before excavation is begun, the information contained on the plot plan (Fig. 6-1) must be transferred to the ground. This is called staking out and is usually done by a surveyor with a transit or leveling instrument (Fig. 6-2).

Careful study is required of the plot plan to locate the building on the lot and establish proper building heights and depths. The shape of the ground may change for proper water drainage. Earth may have to be removed or more brought in to reshape the ground according to plan.

All trees and tree stumps that interfere with the building location must be removed. Building lines must be established and foundation height and depth must be indicated.

Staking out the building is the first and most critical operation of the entire building process. The plot plan should provide all the information necessary for staking out a building. Careful study of the plot plan will show the distance from the front property line to the front building line, the distance from the side property line to the building side, and the distance from the rear property line to the rear house wall (Fig. 6-1).

Generally, the building dimensions found on the plot plan apply to the building foundation. The finish ground shape or contour elevation will also be shown on the plot plan. When all the information has been transferred from the plot plan to the ground, the project is ready for excavation.

PLOT PLAN

Careful study of the plot plan (Fig. 6-1) will show the title of the sheet, the plot and lot numbers of the building site, the scale of the drawing, and the compass bearing or the direction of north. In addition, the key in the lower

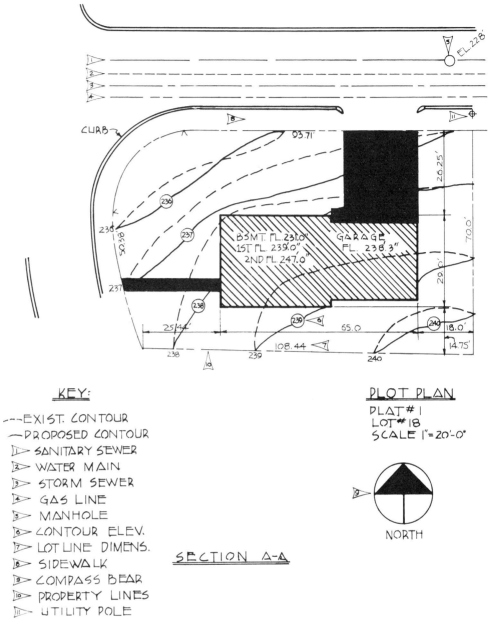

KEY:

---EXIST. CONTOUR
——PROPOSED CONTOUR
1▷ SANITARY SEWER
2▷ WATER MAIN
3▷ STORM SEWER
4▷ GAS LINE
5▷ MANHOLE
6▷ CONTOUR ELEV.
7▷ LOT LINE DIMENS.
8▷ SIDEWALK
9▷ COMPASS BEAR
10▷ PRODERTY LINES
11▷ UTILITY POLE

PLOT PLAN

PLAT # 1
LOT # 18
SCALE 1"=20'-0"

NORTH

SECTION A-A

Figure 6-1 Plot plan.

left corner will explain what the various symbols mean. The street names and the dimensions of the building lot are given.

The building size and location on the lot are necessary for staking out the building. The shape or surface of the ground is indicated by irregular solid and dotted lines. The dotted lines show the ground shape before any change was made. The solid irregular lines show the change in the shape of the ground. In the figure the ground shape at the street corners is indicated by 236. The opposite corner of the lot is indicated by 240. This means that the total shape or pitch of the ground is 4 ft, the lower ground being at the street intersection.

Adjacent to the front door is ground level 238. This level will determine the house floor levels in relation to the ground. The levels shown are basement, 231'-0"; first floor, 239'-0"; second floor, 247'-3"; and garage, 238'-3". The ground level near the front door is 238 ft and the basement level is 231'-0". As 231 ft subtracted from 238 ft is a difference of 7 ft, excavation must be no less than 7 ft below ground level (238 ft) to reach the basement level. Follow that same ground level in front of the garage door, 238 ft, and relate that ground level to the garage floor level of 238'-3", which means that the garage floor level is 3 in. higher than the ground level of 238 ft.

The plot plan shows the entire scope of the construction project. This will include all services, such as electric, water, gas, and sewer, which are to be connected to the house. This drawing is prepared at a smaller scale to show the property lines, angles, ground level, and location of the street. Water, gas, electric, and sewer services were compiled by a land surveyor and are vital to the construction project. In addition, the following information is necessary:

1. North arrow
2. Stakes or other markers locating the lot lines, bearings, and dimensions
3. Lot area in square feet or number of acres
4. Easements or rights-of-way
5. Street location and width; name of existing or proposed streets
6. Width of sidewalk
7. Location of curb and curb cuts, such as a driveway entrance
8. Location, depth, and size of all water and gas lines, telephone lines, and location of overhead or underground electric wires
9. Shape of ground level on lot or contour elevations
10. Location and size of all trees or buildings
11. Outcrop of rock or ledge

All property is recorded in a system of plans or books at the local city or town hall. Each parcel of land is recorded and described, no matter how large or small. All property owners can find their lot, parcel, or tract, regardless of the location. The plot plan also shows the driveway, by a shaded rectangle, from the northern road to the garage. In addition, the front walk is also shown by a shaded area from the western road to the front door of the house.

Before any site work is begun, the site must be visited and studied together with the plot plan, not only to confirm the information contained on the plot plan, but to be sure that it agrees with the site.

If there is an outcrop of rock or ledge within the house location, it will affect the excavation and it may be better to move the house on the lot to avoid these problems. If any redesigning or moving is done, it must conform to the local zoning laws.

The character of the soil must be examined to confirm that the foundation design will be adequate to support the house. The best way to examine the soil is to excavate a pit or hole anywhere on the foundation line. More than one test may be necessary because the site may have been a refuse collection area. The test pit may also show the underground water level. Any trees interfering with the house location must be removed and the branches and stumps hauled away from the site.

Under no circumstance is the project to extend beyond the property lines, including the area used for delivery and storage of building material. The adjacent property may be owned by someone other than the owner of the house under construction.

Careful study of the plot plan will show that the house is 26'-3" back from the property line on the northern road. The total house width is 29'-0" and the house wall at the rear property line is 14'-9", which totals 70'-0" and is the total dimension of the property.

This same rule follows on the rear property line parallel to the northern road. The total lot line dimension is 108'-4". The front wall of the house is 25'-4" back from the western road. The total house length is 65'-0" and the 14'-9" dimension is to the property line, all of which equals the property line dimension of 108'-4".

LEVELING INSTRUMENT

In construction, one of the most important tools used is the transit or builder's level (Fig. 6-2). This is the instrument used in laying out the building from the plot plan to the ground. This is a precision instrument used for locating various points of the building. It consists of a telescope with a focusing lever resting on a three-legged base. It is adjustable for proper leveling of the instrument and revolves in a complete circle for transferring points to any location on site.

The leveling instrument is similar to a carpenter's level except that it is much more accurate and used for layout work and long distances. It sits on a tripod with adjustable legs to make the instrument easier to level while setting up on the ground.

Leveling screws are used to adjust the instrument on the tripod. The telescope part of the instrument rotates on a base and can be used for laying out any angle or sighting a horizontal plane for accurate measurement. The

(a)

(b)

Figure 6-2 (a) Builder's level; (b) transit. (Courtesy of David White Instruments, Division of Realist, Inc.)

telescope will enlarge the object sighting with a power of about 20X. This makes it easier to read a site distance, dimension, or number.

Stakes are driven into the ground to the exact dimension and shape of the building. The leveling instrument will ensure the correct angles at the corners of the building and provide the exact measurement.

Leveling instruments are very delicate and require extreme care. Any damage to the instrument may cause inaccuracies in the layout work.

1. Keep the instrument in the carrying case when not in use.
2. The instrument must be kept dry and clean.
3. Do not overtighten adjustment screws.
4. Never leave the instrument unattended.
5. Use care and caution when carrying the instrument.
6. Always select firm ground when setting up the instrument.
7. Keep the lens clean.
8. Have the instrument checked periodically for accuracy.

TAPING AND STAKING

The very first step in the process of building a house is to locate the house on the land. Usually, the front building line is located first, because it may be the start of other points of the building. All buildings are built or staked out by lines, and generally the outside foundation lines are used for staking out the building. These lines are used for reference in locating the remainder of the building.

The building-line layout must be accurate, using a system of stakes, lines, and batter boards, which include offset stakes. This entire process is accomplished by the surveyor's transit or leveling instrument.

Extreme accuracy is required in transferring the building dimensions from the plan to the ground. This is mostly done with a steel measuring tape. The measuring tape is available for reading feet and inches, decimal parts of a foot, or metric readings. Cloth tapes are not recommended because they will expand and contract or stretch when pulled tightly.

Once the first stake is driven into the ground for the house layout, the other corners are carefully measured according to the house dimension. Usually, a nail is driven into the top of the stake for precision dimensions, and with the use of the measuring tape and leveling instrument, all building dimensions are transferred from the plan to the ground.

The ground stakes for layout work are temporary and will be removed later during excavation for the basement or foundation. The excavation area is larger than the building dimensions to allow enough space to set up the forms. Before these stakes are removed, the dimensions are extended onto batter boards, which provide an extension of the dimensions of the building or stakes.

BATTER BOARDS

After making a survey of the property and before the site is cleared, the surveyor will mark the corners of the house (Fig. 6-3). The next step is to determine lines and grades as an aid in keeping the building true, plumb, and level. This is accomplished by the use and installation of batter boards. Sometimes the height of batter boards is used to establish the height of the foundation walls.

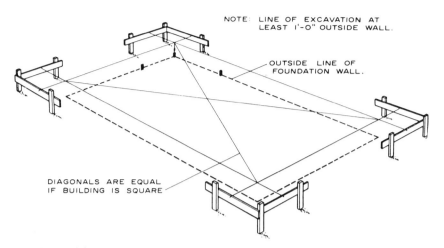

Figure 6-3 Batter boards. (Courtesy of U.S. Department of Agriculture.)

Small wooden stakes are driven into the ground to locate the corners of the house (Fig. 6-4). Nails are driven in the top of the stakes to locate the outside line of the foundation walls. Once the corners have been located, three stakes of suitable lengths of 2 × 4's are driven into the ground at each location (Fig. 6-4). They should be about 4 to 6 ft away from the corner of the foundation to prevent the excavation from disturbing the stakes. Nailed to these stakes are 1 × 6's, horizontally indicating a point of reference, such as the top of the foundation or floor line. Twine is stretched across opposite boards exactly over the nail in the corner stake. When this process is completed, the small corner stakes can be removed to make ready for excavation.

The outside foundation line is the dimension used for building layout. The corner stakes installed previously will be removed because of the building excavation. These stakes represent the corners of the building. This information must be transferred to the batter board so as not to interfere with the building excavation. The batter boards are extended beyond the building dimensions and are an extension of the corner stakes. Batter boards are installed for temporary use as a reference. They are removed when the reference is no longer needed.

Figure 6-4 Staking out. (Courtesy of U.S. Department of Agriculture.)

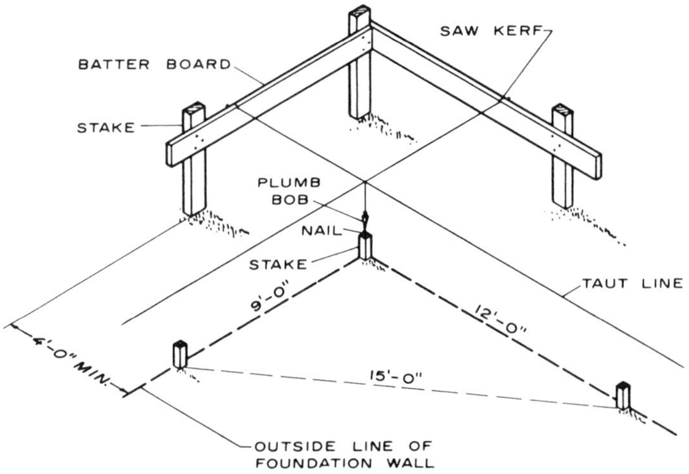

BUILDING LEVELS

The excavator is now able to dig to the proper depth for the house foundation. This information was transmitted from the plot plan to the batter boards. The plan established the distance from the ground or grade to the first floor. The plan also states the distance from the first floor to the basement floor, and from this information the excavation depth below the level of the ground is established.

EASEMENT

In many cases, utility companies will be granted land or aerial use for water lines, sewer lines, electric lines, or other underground utility lines serving the community. These easements are granted to serve the public and to maintain the services and installations. It is agreed that the services and easements will be open at all times in case there is trouble with the lines and excavation is necessary to make repairs. When work or repairs are completed, the ground must be restored to its original condition.

No building or parts of a building are to be constructed over an easement. The location of the easement, if any, will be shown on the plot plan. Other reasons for easements are railroad lines or tracks and access to public water, such as brooks, ponds, streams, lakes, rivers, and oceans for bathing, fishing, skating, boating, or other recreational use.

In addition to easements, any paper street must also be shown. A paper street is an area reserved for building a street in the future.

QUESTIONS

1. Define *staking out*. _____
   _____

2. What instrument is used for staking and locating various points of the building? _____

3. Lot dimensions are shown on:
   A. Plot plan
   B. Building site
   C. Batter boards

4. What are contour elevations, and what do they tell the builder? _____
   _____

5. What are batter boards? _____
   _____

6. A building lot must be surveyed before being staked out.
      True or False

7. Excavation should extend _____ feet beyond the building line.

8. Where will the foundation height be found? _____
   _____

9. It is not necessary to clear the building site before excavation is begun.
      True or False

10. To assure a level building, builders rely on which of the following?
    A. Surveyor
    B. Batter boards
    C. Builder's instrument
    D. Plot plan

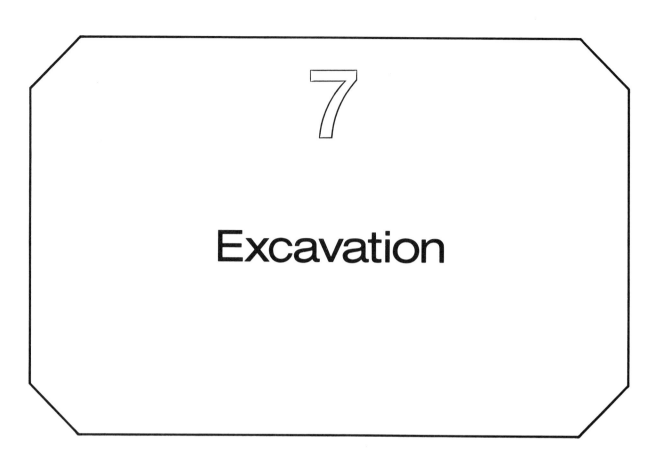

7

Excavation

INTRODUCTION

Once a building has been staked out on a site, excavation is begun. The top-soil is stripped of loam and stockpiled somewhere so as not to interfere with building activity. The loam will later be used for landscaping.

The beginning of the construction activity is preparing the building for foundations (Fig. 7-1). House construction with or without basements re-

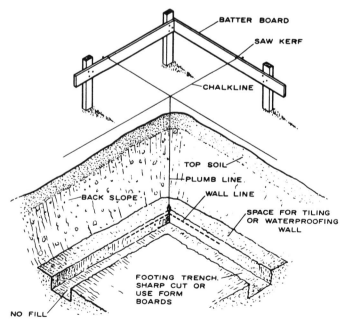

Figure 7-1 Establishing corners for excavation and footing. (Courtesy of U. S. Department of Agriculture.)

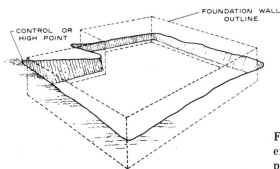

Figure 7-2 Establishing depth of excavation. (Courtesy of U.S. Department of Agriculture.)

quires foundations in the ground. This requires digging or excavating into the ground (Fig. 7-2).

The characteristics of the soil will indicate the type of excavating equipment to be used. If digging is in hard sand, a heavier or stronger machine may be necessary. If the soil is soft, like beach sand, a smaller machine may be used.

Excavation also includes digging trenches for water, sewer, and/or electric lines. Not all excavation is done with machines. Hand digging may be necessary for small holes or for leveling larger areas.

Trees that interfere with the building location must be removed. The tree branches and trunk are cut first, leaving the tree stump, which is removed by machine.

Excess earth will be removed from the site. Occasionally, earth will be used for filling low areas on the building site. If excavation does not provide enough earth for filling in low areas, earth will have to be hauled in from other sources. Enough earth must remain on the building site for filling the hole around the exterior of the foundation. This is called backfilling.

TREE REMOVAL

Any trees within the dimensions of the building must be removed. The tree is cut before excavating is begun, leaving about 3 ft of the tree trunk above the ground. This makes it easier for the machine to remove the stump and the roots, to be carried from the site. No tree limbs or roots are to be used for backfilling because the wood will eventually decay, causing uneven settlement and the wood may attract termites or carpenter ants.

Tree removal should be done by experts because of the danger of falling limbs or trunk. A tree trunk falling in the wrong direction, or touching overhead wires on adjacent property, can cause serious problems to people and may result in serious injury or death.

All trees on the site that are to remain should be protected against injury from building, equipment, and machinery. Boards are usually wired to the tree trunk for protection. Trench work should not be close to remaining trees because the tree may die if the tree roots are seriously cut or injured.

Low branches should be removed from remaining trees. Trees close to the foundation may not survive if the roots are disturbed during excavation. Trees that are barely surviving should be removed, and if the site is heavily wooded, thinning out may be necessary to allow other trees to grow stronger. If solar energy is designed for the house, all trees blocking the sun's rays should be removed.

STRIPPING

Before excavation is begun, the lot is stripped, which means removing the topsoil to a depth of about 6 in. This topsoil is usually a rich soil suitable for growing grass and shrubs. It is very expensive to purchase. The stripped soil is stockpiled on the site out of the way of the activity around the building.

When the building has been completed and the backfill and rough grading or finish ground level have been finished, the stripping or loam is spread in the area to be seeded and planted. After spreading, it should be raked to remove any unwanted objects, such as roots, tree limbs or branches, and rock or foreign material. Before seeding, the topsoil should be fertilized for plant or seed nourishing; after seeding it should be watered and cared for until the plants and seed are fully developed.

MACHINE EXCAVATION

The size of the machine used in excavation is determined by the amount of earth to be removed and the condition of the earth. The machine used for excavation is usually either a bulldozer or a backhoe (Figs. 7-3 and 7-4).

Figure 7-3 Bulldozer. (Courtesy of Caterpillar.)

Figure 7-4 Backhoe. (Courtesy of John Deere.)

If a bulldozer is used, the earth is pushed out. If a backhoe is used, the earth is scooped out and left around the excavated area. Enough earth is left on site to backfill and to bring the ground up to a rough grade. Any excess earth is hauled away from the site.

If hard soil or large rocks are encountered, it may be necessary to use a pneumatic hammer or jackhammer to remove the material. Sometimes it is necessary to use explosives to remove rock.

HAND EXCAVATION

Not all excavation is done by machine. Sometimes a machine will not fit in the space to be excavated. This requires hand excavation.

Trenches of shallow depth may also be excavated by hand. Leveling the bottom of excavated areas may require hand work. If the areas to be excavated by hand are hard, the ground will need to be softened with a pick for earth removal. Hand excavation is strenuous physical labor and should only be done by workers who are physically able to perform such work.

The time involved for hand excavation is much longer than that for machine excavation. This should be taken into account whenever time is an important factor in completion of the project.

TRENCHES

Trenches are used to bury water pipe, sewer pipe, and electric wires. If the trench is deep enough and wide enough, excavation can be done with a backhoe (Fig. 7-5). Some trenches are shallow and narrow and can be done only by hand.

Precautions must be taken in digging trenches. Trench walls that look safe may collapse, resulting in possible death or injury to the worker. Quite often there are warning signs of possible danger. These signs include the trickling of earth from the walls of the trench. Cracks in the surface of the ground above the trench may indicate possible failure.

Figure 7-5 Backhoe digging a trench. (Courtesy of Melroe Company.)

If these signs occur, the trench walls will need to be supported or braced with heavy lumber called shoring or sheet piling. Time, rain, and vibration are other possible causes of trench work failure.

STOCKPILING

All excavated material must be left on the job temporarily for future use. This is called stockpiling. The material must be piled on the property out of the way of construction. It will later be used for backfilling, and all excess earth will be removed from the site. Any tree stumps, branches, or clay should be removed from the site and not reclaimed or reused. The loam or topsoil should not be mixed with the general excavation. It will later be spread and used for planting.

Any excess excavation must be removed from the site. If the finish grade needs to be raised from the original grade or there are holes or depressions that must be filled in, earth removed for the basement can be used provided that it is clean and free of foreign matter. If this earth is not enough to fill up the areas, additional earth must be brought on site from other areas.

If large rock is found, generally the excavation machine can move it, and it can later be used for fill. If the rock is too large for the machine to move, it will need to be dynamited and broken up into smaller pieces.

Occasionally, ledge is found on the site. Ledge is a continuous rock covering a wide area with varying depth. No excavation machine can remove ledge. It must be removed by dynamite. This operation is expensive and it may be best to move the building on the lot to avoid the ledge. If the building location is moved on the site, the zoning laws governing minimum front, side, and rear dimensions must be followed.

BACKFILLING

After all excavation is accomplished, the foundation completed, and the forms have been removed, earth must be placed back into any remaining excavated areas around the exterior of the foundation. This is called backfilling. Care must be taken not to allow heavy boulders used for fill to be pushed by machine and free-roll against the wall. This action may cause the wall to crack or break. This type of damage is difficult and expensive to repair. It may mean rebuilding the entire wall. All ground levels must be brought up according to plan and any excess earth removed from the site.

Occasionally, not enough earth is salvaged from the excavation. Should this happen, more earth must be brought on site from other areas. The final grading is done using the topsoil or loam. It is spread out and made ready for landscaping and planting. If no loam is available on site, it must be brought in from other sources.

COMPACTED SOIL

No building should rest on soil that has been previously disturbed without taking the necessary precautions. If these precautions are not taken, the building will settle and move beyond its capabilities and cause severe damage. All soil that has been previously disturbed must be removed and replaced with gravel that is compacted by machine to make the soil firm and dense enough to carry the weight of the building. This compaction is done in 6-in. layers, one layer at a time.

Any soil not previously disturbed must be tested for load-bearing capacities. The entire weight of the building is being supported by the ground or earth. The characteristics, composition, and quality of the soil will determine how much weight it will support. If the land has been filled in, this soil will not support the same amount of building weight as natural or virgin soil, soil that has never been disturbed. If filled areas have been encountered at the excavated area, one of three solutions must be employed:

1. Design a special foundation footing to support the weight of the building.
2. Excavate deeper until virgin soil has been found, which means a deeper foundation.
3. Compact the soil to make it solid and firm. Compaction can be completed successfully in 6-in. layers, one layer at a time.

One of the reasons why foundations fail and crack is because of bad soil conditions. The weight of the building pushes down on the soil, causing excessive building movement and eventual problems. The soil must be firm and solid enough to support the building weight.

WATER

During the excavation, if water is encountered, special provision must be made to prevent the water from entering the basement.

Underground Water

When the excavation is prepared for the construction of the house foundation, a high underground water table may be found, causing the excavated area to fill with water. Underground water is a natural condition and provision must be made to remove the water from the excavated area to install the forms for the house foundation.

The amount of water found will vary from one location to another. A pump must be used to pump out the water and the excavated area must remain dry until the foundation work has been completed. This means that the pump may need to operate continuously to keep the area free of water.

SHORING

Because working space is necessary to install the house foundation wall forms, an area larger than the house size is excavated around the entire foundation perimeter. This may present a danger to adjacent buildings because the ground may not be firm enough to support its walls. There will thus be a danger of possible collapse of the adjacent building.

If this condition is found, it will be necessary to provide temporary walls to keep the earth from caving in. These temporary walls are called shoring. They consist of wood, concrete, or steel piles driven into the ground to support the earth walls temporarily. Another means of providing shoring is to build temporary walls of heavy timbers and brace the timbered walls with diagonal bracing to support the earth walls until the foundation wall is complete. The temporary walls or shoring can then be removed.

Cave-ins are also dangerous to the work force. It is possible for a worker to be buried alive in an earth cave-in.

UNDERGROUND UTILITIES

Another danger of excavation is the possible accidental cutting of underground water, sewer, electric, or gas lines. Sometimes these underground utilities are not recorded, the records have been lost, or the lines have been rerouted.

Should this happen, work must be stopped to repair the underground lines, and either the building or the underground lines must be moved on the lot. Some areas have a special telephone number to call before excavation is begun, to warn of any underground lines. This is called "dig safe."

ACCESS

When the excavation is completed, access must be provided so that the trucks delivering the concrete (Fig. 7-6) can get close enough to the forms to deposit the concrete. These concrete trucks weigh many tons and any unstable ground may cause the concrete truck to sink into the earth or tip over. If the building is large, more than one access area must be provided so that the concrete can be evenly distributed into the forms.

Usually, a ramp of earth is constructed so that the concrete truck will be higher than the top of the forms. This will allow the concrete to flow from the truck chute into the forms.

Figure 7-6 Concrete delivery. (Courtesy of Navistar International Corporation.)

FROZEN GROUND

A foundation must not be placed on frozen ground. When the ground freezes, the natural water in the ground expands, causing the ground to swell or expand. When the frost thaws, the ground will move or settle back to its original position. Any building on the frozen ground will move with the ground, causing serious damage to the building.

Care should be taken to prevent the excavated ground area from freezing until the foundation is in place. This is usually done by spreading calcium chloride on the ground or by covering the ground area with hay, either of which will prevent the cold from penetrating the ground and causing frost. The amount of frost protection will depend on the geographic location of the building.

QUESTIONS

1. The first step in residential construction is to perform which of the following types of work?
   A. Forms
   B. Foundation
   C. Concrete
   D. Excavation
   E. Grading

2. Name the two methods by which excavation can be completed.
   1. _____
   2. _____

3. Trench work is not required in residential construction.
   True or False

4. Stripping of land means _____
   _____

5. Tree stumps and tree branches can safely be used for fill.
   True or False

6. Define *backfilling*. _____
   _____

7. Name three dangers involved in hand trench work.
   1. _____
   2. _____
   3. _____

8. Define *stockpiling*. _____
   _____

9. There is always enough surplus earth for grading.   True or False

10. Which of the following will help prevent excavated ground from freezing?
    A. Calcium chloride
    B. Hay
    C. Salt
    D. Chloroform

Foundations

INTRODUCTION

The most critical part of the house is the foundation. If problems develop after it is completed, little can be done to correct them.

The entire weight of the building is being supported on the ground. The foundation design will be affected by the characteristics of the ground.

The foundation consists of two parts: footings and walls. The material used for foundations is concrete block, brick, stone, concrete, or wood. Local building codes will determine what material may not be used.

The geographic location of the house will determine the depth of the foundation in the ground, as well as buildings with or without basements. All foundations must extend below the frost line. The local building codes will indicate the minimum depth of the foundation.

Part of the foundation includes support for columns, stairs, garages, piers, porches, decks, and patios. The foundations must conform to the dimensions shown on the plans. If these dimensions are not followed, it will affect the house size, creating endless problems in construction.

FORMS

One way of providing the proper foundation is by placing concrete into forms (Fig. 8-1). These forms are generally constructed of plywood panels or metal panels. The dimensions of the foundation will be found on the foundation or basement plans. Included in the formwork will be the window and door openings, the shelf for brick walls (Fig. 8-2), and holes for passages for pipes to and from the building. The opening for pipes is called a chase. Two separate operations are required for the formwork. The first is to construct a footing, and the second is to construct the foundation wall. Openings in foundation walls require steel for proper design load.

The foundation of a building is the only means of supporting a building on the ground. The size of the foundation (Fig. 8-3) depends on the depth into the ground, the condition of the ground, and the total weight of the building.

FOUNDATION FOOTING

After excavating to the proper depth, the first step in the foundation system is to install the spread footing (Fig. 8-4). The purpose of the spread footing is to distribute the building load over a wider surface of the ground, much like the principle of snowshoes. As a general rule, the size of the concrete spread footing is 12 in. deep and 12 in. wider than the foundation thickness. Two ½-in-diameter steel reinforcing rods are placed about 2 in. from the bottom of the footing along the entire length (Fig. 8-5). The rods reinforce the concrete footing, minimizing or preventing the footing from cracking. The rods are placed about 12 in. apart.

KEY

A key is placed in the top of the footing to stabilize the foundation which will later be placed on top of the footing. This will prevent the foundation from shifting or moving from position. The key is constructed in one of two ways.

In the first method a 2 × 4 laid flat is secured into the forms of the spread footing. The top of the 2 × 4 is flush with the top of the footing. The sides or edges of the 2 × 4 are beveled to make it easy to remove it after the concrete has set (Fig. 8-5).

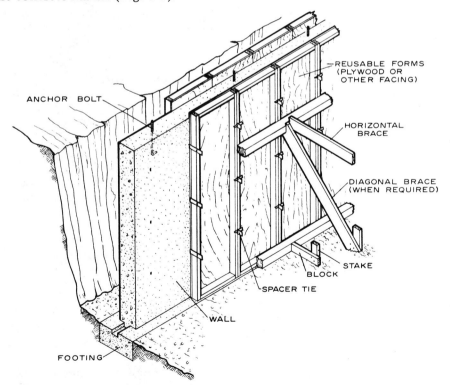

Figure 8-1 Forming for poured concrete walls. (Courtesy of U.S. Department of Agriculture.)

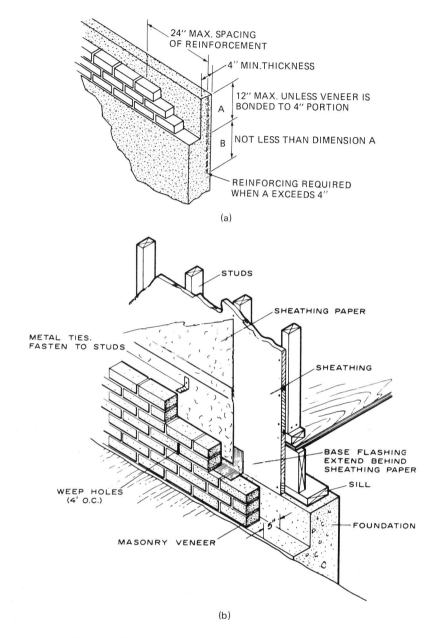

(a)

(b)

Figure 8-2 (a) Stepped wall footings (foundation walls—reduced thickness); (b) wood-frame wall with masonry veneer. (Courtesy of U.S. Department of Agriculture.)

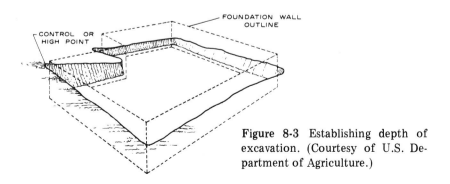

Figure 8-3 Establishing depth of excavation. (Courtesy of U.S. Department of Agriculture.)

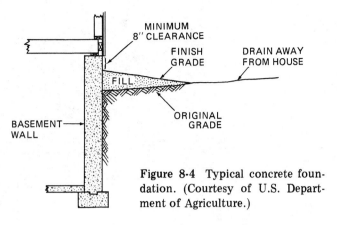

Figure 8-4 Typical concrete foundation. (Courtesy of U.S. Department of Agriculture.)

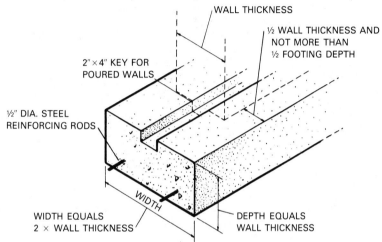

Figure 8-5 Reinforced footing. (Courtesy of U.S. Department of Agriculture.)

The second method is to place ½-in-diameter steel reinforcing bars bent in an L shape (Fig. 8-6). The horizontal leg is placed into the concrete footing while the concrete is still wet, with the vertical leg projecting above the footing about 24 in. The rods are placed about 4 ft apart along the entire length of the footing. When the foundation is placed on top of the footing, the steel rods lock the foundation and the footing together.

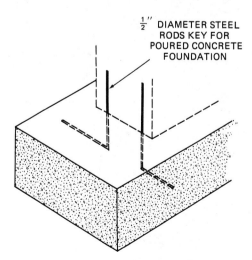

Figure 8-6 Steel rod key. (Courtesy of U.S. Department of Agriculture.)

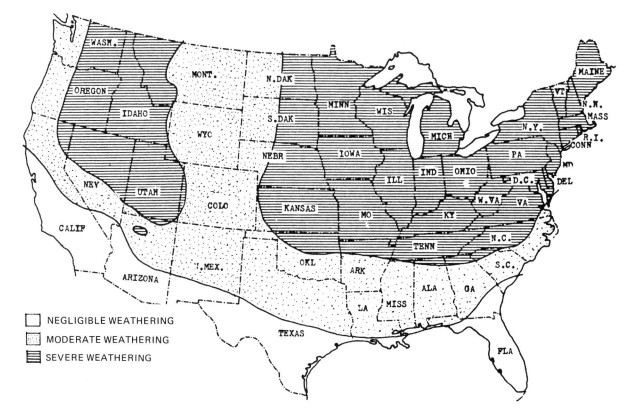

Figure 8-7   Weathering areas. (Courtesy of U.S. Department of Housing and Urban Development.)

Figure 8-8   Average annual frost penetration (in inches) based on state averages. (Courtesy of U.S. Department of Commerce.)

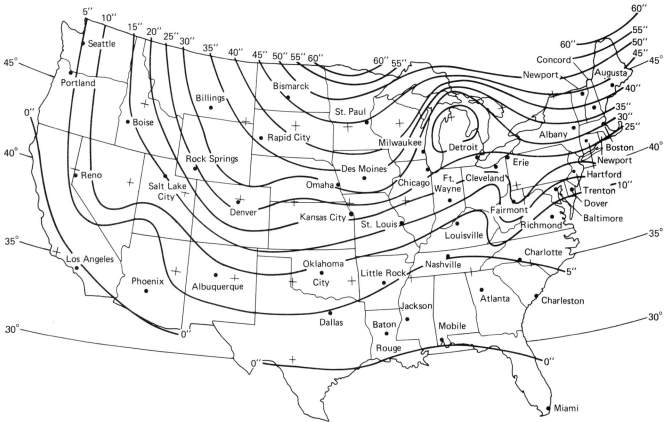

For a building that is not to have a basement, the depth of the footing below the ground is determined by law or building code. It must be deep enough to avoid any damage from ground frost (Figs. 8-7 and 8-8). Geographic location will determine the depth of the foundation, which will vary from 6 in. to 10 ft below the ground.

If the ground surface has a slope, the footing must be placed horizontally, stepping down with the grade (Fig. 8-9). Never place the footing paral-

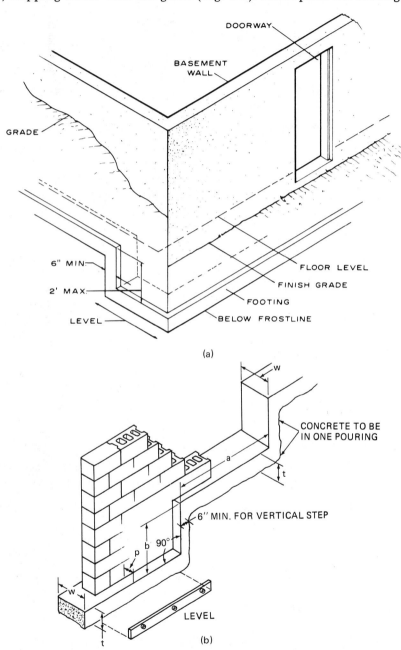

Figure 8-9 (a) Stepped footing; (b) stepped wall footing for masonry. [(a) Courtesy of U.S. Department of Agriculture; (b) courtesy of U.S. Department of Housing and Urban Development.]

a, Horizontal step; b, vertical step; t, footing thickness; p, projection of footing; w, width of footing; all footings and steps should be level; step b should not exceed three-fourths of step a.

lel with the ground slope. The vertical dimension of the step down should not exceed 2 ft.

The foundation of the house must slope with the land in steps. This is to provide a better anchor of the foundation into the ground. If the foundation bottom were built on a straight-line slope, it might cause a sliding action. Such action is prevented by stepping the foundation bottom, making all points on contact with the ground level. The local building code will specify the minimum foundation depth below the ground surface. The foundation spread footing must take the same shape as the foundation. This step-down foundation applies no matter what material is used to construct the foundation.

CONCRETE FOUNDATIONS

When the concrete footing has set, or hardened, the forms are removed, and the foundation forms are placed on top of the concrete footing. After the forms have been installed, concrete is placed in them. Concrete consists of a mixture of cement, sand, stone, and water. When the cement and water are mixed together, a chemical action takes place which solidifies the mass. The sand and stone add volume to the mix. Openings in concrete walls for doors or windows require placing steel rods in the concrete above the opening to help support the load (Fig. 8-10).

The strength of the concrete is determined by the relative amounts of each ingredient in the mix. The plans or specifications will indicate the strength of concrete. One example might be 1:2½:5, which is 1 part cement, 2½ parts sand, and 5 parts stone. Water is controlled by volume.

Concrete can be designed to support loads from 1500 to 5000 lb/in.^{2} by controlling the amount of ingredients in the mix. The stone in the concrete is called aggregate. When being placed in the forms, concrete should not be freely dropped more than 6 ft; otherwise, the ingredients will separate, resulting in inferior-strength concrete. When concrete is used in below-freezing temperatures, antifreeze is added to prevent the water in the mix from freezing.

Concrete mixing can be done by hand or machine. Hand mixing is usually reserved for small amounts of concrete. In machine mixing, called ready-mixed, a rotating drum is used. All dry ingredients are put into the drum and thoroughly mixed together. Later, the proper amount of water is added to

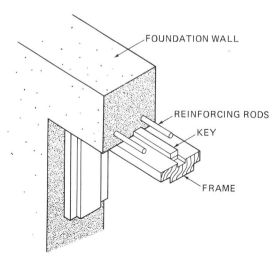

FOUNDATION WALL

REINFORCING RODS

KEY

FRAME

Figure 8-10 Reinforced opening in concrete wall. (Courtesy of U.S. Department of Agriculture.)

the mix. The amount of water added to the mix is important, as it determines the degree of workability. If too much water is added, the mix becomes soupy and loses its strength. If not enough water is added, the mix will flow into the forms, causing voids in the foundation. Water makes a big difference in the strength of concrete.

Special precautions must be taken to bond new concrete to old concrete. This happens when all concrete work cannot be completed in the same day. New and old concrete can be joined if it is done within 2 hours. After that, two stages take place. The first stage, called initial setting, is the beginning of the hardening process. During this initial stage, new concrete and old concrete will not bond after about 7 hours. The second stage, called final setting, takes place next, and during this stage new and old concrete will not bond.

To bond new and old concrete properly, the old concrete surface must be brushed clean and roughened by chipping thoroughly; then the surface must be brushed clean and washed with water. A vertical groove called a key must be formed in the old concrete, or round steel rods spaced about 12 in. apart are left exposed about 18 in. from the old concrete.

Either method will lock the new concrete with the old. When the new concrete is deposited against the old, it must be thoroughly worked against the old by rodding or ramming to form a positive bond. In addition, fine sand, cement, and water are mixed to form grout, which is coated on the old concrete to help bond the new concrete. After the concrete has set, usually the next day, the forms are removed. It takes concrete 28 days to reach its total strength.

Pockets

The location and size of beams must be determined to allow proper support on the foundation. This is accomplished by forming a pocket in the form to provide for support of the beam at a predetermined height, size, and location (Fig. 8-11).

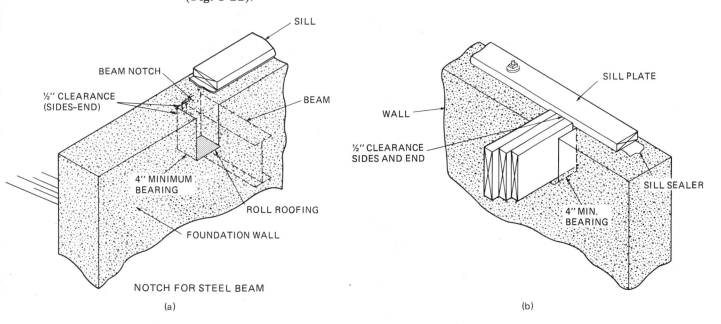

Figure 8-11 (a) Notch for steel beam; (b) built-up wood girder. (Courtesy of U.S. Department of Agriculture.)

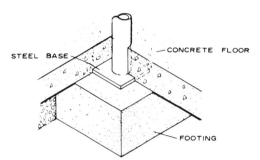

Figure 8-12 Concrete column footing. (Courtesy of U.S. Department of Agriculture.)

Spread Footings

In addition to foundation footings, other units such as columns, chimneys, and fireplaces must be properly supported (Fig. 8-12). Column footings are usually 2 ft square and 1 ft deep. Chimneys and fireplace footings are generally 1 ft deep and 1 ft wider than the length and width of the chimney or fireplace. Example: If the size of the chimney is 2 ft by 4 ft, the footings should be 3 ft by 5 ft and no less than 12 in. deep.

MASONRY FOUNDATION

Where the building codes permit, foundations can also be built of concrete block, stone, or brick (Fig. 8-13). A concrete footing must be installed to support the masonry. The thickness of the wall is determined by the building laws, but in no case will be less than 8 in. thick. A masonry wall 12 in. thick is more common. Care must be taken when installing a masonry foun-

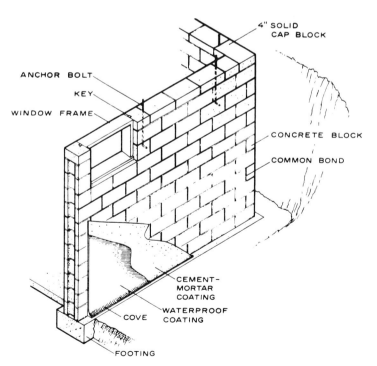

Figure 8-13 Masonry wall waterproofing. (Courtesy of U.S. Department of Agriculture.)

dation to be certain the mortar joints are full and tight, to avoid leakage through the wall. In masonry foundations it is best to use the rod method of tying the wall to the footing. The core of the block is placed over the extended steel rod and filled with mortar. If brick or stone are used, they are bonded by alternating the length of the unit as the wall is built, giving the wall lateral or vertical strength.

Foundation Accessories

Foundations for steps and porches are generally set against the main foundation. When this is done, precautions must be taken to prevent undue settlement of the accessory foundations. Settlement is caused because the soil had to be disturbed to allow ample room for installing the foundation forms. To support the accessory foundation properly, steel reinforcing rods are installed in the main foundation, bent in an L shape (Fig. 8-14). One leg of the L is embedded in the foundation form, the other leg is left extended to tie the two foundations together later. This will minimize or prevent undue settlement of the accessory foundation.

Anchor Bolts

The wood frame of the house is supported by the concrete foundation. The first piece of wood installed in the framing system is called a foundation sill. The foundation sill must be attached to the top of the foundation wall. This is done by installing ½-in.-diameter bolts in the wet concrete, spacing them about 4 ft apart. These bolts are called anchor bolts. Holes are drilled through the wood foundation sill to match the anchor bolts. The nut installed on the anchor bolt will secure the sill to the foundation (Figs. 8-13 and 8-14).

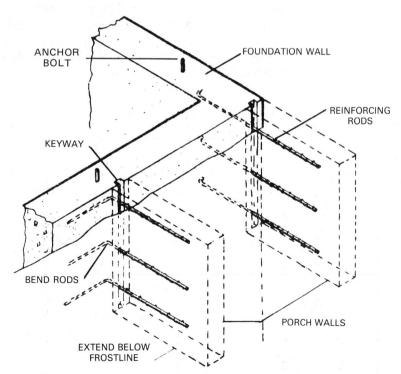

Figure 8-14 Accessory foundation. (Courtesy of U.S. Department of Agriculture.)

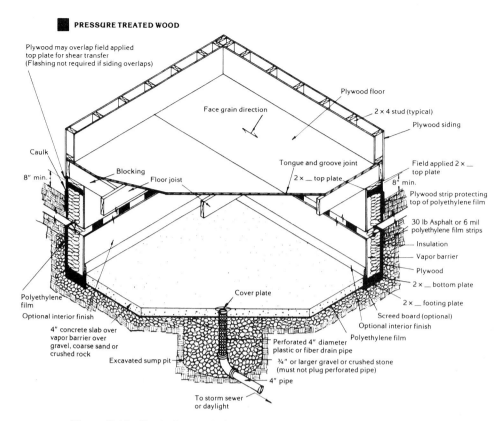

Figure 8-15 Typical wood foundation. (Courtesy of American Plywood Association.)

WOOD FOUNDATIONS

In addition to concrete and masonry foundations, wood foundations are also installed. A good drainage system is essential to keep the basement dry (Fig. 8-15). Gravel is the key element, together with underfloor drains and pipes used to control the water. The gravel will help prevent a buildup of pressure against the wood foundation and will help avoid leaks. The drains and pipe underground can be led to a storm sewer or dry well. On the outside surface, against the studs, pressure-treated exterior plywood of ½ in. minimum thickness will be applied (Table 8-1).

TABLE 8-1

Minimum Plywood Grade and Thickness for Basement Construction

Height of fill (in.)	Stud spacing (in.)	Face grain across studs			Face grain parallel to studs		
		Grade	Minimum thickness (in.)	Identification Index	Grade	Minimum thickness (in.)	Identification Index
24	12	B	$\frac{1}{2}$	$^{32}/_{16}$	B	$\frac{1}{2}$	$^{32}/_{16}$
	16	B	$\frac{1}{2}$	$^{32}/_{16}$	B	$\frac{1}{2}$ (4-ply or 5-layer)	$^{32}/_{16}$
48	12	B	$\frac{1}{2}$	$^{32}/_{16}$	B	$\frac{1}{2}$ (5-layer)	$^{32}/_{16}$
					A	$\frac{1}{2}$	$^{32}/_{16}$
	16	B	$\frac{1}{2}$	$^{32}/_{16}$	A	$\frac{5}{8}$	$^{42}/_{20}$
					B	$\frac{3}{4}$	$^{48}/_{24}$
72	12	B	$\frac{1}{2}$	$^{32}/_{16}$	A	$\frac{5}{8}$ (5-layer)	$^{42}/_{20}$
	16	A	$\frac{1}{2}$	$^{32}/_{16}$	B	$\frac{3}{4}$	$^{48}/_{24}$
86	12	B	$\frac{1}{2}$	$^{32}/_{16}$	A	$\frac{5}{8}$	$^{42}/_{20}$
					B	$\frac{3}{4}$	$^{48}/_{24}$
	16	A	$\frac{5}{8}$	$^{42}/_{20}$	A	$\frac{5}{8}$	$^{42}/_{20}$
		B	$\frac{3}{4}$	$^{48}/_{24}$			

Source: American Plywood Association.

The wood foundation can be built in place or delivered partially pre-built and installed on the site, using 2 × 4's or 2 × 6's (Tables 8-2 and 8-3). The spacing of the studs is determined by the load on the foundation. High-quality lumber must be used and all must be pressure treated to prevent rot and decay. As with concrete and masonry foundations, wood foundations also must extend below the frostline. Full basement, slab on grade, or crawl space can be designed (Fig. 8-16). The quality of soil and the building weight will determine the recommended size of the wood or concrete footing. Wood

TABLE 8-2

Minimum Structural Requirements for Basement Walls

Construction	House width (feet)	Height of fill (inches)	Uniform load conditions					
			Roof—40 psf live; 10 psf dead / Ceiling—10 psf / 1st floor—50 psf live and dead / 2nd floor—50 psf live and dead			Roof—30 psf live; 10 psf dead / Ceiling—10 psf / 1st floor—50 psf live and dead / 2nd floor—50 psf live and dead		
			Lumber species and grade[3]	Stud and plate size (nominal)	Stud spacing (inches)	Lumber species and grade[3]	Stud and plate size (nominal)	Stud spacing (inches)
2 Stories	32 or less	24	D	2×6	16	D	2×6	16
		48	D	2×6	16	D	2×6	16
		72	A B C D	2×6 2×6 2×8 2×8	16 12 16 12	A B C	2×6 2×6 2×8	16 12 16
		86	A B C	2×6 2×8 2×8	12 16 12	A B C	2×6 2×8 2×8	12 16 12
	24 or less	24	D	2×6	16	D	2×6	16
		48	D	2×6	16	D	2×6	16
		72	C D	2×6 2×8	12 16	C	2×6	12
		86	A B C	2×6 2×8 2×8	12 16 12	D	2×8	12
1 Story	32 or less	24	B D D	2×4 2×4 2×6	16 12 16	B D D	2×4 2×4 2×6	16 12 16
		48	D	2×6	16	D	2×6	16
		72	A B D	2×6 2×6 2×8	16 12 16	A C D	2×6 2×6 2×8	16 12 16
		86	A B C	2×6 2×8 2×8	12 16 12	A B D	2×6 2×8 2×8	12 16 12
	28 or less	24	B D D	2×4 2×4 2×6	16 12 16	D	2×4	16
		48	D	2×6	16	B	2×4	12
		72	C	2×6	12	C	2×6	12
		86	D	2×8	12	A B D	2×6 2×8 2×8	12 16 12
	24 or less	24	D	2×4	16	D	2×4	16
		48	B	2×4	12	B	2×4	12
		72	C	2×6	12	C	2×6	12
		86	D	2×8	12	A B D	2×6 2×8 2×8	12 16 12

Source: American Plywood Association.

TABLE 8-3

Minimum Structural Requirements for Crawl-Space Wall Framing

Construction	House width (feet)	Uniform load conditions					
		Roof—40 psf live; 10 psf dead Ceiling—10 psf 1st floor—50 psf live and dead 2nd floor—50 psf live and dead			Roof—30 psf live; 10 psf dead Ceiling—10 psf 1st floor—50 psf live and dead 2nd floor—50 psf live and dead		
		Lumber species and grade	Stud and plate size (nominal)	Stud spacing (inches)	Lumber species and grade	Stud and plate size (nominal)	Stud spacing (inches)
2 Stories	32 or less	B	2 × 6	16	B	2 × 6	16
					D	2 × 6	12
	28 or less	D	2 × 6	12	D	2 × 6	12
	24 or less	D	2 × 6	12	C	2 × 6	16
1 Story	32 or less	B	2 × 4	12	A	2 × 4	16
		B	2 × 6	16	B	2 × 4	12
		D	2 × 6	12	D	2 × 6	16
	28 or less	A	2 × 4	16	B	2 × 4	12
		D	2 × 6	16	D	2 × 6	16
	24 or less	D	2 × 6	16	C	2 × 4	12

Source: American Plywood Association.

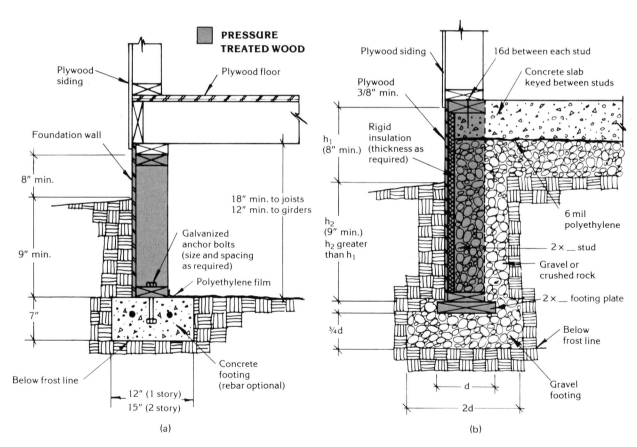

Figure 8-16 (a) Crawl space on concrete footing; (b) concrete slab on grade. (Courtesy of American Plywood Association.)

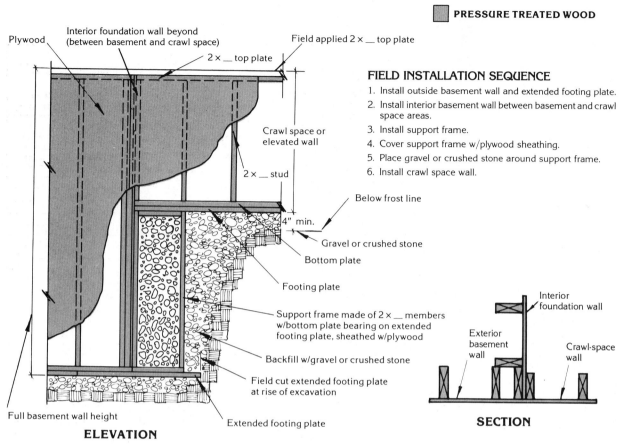

PRESSURE TREATED WOOD

FIELD INSTALLATION SEQUENCE

1. Install outside basement wall and extended footing plate.
2. Install interior basement wall between basement and crawl space areas.
3. Install support frame.
4. Cover support frame w/plywood sheathing.
5. Place gravel or crushed stone around support frame.
6. Install crawl space wall.

ELEVATION

SECTION

Figure 8-17 Stepped footing. (Courtesy of American Plywood Association.)

step-down foundations, to suit ground slope, can be built similar to concrete step-down foundations (Fig. 8-17).

Wood Foundation Insulation

Rigid insulation may be applied over the plywood panel, varying in thickness from ½ to 4 in., or blanket insulation may be installed between the studs either 4 or 6 in. thick.

FOUNDATION WATERPROOFING

If concrete were put under a microscope, it will look like a sponge with millions of cells. Water is lazy and will find the easiest and shortest way to travel through the foundation wall. The exterior surface of all foundations should be waterproofed to prevent water penetration through the wall.

If the foundation is of concrete, one or two coats of asphaltum is applied over the outer concrete surface (Fig. 8-18). If the wall is of masonry, a coating of cement mortar is applied over the outer wall with a cove formed where the wall and footing join. Over this is applied a membrane of roofing

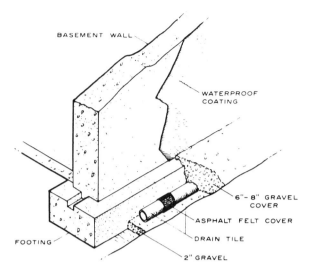

Figure 8-18 Drain tile for soil drainage at outer wall. (Courtesy of U.S. Department of Agriculture.)

paper mopped with asphalt in shingle style, overlapping the paper joints about 6 in. Tar or hot asphalt is then applied over the entire surface to properly seal the masonry and joints (Fig. 8-13).

If the foundation is of wood, the plywood joints are sealed with caulking compound, then the entire exterior surface is covered with a 6-mil thickness of polyethylene (plastic) sheet. This polyethylene covering is spot bonded to the plywood with an adhesive and vertical joints are lapped 6 in. and sealed. Treating the outer surface of the foundation will prevent water penetration through the wall, but more precautions must be taken to prevent water from entering through the basement floor. This is controlled by the installation of foundation drains.

DRAINS

Foundation drains must often be used around a full basement, crawl space, or slab-on-grade foundation to drain away subsurface or underground water. This precaution will prevent damp or wet basement walls or floors.

Drain pipe is installed at or below the area to be protected, along the entire perimeter of the wall, and the drain is pitched away from the building into a storm sewer, drywell, or ditch (Fig. 8-18). Generally, this pipe is 4 in. inside diameter made of clay, concrete, or asphalt composition. It is ordinarily placed at the bottom of the footing, in an envelope of crushed stone. If concrete or clay pipe is used, they are about 12 in. long and are laid with the joints about ¼ in. apart. The top of open pipe joint is covered with a strip of asphalt paper to prevent dirt on stone from falling into and blocking the pipe. If asphalt composition pipe is used, holes are factory drilled around one-half the pipe diameter. Water enters the pipe through these holes.

SUMP PITS

If there is suspicion of a groundwater problem, a sump pit and pump should be installed under the basement floor. This installation is used to control the underground water and to prevent it from entering the basement.

Piping is installed along the inner perimeter of the foundation, under the basement floor, much like the outside drain pipe. The pipe is led to a pit, or a hole in the basement floor about 24 in. in diameter and about 24 in. deep. Water under the ground is led to and contained in the pit and pumped to the outside by a sump pump.

BACKFILLING

After completion of the foundation, removal of the forms, installing of the drains, and waterproofing of the walls, earth is placed around the foundation. This is called backfilling. The backfill is about 6 in. below the finish grade to allow for loam used for seeding, planting, walks, and driveway.

Care must be exercised in backfilling to be certain that no tree stumps, limbs, scrap lumber, or organic material is mixed with the fill or deposited around the foundation. Wood waste will decay, causing eventual cave-in, and more important, will invite termites. The fill used for backfill should be compacted in 6-in. layers to avoid settlement.

Rock or large stone may be used if there is no pressure against the outside foundation wall. If large rock or stone is used, care must be exercised in placing it, not pushing it into the area to be filled. If the stone is pushed in, it may roll against the foundation and crack it. If the foundation cracks, it cannot be repaired; it must be rebuilt. When backfilling, the earth should pitch away from the house to keep surface water from puddling around the house, to avoid water in the basement.

CHASES

It is necessary to provide openings in foundations to pass wiring and piping through the foundation wall under the ground and into the house. The wiring is any electric service that is buried underground, and the piping is water, gas, and sewer lines. These openings are incorporated into the foundation forms and must be planned before concrete is placed in the forms. If provisions are not made in the formwork, the openings will have to be cut through the concrete, which can be a time-consuming job.

In either case the openings must be properly sealed against water entry after the wall or pipe has been installed through the chase. The seal is made with a concrete-like mix without stone, to properly fill and seal the areas around the wire or pipe. This is called grout.

MASONRY VENEER

Brick or stone facing on a house exterior wall is called masonry veneer. Masonry is block, brick, or stone. Provisions must be made at the foundation to support the masonry veneer. The veneer must be planned before the foundation forms are installed because a shelf must be provided on the foundation form top to support the masonry veneer (Fig. 8-2). The outside face of the veneer is flush with the outside face of the concrete foundation. The width of the supporting shelf is 6 in. Concrete block foundations require no special foundation provisions because the masonry veneer is a continuation of the foundation block wall. Masonry veneer cannot be supported on a wood foundation.

TERMITE SHIELDS

The wood foundation sill is the closest wood piece to the ground and one that termites will attack first. Termites resemble ants in size and appearance, and live on the cellulose in the wood. They live in colonies underground. They will enter the building from underground through any small opening within the foundation system. These openings can be small wall cracks, or holes left in the foundation walls for passing pipes. All openings within the foundation must be sealed. A shield must be provided to prevent the termites from attacking the sill (Fig. 8-19). The shield is a nonrust metal such as lead, copper, or aluminum no less than 26-gauge metal, and should be placed

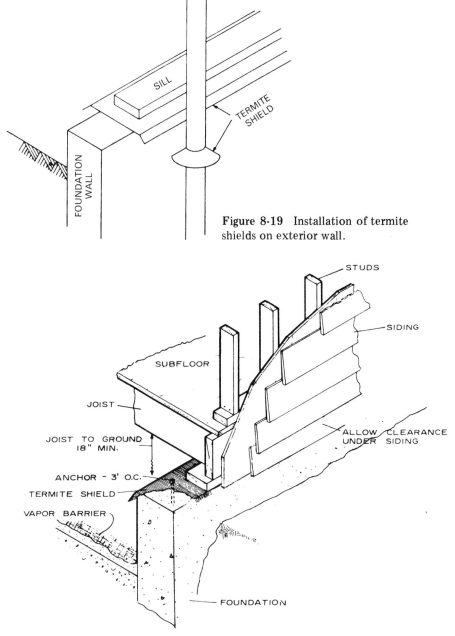

Figure 8-19 Installation of termite shields on exterior wall.

Figure 8-20 Termite shield. (Courtesy of U.S. Department of Agriculture.)

between the top of the foundation and the bottom of the sill. The metal should be no less than 8 in. wide, extending out beyond the outside foundation about 1 in. with a 60° bend. Be sure to overlap and seal the joints of the metal. The same procedure should be followed in locating the transfer of the anchor bolt holes onto the termite shield as for the foundation sill. Longitudinal joints should be locked and soldered (Fig. 8-20). In addition, the wood foundation sill is treated with a preservation, such as creosote, zinc chloride, or penta solutions, before it is bolted to the foundation top. Since termites live on wood, no wood scrap, tree stumps, branches, or lumber waste should be buried underground.

TERMITES

The home of the termite is in the ground (see Fig. 8-21 for the geographic distribution of termite infestation). Termites are attracted to wood, and work their way inside, often leaving no visual sign of their presence. The first indication may be noticed too late to make it worthwhile to correct the damage. These unwanted pests can be found even in the cleanest of homes because they can be brought in with fruits, vegetables, and clothing

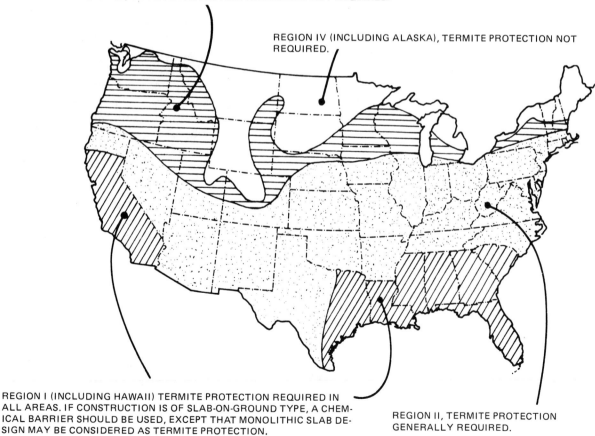

REGION III, TERMITE PROTECTION GENERALLY NOT REQUIRED.

REGION IV (INCLUDING ALASKA), TERMITE PROTECTION NOT REQUIRED.

REGION I (INCLUDING HAWAII) TERMITE PROTECTION REQUIRED IN ALL AREAS. IF CONSTRUCTION IS OF SLAB-ON-GROUND TYPE, A CHEMICAL BARRIER SHOULD BE USED, EXCEPT THAT MONOLITHIC SLAB DESIGN MAY BE CONSIDERED AS TERMITE PROTECTION.

REGION II, TERMITE PROTECTION GENERALLY REQUIRED.

PUERTO RICO IS AN AREA OF SEVERE INFESTATION; ALL LUMBER SHOULD BE PRESSURE TREATED PER AWPI STANDARDS.

Figure 8-21 Geographic distribution of termite infestation. (Courtesy of U.S. Department of Housing and Urban Development.)

or sometimes even by domestic pets. When they are not able to find enough food (wood) in or on the ground, they will emerge from the soil and attack the wood in buildings, taking care to avoid contact with outside air or light. They will gain entrance through any part of the wood structure in contact with the ground through openings in the foundation, around pipes and conduits, or through cracks in the foundation. If none of these are available, they will construct tubes made from mud to reach the wood of the building. They work quickly and quietly, devouring and destroying all wood in their path from the inside of the wood, working their way outside. They will hollow out a board, leaving nothing but the paint. Detection is difficult. They are careful not to eat through the outside surface of the wood, even going so far as to block up any surface hole accidentally broken through. Egg laying of termites increases rapidly within 2 or 3 years after the colony is established, and a colony can consist of several thousand termites. The worker termite will leave the colony seeking wood, because the principal food of termites is cellulose, the main ingredient of wood.

Here are some danger signs that may be encountered: swarms of tiny black or dark brown insects with whitish, opaque wings, thick waists, and curved antennas. These are reproductive termites, which swarm in the spring and fall of the year, then shed their wings, and go underground to start their colony. Watch for clusters of discarded wings. Winged termites are often mistaken for winged ants (Fig. 8-22). The ant has a thin, wasp-like waist with transparent wings and elbow-shaped antennas. Tubes are built in the ground leading from a crack in the foundation to the wood structure of the house. The shelter tubes may be attached to the foundation or may rise directly upward without support. This is a sure sign of termite infestation.

Protection against termites is accomplished by a barrier of toxicant sprayed beneath and around the house which makes it impossible for the termites to cross or pass. The termites above the chemical barrier will die for lack of moisture and those below it will die from lack of food. If any damage has affected the structural portion of the house, it should be replaced. This spraying should be done once a year for lasting protection.

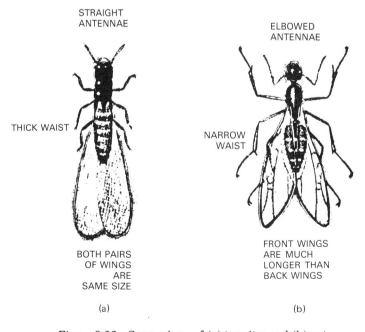

STRAIGHT
ANTENNAE

ELBOWED
ANTENNAE

THICK WAIST

NARROW
WAIST

BOTH PAIRS
OF WINGS
ARE
SAME SIZE

FRONT WINGS
ARE MUCH
LONGER THAN
BACK WINGS

(a)   (b)

Figure 8-22 Comparison of (a) termites and (b) ants.

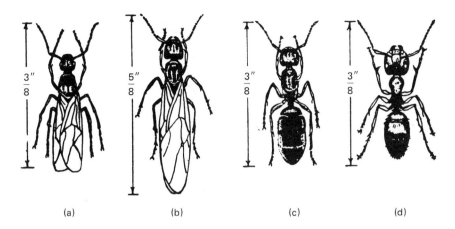

Figure 8-23 Carpenter ants: (a) male; (b) winged female (queen); (c) and (d) workers.

CARPENTER ANTS

Unlike termites, carpenter ants (Fig. 8-23) do not eat wood but nest in wood. They will build tunnel-like galleries in the wood for nesting. These tunnels damage and weaken the wood. Carpenter ants will nest in any wood within the house, and in trees, poles, and posts. They may wander anywhere, but follow a specific trail marked by a visible narrow path of any vegetation. Often, a pile of "sawdust" will be found near a colony in a house, hollow tree, or pole. The ants carry the sawdust out of the wood in building their nests. To prevent damage from carpenter ants, a chemical must be sprayed where the ants have nested.

QUESTIONS

1. What is the main structure supporting a building called? _____

2. What is the purpose of a spread footing? _____
   _____

3. Name two ways of securing the foundation to the spread footing.
   1. _____
   2. _____

4. How is a poured concrete foundation shaped? _____
   _____

5. Describe the method of installing a foundation on a sloped site. _____
   _____

6. How is the strength of concrete determined? _____

7. How is a beam fitted onto a foundation? _____

8. How are chimneys, steps, fireplaces, and columns supported? _____
   _____

9. Name three materials used for masonry foundations.
   1. _____

2. _____

3. _____

10. How are accessory foundations secured to the main foundation? _____

_____

11. What size of studs are used for wood foundations? _____

_____

12. How is a wood foundation insulated? _____

_____

13. Describe the purpose of a foundation drainage system. _____

_____

14. What is backfilling? _____

_____

Floor Framing

INTRODUCTION

A floor framing system provides a safe means of building use for people and furniture. It consists of a foundation sill, columns, beams, floor joists, bridging, and subflooring (Fig. 9-1).

Designing of the floor framing system is controlled by building laws. Floor framing also becomes an integral part of the wall framing system. Two main types of wall framing systems are used, which affect the floor framing: balloon framing and platform framing.

The spacing of the members of the floor, the length and span of the floor, the species and quality of the wood, and the size of the wood are factors that affect the floor framing system. The support of the floor, such as beams, columns, and footings, is also part of the floor framing system.

Three types of floor construction are used in residential building: full basement, crawl space, and slab on grade. The parts of a floor framing system are: foundations, sill, floor joists, bridging, subflooring, beam columns, concrete footings, firestops, and trusses.

FOOTINGS

Two of the main supporting members of the floor framing system are the concrete footing and steel columns (Fig. 9-2). The footings are placed on the ground, and if the house has a basement, the footings are under the basement concrete floor. Generally, the concrete footings are 24 in. square and 12 in. deep. The concrete footings help to spread the load of the floor on the ground.

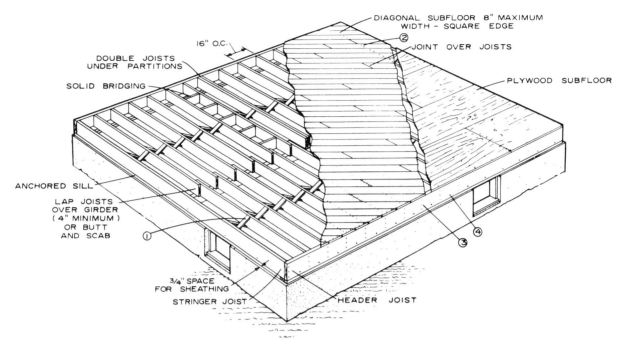

Figure 9-1 Floor framing system. (Courtesy of U.S. Department of Agriculture.)

1, Nailing bridging to joists; 2, nailing board subfloor to joists; 3, nailing header to joists; 4, toenailing header to sill.

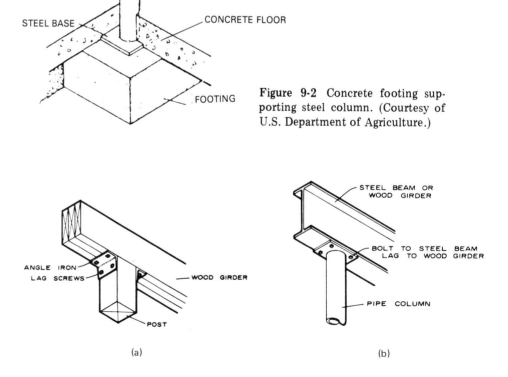

Figure 9-2 Concrete footing supporting steel column. (Courtesy of U.S. Department of Agriculture.)

Figure 9-3 (a) Wood column; (b) steel column. (Courtesy of U.S. Department of Agriculture.)

COLUMNS

One of the main supporting members of the floor framing is the column. The purpose of the concrete footings is to support the columns. The columns can be concrete, concrete block, wood, or steel (Fig. 9-3). The columns are usually 3½-in.-diameter steel pipe with a welded steel plate top and bottom. The steel plate helps to spread the load of the floors onto the column.

The spacing and size of the columns is determined by the load they must support. If the loads are exceptionally heavy, the pipe columns are filled with concrete to support heavier loads. The height or length of the column is set by the ceiling height. If the house has a crawl space and no basement, the columns are called piers (Fig. 9-4). If the house has a floor on the ground, footings, columns, or piers are not necessary; such a system is called slab on grade.

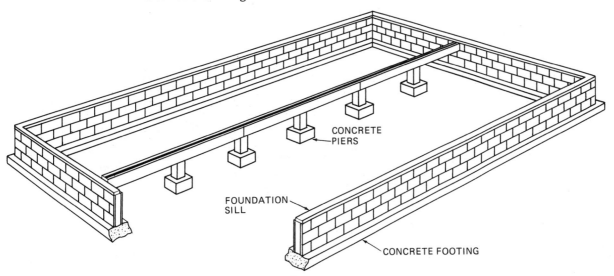

Figure 9-4 Crawl space piers. (Courtesy of U.S. Department of Housing and Urban Development.)

FOUNDATION SILL

The first wood member used for supporting the floor framing system is the foundation sill. The sill is supported by and bolted to the top of the foundation wall with anchor bolts (Fig. 9-5). The sill can be one 2 × 6, two 2 × 6's,

Figure 9-5 Anchor bolts.

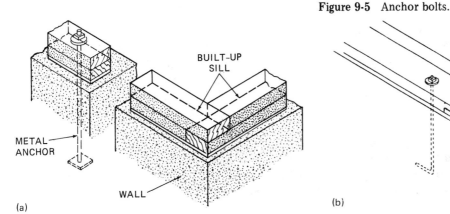

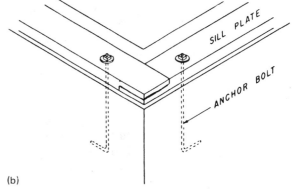

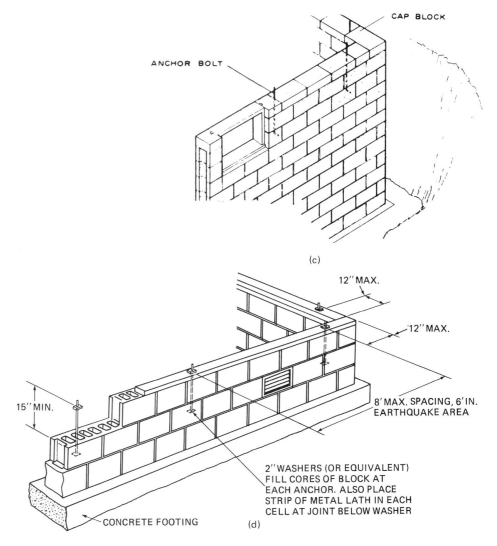

Figure 9-5 (continued) [(c) Courtesy of U.S. Department of Agriculture; (d) courtesy of U.S. Department of Housing and Urban Development.]

or one 4 × 6, all laid flat (Fig. 9-6). The type of framing will determine the type of sill. The sill must be perfectly true, straight, and level.

FOUNDATION SILL SEAL

The foundation top is often uneven. With the foundation sill properly attached to the foundation top, voids are created between the sill bottom and the foundation top. This may not only affect the level of the floor, but will allow cold air to enter the building. A firm, solid bed of mortar must be placed on the foundation top for proper bearing and sealing (Fig. 9-7a). This is a mixture of sand, cement, and water. This mixture not only provides uniform bearing, but also affords leveling of the sill. Occasionally, a soft, rigid sill sealer is used between the foundation top and the sill bottom (Fig. 9-7b). This is successful in sealing against cold air, but not successful in forming a firm, solid bed for supporting the framework to the sill. The wood foundation sill is used to support one end of the floor joists (Fig. 9-8).

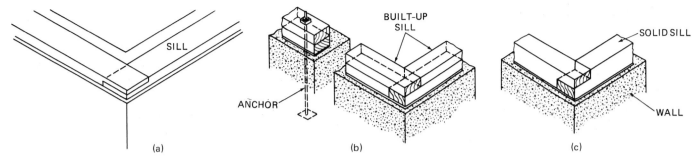

Figure 9-6 Sills: (a) 2×6; (b) two 2×6's; (c) 4×6.

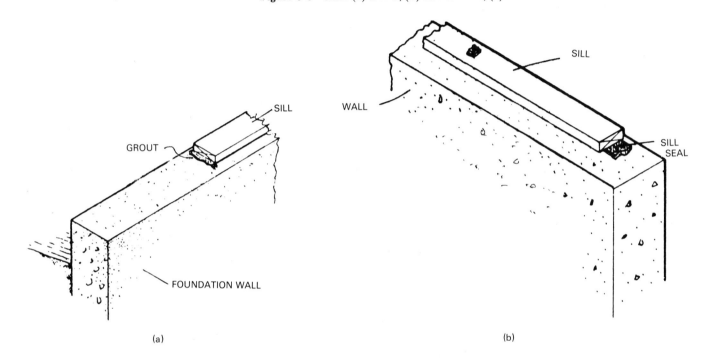

Figure 9-7 (a) Grout sill seal; (b) foundation sill seal.

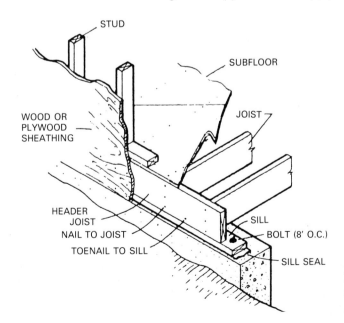

Figure 9-8 Joist support at sill. (Courtesy of U.S. Department of Agriculture.)

BEAMS AND GIRDERS

The purpose of the columns is to support the beam. The greater the load and the greater the spacing of the columns, the larger the beam size. Beams can be solid wood; several smaller wood members bolted together, called builtup beam; or steel beam (Fig. 9-9). If a steel beam is used, wood must be bolted to the steel to allow nailing the floor joists (Fig. 9-10). The other ends of the beam are supported by the foundation walls (Fig. 9-11). Care must be taken in splicing wood beams. Splicing must be done on a column to properly support the loads on the beam (Fig. 9-12). Steel beams are usually one length, and can be designed without columns. Girders are wood structural member framing into a beam for supporting floor joists. Girders are not used in residential construction except for unusual loading conditions.

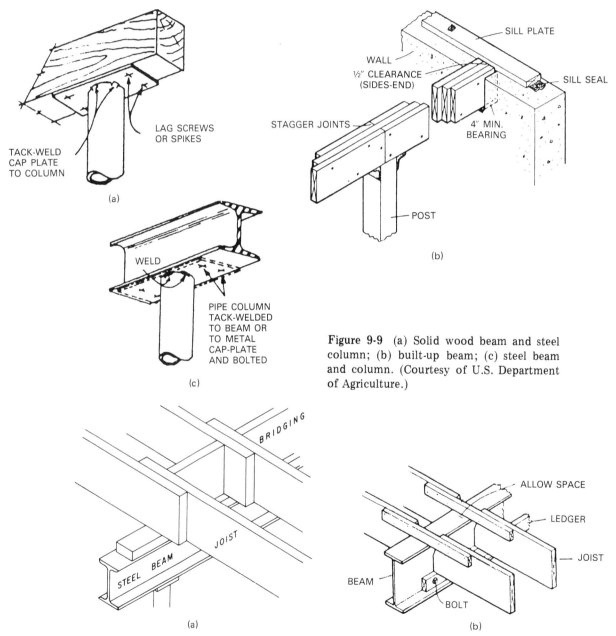

Figure 9-9 (a) Solid wood beam and steel column; (b) built-up beam; (c) steel beam and column. (Courtesy of U.S. Department of Agriculture.)

Figure 9-10 (a) Joists resting on steel beam; (b) joist bolted onto steel beam. (Courtesy of U.S. Department of Agriculture.)

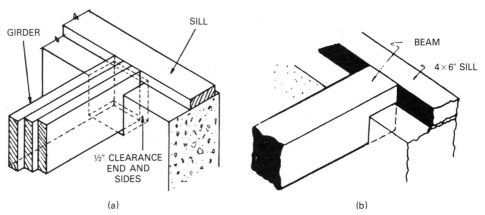

Figure 9-11   Foundation beam supports. [(a) Courtesy of U.S. Department of Agriculture.]

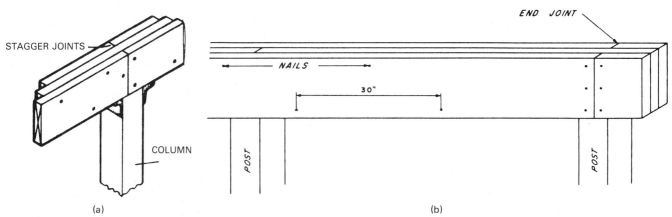

Figure 9-12   (a) Spliced wood beam; (b) arrangement of nailing for built-up beams or girders. [(a) Courtesy of U.S. Department of Agriculture.]

FLOOR JOISTS

Another member of the floor framing family is the floor joist (Figs. 9-10 and 9-13). These members are usually 2 in. thick and from 6 to 12 in. deep. They are generally spaced 16 in. apart. The size and spacing of the floor joists are determined by floor loads (Table 9-1), span (distance from beam

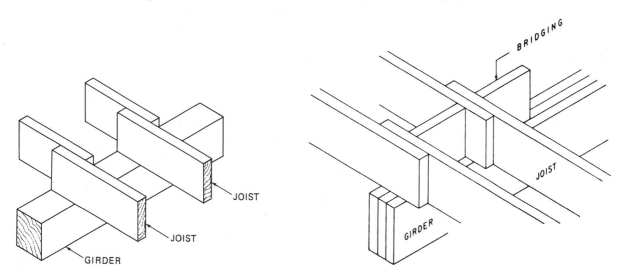

Figure 9-13   Floor joists. (Courtesy of U.S. Department of Agriculture.)

TABLE 9-1

Floor or Ceiling Live Loads

Location	Live Load (psf)
Dwelling rooms (other than sleeping quarters)	40
Dwelling rooms (sleeping quarters and attic floors)	30
Ceiling joist-attics (served by permanent or disappearing stair)	30
Ceiling joist-attics (limited storage roof slope over 3 in 12)	20
Ceiling joists-attics (without storage roof slope 3 in 12 or less)	10
Stairs	60
Public stairs and corridors (two family dwellings)	60
Garages and carports (passenger cars)	75
Balconies and porches	60
Sidewalks and driveways	250

to foundation; Table 9-2), and building laws. Floor joists are doubled under parallel walls above to help support the extra weight of the wall (Fig. 9-14). Joists should never be supported by the chimney.

It is not unusual for chimneys to leak if they are not properly constructed. This happens when the mason does not take the time to seal the mortar joints between brick courses or to seal the clay pipe inside the chimney, called the flue lining.

The smoke and heat inside the chimney will find its way through these defects in the chimney, causing possible fire to the house or extensive smoke damage. To guard against this possibility, most building codes will demand no less than 2 in. of clearance between chimneys and all structural wood framing members (Fig. 9-15).

The same reasons apply for not using the chimney as a column or means of supporting floor framing. The chimney must be built as a separate structure completely independent from the rest of the house.

One end of the floor joist will sit on the foundation sill. The other end will sit on top of the beam (Fig. 9-16). To save space, the floor joists will sometimes rest into the beam instead of on top of the beam by the use of metal joist hangers (Fig. 9-17).

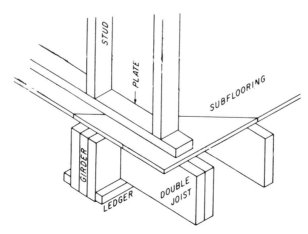

Figure 9-14 Double joists under nonbearing partitions.

TABLE 9-2

Floor Joist Span

		SOUTHERN YELLOW PINE — 30 LB. LIVE LOAD			
JOIST SIZE (NOMINAL)	SPACING OF JOISTS O. C. IN INCHES	LUMBER GRADES			
		NO. 1 DENSE KILN-DRIED 2" DIM.	NO. 2 DENSE KILN-DRIED 2" DIM.	NO. 1 DENSE 2" DIM.	NO. 2 DENSE 2" DIM.
2 x 6	12	12'- 5"	12'- 5"	12'- 5"	12'- 5"
	16	11'- 4"	11'- 4"	11'- 4"	11'- 4"
	24	10'- 2"	10'- 2"	10'- 0"	9'- 2"
2 x 8	12	16'- 1"	16'- 1"	16'- 1"	16'- 1"
	16	14'- 9"	14'- 9"	14'- 9"	14'- 9"
	24	13'- 1"	13'- 1"	13'- 1"	12'- 4"
2 x 10	12	19'- 11"	19'- 11"	19'- 11"	19'- 11"
	16	18'- 3"	18'- 3"	18'- 3"	18'- 3"
	24	16'- 2"	16'- 2"	16'- 2"	15'- 7"
2 x 12	12	23'- 9"	23'- 9"	23'- 9"	23'- 9"
	16	21'- 9"	21'- 9"	21'- 9"	21'- 9"
	24	19'- 2"	19'- 2"	19'- 2"	18'- 11"

		SOUTHERN YELLOW PINE — 40 LB. LIVE LOAD			
JOIST SIZE (NOMINAL)	SPACING OF JOISTS O. C. IN INCHES	LUMBER GRADES			
		NO. 1 DENSE KILN-DRIED 2" DIM.	NO. 2 DENSE KILN-DRIED 2" DIM.	NO. 1 DENSE 2" DIM.	NO. 2 DENSE 2" DIM.
2 x 6	12	11'- 5"	11'- 5"	11'- 5"	11'- 5"
	16	10'- 5"	10'- 5"	10'- 5"	10'- 1"
	24	9'- 2"	9'- 2"	8'- 11"	8'- 3"
2 x 8	12	14'- 9"	14'- 9"	14'- 9"	14'- 9"
	16	13'- 6"	13'- 6"	13'- 6"	13'-6"
	24	12'- 0"	12'- 0"	11'- 11"	11'- 0"
2 x 10	12	18'- 3"	18'- 3"	18'- 3"	18'- 3"
	16	16'- 9"	16'- 9"	16'- 9"	16'- 9"
	24	14'- 10"	14'- 10"	14'- 10"	14'- 10"
2 x 12	12	21'- 9"	21'- 9"	21'- 9"	21'- 9"
	16	19'- 11"	19'- 11"	19'- 11"	19'- 11"
	24	17'- 7"	17'- 7"	17'- 7"	16'- 11"

		LARCH AND DOUGLAS FIR — 30 LB. LIVE LOAD				
JOIST SIZE (NOMINAL)	SPACING OF JOISTS O. C. IN INCHES	LUMBER GRADES				
		SELECT STRUCTURAL	DENSE CONSTRUCTION	CONSTRUCTION	STANDARD	UTILITY
2 x 6	12	11'- 4"	11'- 4"	11'- 4"	11'- 4"	8'- 4"
	16	10'- 4"	10'- 4"	10'- 4"	10'- 4"	7'- 2"
	24	9'- 0"	9'- 0"	9'- 0"	9'- 0"	5'- 10"
2 x 8	12	15'- 4"	15'- 4"	15'- 4"	15'- 4"	12'- 4"
	16	14'- 0"	14'- 0"	14'- 0"	14'- 0"	10'- 8"
	24	12'- 4"	12'- 4"	12'- 4"	12'- 4"	8'- 8"
2 x 10	12	18'- 4"	18'- 4"	18'- 4"	18'- 4"	16'- 10"
	16	17'- 0"	17'- 0"	17'- 0"	17'- 0"	14'- 8"
	24	15'- 6"	15'- 6"	15'- 6"	15'- 6"	12'- 0"
2 x 12	12	21'- 2"	21'- 2"	21'- 2"	21'- 2"	19'- 8"
	16	19'- 8"	19'- 8"	19'- 8"	19'- 8"	17'- 0"
	24	17'- 10"	17'- 10"	17'- 10"	17'- 10"	14'- 0"

		LARCH AND DOUGLAS FIR — 40 LB. LIVE LOAD				
JOIST SIZE (NOMINAL)	SPACING OF JOISTS O. C. IN INCHES	LUMBER GRADES				
		SELECT STRUCTURAL	DENSE CONSTRUCTION	CONSTRUCTION	STANDARD	UTILITY
2 x 6	12	10'- 6"	10'- 6"	10'- 6"	10'- 6"	7'- 4"
	16	9'- 8"	9'- 8"	9'- 8"	9'- 8"	6'- 4"
	24	8'- 4"	8'- 4"	8'- 4"	8'- 2"	5'- 2"
2 x 8	12	14'- 4"	14'- 4"	14'- 4"	14'- 4"	10'- 0"
	16	13'- 0"	13'- 0"	13'- 0"	13'- 0"	9'- 6"
	24	11'- 6"	11'- 6"	11'- 6"	11'- 0"	7'- 10"
2 x 10	12	17'- 4"	17'- 4"	17'- 4"	17'- 4"	15'- 2"
	16	16'- 2"	16'- 2"	16'- 2"	16'- 2"	13'- 0"
	24	14'- 6"	14'- 6"	14'- 6"	14'- 0"	10'- 8"
2 x 12	12	20'- 0"	20'- 0"	20'- 0"	20'- 0"	17'- 8"
	16	18'- 8"	18'- 8"	18'- 8"	18'- 8"	15'- 4"
	24	16'- 10"	16'- 10"	16'- 10"	16'- 10"	12'- 6"

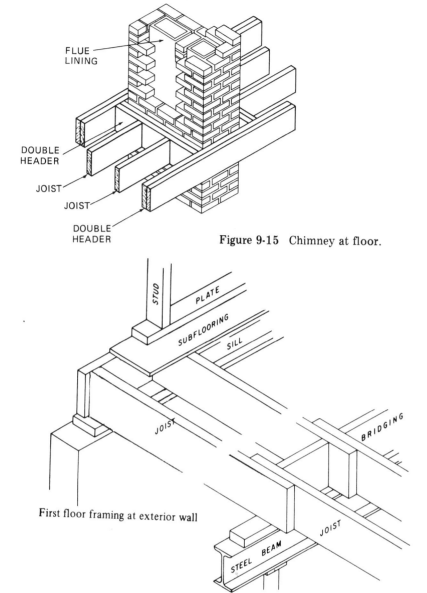

Figure 9-15 Chimney at floor.

First floor framing at exterior wall

Joists resting on steel beam.

Figure 9-16 Floor joist supports.

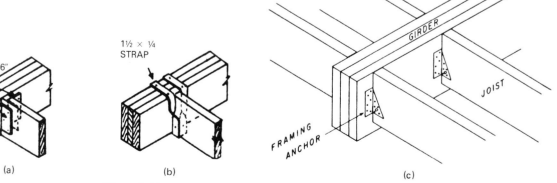

Figure 9-17 Framing floor joists into the side of wood girders: (a) steel angle; (b) steel joist hanger; (c) framing anchors. [(a) and (b) Courtesy of U.S. Department of Housing and Urban Development.]

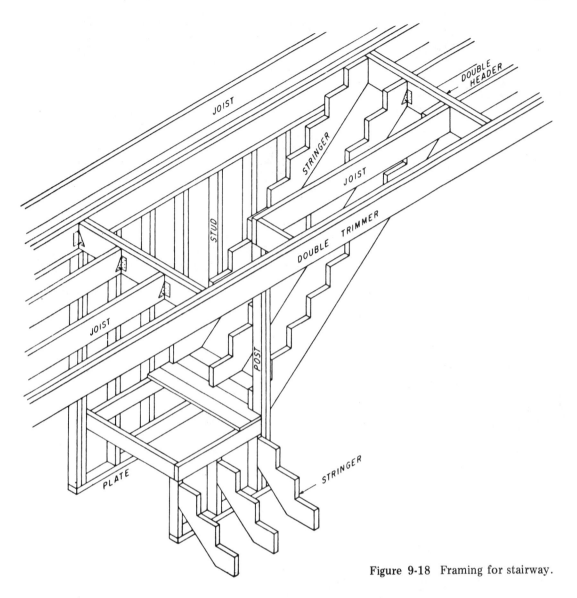

Figure 9-18 Framing for stairway.

All openings in the floor framing or joists spaced more than the usual 16 in. apart require double joists around the perimeter of the opening. These are called double headers and will occur at stair openings (Fig. 9-18) and chimney or fireplace openings (Fig. 9-19). The purpose of the double header is to carry the load normally supported by the missing floor joist in the stair or chimney opening. The double joist acts as a builtup beam.

TRUSSES

Occasionally, the span is too great for the loads that floor joists will carry. When this happens, trusses are used in place of floor joists. These trusses are built of a series of wood members bolted or nailed together, forming one unit or truss. Trusses are used when the span of the floor joists exceeds the distance required by the building code, or when the floor load is too heavy for the floor joists to carry. Great spans and loads are permitted with the use of trusses (Fig. 9-20).

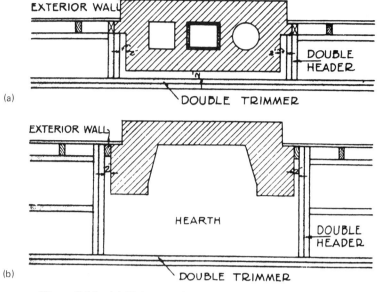

(a)

(b)

Figure 9-19   (a) Chimney above fireplace; (b) plan of fireplace.

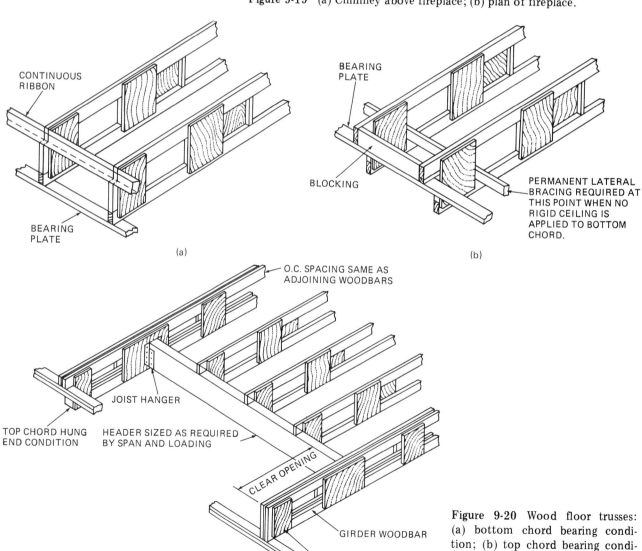

(a)

(b)

(c)

Figure 9-20 Wood floor trusses: (a) bottom chord bearing condition; (b) top chord bearing condition; (c) end conditions. (Courtesy of Wood Fabricators, Inc., North Bellerica, Mass.)

CANTILEVERS

Whenever a floor extends beyond the foundation, or hangs over, it is called a cantilever. If the cantilever is in the same direction or parallel to the floor joists, no alteration of floor framing is involved; the floor joists are simply extended to the desired projection within the limits of proper support (Fig. 9-21). If the cantilever is opposite the direction of the joists, the joists, in part, are reversed in the direction of the cantilever.

There is a limit to how far a floor joist can extend beyond the foundation wall. A cantilever system is used often to support bay windows and garrison-style homes, where the second floor extends beyond the wall (Fig. 9-22).

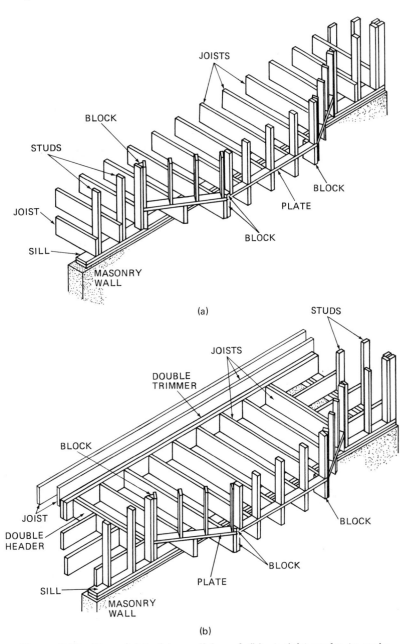

Figure 9-21 Floor joists (a) parallel, and (b) at right angles to main joists.

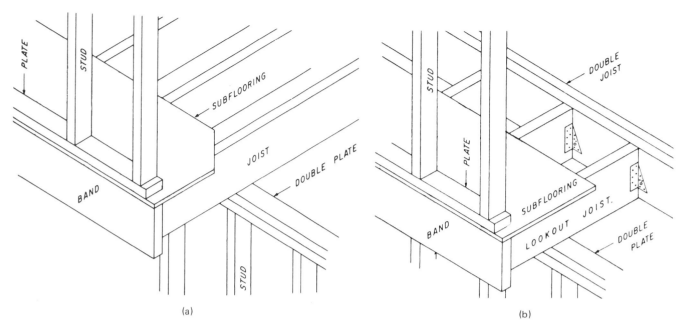

Figure 9-22 Overhang of exterior wall at second floor: (a) joists at right angles to wall below; (b) joists parallel to wall below.

BRIDGING

Whenever heavy loads such as pianos, refrigerators, or water beds are placed on floors, the load is concentrated in one area of the floor. This is called a concentrated load. These loads must be distributed over a greater area of the floor space than they occupy. This is accomplished by bridging the floor joists. There are three types of bridging: wood cross-bridging, metal cross-bridging, and solid bridging. As a general rule, one row of bridging is installed between every floor joist midpoint between the outer foundation wall and the beam (Fig. 9-23).

Wood cross-bridging consists of a 1 × 3 nailed top and bottom. Metal bridging consists of light-gauge metal shaped to help distribute the load, installed similar to wood cross-bridging. Solid wood bridging consists of members of the same size as the floor joists cut to length to fit between the spacing of the joists.

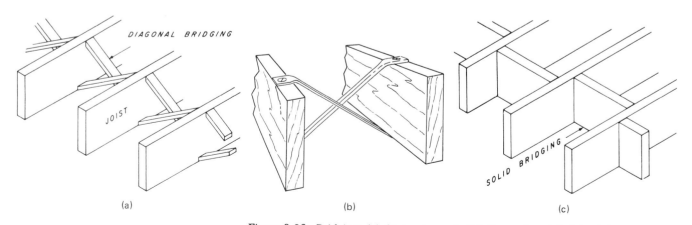

Figure 9-23   Bridging: (a) diagonal wood; (b) diagonal metal; (c) solid wood.

BALLOON FRAMING

One of two types of floor framing with joists is called balloon framing; the other is called platform framing. This choice of framing types takes place at the foundation sill. Balloon framing is recommended for buildings more than one story high. The exterior wall studs are without joints, of one piece from the foundation sill to the second floor ceiling. This type of framing provides a stronger, sturdier building (Fig. 9-24). The foundation sill is one 4 × 6 or two 2 × 6's bolted to the foundation (Fig. 9-6).

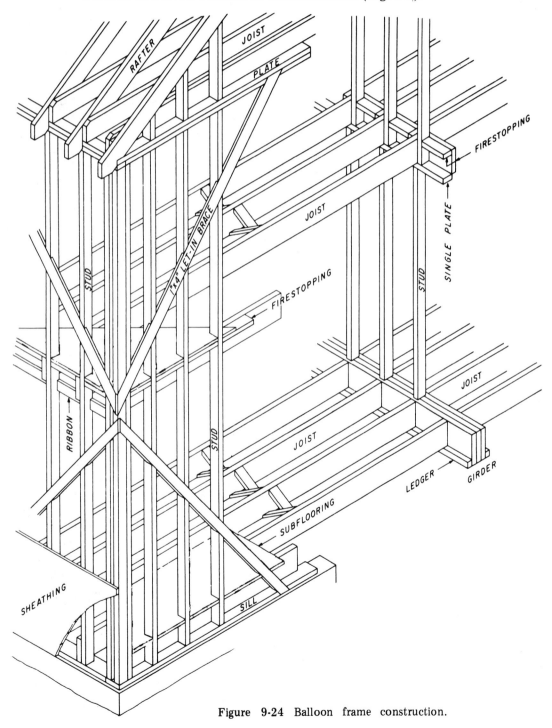

Figure 9-24 Balloon frame construction.

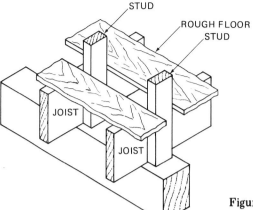

Figure 9-25 Platform floor framing and beam.

Figure 9-24 shows the face of the sheathing and the face of the foundation on the same plane. This indicates a continuous joint around the entire building between the foundation top and the bottom of the sheathing. Strong winds or a driving rain may penetrate this joint. If the back of the sheathing and the face of the foundation are on the same plane, the sheathing could be extended about 1 in. below the foundation, and this will seal the joint between the foundation and the sill.

The outer edge of the sill is in line with the outer face of the foundation. The floor joists are extended to the outer face of the foundation sill. When the exterior walls are constructed, the studs are supported on top of the foundation sill alongside the floor joists.

The floor joists, studs, and foundation sill are nailed together. Construction of the wall over the beam is similar (Fig. 9-25). The supporting interior wall on the first floor rests on the top of the beam alongside the floor joists, and the two are nailed together. The inner supporting wall on the first floor supports the floor joists on the second floor (Fig. 9-24). The second-floor joists are supported by a 1 × 4 wood ribbon notched into the exterior wall studs flush with the inside stud line (Fig. 9-24).

PLATFORM FRAMING

The second type of framing is called platform. This system is used on a single-story house. The foundation sill is generally a 2 × 6 laid flat, bolted to the foundation flush with the outside foundation line (Fig. 9-26).

Along the entire perimeter of the foundation sill and on top of the foundation sill is nailed a member called a header or band joist. The outer edge of the band joist is flush with the outer edge of the foundation sill. The floor joists are nailed to this header and also to the foundation sill.

The subfloor is then applied, extending it to the outer edge of the header. This forms a platform to allow the carpenters to construct the walls on the subfloor platform and erect it in position completely assembled on top of the subfloor. Firestops are not required with platform framing because extending the subfloor to the outer edge of the wall acts as a firestop, blocking the space between the studs.

SUBFLOORS

Over the joists or trusses is nailed the first of two thicknesses of floor, called the subfloor. This subfloor not only provides a nailing surface for the finish floor but also reinforces and braces the structural part of the floor framing

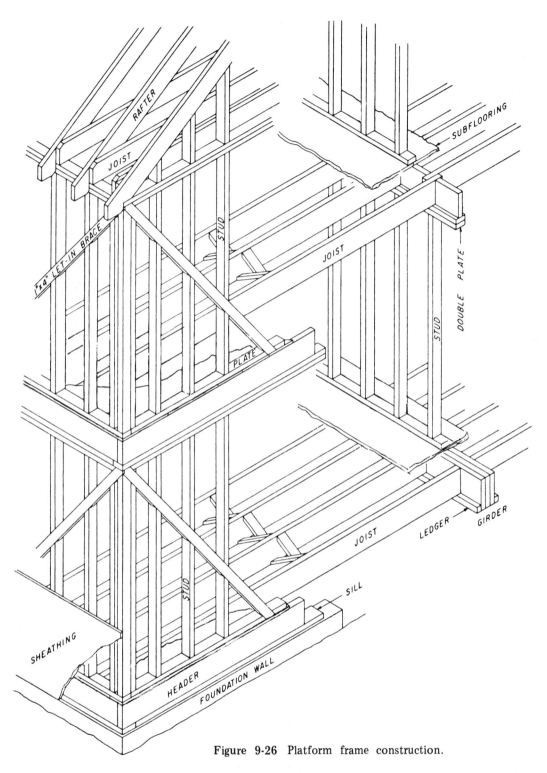

Figure 9-26 Platform frame construction.

system, which includes the floor joists, bridging, beam, and columns. Usually, the subfloor is ⅝-in. plywood nailed to the floor joists with screw nails or coated nails for a firm hold (Fig. 9-27). Occasionally, the plywood subfloor is glued to the joists, being careful to follow manufacturer's directions. Nailing or gluing will produce the same results. The 8-ft dimensions of the plywood subfloor are laid perpendicular to the floor joists, being careful to stagger the plywood joints.

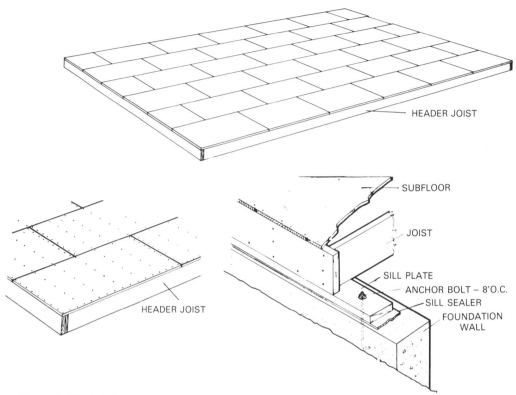

Figure 9-27 Subflooring. (Courtesy of U.S. Department of Housing and Urban Development.)

Gluing the Subfloor

An alternative method of applying the plywood subfloor to the floor joists is by gluing the plywood to the floor joists. This method does not eliminate nailing the plywood subfloor to the floor joists, but it does allow the nails to be spaced farther apart because the glue is also providing some holding power. When plywood subfloor is nailed only to the floor joists, a square-edge plywood is used; when the plywood is glued to the floor joists, a tongue-and-groove plywood is used. The tongue-and-groove edge locks the plywood panels together (Fig. 9-28).

(a)   (b)

Figure 9-28 Gluing plywood. (Courtesy of American Plywood Association.)

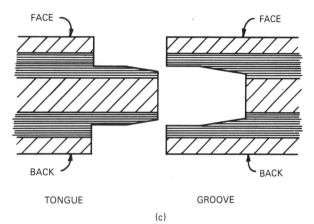

FACE   FACE

BACK   BACK

TONGUE   GROOVE

(c)

Figure 9-28 (continued)

FIRESTOPS

Only balloon framing requires firestops. The purpose of the firestops is to seal the spaces between the studs to avoid a fire from being drawn up into the studs created by the space between the studs inside the wall. A fire could rapidly spread through drafts in the wall.

These air spaces must be blocked with fillers such as brick, wood, concrete sand, or mineral wool; these seal the wall against draft action. The system is repeated at all floor levels and at all partitions resting on the main beam (Fig. 9-29) and columns.

LOADING

In the design of building, two types of loading are considered, live load and dead load. Live load is the weight to be supported by the floor, such as furniture, equipment, people, and storage. Dead load includes the weight of the material or lumber used to build the floor. The total of these two loads is called the total load. Local building laws will determine what loads are required for structural design. It is this load that will determine the size and spacing of floor joists or trusses (Table 9-2 on page 127).

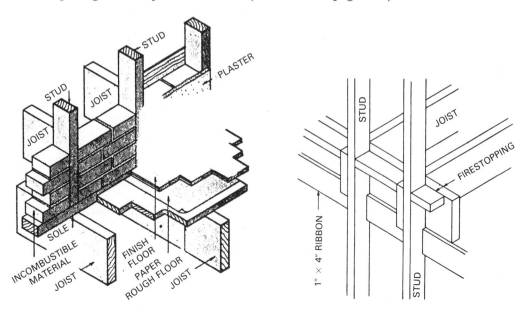

Figure 9-29 Firestops.

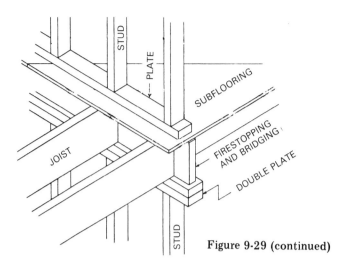

Figure 9-29 (continued)

SLAB-ON-GRADE CONSTRUCTION

In buildings designed with basements or crawl spaces, floor joists are used. In buildings that have no basement or crawl space, the concrete floor is placed directly on the ground.

All piping for heating and plumbing and all electric wiring must be installed or "roughed out" on the ground under the concrete floor before the concrete floor is placed. Stubs of short lengths of pipe and wiring are left above the concrete floor to be continued and completed later.

The ground must be prepared to receive the concrete, to avoid any cracking of the floor. Steel mesh is placed in the concrete to prevent the floor from cracking. In addition, moisture within the ground must not be allowed to penetrate through this concrete floor and into the house. To prevent this from happening, a vapor barrier such as polyethylene is placed on top of the ground under the concrete floor. Provisions must also be taken to prevent the escape of heat from within the house through the concrete floor.

A rigid type of insulation such as Styrofoam is placed along the outer perimeter of the building under the concrete floor (Fig. 9-30). No beams,

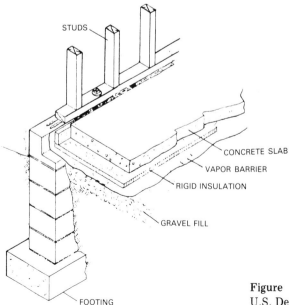

Figure 9-30 Slab on grade. (Courtesy of U.S. Department of Agriculture.)

footing, or columns are required in slab-on-grade construction. All studs in contact with the concrete must be treated against rot, or a waterproof paper or plastic must be installed between the bottom of the shoe and the top of the concrete.

WOOD-OVER-CONCRETE CONSTRUCTION

If wood flooring or other flooring is installed as a finish floor over a concrete slab on grade, it can be installed directly by applying adhesive (Fig. 9-31a). An alternative method is to install 2 X 3's onto the concrete, much like floor joists, to allow a nailing surface for the wood finish floor. These are called screeds or sleepers. Screeds must be treated to prevent rotting (Fig. 9-31b).

If the concrete floor is used as a base for gluing the wood finish floor, care must be exercised in finishing the concrete base to a perfect, even, level finish. If the concrete floor is not perfect, all the defects will show in the finish wood floor. In addition, extreme care must be used to ensure a dry

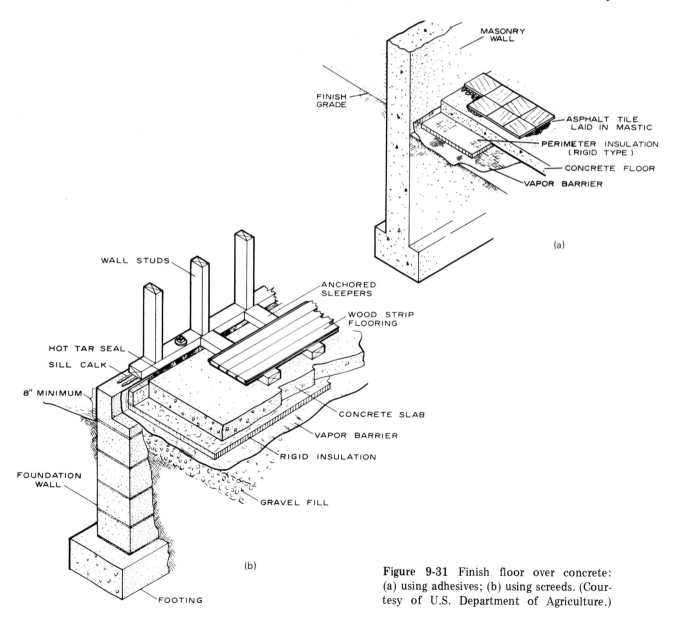

Figure 9-31 Finish floor over concrete: (a) using adhesives; (b) using screeds. (Courtesy of U.S. Department of Agriculture.)

concrete floor; otherwise, dampness, moisture, or water will warp, twist, and mar the wood finish floor. Moisture will break down the adhesive, causing the wood floor to come loose from the concrete floor.

CRAWL SPACES

Another type of construction is one without a basement or part basement, called a crawl space (Fig. 9-32). Everything remains the same as with a full basement except that there is no basement. The height between the ground and the underside of the first floor is only enough to crawl in to make repairs to electric wiring, heating, or piping. This type of construction is used if the area has a high water table or if there is ledge on the land, making it too costly to construct a basement.

A high water table is an area where the natural underground water is close to the surface of the ground. If a house with a basement were to be built in such an area, the possibility exists that the basement will be flooded. Crawl-space construction will help to solve this problem.

This type of construction must have cross-ventilation in the crawl space; otherwise, dampness, moisture, and lack of air will cause the framing to rot. Cross-ventilation is accomplished by installing screened louvers on at least two opposite walls of the foundation above ground. In cold climates, this ventilation will also cause the freezing cold air to find its way into the crawl space. It becomes necessary to insulate the space between the floor joists and also to insulate the water pipes and heating ducts. Access to the crawl space can be through a trap door in the floor in one of the closets or through a small door designed in the foundation, much like a basement window.

Like a full basement house, columns, beams, and floor joists are re-

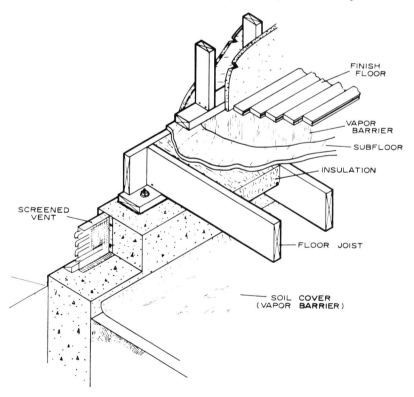

Figure 9-32 Crawl space. (Courtesy of U.S. Department of Agriculture.)

quired in crawl-space construction. The foundation is not as deep in the ground as is the full basement because there is no need for a foundation deeper than is required by the local building code.

QUESTIONS

1. Name two structural means of supporting floors.
    1. _____
    2. _____
2. What is the first wood member used in the framing system called?
    _____
3. How is a foundation sill secured to the foundation? _____
    _____
    What is the spacing? _____
    _____
4. Name two means of sealing a sill to a foundation.
    1. _____
    2. _____
5. Name three types of beams.
    1. _____
    2. _____
    3. _____
6. What determines the size of floor joists? _____
    _____
7. How are openings in floor framing treated? _____
    _____
8. What means are used to support floors when the length of the span precludes the use of floor joists? _____
    _____
9. What type of framing is recommended for a building with one floor above the foundation? _____
    _____
10. What type of framing is recommended for a building with more than one floor above the foundation? _____
    _____
11. What can be used to protect the spaces between studs in balloon framing? _____
    _____
12. How many stories are recommended in platform framing? _____
    _____
13. What is the term used to describe framing that extends beyond the means of support? _____
14. Name two types of loading.
    1. _____
    2. _____
15. How are heavy, concentrated loads distributed over floor joists? _____
    _____
16. What is the first layer of floor called? _____
17. Name the type of floor construction used in buildings with no basement or crawl space. _____

10

Wall Framing

INTRODUCTION

After the floor framing system is completed, including the subflooring, the framing of the walls begins, using wood or steel studs spaced 16 or 24 in. apart. Careful planning of the walls, called partitions, provides for layout of the rooms in the house. The location of the partitions determines the size of the rooms. Partitions make up the interior and exterior walls of the house.

There are two types of partitions. One, called a bearing partition, is used to support a part of the building, usually a floor, ceiling, or roof. The second type, called a nonbearing partition, does no work within the house except to separate or divide space. Another name for a nonbearing partition is "curtain wall."

The members that make up the partitions are called studs. Metal or wood studs can be used. The length of the stud determines the height of the wall or ceiling. Wood and metal studs are covered with any of a wide range of materials, which have no great structural strength but act as a finish, or "cosmetic."

When a house is altered or remodeled, walls can be removed, including bearing partitions. When a bearing partition is removed, a beam must be installed in its place to carry the load that the bearing partition carried. All walls must be laid out very carefully to be sure that they are plumb and straight.

A typical wall is made up of a sole or shoe, studs, top plates, and headers. The sole or shoe is of the same dimension as the stud and is nailed flat onto the subfloor. The studs are nailed to the shoe in a vertical position 16 or 24 in. apart, and at the ceiling level or at the top of the studs, the plate or plates are nailed flat, which ties the entire wall assembly together. Provisions must be made in walls for doors and windows, which are installed later.

WOOD STUDS

Some of the species of wood used for studs are: fir, hemlock, spruce, and pine. Generally, 2 × 4 studs placed 16 in. apart are used for bearing walls, which include exterior walls. Occasionally, 2 × 6 studs placed 24 in. apart are used for exterior walls only. The reason for this is to allow for thicker insulation between the studs, for greater energy savings.

It is not unusual to construct nonbearing walls with 2 × 3 studs placed 16 in. apart, since the nonbearing walls are not doing any work except to divide spaces. Studs are used for the interior and exterior wall framing system and form a structural skeleton for the building (Fig. 10-1).

Care must be used in the selection of wood studs to be certain that the pieces are straight, square, and sound. Defective studs must not be used, or the structural integrity of the building may be affected.

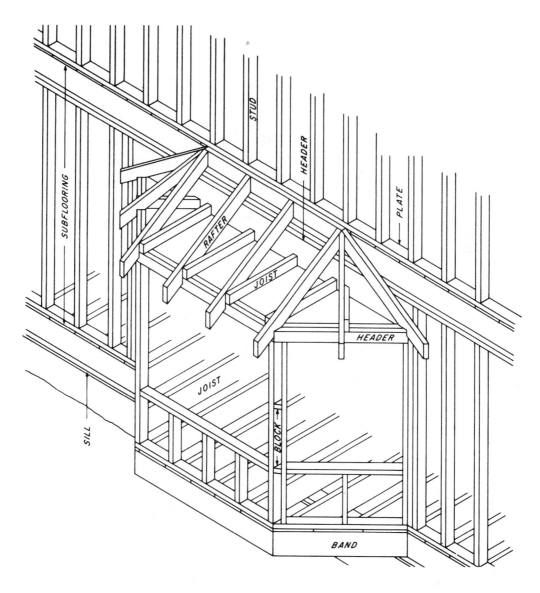

Figure 10-1   Wood studs.

METAL STUDS

Galvanized or zinc-coated light-gauge steel studs are sometimes used instead of wood studs (Figs. 10-2 and 10-3). Galvanized or zinc coating is a chemical coating over the stud to help reduce rust. The thickness of the light steel is 12, 14, 16, 18, 20, 22, or 25 gauge. The thickness or gauge is selected by the weight the wall must carry and the height of the wall. Metal or steel studs will not warp, shrink, or swell and are easily cut from lengths of up to 32 ft by a power saw with an abrasive blade.

Like wood studs, metal studs are fastened to a runner or track at the floor and ceiling. The vertical studs are then screwed or welded to the top and bottom runners. The tracks are unpunched sections attached to the floor. They are wider than the studs and are usually of the same metal thick-

Figure 10-2 Steel stud wall framing. (Courtesy of Wheeling Steel Framing.)

(a)

Figure 10-3 Assembled steel stud wall. (Courtesy of Zinc Institute, Inc.)

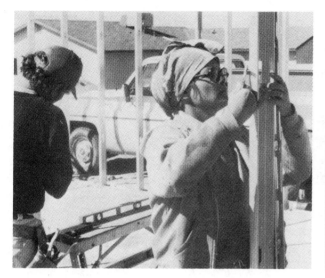

(b)

Figure 10-3 (continued)

ness. The vertical studs must be braced by diagonal members called bridging and are used to strengthen the wall and to prevent the studs from twisting or rotating.

Metal studs can be bearing walls or nonbearing walls spaced 16 or 24 in. apart. Holes are preformed in the studs to allow for the passage of electric wires or piping within the partition or wall (Fig. 10-4). If drywall or plasterboard is used as a wall finish, it is screwed into the steel studs with a self-tapping screw.

Steel studs are manufactured in a roll-forming process. Flat steel strips are passed through roll-bearing dies which form any shape desired in a wide range of sizes, lengths, and thicknesses (Fig. 10-5).

(a)

(b)

Figure 10-4   Pipe and wire through studs. (Courtesy of Zinc Institute, Inc.)

(a)   (b)

(c)

Figure 10-5 Metal stud roll forming. (Courtesy of Zinc Institute, Inc.)

BEARING PARTITIONS

Any wall that supports a floor, ceiling, or roof is called a bearing partition (Fig. 10-6). The studs used to construct a bearing wall can be of wood or metal. Generally, bearing interior walls are built from 2 × 4 wood studs spaced 16 in. apart. Provisions must be made in the wall assembly for doors and window openings. Occasionally, exterior walls are constructed from 2 × 6 wood studs placed 24 in. apart or 2 × 4 wood studs spaced 16 in. apart. The difference is in the stud size, which determines the thickness of insulation in the walls. A 2 × 4 stud wall will accept a 4-in.-thick insulation, whereas a 2 × 6 stud wall will accept a 6-in.-thick insulation.

The studs are nailed to a shoe or sole plate, which is a wood stud laid flat and nailed to the subfloor. The purpose of the shoe is to help distribute

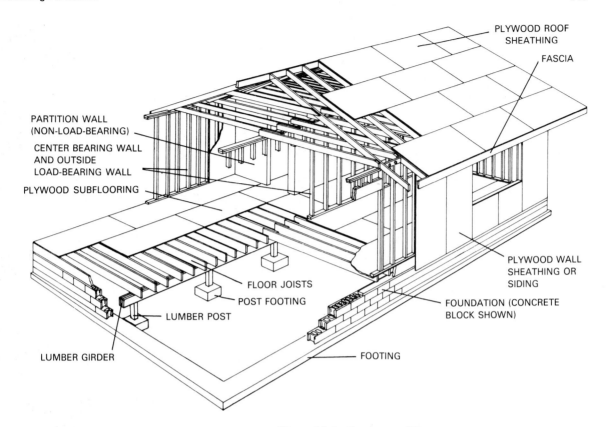

Figure 10-6 Bearing partitions.

over a wider surface of the floor area the weight supported by the bearing wall. The concept of a bearing wall or partition can be understood more easily by visualizing the studs as a series of wood columns spaced closely together. On top of the wood studs is a double plate or two studs laid flat. This double plate acts as a wood beam supported by the wood studs or columns. This entire assembly is to support a floor, ceiling, or roof. Extreme care must be used in the assembly of a bearing wall to be certain that all studs are properly spaced, sound, straight, true, and plumb with proper nailing.

NONBEARING PARTITIONS

Any wall or partition that does nothing to support a ceiling, floor, or roof is called a nonbearing wall (Fig. 10-7). The purpose of a nonbearing wall is only to divide space. Nonbearing walls are sometimes called curtain walls.

The parts of a nonbearing wall are the sole or shoe, studs, and plate. Nonbearing walls may be constructed of 2 × 3 wood studs placed 16 in. apart, or metal studs of the size and thickness needed for proper stiffness. The shoe or sole is nailed flat onto the subfloor and the studs are attached to the shoe with 16 in. spacing. The single plate is attached to the top of the studs. The ceiling joists are installed before the nonbearing partitions are erected, allowing the top plate to be nailed to the underside of the ceiling joists. Much like the bearing walls, the studs in a nonbearing wall must be sound, straight, true, and plumb, and provisions must be made in the wall assembly for door openings.

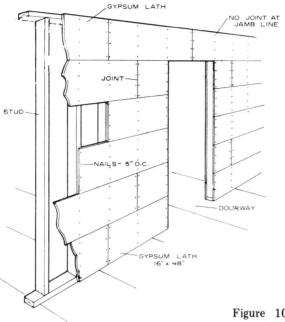

Figure 10-7 Nonbearing partition. (Courtesy of U.S. Department of Agriculture.)

MASTER STUDS

Once the length of the stud for the walls has been determined, one stud is measured for proper length and is used as a master stud to cut all studs the same length. This reduces error in not having to measure all studs separately. Caution must be used in measuring the master stud because if an error is made on the master stud, all the studs will be in error. Such an error can be costly. The distance from floor to ceiling determines the length of the master stud.

WALL LAYOUT

Before wall framing can be constructed, door and window sizes must be determined. The manufacturer of the units will recommend what size opening is required for proper placement of doors or windows. This opening is called a rough opening (Fig. 10-8). The location of doors and windows will be found by the dimensions on the plans. These dimensions will be to the center of the doors and windows.

It must be decided if platform framing or balloon framing will be used (Fig. 10-9). If platform framing is selected, a shoe or sole plate is secured to the subfloor. This shoe or sole plate is the same size as the wall framing laid flat (2 in. dimension vertical). If balloon framing is selected, no sole plate or shoe is required. The studs are secured to the top of the foundation sill and nailed adjacent to the floor joists. Platform or balloon framing requires top plates of two 2 × 4's or two 2 × 6's (depending on stud dimension). These are nailed flat on top of the studs (2 in. vertical dimension). The length of the studs determines the height of the wall.

If wall framing is built over a slab on grade, a shoe or sole plate is secured to the concrete slab by preinstalled anchor bolts (Fig. 10-10). This shoe should be treated against penetration of moisture by either sealing with a preservative or installing a tarpaper strip between the concrete floor and the sole plate.

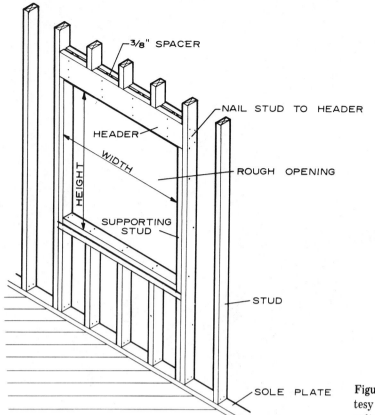

Figure 10-8 Rough opening. (Courtesy of U.S. Department of Agriculture.)

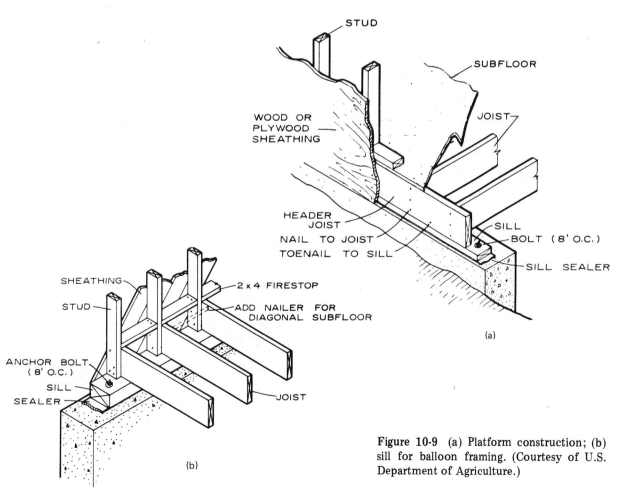

(a)

(b)

Figure 10-9 (a) Platform construction; (b) sill for balloon framing. (Courtesy of U.S. Department of Agriculture.)

149

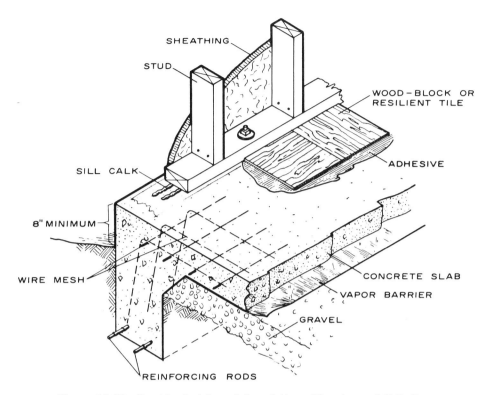

Figure 10-10 Combined slab and foundation. (Courtesy of U.S. Department of Agriculture.)

Most often, the entire wall framing assembly will be built on the floor and raised in place when completed. Whenever a stud exceeds the 16- or 24-in. spacing, because of the door or window sizes, provisions must be made in the wall construction to strengthen this larger stud spacing. This added spacing will affect the loads being carried by this partition. These loads may be another floor level above, or the load of the ceiling and roof. To make up for the added spacing and to carry the load above, a short beam called a header is installed across and above the opening. The size of this header is usually determined by the load and the span (Fig. 10-8).

The span is the distance across the opening or the length of the beam. The wall assembly above and below the opening is made up of the usual spacing of the studs 16 or 24 in. apart. This spacing must not be varied or interrupted. Around the area of the door or window opening, the studs are doubled to reinforce the wall.

CORNERS

Special treatment is required at wall corners for both inside and outside corners (Fig. 10-11) and where partitions meet (Fig. 10-12). The reason for special treatment is to provide a nailing surface on all walls where they meet. This can be accomplished by using at least three studs nailed together in such a shape as to allow a surface on each wall for the application of finish.

BRACING

All exterior and interior corners must be braced to prevent racking, or leaning of the wall from high winds. This is done by applying wood members at a 45° angle at all exterior and interior corners. These 45° wood members

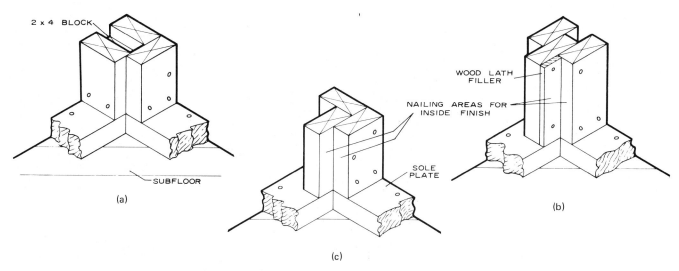

Figure 10-11 Stud assembly: (a) standard outside corner; (b) special corner with lath filler; (c) special corner without lath corner. (Courtesy of U.S. Department of Agriculture.)

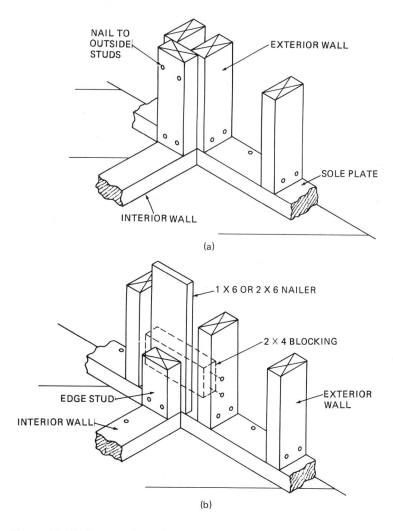

Figure 10-12 Intersection of interior and exterior walls: (a) doubled studs on outside wall; (b) partition between outside studs. (Courtesy of U.S. Department of Agriculture.)

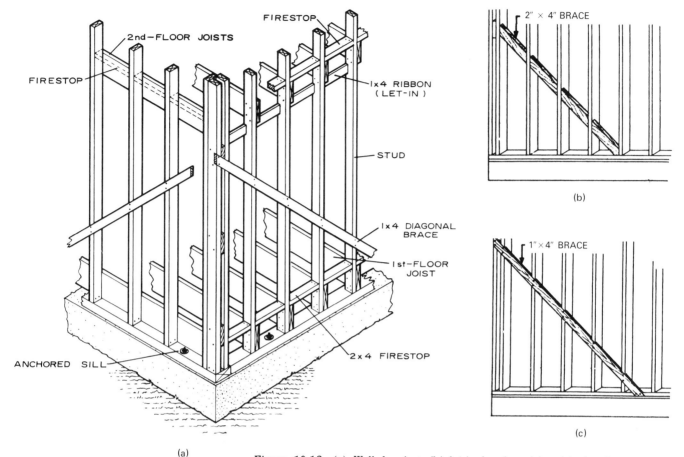

(a)

Figure 10-13 (a) Wall bracing; (b) let-in bracing; (c) cut-in bracing. (Courtesy of U.S. Department of Agriculture.)

can be 1 × 4's cut into the studs to make the exterior bracing flush with the exterior of the studs. This is called let-in bracing. They can also be short studs nailed between the studs at a 45° angle (Fig. 10-13).

SECOND-FLOOR CONSTRUCTION

In a house with two floors, balloon framing construction is recommended, because the length of the stud is continuous from the foundation sill to the double plate of the second-floor ceiling (Fig. 10-14). This makes for a stronger building. The second-floor joists are being supported by a continuous 1 × 4 let-in called a ribbon and are also nailed to the side of the stud. If platform framing is used in a two-story house, the first-floor framing is repeated at the second floor, creating a joint in the walls between floors. This system is not as strong as balloon framing because of the separation of framing at the floor levels (Fig. 10-15).

NAILING

The only means of fastening two pieces of wood together in framing a wall is by nailing. Proper size, type, and length of nail must be used to hold all the component parts together. Nail sizes are classified by "penny," an English system of weight. The larger the penny number, the larger the nail size. The symbol used is "d" (Fig. 10-16).

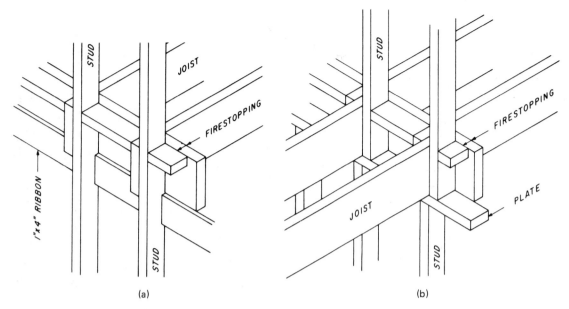

Figure 10-14 Balloon framing for a two-story house: (a) at exterior wall; (b) over bearing partition.

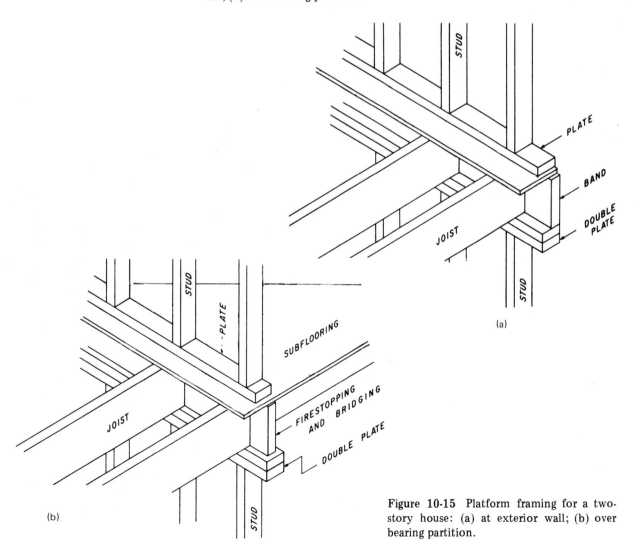

Figure 10-15 Platform framing for a two-story house: (a) at exterior wall; (b) over bearing partition.

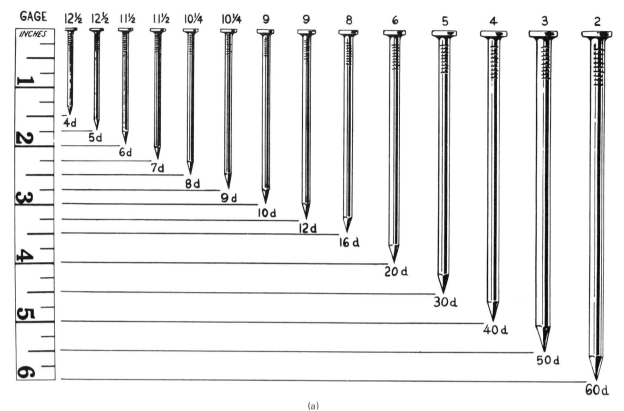

(a)

Recommended Nailing Schedule

Joist to sill or girder, toe nail	3–8d	Continuous header, two pieces	16d @ 16 in. oc
Bridging to joist, toe nail each end	2–8d		along each edge
Ledge strip	3–16d	Ceiling joists to plate, toe nail	3–8d
	at each joist	Continuous header to stud, toe nail	4–8d
1 × 6 subfloor or less to each joist, face nail	2–8d	Ceiling joists, laps over partitions, face nail	3–16d
Over 1 × 6 subfloor to each joist, face nail	3–8d	Ceiling joists to parallel rafters, face nail	3–16d
2-in. subfloor to joist or girder,		Rafter to plate, toe nail	3–8d
blind and face nail	2–16d	1-in. brace to each stud and plate, face nail	2–8d
Sole plate to joist or blocking, face nail	16d @ 16 in. oc	1 × 8 sheathing or less to each bearing, face nail	2–8d
Top plate to stud, end nail	2–16d	Over 1 × 8 sheathing to each bearing, face nail	3–8d
Stud to sole plate, toe nail	4–8d	Builtup corner studs	16d @ 24 in. oc
Doubled studs, face nail	16d @ 24 in. oc	Builtup girders and beams	20d @ 32 in. oc
Doubled top plates, face nail	16d @ 16 in. oc		along each edge
Top plates, laps and intersections, face nail	2–16d		

(b)

Figure 10-16 (a) Sizes of common nails; (b) recommended nailing schedule using common nails.

Nail Sizes

Nails vary in size from 4d to 60d, with lengths as follows (in inches):

4d	1½	10d	3	40d	5
5d	1¾	12d	3¼	50d	5½
6d	2	16d	3½	60d	6
7d	2¼	20d	4		
8d	2½	30d	4½		

There are many types of nails, but those most commonly used for framing are classified as common nails.

Common Nails

All framework is assembled with common nails. These nails have a wide head to allow greater holding power. How two pieces of wood are joined together and the thickness of the pieces determine the nail length. If the nails are too large, the wood may split, causing weakness at the joint, thereby affecting the strength of the framework.

Toe Nailing

When studs are nailed to foundation sills, nails are driven at an angle called toe nailing. Toe nailing is also sometimes used to nail the end of a horizontal member into a vertical member. This type of nailing is not as strong as direct nailing a member through the thickness of the wood into another member (Fig. 10-17). See Fig. 10-16 for the number and size of nails recommended.

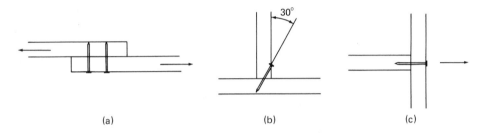

(a)   (b)   (c)

Figure 10-17 Methods of loading nails: (a) nail perpendicular to load; (b) toenailing; (c) nail in withdrawal.

BLOCKING

Whenever any hardware item, such as tub grab bars, hand rails, or towel racks, is to be attached to the finish wall or joining of a wall paneling, provision must be made to allow for fastening to the wall; this is called blocking. Blocking is attached between the studs in the form of horizontal 2 × 4's or plywood panels cut to fit between the studs (Fig. 10-18). This occurs

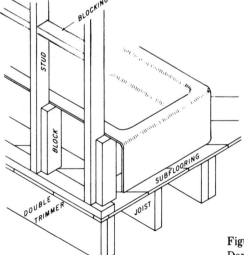

Figure 10-18 Blocking. (Courtesy of U.S. Department of Agriculture.)

whenever the 16- or 24-in. spacing of the studs is too far apart to fasten the hardware to more than one stud.

SHEATHING

When the exterior framework is completed, it is covered with sheathing. This sheathing can be plywood, man-made composition panels, or $\frac{3}{4}$-in.-thick wood boards. Sheathing serves two purposes: to help strengthen the exterior walls and to provide a nailing surface for applying the exterior finish.

Plywood

If plywood is used, it will either be $\frac{1}{2}$ or $\frac{5}{8}$ in. thick. The panels are $4'-0'' \times 8' \times 0''$ and the $8'-0''$ dimension should be positioned horizontal to the studs. Joints should be staggered and a space of about $\frac{1}{8}$ in. should be allowed between the panels for expansion. These plywood panels should be well nailed to the studs (Fig. 10-19).

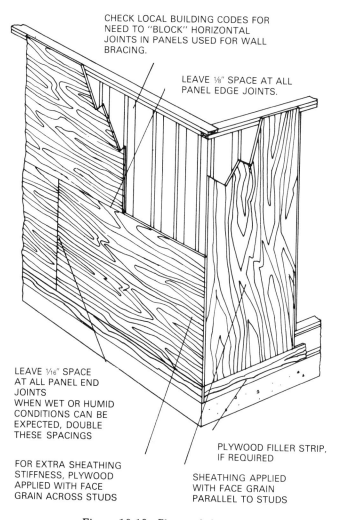

CHECK LOCAL BUILDING CODES FOR NEED TO "BLOCK" HORIZONTAL JOINTS IN PANELS USED FOR WALL BRACING.

LEAVE ⅛" SPACE AT ALL PANEL EDGE JOINTS.

LEAVE 1/16" SPACE AT ALL PANEL END JOINTS WHEN WET OR HUMID CONDITIONS CAN BE EXPECTED, DOUBLE THESE SPACINGS

FOR EXTRA SHEATHING STIFFNESS, PLYWOOD APPLIED WITH FACE GRAIN ACROSS STUDS

PLYWOOD FILLER STRIP, IF REQUIRED

SHEATHING APPLIED WITH FACE GRAIN PARALLEL TO STUDS

Figure 10-19 Plywood sheathing.

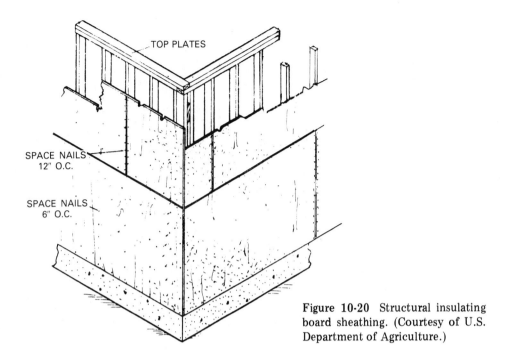

Figure 10-20 Structural insulating board sheathing. (Courtesy of U.S. Department of Agriculture.)

Composition Panels

A variety of man-made panels are available in thicknesses of $\frac{3}{8}$, $\frac{1}{2}$, and $\frac{5}{8}$ in. Some panels have an insulation value. The joints should be staggered. Composition panels do not add as much strength to the framework as does plywood. These panels should be applied with the long dimension horizontally, following the manufacturers' direction for nailing. When the exterior finish is nailed into the composition panel, the holding power of the nail into the panel is not as strong as with plywood (Fig. (10-20).

Boarding

Seldom used for sheathing, but available, is $\frac{3}{4}$-in.-thick boarding. The width of the boards is 6 or 8 in. They are nailed to the studs horizontally or diagonally. All joints should be staggered. Greater strength is afforded to the framework if the boarding is applied diagonally. There is also more waste because both ends of each board must be cut at an angle (Fig. 10-21).

ARCHES

Whenever an arch is to be framed into a wall, regardless of the size or shape, it must be done with tangents (Fig. 10-22). The length of the tangents depends on the curvature of the arch. The exact shape or curve of the arch is accomplished by shaping a metal corner bead which is nailed to the wood-frame tangents. The finished wall material is shaped to the metal bead forming the arch.

MASONRY VENEER

Provisions must be provided to support brick or stone veneer. Veneer is classified as masonry nonsupporting of brick or stone. Generally, a veneer wall is 4 in. thick. The foundation wood sill is installed flush with the inside

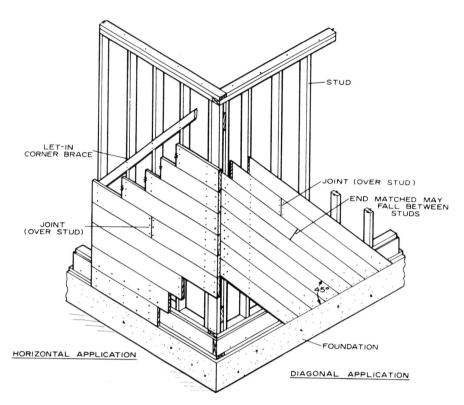

Figure 10-21   Boarding sheathing. (Courtesy of U.S. Department of Agriculture.)

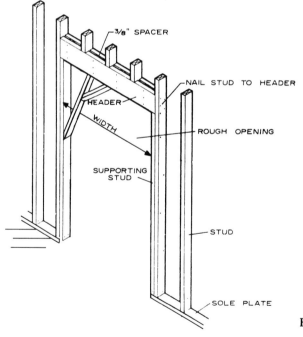

Figure 10-22   Arch framing.

of the 12-in.-thick foundation wall, leaving a 6-in. shelf for supporting the veneer on the outside of the foundation wall (Fig. 10-23). The veneer is not only nonbearing, but is also nonsupporting in height. Corrugated metal ties are nailed to the sheathing about 2 ft apart and are built into the stone or brick joints to help support the wall from falling forward. The wood-frame wall is used to help hold the veneer to the framework.

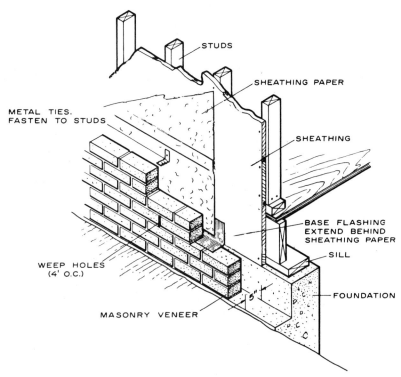

Figure 10-23 Wood frame wall with masonry veneer. (Courtesy of U.S. Department of Agriculture.)

QUESTIONS

1. The types of studs used for wall framing are: _____
    _____ .

2. The two types of partitions are nonbearing and bearing.
    True or False

3. Which of the following must be known before walls can be laid out?
    A. Window size
    B. Type of wall finish
    C. Type of studs used
    D. Door size
    E. Door type or style
    F. Window type or style

4. Define *master stud*. _____
    _____

5. Name three types of sheathing.
    1. _____
    2. _____
    3. _____

6. More nails used to fasten framework together makes a better frame.
    True or False

7. Define *masonry veneer*. _____
    _____

8. Steel studs require no bracing.   True or False

9. Why is corner framing different from straight wall framing? _____
    _____

10. Studs can be bent to form arches.   True or False

11

Ceiling Framing

INTRODUCTION

After exterior and interior walls are plumbed and braced, ceiling joists can be positioned and nailed in place. They are normally placed across the width of the house. The partitions of the house are usually located so that ceiling joists of even lengths (10, 12, 14, and 16 ft or longer) can be used without waste to span from exterior walls to load-bearing interior walls. The sizes of the joists depend on the span, wood species, spacing between joists, and the load on the second floor or attic (Table 11-1). The correct sizes for various conditions can be found in joist tables or are designated by local building requirements. When preassembled trussed rafters (roof trusses) are used, the lower chord acts as the ceiling joist. The truss also eliminates the need for load-bearing partitions.

Ceiling joists are used to support ceiling finishes. They often act as floor joists for second and attic floors and as ties between exterior walls and interior partitions. Since ceiling joists also serve as tension members to resist the thrust of the rafters of pitched roofs, they must be securely nailed to the plate at the outer and inner walls.

A ceiling framing is an assembly below the roof. Other ceilings are carried on floor joists, as in a two-story house, where the second floor is the same framing for the first-floor ceiling. Construction framing of a ceiling is similar to that of joist construction. The main members, called ceiling joists, are much like floor joists. The span, load, spacing, and species of wood determine the size of the ceiling joists. They are usually spaced 16 in. apart, although 12-in. spacing is not uncommon. As a rule, ceiling joists run across the narrow dimension or shortest span of the building.

TABLE 11-1

Ceiling Joist Span

SOUTHERN YELLOW PINE			
		LUMBER GRADES GRADES	
JOIST SIZE	SPACING OF JOISTS O.C.	NO. 1 KILN-DRIED	NO.2 KILN-DRIED
LIMITED ATTIC STORAGE			
2 x 6	12	14'- 4''	14'- 4''
	16	13'- 0''	13'- 0''
	24	11'- 4''	11'- 4''
2 x 8	12	18'- 4''	18'- 4''
	16	17'- 0''	17'- 0''
	24	15'- 4''	15'- 4''
2 x 10	12	21'- 10''	21'- 10''
	16	20'- 4''	20'- 4''
	24	18'- 4''	18'- 4''
NO ATTIC STORAGE			
2 x 6	12	17'- 2''	17'- 2''
	16	16'- 0''	16'- 0''
	24	14'- 4''	14'- 4''
2 x 8	12	21'- 8''	21'- 8''
	16	20'- 2''	20'- 2''
	24	18'- 4''	18'- 4''
2 x 10	12	24'- 0''	24'- 0''
	16	24'- 0''	24'- 0''
	24	21'- 10''	21'- 10''
DOUGLAS FIR AND LARCH			
LIMITED ATTIC STORAGE			
2 x 6	12	14'- 4''	14'- 4''
	16	13'- 0''	13'- 0''
	24	11'- 4''	11'- 4''
2 x 8	12	18'- 4''	18'- 4''
	16	17'- 0''	17'- 0''
	24	15'- 4''	15'-'4''
2 x 10	12	21'- 10''	21'- 10''
	16	20'- 4''	20'- 4''
	24	18'- 4''	18'- 4''
NO ATTIC STORAGE			
2 x 6	12	17'- 2''	17'- 2''
	16	16'- 0''	16'- 0''
	24	14'- 4''	14'- 4''
2 x 8	12	21'- 8''	21'- 8''
	16	20'- 2''	20'- 2''
	24	18'- 4''	18'- 4''
2 x 10	12	24'- 0''	24'- 0''
	16	24'- 0''	24'- 0''
	24	21'- 10''	21'- 10''

JOISTS

The ceiling is constructed in a manner similar to that of the floor framing. The members that support the ceiling are called joists and are spaced 16 in. on center. Usually, the ceiling joists are smaller than the floor joists because the loads to be supported are less than those of the floor joists.

Ceiling joists are supported by the exterior wall on one end and a bearing partition on the other end. In both cases, they are nailed to the double plate on top of the partitions (Fig. 11-1). No bridging is required at ceiling joists.

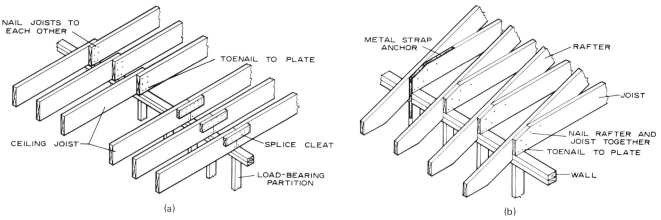

Figure 11-1 Ceiling joist connections: (a) at center partition with joists lapped or butted; (b) at outside wall. (Courtesy of U.S. Department of Agriculture.)

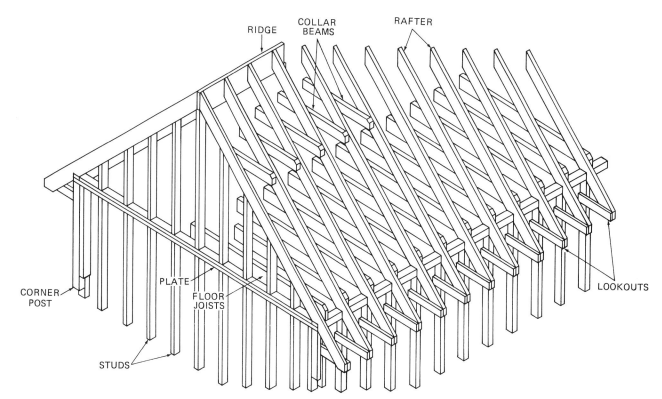

Figure 11-2 Two-story framing.

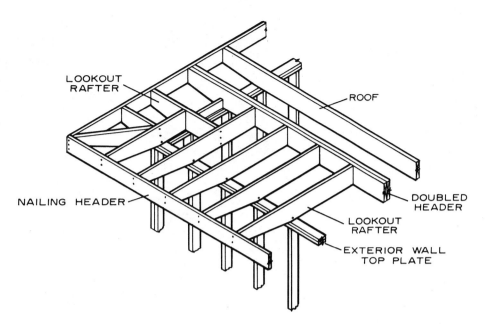

LOOKOUT
RAFTER

ROOF

NAILING HEADER

DOUBLED
HEADER

LOOKOUT
RAFTER

EXTERIOR WALL
TOP PLATE

Figure 11-3   Extended ceiling joists. (Courtesy of U.S. Department of Agriculture.)

In a two-story house, the floor joists on the second floor become the ceiling joists on the first floor (Fig. 11-2). In that case, bridging is necessary. When the ceiling joists have no floor above and the roof design, such as a flat roof, has an overhang, the ceiling joists extend beyond the exterior wall to the same dimension as the roof rafters (Fig. 11-3). This extension is necessary to apply the finish to the underside of the roof overhang. The roof and ceiling overhang dimension will be given on the building plans. When the overhang is in the same direction as the ceiling joists, it is a simple matter to extend the ceiling joists beyond the exterior wall, but if the overhang is in the opposite direction of the ceiling joists, the joists' direction must be changed to run in the same direction as the overhang. This is done by doubling the ceiling joists at the point of direction change. This joist doubling acts as a beam to help support the change of direction. There is a limit to how much ceiling joists can overhang without additional support.

Ceiling joists serve several purposes. They form a nailing surface for the finish ceiling. They tie all exterior and interior walls together and serve as a main floor or an attic floor. Caution must be used in designing ceiling joists for an attic floor because if at a later date the attic floor is to be used as a living floor, the ceiling joists become floor joists and may not be strong enough to carry the load.

OPENINGS

Any opening larger than 16-in. spacing of the ceiling joists requires special framing with double headers (Fig. 11-4). This means doubling the ceiling joists around the perimeter of the opening. The reason for doubling is to transfer the load from the opening to the double joist. The double joists act as a beam to support the load.

These large openings are required for chimneys, stairs, skylights, heating ducts, and access panels. The dimensions of these openings should be shown on the plans. There are two ways of framing ceiling joists for openings. One

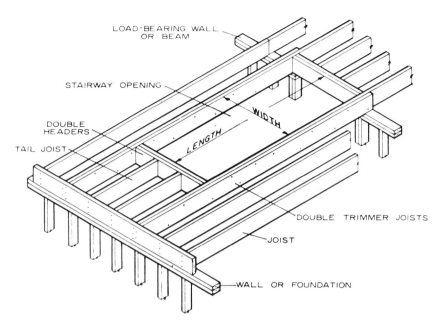

Figure 11-4 Opening in joists for stairs. (Courtesy of U.S. Department of Agriculture.)

is by nailing and the other is by joist hangers. The joist hanger method may be faster and more convenient. Care must be taken in locating the openings by double-checking the dimensions on the plans. If the opening in the ceiling is for stairs, the same opening will apply in the floor, and if the two openings do not line up, the stairs will be affected.

FLAT ROOFS

In the design of flat or nearly flat roofs, the ceiling joists often also act as roof rafters. In this case, the loads supported by roof are greater than the loads supported by only the ceiling, because the same members are used for support of the ceiling and the roof (Fig. 11-3). The total composition of the roofing materials determines part of the total load supported by the roof rafters, which in this case are also ceiling joists.

Future planning is important in flat-roof construction, for a possible addition later. If the roof is later to be used as a floor, larger members must be used to support the heavier floor loads.

NAILING

Nailing of ceiling joists to wall plates is done by toe nailing, using 6d common nails, usually two nails on each side of the joist and one on the end of the joist. If the larger joists are nailed together, such as doubling around openings, they are nailed together with 10d common nails. The shorter joists framing into the double headers can be nailed or supported by metal joist hangers.

FURRING

Ceiling joists must be prepared to receive a finished ceiling. The choice of a finished ceiling is wide and varied. Among the most popular and widely used finish ceiling materials are plasterboard and drywall. Another possible finish,

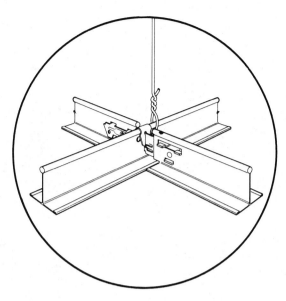

Figure 11-5 Suspended acoustical tile.

not often used, is wet plaster. A third possibility is an acoustical suspended tile ceiling, or acoustical tile attached to the ceiling joists.

Preparing the ceiling joists depends on the finish selected. If suspended acoustical tile is selected, no preparation is required. The acoustical tile is hung or suspended from the ceiling joists with wired metal runners (Fig. 11-5).

Drywall or plasterboard requires the installation of furring strips, sometimes called strapping. The furring strips are 1 × 3's wood nailed perpendicular to the bottom of the ceiling joists spaced 16 in apart. The drywall will be nailed or screwed to the furring strips (Fig. 11-6).

If acoustical tile is selected, the furring strips are placed 12 in. apart to allow the acoustical tile to be glued, stapled, or nailed to the furring strips (Fig. 11-7). In either case, the furring strips must be straight and level because the bottom of the ceiling joists are not in perfect alignment. If the furring strips are not in perfect alignment, the ceiling finish will show waves, out of plumb and uneven. Perfect alignment of the furring strips is accomplished by stringing a line from one end of the room to the other and shimming the furring strips with wood shingles.

If wet plaster is selected for the finish ceiling, the same procedure is used as with drywall or plasterboard. Gypsum lath, which has a plaster base, is secured to the furring strips and the finish plaster is applied over the gypsum lath. Metal lath is also used for wet plaster. Metal lath is applied to the furring strips and the wet plaster is applied to the metal lath (Fig. 11-8).

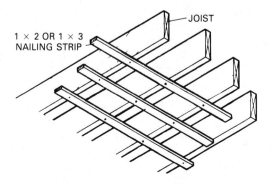

JOIST

1 × 2 OR 1 × 3 NAILING STRIP

Figure 11-6 Furring strips.

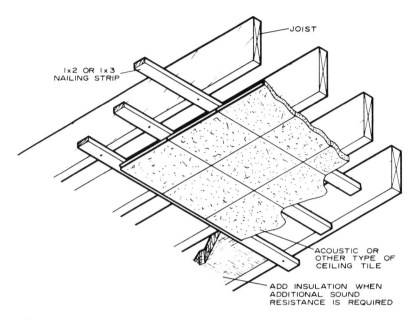

Figure 11-7   Acoustical tile ceiling. (Courtesy of U.S. Department of Agriculture.)

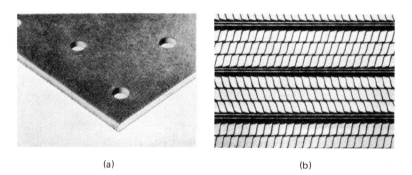

(a)   (b)

Figure 11-8   (a) Perforated gypsum lath; (b) $\frac{1}{8}$-in. flat rib lath.

TRUSSES

When units are preassembled as trusses (Fig. 11-9), the ceiling rafters and roof rafters act as a single unit. The advantage of trusses is that interior bearing partitions are not required. The trusses are supported by the exterior walls and usually span the short dimension of the house width. Sometimes, because of added strength in the assembled units, the trusses may be spaced 24 in. apart instead of the usual ceiling rafter spacing of 16 in. The same preparation for the ceiling finish is required of trusses as of single ceiling joists.

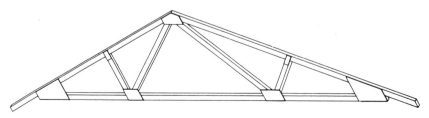

Figure 11-9   Truss.

QUESTIONS

1. Define *ceiling joist*. _____

_____

2. Which of the following types of bridging is required for ceiling joists?
   A. Cross
   B. Metal
   C. Solid
   D. None of the above

3. Ceiling joists become floor joists in two-story buildings.
   True or False

4. The floor load for ceiling joists is the same as for floor joists.
   True or False

5. Openings for chimneys and fireplaces are framed in the same way as floor openings but different than roof framing.   True or False

6. Flat roofs cannot double as ceiling joists.   True or False

7. Onto what are ceiling joists nailed? _____

_____

8. Name an alternative method of supporting headers besides nailing.

_____

9. Define *furring strips* or *strapping*. _____

_____

10. (a) What is a preassembled unit of ceiling and roof called? _____

_____

   (b) Name three advantages of using such an assembly.
      1. _____
      2. _____
      3. _____

12

Roof Framing

INTRODUCTION

Before any finish roof covering can be installed, a frame must be provided to support the roof covering. Roof framing is similar to floor framing or ceiling framing. The members making up the roof framing can be flat or pitched, depending on the roof design. The members of the roof framing are rafters, ridge, valley, hip, collar beam, and sheathing. Before any roof framing can be designed or built, the span, run, rise, roof overhang, and roof pitch must be determined.

A roof framing member can be prebuilt, called a truss. Instead of each roof framing member being installed separately, all the members are assembled together on the ground and the entire assembled unit is installed for the roof. In either case, the roof is supported by the exterior walls and/or by bearing partitions.

Information necessary for designing the roof includes data on the roof load and wind load. The roof load includes the weight of all the roofing material plus the force of the wind against the roof.

Within the roof framing, skylights and dormer windows can be designed and built. Flat roofs are sometimes used as a deck. There are many roof designs to choose from, depending on the style of architecture selected.

ROOF STYLE

There are many styles of roof design, including flat and pitched. Generally, the roof style is a clue to the aesthetic design of the house. It is important to know if the roof is flat or pitched because the selection of roof covering is determined by the roof pitch. The geographic location of the house will also play a significant part in roof design. Areas that have an annual heavy snowfall will have steeply pitched roofs to allow snow to slide from the roof. Areas that have mild or warm climates may have flat roofs or nearly flat

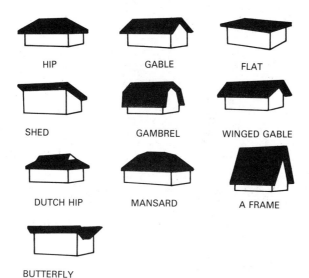

Figure 12-1 Roof designs.

roofs with a slight pitch, to help keep the building cool during hot weather. Roofs are also designed to allow more living space on second-floor levels such as by using a mansard roof. Roofs with a flat pitch sometimes also serve as ceiling framing, using the same framing member for both roof framing and ceiling framing. The various roof styles are as follows (Fig. 12-1):

Hip: pitched on all sides.

Gable: most popular, and easy to ventilate.

Flat: most economical and easy to construct. A dead-level roof is not recommended because water remaining on the roof can cause serious problems should a roof leak occur. Sometimes so-called "flat" roofs are pitched about ½ in./ft, just enough to shed water.

Shed: similar to a flat roof, but has a greater pitch.

Gambrel: double-pitched roof on each side; provides additional second-floor space.

Mansard: double-pitched roof nearly flat on top with steeply pitched sides.

A-frame: provides both interior ceiling, wall and roof; adds more cubic space to a building.

Butterfly: provides more light and ventilation, but may cause drainage problems at the low point.

ROOF TERMS

Following are terms making up the roof assembly (see Fig. 12-2 for illustrations of most of these parts).

Common rafter: main roof support, running from top plate of wall to ridge

Hip jack or rafter: main support from top of plate to ridge, where roof pitch changes direction

Valley rafter: main support from top plate to ridge in the hollow or change of roof pitch direction

Ridge or ridgeboard: highest part; roof connecting both sides

Hip rafter: successively shorter rafters to complete the pitch of the hip

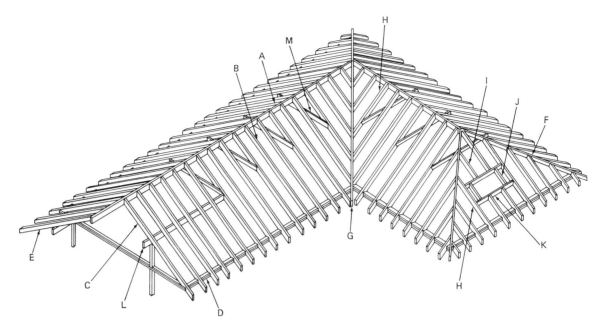

Figure 12-2 Roof framing parts. (From Mortimer P. Reed, *Residential Carpentry*. Copyright 1980, John Wiley & Sons, Inc., New York.)

A	Ridgeboard	H	Jack rafter
B	Common rafter	I	Cripple rafter
C	End rafter	J	Trimmer rafter
D	Rafter plate	K	Header
E	Fly rafter	L	Purlin
F	Hip rafter	M	Collar beam
G	Valley rafters		

Valley jack or rafter: successively shorter rafters, completing the pitch of the valley

Cripple jack or rafter: fill-in of main roof between hip and valley

Collar tie or beam: beam that ties two opposite rafters together

Overhang: portion of roof beyond wall surface

Soffit: underside of roof overhang

Bird's mouth: angle cut at the bottom of the rafter sitting on the wall plate

Plumb cut: cut fitting against ridge

Tail cut: roof overhang cut

Gable: wall surface at roof's end

One of the most difficult parts of a house to construct is the roof framing. Not only is it used as a means of applying the finish roofing material, but more important, it provides shelter. Faulty roofs create no end to problems, causing leaks that will damage not only the house but furniture as well. Each part of the roof assembly must be joined perfectly and secured to each other for proper strength. One roof part depends on another, all working together for a sound safe roof. The entire roof assembly is made up of a series of angle cuts based on the roof pitch and roof shape or style. The size of the members of the roof framing is determined by length, span, and load (Table 12-1).

TABLE 12-1

Rafter Span

A. Maximum spans for rafters: Roof load of 30 lb/ft^2 uniformly distributed for slopes of 20 in. or more.

American standard lumber sizes (in.)		On center (in.)	Maximum clear span—plate to ridge					
			S. pine and Douglas fir		Western hemlock		Spruce	
Nominal	Net		Unplastered	Plastered	Unplastered	Plastered	Unplastered	Plastered
2 × 4	1⅝ × 3⅝	16	7'- 8"	6'-10"	7'- 4"	6'- 6"	7'- 0"	6'- 2"
		24	6'- 3"	6'- 0"	6'- 0"	5'- 8"	5'- 9"	5'- 5"
2 × 6	1⅝ × 5⅝	16	11'- 9"	10'- 6"	11'- 3"	10'- 1"	10'- 9"	9'- 7"
		24	9'- 8"	9'- 3"	9'- 3"	8'-10"	8'-10"	8'- 5"
3 × 6	2⅝ × 5⅝	16	14'-10"	12'- 3"	14'- 1"	11'- 9"	13'- 6"	11'- 1"
		24	12'- 3"	10'-10"	11'- 9"	10'- 4"	11'- 1"	9'-10"
2 × 8	1⅝ × 7½	16	15'- 7"	14'- 0"	15'- 0"	13'- 4"	14'- 3"	12'- 9"
		24	12'-10"	12'- 3"	12'- 4"	11'- 9"	11'- 9"	11'- 2"
3 × 8	2⅝ × 7½	16	19'- 5"	16'- 1"	18'- 7"	15'- 5"	17'- 9"	14'- 7"
		24	16'- 1"	14'- 3"	15'- 5"	13'- 7"	14'- 9"	12'-11"
2 × 10	1⅝ × 9½	16	19'- 7"	17'- 6"	18'- 9"	16'-10"	17'-11"	15'-11"
		24	16'- 3"	15'- 6"	15'- 6"	14'-10"	14'-10"	14'- 0"
2 × 12	1⅝ × 11½	16	23'- 6"	21'- 2"	22'- 6"	20'- 3"	21'- 6"	19'- 3"
		24	19'- 6"	18'- 8"	17'-10"	17'-10"	17'-10"	17'-10"

B. Low-slope roof rafters: Roof slope 3 in 12 or less.

		Not supporting finished ceiling						Supporting finished ceiling					
2 × 6	12	14 4	14 4	14 4	14 4	11 4	9 6	13 8	13 8	13 8	13 8	10 6	8 10
	16	13 0	13 0	13 0	12 10	9 8	8 4	12 4	12 4	12 4	11 10	9 0	7 8
	24	11 4	11 4	11 4	10 6	8 0	6 8	10 10	10 8	10 8	9 8	7 4	6 2
2 × 8	12	18 4	18 4	18 4	18 4	17 6	15 4	17 8	17 8	17 8	17 8	16 2	14 2
	16	17 0	17 0	17 0	17 0	15 0	13 4	16 4	16 4	16 4	16 2	14 0	12 4
	24	15 4	15 4	15 4	14 4	12 4	10 10	14 6	14 6	14 6	13 2	11 4	10 0
2 × 10	12	21 10	21 10	21 10	21 10	21 10	20 8	21 0	21 0	21 0	21 0	21 0	19 0
	16	20 4	20 4	20 4	20 4	20 4	18 0	19 6	19 6	19 6	19 6	19 2	16 8
	24	18 4	18 4	18 4	18 0	16 6	14 8	17 8	17 8	17 8	16 8	15 8	13 6
2 × 12	12	24 0	24 0	24 0	24 0	24 0	24 0	24 0	24 0	24 0	24 0	24 0	23 0
	16	23 6	23 6	23 6	23 6	23 6	21 10	22 6	22 6	22 6	22 6	22 6	20 0
	24	21 2	21 2	21 2	21 2	20 0	19 6	20 4	20 4	20 2	20 2	18 6	16 4

C. Rafters: Roof slope over 3 in 12.

		Light roofing						Heavy roofing					
2 × 4	12	10 10	9 6	8 0	7 4	5 8	5 2	9 4	8 2	6 10	6 4	4 10	4 4
	16	10 0	8 4	7 0	6 4	5 0	4 6	8 0	7 2	6 0	5 6	4 2	3 10
	24	7 4	6 10	5 2	5 2	4 0	3 8	6 8	5 10	5 0	4 6	3 6	3 2
2 × 6	12	16 10	16 10	16 10	16 10	13 4	11 2	15 6	15 6	15 6	14 10	11 4	9 6
	16	15 8	15 8	15 8	15 0	11 6	9 8	14 4	14 0	14 2	12 10	9 8	8 4
	24	13 10	13 6	13 6	12 2	9 4	7 8	12 6	11 6	11 8	10 6	8 0	6 8
2 × 8	12	21 2	21 2	21 2	21 2	20 10	18 0	19 8	19 8	19 8	19 8	17 6	15 4
	16	19 10	19 10	19 6	19 0	17 8	15 8	18 4	18 4	18 4	17 6	15 0	13 4
	24	17 10	17 10	17 10	16 8	14 4	12 8	16 6	15 8	15 10	14 4	12 4	10 10
2 × 10	12	24 0	24 0	24 0	24 0	24 0	24 0	23 6	23 6	23 6	23 6	23 0	20 8
	16	23 8	23 8	23 8	23 8	23 8	21 0	21 10	21 10	21 10	21 10	20 4	18 0
	24	21 4	21 4	21 4	21 0	19 8	17 2	19 8	19 8	19 8	18 0	16 2	14 8

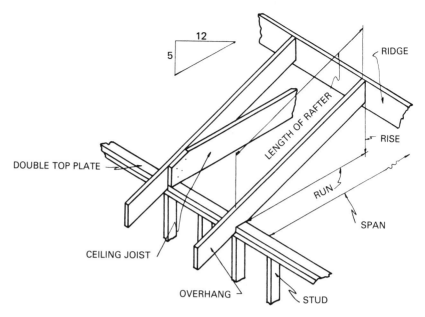

Figure 12-3 Roof pitch and slope.

PITCH AND SLOPE

The angle of the roof in proportion to the rise is called a pitch (Fig. 12-3). The pitch is indicated as a fraction. For example: If the roof rise were 5 ft and the total width were 25 ft, the pitch would be $^{5}/_{25} = ^{1}/_{5}$ pitch.

The slope of the roof is related to the rise and the run.

As shown, 5 is the rise or vertical dimension of the run or horizontal dimension; 12 indicates that for every 12 in. in run, or horizontal dimension, the roof will rise 5 in.

FRAMING SQUARE

The tool used to lay out the roof rafters is the framing square, sometimes called a steel square or carpenter's square (Fig. 12-4). It is an L-shaped tool with two legs of unequal length. The long 24-in. leg is called the body; the shorter 16-in. leg is called the tongue. Once the rise and run are known, these numbers are read on the framing square and marked off on the roof rafter for various cuts.

Use of the framing square for roof rafter cuts requires several steps, called units. Once the run and rise are known. the framing square is placed on the roof rafter and the figures read from the framing square are aligned on the stock and marked. The figures on the framing squares must be in perfect position with the edge of the stock or roof rafters. This is to assure an accurate cut. This process is repeated several times until the total length of the roof rafter has been marked or laid out. This process will give the angle cuts of ridge, tail and bird's mouth of all rafters, including those of different lengths, such as a hip roof.

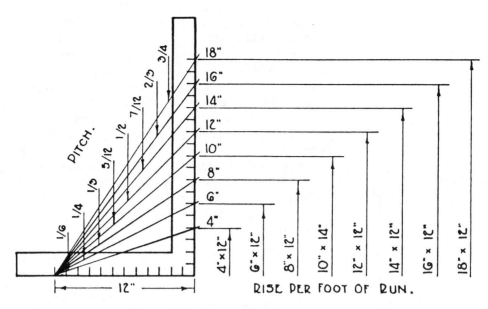

Figure 12-4 Carpenter's square and roof pitches.

RAFTER FRAMING

Several factors are determined before the size of roof rafters is selected: the amount of load the roof is to support, which is determined by the local building laws; the shape of the roof; the length of the run; the quality and species of framing lumber; and the spacing of the roof rafters.

Once this information is known, the roof framing can be installed one rafter at a time, or the entire roof and ceiling can be installed in place using a truss (Fig. 12-5). The weight of the roof includes the wind load and snow load. The selection of roof covering material will determine the size of the framing members.

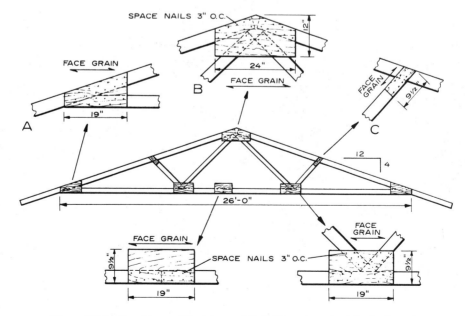

Figure 12-5 Roof truss. (Courtesy of U.S. Department of Agriculture.)

Each rafter is cut using the framing square, based on the dimensions required, and nailed into place. The rafters from both sides of the roof are connected to a ridge board (Fig. 12-6). Because of the angle cut of the wood rafter, the ridge board is larger than the roof rafter size, usually 2 in. larger or wider. The ridge board runs the entire length of the roof and helps to distribute the roof load among several roof rafters working in unison or as one unit. The hip rafters and valley rafters serve the same function as the ridge board (Fig. 12-7). In determining the total length of the roof rafter, the roof overhang must be known and the style of the finish wood trim must be known to determine the type of angle cut to put at the rafter end.

The end of the roof is called a gable (Fig. 12-8). This is the joining of the wall and the roof, and if the gable end has an overhang, special roof framing is required which reverses the direction of the roof rafters (Fig. 12-9). Most often roof rafters are placed 16 in. on center, and occasionally they are placed 24 in. on center.

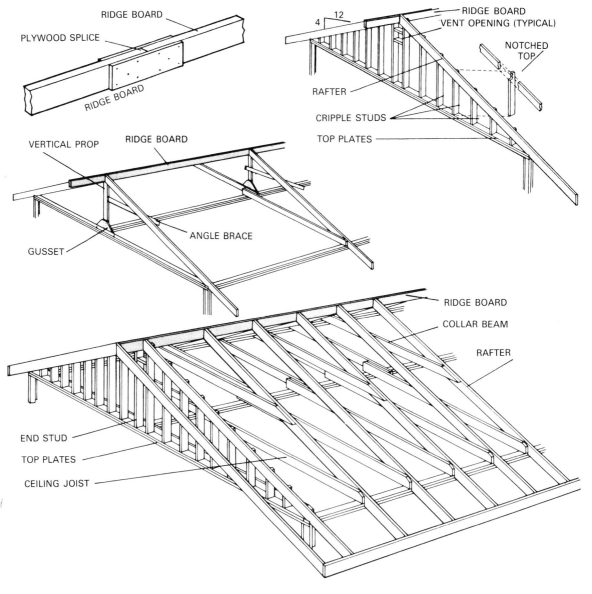

Figure 12-6   Ridge board.

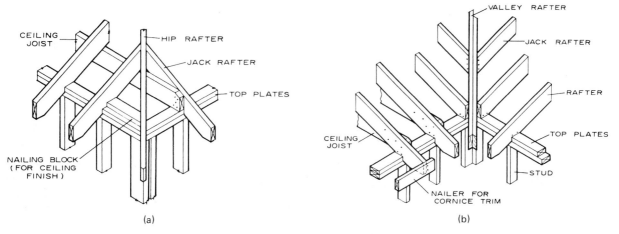

Figure 12-7 (a) Hip rafter; (b) framing at a valley. (Courtesy of U.S. Department of Agriculture.)

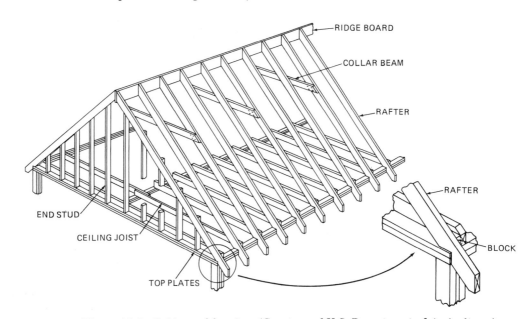

Figure 12-8 Gable roof framing. (Courtesy of U.S. Department of Agriculture.)

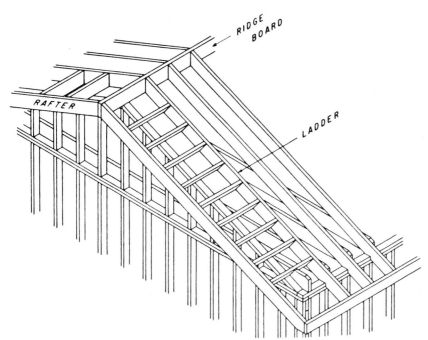

Figure 12-9 Roof framing for overhang at gable end.

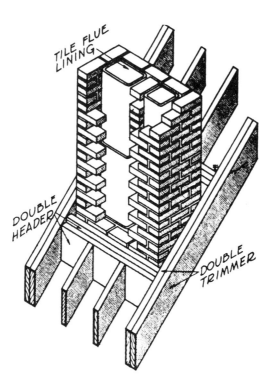

Figure 12-10 Chimney at roof.

Any and all projections through the roof, such as chimneys and sky-lights, use the same framing technique as that used for floor framing and ceiling framing. The entire perimeter of the roof opening is doubled, with the opening at least 2 in. larger than the unit being framed (Fig. 12-10). The reason for doubling the opening is to add to the roof the strength lost by the size of the opening, which is larger than the spacing of the roof rafters.

Another member of the roof framing system is the collar beam. A collar beam is a horizontal wood member nailed to both sides of the roof rafters, usually midway between the ceiling rafters and the roof ridge board. The purpose of the collar beam is to add strength and stiffness to the roof rafters and to help support the roof load. Collar beams also serve as an attic ceiling support (Fig. 12-8).

Gambrel roof framing consists of two sets of roof rafters, each with a different pitch, separated with a horizontal wood member called a purlin (Fig. 12-11). The purlin acts in the same capacity as the ridge board.

SHEATHING

When the roof framing is completed, the entire framework is covered with plywood, called sheathing (Fig. 12-12). The sheathing not only provides a surface for applying the finish roof covering, but also stiffens and reinforces the structural members of the roof framing. The thickness of the plywood is determined by the spacing of the roof rafters. If the roof rafters are spaced 16 in. apart, the plywood roof sheathing is usually $\frac{1}{2}$ in. thick. If the roof framing members are spaced 24 in. apart, the plywood sheathing thickness may be $\frac{5}{8}$ in. The sheathing is applied over roof rafters or trusses. When installing plywood, the short or 4-ft dimension is placed parallel to the roof rafters, and the long or 8-ft dimension is parallel to the long wall or perpendicular to the roof framing members. Plywood has greater strength in that position.

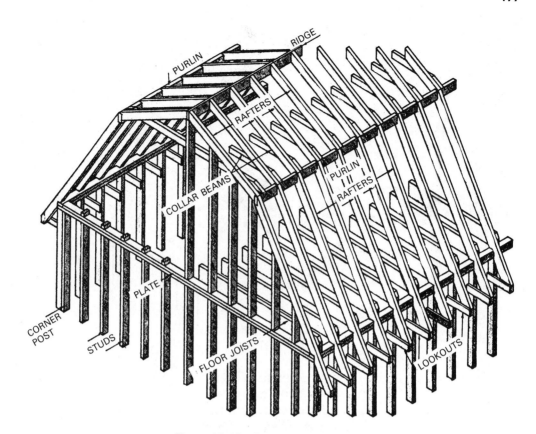

Figure 12-11 Gambrel roof construction.

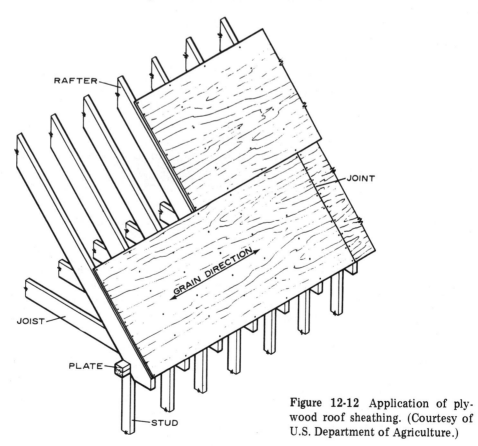

Figure 12-12 Application of plywood roof sheathing. (Courtesy of U.S. Department of Agriculture.)

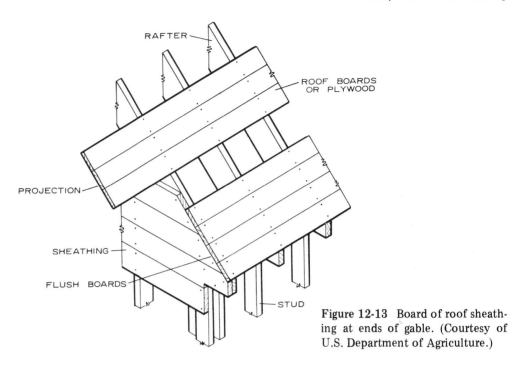

Figure 12-13 Board of roof sheathing at ends of gable. (Courtesy of U.S. Department of Agriculture.)

It is not unusual to use 1 × 6's for roof sheathing instead of plywood (Fig. 12-13), or man-made panel products similar to wall sheathing. Any man-made panel used must be approved by the local building inspector. The sheathing is nailed into every rafter member, spacing the nails about 18 in. apart, the length of the rafter.

DORMERS

Frequently a second floor is tucked away under the roof slope. To provide windows at this level, the roof is prepared for dormer windows. A dormer is a projection above the roof pitch. The main purpose is to provide for light and ventilation and additional interior space. Dormers also contribute to the aesthetic value of the building.

There are two types of dormers (Fig. 12-14):

1. *Gable dormer:* projection between the wall plate and the roof ridge; one or more windows wide
2. *Shed dormer:* continuous for most or all of the building length

Like the floor and ceiling, once the size and location of the dormer is established, the roof rafters are doubled around the perimeter of the opening. The dormer wall is constructed much like a typical exterior wall and conventional roof, with framing members spaced 16 in. apart. After framing of the dormers, the walls and roof are covered with sheathing.

ROOF TRUSSES

Another alternative method of roof framing is accomplished with trusses (Fig. 12-15). A truss is a series of wood members assembled together to form the framework for the roof and the ceiling or attic floor. Trusses require no

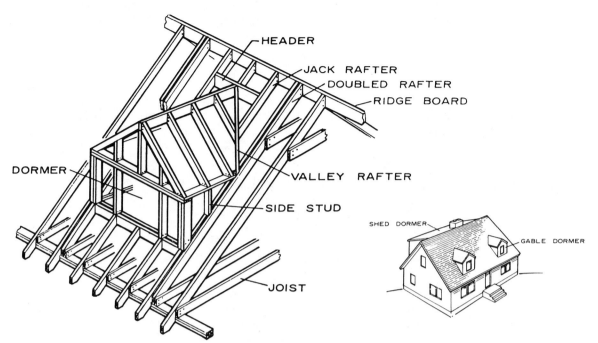

Figure 12-14 Roof dormers. (Courtesy of U.S. Department of Agriculture.)

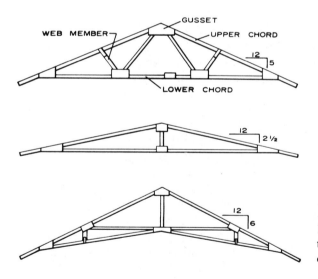

Figure 12-15 Roof trusses. (Courtesy of U.S. Department of Agriculture.)

interior bearing partition but are supported entirely by the exterior wall. This allows freedom of interior partition location without affecting the structural integrity of the building.

Most often, trusses are built on the ground or in a woodworking shop and delivered to the job site ready for erection. Trusses can be built while the rest of the house framing is being constructed. This system will speed the construction completion date. Trusses can be designed and built for flat or pitched roofs and allow a variety of design possibilities without interior columns or partitions.

Hundreds of feet can be spanned with trusses. A trussed roof does not adapt itself to roof dormers easily because of the increased spacing required by the dormer. Trusses are very adaptable to a cathedral-type ceiling, with the roof and the ceiling as one. The wood truss members can be exposed or finished. If roof trusses are used, adding another floor to the house may require removing the roof trusses and using conventional framing of floor joists and roof rafters installed separately.

LOAD SPAN TABLES

To determine the size of lumber required for roof framing, several factors must be known:

1. Roof pitch or slope
2. Roof load (determined by building code)
3. Span or length of roof rafter
4. Finish of ceiling (if any)
5. Species of wood used for framing
6. Material of roof covering
7. Spacing of roof framing members

Once this information is known, the size of lumber required for roof framing can be selected from the rafter tables (Table 12-1).

GABLES

The vertical end of the building is called a gable and is found only on roofs that have a gable design or a roof with only two sides pitched. Gables will not be found on a hip roof or mansard roof or flat roof because the end of the building has a sloped or pitched roof (except the flat roof). A gable is an extension of the end wall of the building, continuing up to the underside of the roof.

The framing of a gable is no different from that of any other exterior wall of the house, except that each stud is longer than the preceding stud because of the roof pitch. These studs are of the same size and spacing as the exterior walls and rest on a double plate extending up to the underside of the roof rafters. Usually, screened louvers or vents are installed in the gable to provide air circulation into the attic space (see Fig. 13-1b, page 184). The framing for the louvers is the same as for a window. The screen, usually on the inside, is to keep out winged animals such as insects, birds, or bats. Attic ventilation should also be provided under the soffit or roof overhang (see Figure 13-1a, page 184). This will allow air to enter and leave the attic space. On a dormer, the vertical wall, where the windows are located, is also called a gable.

QUESTIONS

1. Name three different roof styles.
   1. _____
   2. _____
   3. _____
2. A soffit is the soft underside of the roof framing members.
   True or False

3. A cripple jack is which of the following?
   A. Main support from the top plate to the ridge
   B. Cut filling against the ridge
   C. Fill-in of main roof between hip and valley
   D. None of the above

4. Define the following symbol:

   _____

5. What tool is used to lay out roof rafters? _____

6. Name three factors that must be known before a roof can be designed.
   1. _____
   2. _____
   3. _____

7. Sheathing is used for which of the following?
   A. Span table
   B. Dormer framing
   C. Roof bracing
   D. Attached roof covering

8. Dormers are easier to construct when roof trusses are used.
     True or False

9. Name two types of dormers.
   1. _____
   2. _____

10. Trusses are never used for cathedral-type ceiling framing.
     True or False

13

Roof Covering

INTRODUCTION

Roof covering provides protection and shelter from the elements. Roof shelter is one of the oldest forms of shelter, starting with a plant leaf for roof covering and extending to our modern system of roof design. The choice of material for roof covering is wide and varied, depending on geographic location, aesthetics, and budget.

Flashing is an integral part of roof covering, providing a seal against leakage for all roof projections, such as chimneys, skylights, pipes, and the joining of roofs with separate pitches. In addition, flashing is also used to seal the joint between roofs and walls.

Roof drainage is designed according to the type of roof and the roofing material, with the purpose of draining any water, melting ice, or snow from the roof as quickly as possible. Gutters and conductors are generally used for roof drainage. Included in the choice of material for roof covering are:

1. Shingles
   a. Asphalt
   b. Wood
   c. Fiberglass
   d. Slate
   e. Tile
2. Tar and gravel roofing
3. Roll roofing
4. Single-ply roofing
5. Metal roofing
   a. Copper
   b. Terne

     c. Lead
     d. Galvanized
     e. Stainless steel
     f. Aluminum

The life of a roof will vary from 5 years to the life of a building, depending on the use and selection of material. The roof is a very important part of the structure and should reflect the final appearance of the building. The roof must be functional, and its shape contributes importantly to the style of the house.

VENTILATION

One of the most important aspects of a home's construction to check before roofing work is performed is whether the attic area under the roof is adequately vented. No matter what type of roofing product is applied, improper ventilation will lead to such problems as premature roof failure, blistering, and buckling.

Energy conservation measures, such as insulation, weather stripping, and caulking, all tend to make a home more airtight and confine water vapor within the house. Although there is some passage of water vapor through the walls, vapor tends to gravitate to and accumulate under the roof deck. Condensation occurs in winter when this warm, moist air comes in contact with the cold underside of the deck. Vapor barriers will reduce but not eliminate the amount of water vapor passing to the roof.

With proper ventilation, air will circulate freely under the roof deck, carrying away the water vapor before it can condense. One of the most common methods is a combination of eaves or soffit vents and ridge vents, which provides a natural draft ventilation from the bottom to the top of the attic space. Another is a combination of eaves or soffit vents and gable vents. If eaves or soffit vents are not used, properly sized gable vents alone usually suffice (Fig. 13-1). Louver and vent openings should not be covered during the winter. Eaves or soffit vents should not be blocked by insulation.

Vent openings should conform to or exceed current construction standards. These usually call for a minimum of 1 square foot of free vent opening for each 150 ft^2 of attic surface where the attic has no vapor barrier. If a vapor barrier is present or if half of the vent openings are along the ridge and the other half at the eaves or soffit, a minimum of 1 ft^2 of free vent opening for each 300 ft^2 of attic space should be provided. On mansard roofs, ventilation ratios should be at least three times those stated. When calculating the net free vent opening, be sure to take screening into consideration, because screens can significantly reduce the free area of the vent.

Materials for roof covering are classified by weight, called a square. A square is an area 10 ft by 10 ft or 100 ft^2. The weight of the roofing material is measured by the square. Covering a roof consists of a number of operations and must be followed in proper sequence.

Moisture control is important in roof design and drainage, to avoid roof failure. Sometimes moisture vapor from within the building will rise to the attic, condensing into water vapor on the underside of the roof or sheathing, causing the sheathing to warp or buckle. Louvers in the roof or roof gables will prevent this from happening. Light roof colors reflect heat and help keep the attic cooler. Dark roof colors absorb heat.

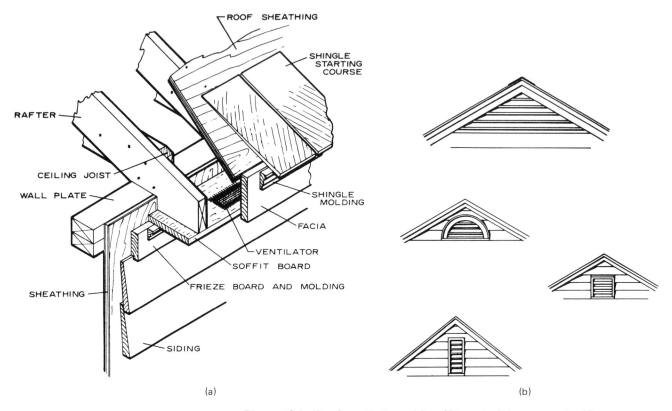

Figure 13-1 Roof ventilation: (a) soffit vent; (b) eaves vents. (Courtesy of U.S. Department of Agriculture.)

ROOFING

The purpose of covering the roof is to seal the structure against sun, rain, snow, dust, and to some degree, fire. The material used for roof covering is determined by the slope of the roof. Because of the vast amount of space covered, the material selected must be aesthetically pleasing as well as functional. Some parts of the exterior must be completed before other parts. The roof is one of them.

Care must be taken to properly seal the roof against leakage at valleys, hips, and areas of projection through the roof, such as chimneys, piping, skylights, dormers, vents, roof-mounted equipment, and roofs terminating against walls.

As soon as the roof framing and sheathing are completed, the roof covering is installed to seal the building from rain or snow. This will allow the work force to work inside the house during inclement weather, postponing the exterior finishing until dry days.

TERMS

To better understand the language of roofing, some additional terms must be defined.

Exposure: that part of the roof shingles that is visible or exposed to the weather

Coverage: number of thicknesses of roof covering

Toplap: portion of the shingle not visible or exposed, but covered by subsequent rows of shingles

Butt: thick part of the wood shingle

Underlayment: felt paper applied over the sheathing to protect the sheathing until the roofing is completed

Square: unit of measure for all roofing, 100 ft^2 of area (length $\times$ the width of the roof area and divide by 10 = the number of squares)

Blind nailing: nails covered by succeeding shingle course

Course: layers of shingles

Fishmouth: a buckle or rise in shingles due to buckling in the felt paper

Granules: crushed stone on the surface of shingles

PREPARATION

Before any roof is covered, a material selection must be made and all material must be on site. All roof projections, such as skylights, pipes, and chimneys, must be in place and completed, and the deck must be dry.

The first application, regardless of the roofing material selected, is to cover the entire roof with 15-lb felt tarred paper (Fig. 13-2). A heavier paper should not be used because it will trap condensation and moisture between the roof sheathing and the felt paper, causing decay of the roof sheathing and structural damage to the roof framing. When applying felt paper, care should be taken to avoid wrinkles in the paper because wrinkles will cause a chain reaction—wrinkles will appear on the finish roofing, causing distortion.

A 15-lb felt tarred paper is one that weighs 15 lb a square. This underlayment serves three purposes:

1. Protects sheathing until roof is completed
2. Prevents penetration of moisture after the roofing is completed
3. Provides a buffer between the shingles and sheathing

Beginning at the roof bottom, or overhang, the roof sheathing is covered with this paper, overlapping each row 2 in. The top lap is always on the downslope of the roof. If any end lap is necessary, it should be a minimum of 4 in. No nails are to be exposed on any roof-covering material.

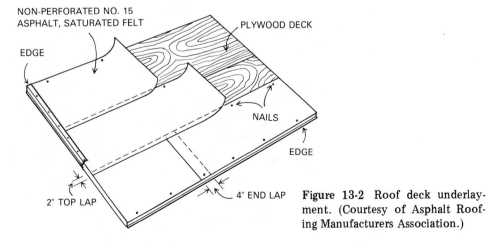

NON-PERFORATED NO. 15
ASPHALT, SATURATED FELT

PLYWOOD DECK

EDGE

NAILS

EDGE

2″ TOP LAP

4″ END LAP

Figure 13-2 Roof deck underlayment. (Courtesy of Asphalt Roofing Manufacturers Association.)

MATERIALS

The roof pitch or slope and wind resistance determines, to some extent, the material used. Roofs with a pitch of less than 3 in./ft require a roofing material with a complete seal without joints because the shallow roof pitch does not shed the water from the roof fast enough; on the other hand, steep roofs or roofs with a slope or pitch of 3 in. or more permits the water to fall from the roof faster and a roofing material with joints is permitted. The following roofing material is recommended.

Tar and Gravel (Built-Up Roofing)

This is a roof covered with four or five plies of roofing felts, each course sealed with asphalt or tar (Fig. 13-3). Over the final ply is mopped hot asphalt, which is covered with small stone called gravel, spread at about 300 lb per roofing square. The gravel protects the roofing felts and reflects the heat from the sun.

Single-Ply Roofing

This is a roof covering, usually polyvinyl chloride (PVC) or rubber, applied in a single thickness (Fig. 13-4). The joints are heated, which causes the material to fuse together forming a seal.

The single-ply roof must be held in place by mechanical fasteners or stone, called a ballast (Fig. 13-5). This is necessary to prevent the wind from lifting the roof covering. Wind lifting the roof is called negative pressure.

Metal Roofing

Roofing can be built of any nonrusting metal, such as aluminum, copper, galvanized metal, which is zinc coated, or terne, which is tin-coated metal. Light-coated galvanized sheets will rust in time and should be coated with at least 2.0 oz ft^2 for permanent protection against rust. Aluminum roofing

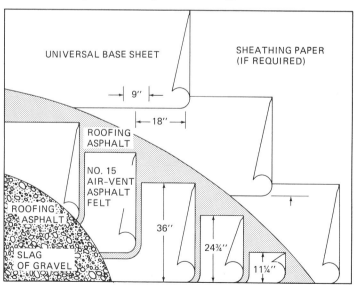

Figure 13-3   Tar and gravel built-up roofing.

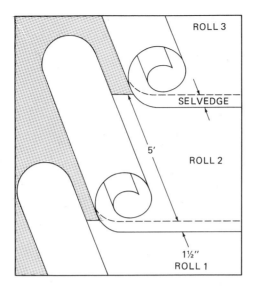
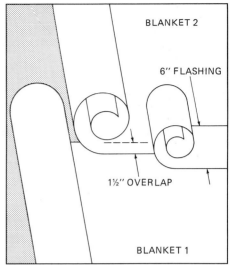

Figure 13-4   Single-ply roofing. (Courtesy of B.F. Goodrich Company.)

Figure 13-5 Roof stone ballast, smooth washed river bed stone, ¾ to 1½ in. in diameter. (Courtesy of Gates Engineering.)

is not recommended in seacoast areas subjected to wind-driven saltwater spray. Aluminum roofing should not be in direct contact with other metals. An asphalt paint is recommended to separate the two metals; otherwise, a chemical action takes place that will eventually break down the aluminum. The joints can be soldered or lapped and locked. The metal can be applied in a flat seam, standing seam, cross seam, or batten seam (Fig. 13-6).

Asphalt Roofing Products

Asphalt roofing products are classified in three broad groups: shingles, roll roofing, and saturated felts. Shingles and roll roofing are outer roof coverings, meaning that they are exposed to the weather and designed to withstand the elements. Saturated felts are inner roof coverings, meaning that they provide the necessary underlayment protection for the exposed roofing materials.

As outer roof coverings, shingles and roll roofing contain the three basic components that provide protection. These components are:

1.   A base material made of an organic felt or fiberglass mat which provides the matrix that supports the other components and gives the product the strength to withstand manufacturing, handling, installation, and service conditions

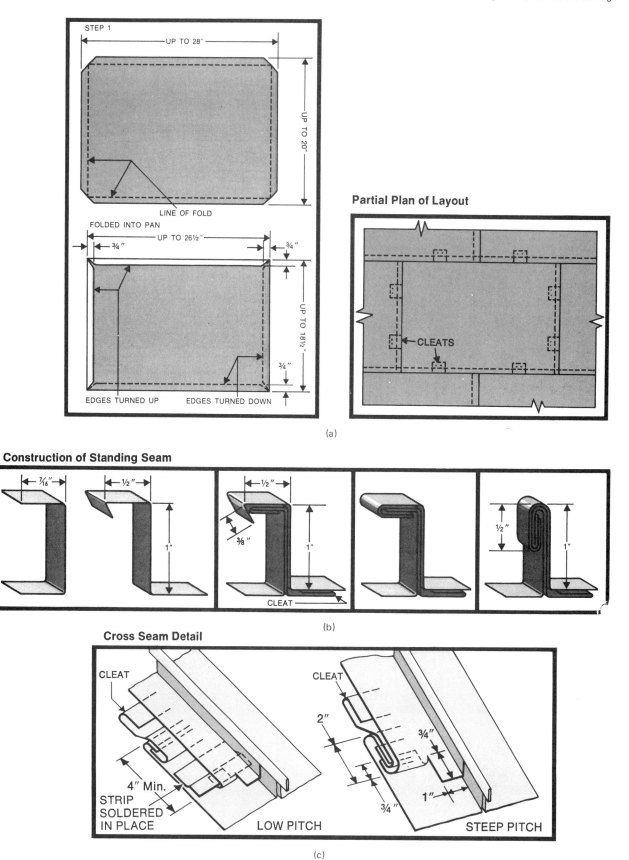

Figure 13-6   Metal roofing: (a) flat seam. (b) standing seam; (c) cross seam.

Batten Seam

Finishing Batten End

Ridge

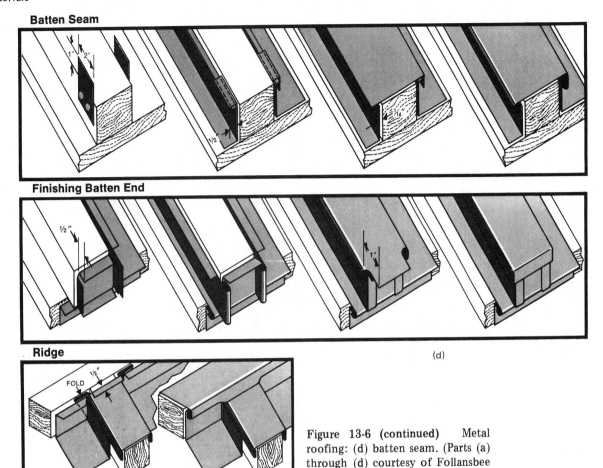

(d)

Figure 13-6 (continued) Metal roofing: (d) batten seam. (Parts (a) through (d) courtesy of Follansbee Steel Corporation.)

2. A specially formulated asphalt coating which provides the long-term ability to resist weathering and remain stable under severe service temperature extremes

3. A surfacing of ceramic-coated mineral granules which shields the asphalt coating against the sun's rays, adds color to the product, and provides fire resistance

Shingles. Asphalt shingles are the most common roofing material used today. They are manufactured as strip shingles, interlocking shingles, and large individual shingles (Table 13-1). Strip shingles are rectangular, measuring approximately 12 in. wide by 36 in. long, and may have as many as five cutouts along the long dimension. Cutouts separate the shingle's tabs, which are exposed to the weather and give the roof the appearance of being comprised of a larger number of individual units (Fig. 13-7). Strip shingles are also manufactured without cutouts to produce a different effect.

Many of the shingles are available with strips or spots of a factory-applied, self-sealing adhesive which is a thermoplastic material activated by the heat of the sun after the shingle is on the roof (Fig. 13-8). Exposure to the sun's heat bonds each shingle securely to the one below for greater wind resistance. This self-sealing action takes place within a few days during the spring, summer, and fall. In winter, the self-sealing action varies depending on geographical location, roof slope, and orientation of the house on the site.

TABLE 13-1

Typical Asphalt Shingles

PRODUCT	Configuration	Per Square			Size		Exposure
		Approximate Shipping Weight	Shingles	Bundles	Width	Length	
Self-sealing random-tab strip shingle 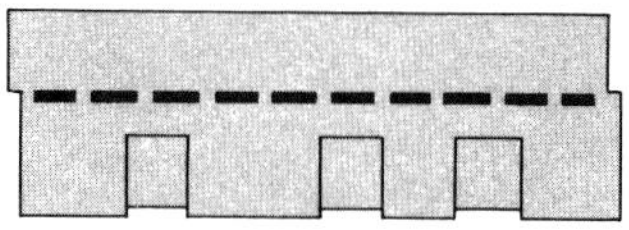 Multi-thickness	Various edge, surface texture and application treatments	240# to 360#	64 to 90	3, 4 or 5	11½" to 14"	36" to 40"	4" to 6"
Self-sealing random-tab strip shingle 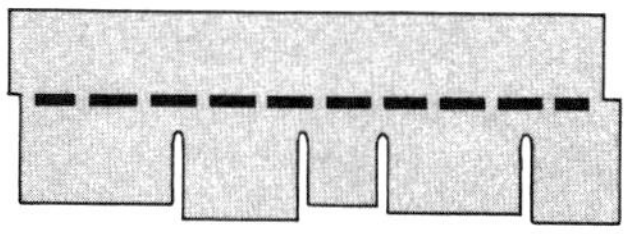 Single-thickness	Various edge, surface texture and application treatments	240# to 300#	65 to 80	3 or 4	12" to 13¼"	36" to 40"	5" to 5⅝"
Self-sealing square-tab strip shingle 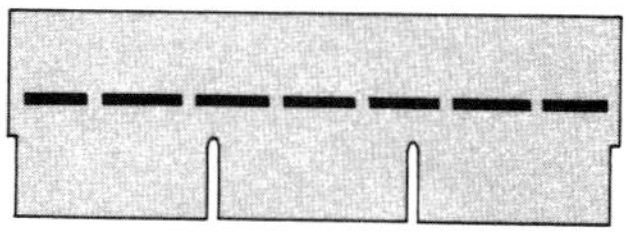 Three-tab	Two-tab or Four-tab	215# to 325#	65 to 80	3 or 4	12" to 13¼"	36" to 40"	5" to 5⅝"
	Three-tab	215# to 300#	65 to 80	3 or 4	12" to 13¼"	36" to 40"	5" to 5⅝"
Self-sealing square-tab strip shingle 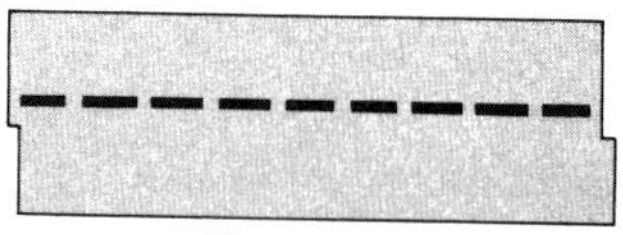 No-cutout	Various edge and surface texture treatments	215# to 290#	65 to 81	3 or 4	12" to 13¼"	36" to 40"	5" to 5⅝"
Individual interlocking shingle 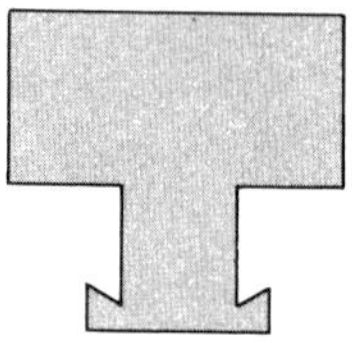 Basic design	Several design variations	180# to 250#	72 to 120	3 or 4	18" to 22¼"	20" to 22½"	—

Source: Asphalt Roofing Manufacturers Association.

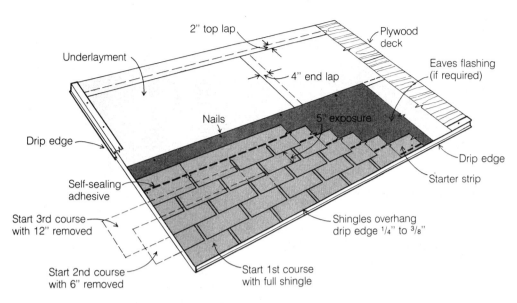

Figure 13-7 Application of shingles. (Courtesy of Asphalt Roofing Manufacturers Association.)

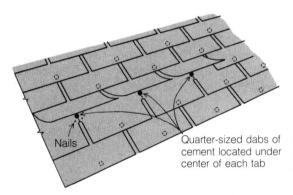

Figure 13-8 Self-sealing adhesive asphalt roofing shingles. (Courtesy of Asphalt Roofing Manufacturers Association.)

Ceramic-coated mineral granules, applied to the top surface of strip shingles during the manufacturing process, make possible a wide variety of colors, ranging from black and white to hues of red, brown, and green. The tabs of a strip shingle may be trimmed or offset to obtain straight or staggered butt lines, respectively. They also may be embossed or built up from a number of laminations of base material to give a three-dimensional effect. These shingle characteristics—staggered butt lines, embossing, and laminations—can be combined in various ways to create textures on the finished roof surface that resemble wood, slate, and tile.

Interlocking shingles are designed to provide resistance to strong winds. The shingles come in various shapes and with various types of locking devices that provide a mechanical interlock on the roof. Large individual shingles are generally rectangular or hexagonal in shape.

Roll Roofing. As the name implies, roll roofing is manufactured, packaged, and shipped in rolls. The roofing is approximately 36 in. wide, 36 to 38 ft long, and varies in weight from 40 to 90 lb per square. The product may be obtained as smooth-surfaced roll roofing or with mineral granules embedded in the top surface in the same manner as shingles (Table 13-2).

Some mineral-surfaced roll roofings are manufactured with a granule-free selvage edge that indicates the amount by which each succeeding course

TABLE 13-2

Typical Asphalt Rolls

PRODUCT	Approximate Shipping Weight		Squares Per Package	Length	Width	Selvage	Exposure
	Per Roll	Per Square					
Mineral surface roll	75# to 90#	75# to 90#	1	36' to 38'	36"	2" to 4"	32" to 34"
Mineral surface roll (double coverage)	55# to 70#	110# to 140#	½	36'	36"	19"	17"
Smooth surface roll	50# to 86#	40# to 65#	1 to 2	36' to 72'	36"	2"	34"
Saturated felt (non-perforated)	45# to 60#	11# to 30#	2 to 4	72' to 144'	36"	2" to 19"	17" to 34"

Source: Asphalt Roofing Manufacturers Association.

should overlap the preceding course. The manufacturer's recommendations with respect to top lap as well as side and end lap should be followed because the amount of overlap determines how much of the material is exposed to the weather and the extent of "coverage" to the roof surface: that is, whether most of the surface has a single or a double layer of roll roofing. In addition to its use as a roof covering, roll roofing is an important flashing material.

Saturated Felts. This type of material consists of a dry felt impregnated with an asphalt saturant. It is used primarily as an underlayment for asphalt shingles, roll roofing, and other types of roofing materials, and as sheathing paper. Saturated felts are manufactured in various weights, the most common being No. 15 (weighing approximately 15 lb per square) and No. 30 (weighing approximately 30 lb per square).

Advantages of Asphalt Roofing Products. The dominant leadership of asphalt roofing products through the years has not evolved as a matter of chance. It is based on proven product performance that goes far beyond the basic roofing requirement of providing a covering that shields a building's inhabitants from the weather.

The product's characteristics include the following:

1. *Weather resistance.* As a result of constant research and testing of the product and its application, asphalt roofing resists heat, cold, water, and ice.
2. *Fire resistance.* Asphalt roofing products are manufactured to comply with the Underwriters' Laboratories standards for fire resistance. The importance of fire-resistant roofs cannot be overemphasized because roofs are particularly vulnerable to fire from external sources such as sparks emitted by nearby fires.
3. *Wind resistance.* Asphalt roofing that bears the Underwriters' Laboratories "Wind-Resistant" label has been tested to withstand winds up to gale force.
4. *Adaptability.* Because of their flexibility and strength, asphalt roofing products can be applied on a wide variety of roof styles.
5. *Beauty.* Asphalt roofing is available in many appealing colors and dimensional depths that provide bold roof textures. The wide range of asphalt roofing products introduced in recent years offers much greater flexibility in choosing colors for a building's exterior than is available with any other type of roofing material.

Selecting the Right Asphalt Roofing Product. There is an asphalt roofing product to meet every roofing requirement, but no product is necessarily the best for every job. On many jobs, several alternatives may exist. The "right" product should be chosen based on a number of considerations, including roof slope, coverage, local wind conditions, and aesthetics.

Slope: Of all the factors to consider in choosing an asphalt roofing product, one of the most critical is the slope of the roof, because it affects the surface drainage of water and thereby dictates the limits within which shingles or roll roofing may be used. Free drainage is essential to the overall performance of both types of asphalt roof covering and can make the difference between a weathertight roof and one that leaks. The slope of a roof is very often a function of the style of a roof (Fig. 13-9). In general, asphalt shingles

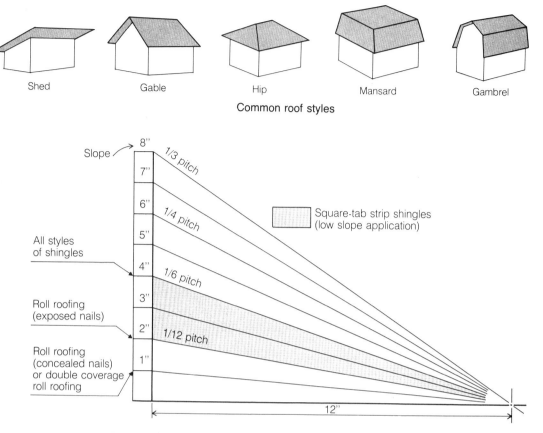

Figure 13-9 Minimum pitch and slope requirements for various asphalt roofing products. (Courtesy of Asphalt Roofing Manufacturers Association.)

may be used on roof slopes between 4 and 21 in./ft using standard application methods. Beyond this maximum slope, special steep slope application procedures must be followed. Square-tab strip shingles may be used on slopes between 2 and 4 in./ft if special low-slope application procedures are followed.

The minimum slope on which roll roofing may be used depends on the application method and the type of roll roofing. Roll roofing may generally be used on roof slopes down to 1 in./ft.

Double-coverage roll roofing which provides a top lap of 19 in. may also be used on slopes down to 1 in./ft. In general, roll roofings should not be used on slopes of less than 1 in./ft unless specified by the manufacturer.

Coverage and Exposure: Exposure is that portion of the roofing exposed to the weather after the roofing is installed. The exposure for various asphalt roofing products is specified by the manufacturer.

Coverage is an indication of the amount of weather protection the asphalt roofing provides. Depending on the number of plies or layers of material that lie between the exposed surface of the roofing and the deck, the material is designated as single, double, or triple coverage. Where the number of plies varies, coverage is usually considered to be that which exists over most of the roof area. For example, where no significant roof area has less than two thicknesses of material, the installation would be considered double coverage.

Asphalt roll roofings are generally considered single-coverage products because they provide a single layer of material over the greater part of the roof area. An exception is roll roofing applied with a 19-in. overlap and 17-in. exposure, which is considered double-coverage material. Asphalt strip shingles are also considered double-coverage materials because their top lap is 2 in. or more greater than their exposure.

Wind: Self-sealing shingles and interlocking shingles were originally available only in high-wind areas. However, both types are now generally available. It is recommended that these shingles be chosen wherever high winds are anticipated. Free-tab shingles—those without a factory-applied adhesive—may be made more resistant to wind by cementing each tab in place as the shingles are being installed.

Aesthetics: One of the most significant developments in asphalt roofing shingles has been the aesthetic freedom they now offer. There is a range of color available to match everyone's imagination in designing the exterior of a home. For example, in addition to such standard colors as white, black, and the light pastels, asphalt roofings are available in numerous blends or mixes of red, brown, and green. If the intent is to relate the building to a natural environment, the latter colors should be considered. They may also be employed to complement and reinforce the natural colors of other building elements, such as brick walls or wood siding.

Roof color can also be utilized in the design of a home to obtain certain psychological effects. For example, a small house may be given added dimension by a light-colored roof that will direct the eye upward and help create a sense of airiness. Dark colors on a tall or steeply sloped building will help create the opposite effect, bringing the structure down in scale visually.

In addition to color, the use of laminated asphalt shingles can contribute to the overall architectural effect of a building. Many of these shingles offer the "look" of wood but have the long-term wear and fire safety of asphalt shingles. Others offer the "look" of slate and tile. All create interesting visual effects of light and shadow over the roof expanse because of their three-dimensional construction.

Porcelain Enamel Shingles

Porcelain enamel shingles (Fig. 13-10) are manufactured of light-gauge steel similar to aluminum with a finish of porcelain enamel. The color is permanent and offers a long-lasting roof covering.

Mineral Fiber Shingles

Mineral fiber shingles are much like asphalt or fiberglass shingles. They are made from asbestos fiber and portland cement. They are formed in molds under pressure and provide a finish that is resistant to rot and decay and offers a fireproof roof covering.

Concrete Tile

Concrete tile (Fig. 13-11) is a roof covering made of lightweight concrete. A variety of design and color is offered and concrete tile looks much like clay tile when applied. Because of the weight of the material used in the manufacture of the shingles, a strong wood roof framing system is required.

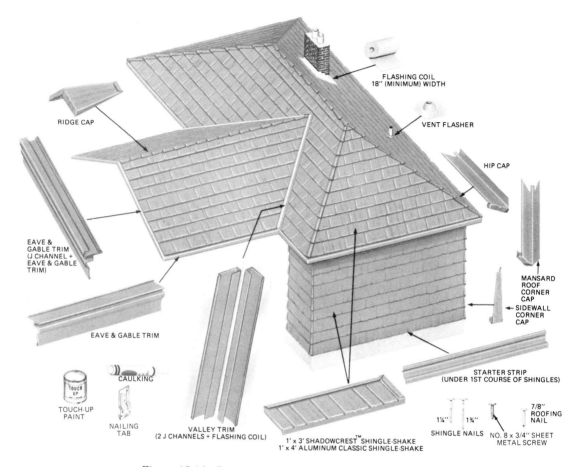

Figure 13-10 Porcelain enamel roofing shingles. (Courtesy of Reynolds Metals Company.)

Figure 13-11 Concrete tile roofing. (Courtesy of Life-tile Corporation.)

Aluminum Roofing

Aluminum roofing is a metal product made from light-gauge shaped aluminum with a permanent baked-on coloring (Fig. 13-10).

Tile

Tile (Fig. 13-12) is a clay product with natural earth colors. It is offered in a variety of shapes, and like concrete, because of its weight, requires a heavier roof framing system.

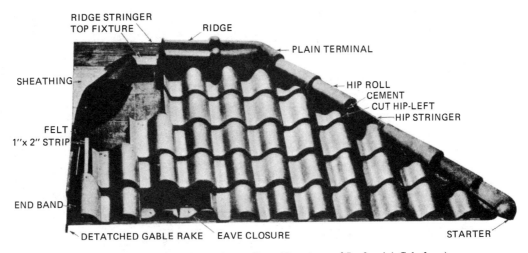

Figure 13-12   Clay tile roofing. (Courtesy of Ludowici-Celadon.)

Wood Shingles

Wood shingles are made of cedar, redwood, and cyprus, all of which are decay resistant, and are of two varieties. One is called shakes (Fig. 13-13a), which is a hand-split shingle, and the other (Fig. 13-13b) is a machine-sawed shingle. The hand-split wood shingle varies in thickness and offers a pleasing

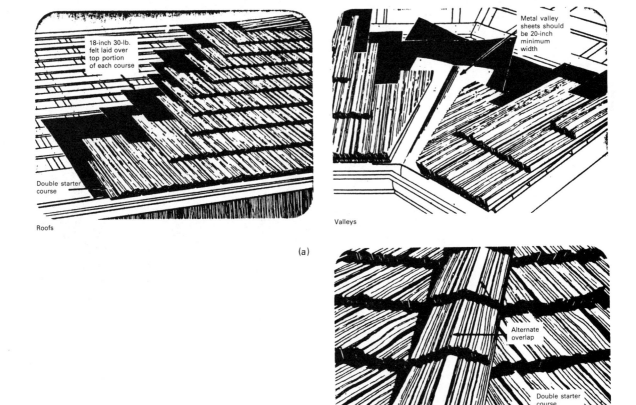

Figure 13-13   (a) Roofing shakes.

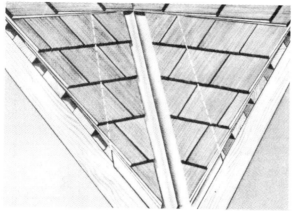

● Valleys should extend far enough under the shingles to insure complete drainage, with water-stop as shown if necessary.

● How the recommended modified "Boston" hip is made.

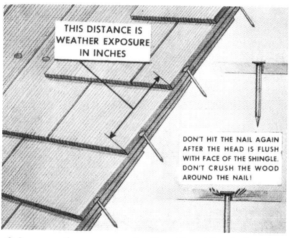

● Proper weather exposure and nailing will provide a 3-ply roof.

● Drip from gables and the formation of icicles can be prevented by this simple expedient.

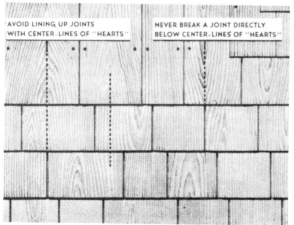

● Flat-grain shingles in Red Label and No. 3 Black Label grades should be properly applied as shown above.

● In over-roofing, new flashings should be placed around chimneys without removing the old.

(b)

Figure 13-13 (continued)   (b) Machine-sawed shingles.

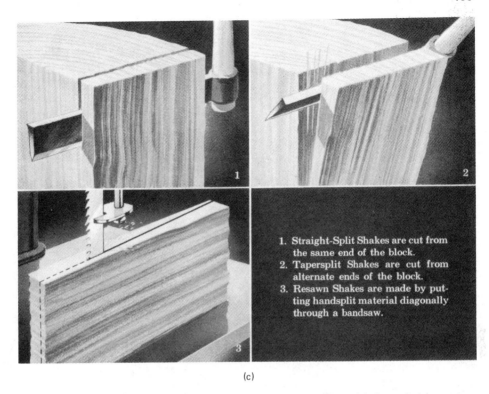

1. Straight-Split Shakes are cut from the same end of the block.
2. Tapersplit Shakes are cut from alternate ends of the block.
3. Resawn Shakes are made by putting handsplit material diagonally through a bandsaw.

(c)

Figure 13-13 (continued) (c) Cutting shakes and shingles. (Parts (a) through (c) courtesy of Red Cedar Shingle and Handsplit Shake Bureau.)

shadow effect on the roof. The machine-sawed wood shingles are uniform in size and wedge shaped (Fig. 13-13c). There are several qualities of wood shingle available. Wood shingles used for roofing are treated with a fire-retardant chemical. Some building codes may prohibit the use of wood roof shingles. Wood roof shingles are applied with a $\frac{1}{4}$-in. space between them to allow for expansion of the wood; otherwise, the shingle will cup. A variety of patterns are available in applying wood roof shingles.

Slate Shingles

Slate is a natural quarried rock product split into thin sheets used for roof covering (Fig. 13-14). The marked cleavage of the slate rock lends itself to a natural, irregular, and pleasing roof surface with natural color variations

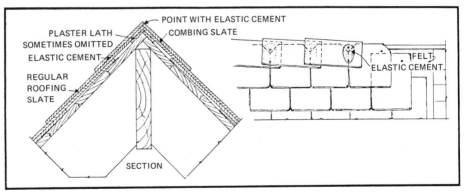

(a)

Figure 13-14 Slate roofing: (a) saddle ridge.

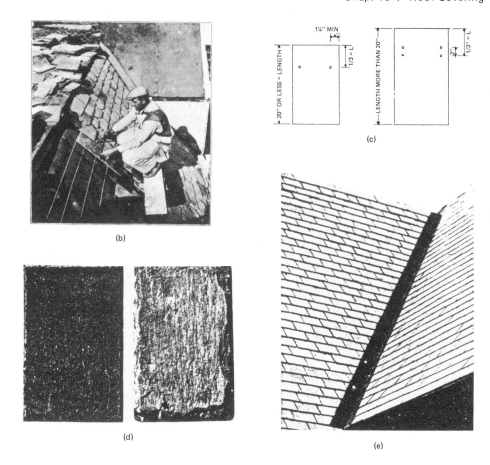

Figure 13-14 (continued) Slate roofing: (b) laying slate; (c) location of nail holes; (d) smooth and rough slate; (e) open valley. (Courtesy of Hilltop Slate, Inc.)

from blacks and grays, blues and greens, and browns and reds. A slate roof will usually outlast the life of the building. They require a stronger roof framing system because of the weight of the shingles, and the roof pitch should be no less than 6 in.

Fiberglass Shingles

Fiberglass shingles are much like asphalt shingles, except that these shingles are made of fiberglass. They are a little lighter in weight and offer a flame-resistant roof covering. Fiberglass shingles resist warping, cupping, and curling and will not absorb moisture, which is the cause of blistering and rotting.

FLASHING

All roof projections, such as skylights, pipes, dormers, chimneys (Fig. 13-15), and meeting of different-angled roofs called valleys, must be sealed to avoid any leaks. Roofs that butt walls must also have protection against leaks (Fig. 13-16). This protective seal is called flashing. The flashing may be a nonrusting metal such as copper, lead, or aluminum or can be a heavy, reinforced fabric.

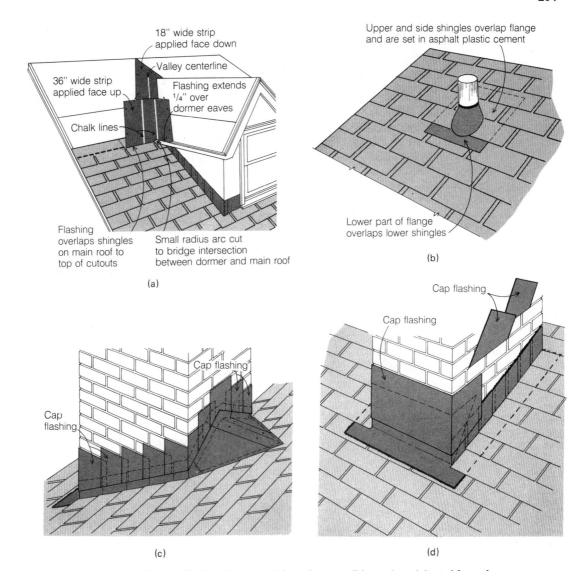

18" wide strip applied face down

Valley centerline

36" wide strip applied face up

Flashing extends ¼" over dormer eaves

Chalk lines

Flashing overlaps shingles on main roof to top of cutouts

Small radius arc cut to bridge intersection between dormer and main roof

(a)

Upper and side shingles overlap flange and are set in asphalt plastic cement

Lower part of flange overlaps lower shingles

(b)

Cap flashing

Cap flashing

Cap flashing

Cap flashing

(c)   (d)

Figure 13-15   Flashing: (a) at dormer; (b) at pipe; (c) at side and rear of chimney; (d) at side and front of chimney. (Courtesy of Asphalt Roofing Manufacturers Association.)

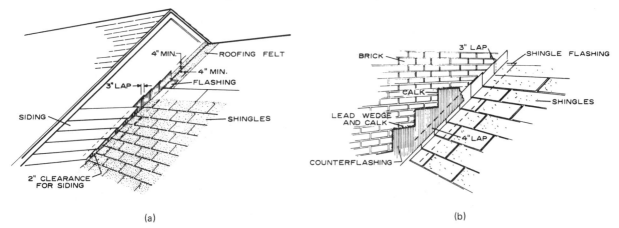

ROOFING FELT

4" MIN.

4" MIN.

3" LAP

FLASHING

SIDING

SHINGLES

2" CLEARANCE FOR SIDING

(a)

BRICK

3" LAP

SHINGLE FLASHING

CALK

SHINGLES

LEAD WEDGE AND CALK

4" LAP

COUNTERFLASHING

(b)

Figure 13-16   Flashing wall and roof: (a) wood siding wall; (b) brick wall. (Courtesy of U.S. Department of Agriculture.)

Valleys

Two angled roofs joining together from different directions on the inside line is called a valley. Care must be taken at this joint to avoid roof leakage. Water draining from the roof is concentrated at this point. This joint is sealed with flashing applied under the roof covering. There are two types of valleys, the open valley and the closed (or "woven") valley (Fig. 13-17). The open valley stops the roof shingles at the flashing, exposing the metal flashing. The closed valley is flashed with the shingles, weaving the shingles at the valley.

Hips

Much like the valley, a hip consists of two angled roofs joined together on the outside line (Fig. 13-18). The hip is constructed and sealed with the same roofing shingles as those used on the entire roof, similar to the ridge.

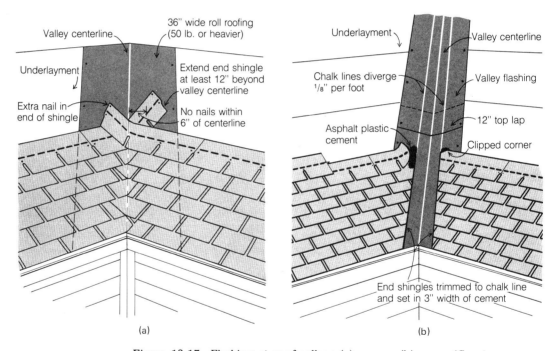

Figure 13-17 Flashing at roof valley: (a) woven; (b) open. (Courtesy of Asphalt Roofing Manufacturers Association.)

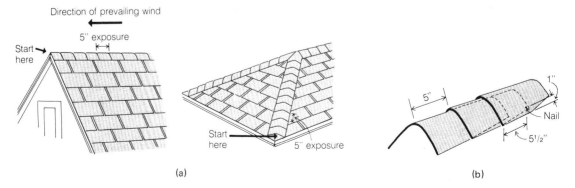

Figure 13-18 Roof hip and ridge shingles: (a) application; (b) fastener location. (Courtesy of Asphalt Roofing Manufacturers Association.)

Ridges

The ridge is the uppermost part of the roof, joining different slopes together. The ridge is sealed much like the hip except that the ridge is on a level plane (Fig. 13-18).

QUESTIONS

1. Define the following terms.
   (a) Square _____
   _____
   (b) Exposure _____
   _____
   (c) Granules _____
   _____

2. Roof covering may be installed directly onto the roof sheathing.
      True or False

3. What roof pitch is recommended for a tar-and-gravel roof? _____
   _____

4. Metal for roofing may be which of the following?
   A. Alloy
   B. Steel
   C. Wrought iron
   D. All of the above
   E. None of the above

5. What is the most popular roof covering? _____

6. Wood roof shingles are not allowed according to building codes.
      True or False

7. Define *flashing.* _____
   _____

8. Closed and open valleys are the same.   True or False

9. *Hip* applies to which of the following?
   A. Roof trim
   B. Roof ventilation
   C. Two angled roofs joining

10. Define *ridge.* _____
    _____

14

Insulation and Vapor Barrier

Hot or warm air is attracted to cold air. The heat used in a house is being drawn around the outside cold walls of the house. The material used for construction, the amount of glass in the walls, and the ceiling height are the factors that determine how much lost heat has to be replaced, for comfort, by the heating system. The greatest single material causing heat loss is glass.

The purpose of insulating a house is to reduce the heat loss through the walls, floor, and ceiling. Hot or warm air rises and a great amount of heat is also lost through the ceiling or roof. The denser the insulation, the less heat is lost to the outside. The thicker the insulation, the less heat is lost to the outside.

The same principle applies in reverse in warm or hot climates. The insulation helps to keep the inside of the building cool when the outside temperature is hot.

Another characteristic of heat is that the natural moisture inside a house moves with the heat toward the colder wall surface. This moisture is generated by steam from baths and showers, cooking, and the breath of the occupants. Steps must be taken to prevent this moisture from going through the cooler exterior walls, which could cause serious damage to the house. This preventive mechanism is called a vapor barrier.

The effectiveness of insulation is measured by the R value and the U value. Five different types of insulation are available: (1) rigid, (2) loose or fill, (3) batts, (4) blanket, and (5) foam. All are available in various thicknesses.

HEAT TRANSFER

There are three ways in which heat moves or is transferred. The first is radiation, which is heat transferred from one surface to another. An example of radiation is the heat from the sun, which warms all objects in contact with the sun. Another example is the heat from an open fire, such as a fireplace, which is radiated into the room. A second way is conduction, which is heat traveling through actual contact. The handle of a hot pan is one example of heat conduction. The handle may not be in direct contact with the burners of a range, but the pan is, and the heat from the pan travels to the pan handle. A third type is convection. This is heat that is transferred through liquid or gas. Air is one form of gas, and the heat generated from a warm-air furnace is forced into various rooms through the gas or air within the room. Another example of convection is water heated from a boiler, which is carried through pipes into baseboards and radiators. Another type of heat loss within a house is by means of infiltration. This is loss of heat through the space around doors and windows. Figure 14-1 shows recommendations for an energy-efficient home.

Figure 14-1 An energy-efficient home. (Courtesy of Owens/Corning Fiberglass Corp.)

1. Insulation in ceilings, walls, and floors to the R-value levels recommended by the map.
2. Vapor barriers required for ceilings, walls, floors, and as a ground cover in crawl spaces.
3. Insulation of slab-on-grade construction with perimeter insulation placed along and under edges of foundation before slab is poured.
4. Double-glazed windows or single-glazed with storm sash are required. Total glass area should be minimized.
5. Storm door and standard door used in combination, or an insulated door.
6. Insulated air-handling ducts should be Duct System (1 in. wall thickness or greater) or sheet metal ducts insulated with 2 in. of Duct Wrap with vapor barrier, and where possible keep ducts within the conditioned space.
7. Windows and doors designed to limit air leakage and weather-stripped.
8. Caulking and sealing at various critical locations to reduce air infiltration.
9. Adequate ventilation and provision for exhausting moisture or dehumidifying air.
10. Properly sized heating and cooling equipment.

Heat is measured by a unit called the British thermal unit (Btu), which is the amount of heat necessary to raise the temperature of 1 pound of water 1 degree Fahrenheit.

INSULATION VALUES

All insulation is rated by a value known as R, which is a measurement of heat passing through the insulation, or the resistance to heat flow. The higher the R value, the better the insulation. R value varies from R-11 for 3½-in. fiberglass insulation to R-38 for 12-in. fiberglass insulation. The R values are printed on the insulation package. Figure 14-2 shows recommended R values for the various zones within the United States.

Another value of insulation is known as the U value. This is a measure of the amount of heat passing through 1 ft^2 of insulation in 1 hour with a temperature difference of 1°F from one side of the wall to the other. The lower the U value, the better the insulation. An uninsulated wall may have a U value of 0.20. With 3 in. of insulation, the U value may drop down to 0.04 in the same wall. The U value is the amount of heat lost through a building section of floor, wall, or ceiling.

A phenomenon known as the "cold effect," caused by the feel of cold surfaces, such as furniture, floors, walls, and ceilings, causes a person to feel cold even though the room temperature is comfortable. This is caused by the body losing heat to these cooler surfaces, or heat loss through conduction.

Another value of heat measurement is the K value. This is the amount of heat lost per hour through a given single building material 1 in. thick, 12 in. wide, and 12 in. long. The difference between U value and K value is the measurement from only one type of building material, whereas the U value is the total of a combination of K factors.

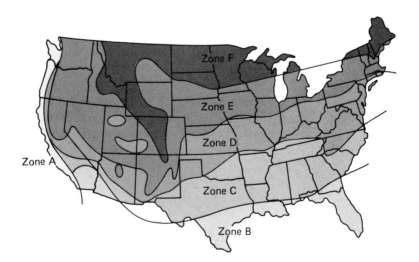

Figure 14-2 Recommended levels of insulation for both heating and cooling.

	Ceilings	Walls	Floors
Zone A	R-19	R-11	R-11
Zone B	R-26	R-13	R-11
Zone C	R-26	R-19	R-13
Zone D	R-30	R-19	R-19
Zone E	R-33	R-19	R-22
Zone F	R-38	R-19	R-22

TYPES OF INSULATION

There are many types, forms, and thicknesses of insulation. Insulation is light in weight because the principal ingredient is air. The air is trapped by hundreds of tiny cells. The material forming the cells may be mineral, glass, fibers, vegetable, wood, cotton, corn or sugarcane stalks, animal hair, or a variety of chemicals or foams.

There are five different types of insulation: blanket, batt, rigid, loose or fill, reflective, and foam (Fig. 14-3).

1. *Rigid:* board-type insulation measuring generally 24 in. by 88 in. and in thicknesses of ½ in. up to 3½ in. It is made of various mineral, wood, and vegetable products and glass (Fig. 14-4a). It is used principally over foundations under concrete floors on grade and on flat roofs. It is also formed to fit the core of masonry units, such as concrete block (Fig. 14-4b).

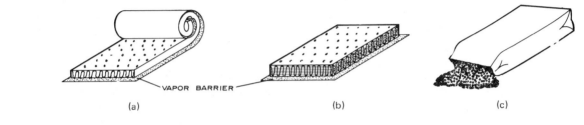
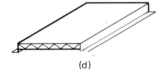

(a)   (b)   (c)

(d)   (e)

Figure 14-3 Types of insulation: (a) blanket; (b) batt; (c) fill; (d) reflective (one type); (e) rigid. (Courtesy of U.S. Department of Agriculture.)

(a)

Figure 14-4 (a) Rigid insulation; (b) form-fitted insulation. [(a) Courtesy of Pittsburgh Corning Corporation; (b) courtesy of Korfil Incorporated.]

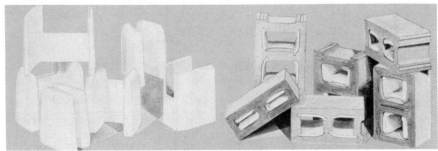

(b)

(a)

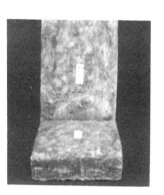

Figure 14-5 (a) Faced insulation;
(b) unfaced insulation. [(a) Courtesy of Owens/Corning Fiberglass
Corp.; (b) courtesy of Manville
Corp.]

(b)

Figure 14-6 Fiberglass blowing
wool. (Courtesy of Owens/Corning
Fiberglass Corp.)

2. *Blanket/batt:* can be in the shape of a batt or blanket. Batt insulation is 15 in. and 23 in. wide and 2 and 4 ft long in thicknesses
from 2 to 12 in. Blanket or batt insulation is manufactured of
loosely felted mats of vegetable or mineral fibers. Blanket insulation is 2 to 12 in. thick and 15 to 23 in. wide. The batt or blanket
can be faced with a variety of covers, including a vapor barrier
(Fig. 14-5a), or it can be unfaced (Fig. 14-5b).

3. *Loose (or fill):* made from various materials in bulk form (Fig.
14-6), is free flowing, and is either blown or poured in place between the studs, rafters, or joists. This type of insulation is best
used in homes being altered or remodeled, where the framework is

not exposed. It is manufactured from glass, rock wool, wood fibers, bark, cork, vermiculite, perlite, gypsum, and sawdust.

Holes need to be made in the exterior wall to blow the insulation in place; the holes are later patched. The blown-in procedure will fill the spaces between the studs, rafters, or joists. This type of insulation can also be poured in the core of concrete block (Fig. 14-7). There is no built-in vapor barrier with loose insulation. A separate vapor barrier must be installed.

4. *Reflective:* usually a single-sheet type of insulation using mostly aluminum foil (Fig. 14-8). It acts as a vapor barrier as well and is designed to reflect the heat inside the building. Frequently, this single sheet of reflective insulation is part of another type of insulation, such as a batt or blanket. It is also attached to wallboard, gypsum lath, and other types as rigid insulation.

Figure 14-7 Masonry fill insulation. (Courtesy of W. R. Grace & Co.)

Figure 14-8 Reflective insulation. (Courtesy of Owens/Corning Fiberglass Corp.)

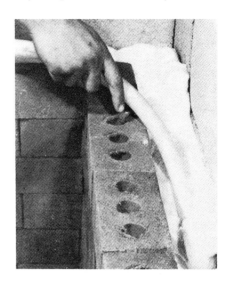

Figure 14-9   Foam insulation. (Courtesy of Intron.)

In summer, the reflective insulation will reflect the heat from the sun back outside the wall, keeping the building inside cooler. In winter the reflective insulation will reflect the heat from the house back into the house, helping to keep the house warm.

To be effective, this type of insulation must have at least a ¾-in. air space around it. If it is in contact with any other building material, it will not be reflective.

5. *Foam:* mixture of urea-formaldehyde resin, pumped into walls between studs of new and existing buildings (Fig. 14-9). Foam is also manufactured as rigid board insulation. Like loose or poured insulation, foam is best used on houses that are being altered or remodeled, where the framework is not exposed. Holes are made in the wall and the foam insulation is pumped into the space between the studs in liquid form, which solidifies in about 10 hours. It cures in about 30 days. The holes in the exterior walls are later patched.

INSULATION APPLICATION

For insulation to be effective, it must block all spaces in the floor, walls, ceiling, or roof. The insulation must be carefully cut and placed in position to assure a proper tight fit. A 6-in.-thick insulation compressed into 3 in. will not give a full 6-in. value. The insulation should be fully thick when placed in position. Blanket insulation has flanges along the edge for stapling into the stud, joist, or rafter face. Tension wires or a network of crossed light-gauge wire is sometimes used to hold insulation in floor spaces, without a finished ceiling. Insulation in the attic is held in place by the finished ceiling below.

Rigid insulation is glued onto vertical wall surfaces. The inside and outside wall finish will hold loose or blown insulation in the wall.

CONDENSATION

All air contains moisture. The warmer the air, the more moisture it will hold. When the warm air within the house moves toward the cold outside wall surface, it can no longer hold the moisture and it is released in the form of drops of water. This is called condensation. An example of this can be seen on the outside of a cold glass, can, or soft-drink bottle. This moisture or water droplets runs down the surface of the container and forms a small puddle of water. The same thing happens inside a framed wall, floor, or ceiling.

Moisture created inside the house through normal living from cooking, clothes washing and drying, humidifiers, and showers is condensation. This heated moisture is drawn to the outside walls from the colder outside temperature. When the condensation is cooled, it turns into water. When this water is trapped inside the partition, it can cause serious problems to the wood framework of the house, such as wood decay. In addition, it will cause paint to peel. A vapor barrier on the heated side of the floor, wall, or ceiling will prevent the passage of cooled vapor. It is nothing more than a seal to trap the condensation from going through the wall. The condensation is then released through the opening of doors, windows, and exhaust fans.

Vapor Barrier

Insulation can be applied with a built-in vapor barrier. It is a waterproof facing over the fiberglass blanket or batt insulation. If the insulation has no vapor barrier, it is called unfaced. The vapor barrier is placed on the heated side of the building. Some rigid-type insulation is made of a material that creates a natural vapor barrier.

Another type of vapor barrier is polyethylene, which is applied on the inside face of studs, ceiling joists, and floor joists. For this purpose a 6-mil thickness is recommended. In slab or grade construction, the polyethylene vapor barrier is placed between the ground and the underside of the concrete floor.

Ventilation

All areas such as crawl spaces, attics, and generally closed areas require the passage of air for ventilation. This is done with screened louvers or electric fans. If the air is not ventilated, it will retain dampness and moisture and can create serious structural damage. Provisions must be made for air to enter and exit the enclosed areas (Fig. 14-10). In crawl spaces the ventilation is usually accomplished by screened openings in the foundation. In the case of an attic space, screened vents are installed under the roof overhang with louvers on the top of the roof. The larger the space, the more air movement is required. An attic fan is more effective than louvers for ventilation.

Terms

Degree-days: a measure of climate conditions over an entire heating period. The difference between 65°F and the mean or average temperature is determined. The sum of these differences is called the degree-days for that area.

Dewpoint: when the air becomes saturated with vapor and is on the verge of the moisture condensing into water, this is known as 100% relative humidity.

Emittance: the ability of a material to give off heat as radiant energy.

Vapor pressure: pressure created by water vapor in a given space.

First law of thermodynamics: constant relation between the amount of heat gained and the amount of energy lost.

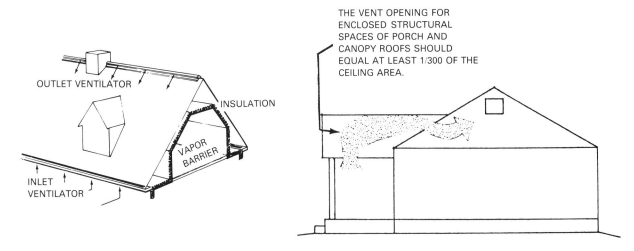

Figure 14-10   Ventilation. (Courtesy of U.S. Department of Agriculture.)

Moisture Vapor

Air contains moisture in the form of vapor which is absorbed by most building materials. All building materials are studied to consider the behavior of moisture, especially from a vapor to a liquid. Condensation will occur in buildings in any climate where there is a source of vapor, especially in cold climates (see Fig. 14-11), where houses are built smaller and tighter.

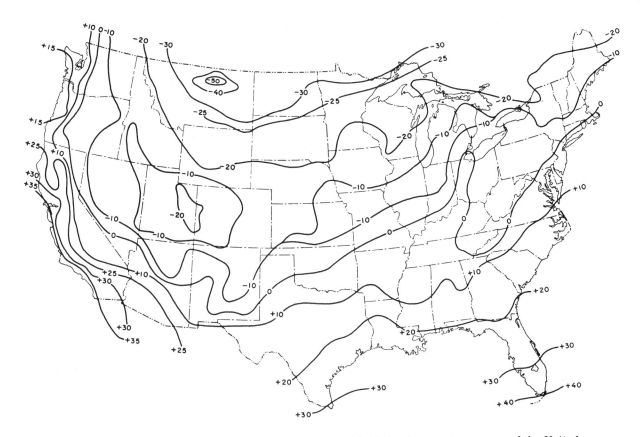

Figure 14-11   Average outside design temperature zones of the United States. (Courtesy of U.S. Department of Agriculture.)

Houses must be built to allow this vapor moisture to escape. This moisture is created in the house from cooking, laundering, bathing, breathing, perspiration, humidifiers, automatic washers and dryers, and the bare earth in a crawl space or around basement walls. Moisture vapor will move through the air within the house or will be absorbed by building materials inside the house. This moisture vapor will move to the outside walls of the house because the warm air within the house is drawn to the outside colder air through the outside walls.

The air within a building must be treated through heating or cooling to make the living area more comfortable and healthful. In addition, fuel consumption and costs are important. The two factors that must be considered to bring about this comfort are the temperature and humidity of the air within the building. In cold winter climates the problem is to provide heat and comfortable humidity, and in the summer, the problem is to cool the air. This is done in part by the proper use of insulation in the walls, floors, ceilings, and/or roof.

Air infiltration is reduced by following good construction practices, which reduce or eliminate cracks and other openings through walls, around cornices, above sills, through roof construction, and around cracks of doors and windows. This is accomplished by sealing these openings with caulking and insulation.

The most comfortable temperature is between 70 and 75°F, with a relative humidity of 35 to 40%. Still air is the best insulation available. Air is almost always moving and is seldom still. The slightest change in air temperature will move the air and make it expand or contract. The warmer the air becomes, the lighter it is and it will float above the cooler air, which is heavier air. The objective is to reduce air movement as much as possible and to keep still air still.

Insulation is a lightweight material such as expanded polystyrene or urea-formaldehyde foam or glass wool that prevents the passage of heat through a building by conduction. These materials are successful because of their very low thermal conductivity or their ability to stop heat from passing through. They all contain pockets of trapped still air or gas, and that is why air is a good insulator.

Because these materials are porous and filled with still air, they are light but have no strength. Insulation works best where applied on the outside of a building because the material used for building the wall is kept close to the temperature inside the building. This will also prevent condensation within the walls. If insulation is placed outside the building wall, it has to be protected, and this adds to the cost of the building. The next-best location for the placement of insulation is inside the wall.

Condensation can happen in all heated buildings when the outside air temperature is near or at the freezing point. A good example of this is the ice that forms on windows in cold weather. If controlled, condensation is not damaging or harmful. If the droplets of water formed when the outside temperature drops are reevaporated during the day, they will not cause any damage. If the water droplets remain in liquid form, they can cause severe damage to the building material by causing rot and deterioration, such as corrosion in metals, peeling of paint, and dry rot in wood.

Condensation is controlled by the installation of a vapor barrier and must be placed on the warm side of the building so that the air will retain its low relative humidity until it hits the barrier. This means that the water vapor is trapped inside the building. If it were allowed to pass through the wall, it will cause condensation instead of preventing it.

Vapor barriers can be made from polyethylene film, plastic, aluminum foil, asphalt-saturated paper, or a combination of these materials. The vapor barrier must be carefully installed, with no voids or breaks, and all seams must be sealed because if there are any breaks, the vapor will go through and escape, causing damage to the building. Some insulating materials have a built-in vapor barrier.

QUESTIONS

1. Cold air is attracted to warm air.   True or False
2. Name three ways in which heat can be transferred.
     1. _____
     2. _____
     3. _____
3. Btu is a measurement of the bottom and top units.   True or False
4. Match the following:
   R   measure of heat flow
   U   heat loss in time
   K   resistance to heat flow
5. Name five types of insulation.
     1. _____
     2. _____
     3. _____
     4. _____
     5. _____
6. Any type of insulation can be applied in any area.   True or False
7. Condensation is the total amount of heat condensed into one unit.
        True or False
8. Vapor barriers are used to control which of the following?
   A. Heat
   B. Cooling
   C. Moisture
   D. Cost
9. What will be the effect of areas that do not have ventilation? _____
_____
10. What areas should be ventilated? _____
_____

15

Doors and Windows

INTRODUCTION

Windows are used primarily for light and ventilation. Doors are used for allowing or preventing entry from one area to another. A selection of door and window size must be made before framing any wall. This is to allow proper fit of the unit in place within the wall. The space between the stud opening for the unit is called the rough opening. The rough opening is larger than the window and door size, to allow for proper fitting, leveling, and squaring the unit. The size of the rough opening is recommended by the manufacturer. The same principle applies for doors and windows in masonry walls.

Window types include double hung, casement, sliding, fixed, awning, bay, and bow, all of which are manufactured from wood, aluminum, vinyl, steel, or bronze.

Window sizes are standard for most manufacturers and vary from $1'-0''$ to $3'-9''$ wide for single units and $3'-0''$ to $6'-5''$ high for a single unit. Door types include hinged, sliding, bifold, overhead, and folding. Doors are manufactured from steel, wood, aluminum, and composition paneling. Two types or styles of doors are available, flush or panel.

Once the size of the opening is prepared, the installation of the units must be square, level, plumb, and secured. All nailing is to the sides and top of the units, into the studs. No nails are driven into the window or door sill; otherwise, a water leak is caused, with serious damage to the units.

Door and window parts are labeled for proper identification. The part of the window that is nailed to the wall is called the frame. The part of the window that operates or moves within the frame is called the sash. The part that the door fits into in the wall is called a frame. The upper or top part of the door or window frame is called the head. The bottom part is called the sill, and the side is called the jamb.

The location and use of the door determine the style and size of the door. Many types of doors and as many ways of installation in the wall are available. In addition, there are as many different wall conditions as there are methods of installation. To prepare the wall for the door, the door size must be known before framing begins.

Generally, doors and frames are considered inside trim or finish, and are one of the last items to be installed. The units are manufactured at the factory or mill and are ready for installation upon delivery to the job.

Windows provide shelter and admit light. There is a wide selection of window sizes and styles. Much like doors, the size and style of windows must be selected before the wall framing is started. The units are built in the shop or factory or mill and are ready for installation when delivered on the job.

The installation is usually done when the roof has been completed and before the exterior wall is finished. The windows must be installed before the exterior finish is installed. In addition, installation of the windows allows workers some degree of comfort and protection against the elements while working inside.

DOORS

There are two areas for doors, interior and exterior. Doors are factory-built, ready for installation.

Door sizes begin at 12 in. wide to a maximum of $3'-0''$ wide in multiples of 2 in. Door heights are $6'-6''$, $6'-8''$, and $7'-0''$, except for overhead doors. Exterior door thickness is $1\frac{3}{4}$ in. and interior door thickness is $1\frac{3}{8}$ in. Doors are built in a number of designs to fit all styles of houses. The traditional style is the panel type (Fig. 15-1a). Each part of this door has a name: stiles, which are the solid vertical member; rails, which are the solid horizontal or cross-member; and in between the stiles and rails are the panels. There is a variety of panels to choose from, including glass. Doors without panels are called flush doors (Fig. 15-1b).

Two types of doors are manufactured: solid core and hollow core (Fig. 15-2). The solid-core door, which is a flush panel door, has solid wood throughout the door's thickness. Several narrow strips of wood or particleboard are glued together, making one solid mass of wood of door size. Covering both sides is glued a thin layer of choice species wood called a veneer.

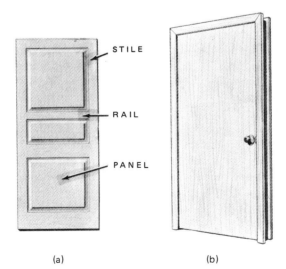

STILE

RAIL

PANEL

(a)   (b)

Figure 15-1 Doors: (a) panel; (b) flush. (Courtesy of Brockway Smith Company.)

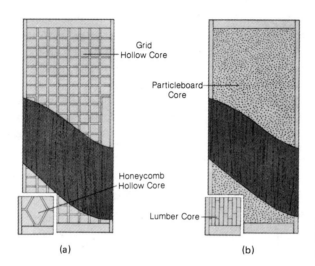

Grid
Hollow Core

Particleboard
Core

Honeycomb
Hollow Core

Lumber Core

(a)   (b)

Figure 15-2 Doors: (a) standard hollow core; (b) standard solid core. (Courtesy of Cal-Wood Door.)

A hollow-core door is also a flush panel door. This consists of a rectangular wood frame much like a picture frame, which is the door size, and to this frame is glued on both sides a thin wood veneer of selected wood. Between the veneers is a hollow space, yielding the name "hollow-core door." Sometimes the space between the veneers will have a corrugated heavy paper filler to make the door stronger, or a honeycomb is used. Exterior doors should be solid core to minimize warping, which is caused by a difference in moisture content on the two faces of the door.

Doors fit into or close into a frame (Fig. 15-3), which is about $\frac{1}{16}$ in.

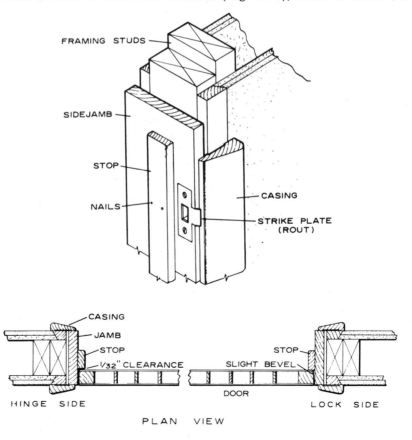

FRAMING STUDS

SIDEJAMB

STOP

NAILS

CASING

STRIKE PLATE
(ROUT)

CASING
JAMB
STOP
1/32" CLEARANCE

STOP
SLIGHT BEVEL

DOOR

HINGE SIDE   LOCK SIDE

PLAN VIEW

Figure 15-3 Door frame. (Courtesy of U.S. Department of Agriculture.)

larger than the door size. The frame, like the door, generally is factory built ready for assembly. Doors swing on butts, sometimes called hinges, which are screwed to the door and frame (Fig. 15-4). The depth or frame thickness varies according to the full finish dimension of the partition. Some door frames are adjustable to accommodate the partition thickness (Fig. 15-5).

Doors preinstalled in frames, including all hardware, are available, or doors and frames can be purchased separately and after fitting the door and frame, the hardware is installed. Doors and frames for residential use are also manufactured from metal with an insulation filler for heat loss and sound control.

Local building laws may insist on a fire door, which is a door with a fire rating in terms of time (Fig. 15-6). If the door label reads "1½-hour door," this means that if there is a fire in the building, the door will withstand burning for 1½ hours. Fire-rated doors can be had up to a 4-hour rating. Fire-rated doors are used to protect the building and the people in hazardous areas such as an attached garage. The wall between the house and the garage is considered a fire wall and the door in that wall must have a fire rating. If the door has a fire rating, so must the door frame.

The swing of the door is optional (Fig. 15-7) and must be considered carefully so as not to interfere with the function of the house.

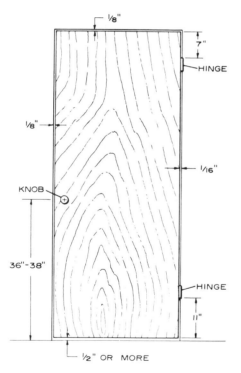

Figure 15-4 Door swing. (Courtesy of U.S. Department of Agriculture.)

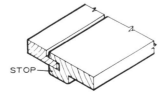

Figure 15-5 Adjustable door frame. (Courtesy of U.S. Department of Agriculture.)

Fire Doors

1 HOUR FIRE DOOR — ROTARY CUT NATURAL BIRCH

for Class "B" Openings

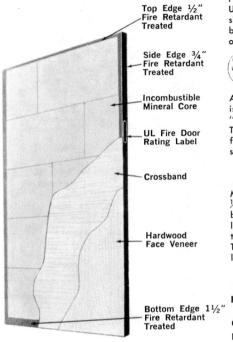

Top Edge ½"
Fire Retardant
Treated

Side Edge ¾"
Fire Retardant
Treated

Incombustible
Mineral Core

UL Fire Door
Rating Label

Crossband

Hardwood
Face Veneer

Bottom Edge 1½"
Fire Retardant
Treated

Fire Doors have been tested and rated by Underwriters' Laboratories, Inc. for fire resistance, heat transmission and structural stability . . . labeled for 1 hour Class "B" openings.

A metal label similar to the one illustrated is secured to the hinge edge of each Class "B" fire door and stipulates 1 hour rating. This metal label is located one-third down from the top edge of door on the hinge stile edge.

INSTALLATION

Maximum clearance for Fire Doors shall be $\frac{1}{16}$" at the sides and top . . . ¼" at the bottom. In fitting door to opening to establish proper width clearance and bevel, plane the lock stile edge only (opposite UL label). The installed door must always have the label on the hinge stile.

CONSTRUCTION FEATURES

Faces: Standard thickness rotary cut Birch veneers.

Core: Incombustible mineral sections.

Edge Banding: Fire retardant treated.

Figure 15-6   Fire door specifications. (Courtesy of Brockway Smith Company.)

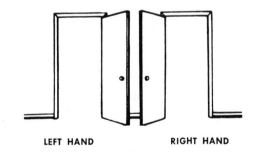

LEFT HAND   RIGHT HAND

Figure 15-7   Door swing. (Courtesy of Brockway Smith Company.)

When the door opens to you and the knob is on the left, it is a left-hand door. When the knob is on the right, it is a right-hand door.

Door Types

Door types are manufactured in a number of uses (Fig. 15-8).

Hinged: hangs on butts, sometimes known as hinges.

Folding: as the name implies. By design, some door openings are larger than single door widths, so two or more doors are required to fill the

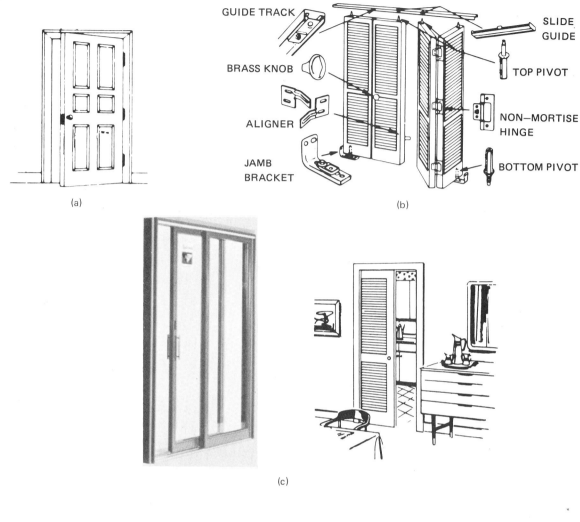

(a)

GUIDE TRACK

SLIDE GUIDE

BRASS KNOB

TOP PIVOT

ALIGNER

NON—MORTISE HINGE

JAMB BRACKET

BOTTOM PIVOT

(b)

(c)

(d)

(e)

Figure 15-8 Doors: (a) hinged; (b) bifold; (c) sliding; (d) overhead; (e) folding. [(a)–(c) Courtesy of Brockway Smith Company; (d) courtesy of Stanley Door Systems; (e) courtesy of Pella/Rolscreen Co.]

opening; commonly used for closets. Another name for folding doors is "bifold."

Sliding: most often, glass doors used on patios, but also used inside the house. This door slides into a wall or partition. Also known as pocket doors, sliding doors are often used in closets, with an overhead track for suspending the door.

Overhead: garage doors made up of several hinged sections.

Access: small door used to gain access to the attic or crawl space under the floor.

Bulkhead: separate exterior entrance to the basement.

Accordion: folds like an accordion; used where door swing might be a problem.

Pass: walk-through door in a larger door such as an overhead door.

Fire: has some fire protection; used in a common wall between a house and an attached garage.

Storm: outer door of wood or aluminum used together with the main door. Storm doors can also be screened. This type of door is also known as a combination door.

Bypass: similar to a sliding door; one part of the door slides or passes behind the other.

Door Frames

Doors of all types must fit into a frame. The frame can be of wood or metal, and the size of the door frame must match the size and thickness of the door. Like doors, frames have named parts (Fig. 15-9). The top of the door frame is called the head and the sides of the door frame are called the jamb.

The thickness of wood used to construct factory-built door frames varies from $1\frac{1}{8}$ to $1\frac{3}{4}$ in.

The width of door frames is determined by the finished wall or partition thickness. If a wall were built of 2 × 3 studs, the door frame would not be as thick as a wall built of 2 × 4 studs. The total wall thickness includes the studs and the wall finish on both sides of the studs.

Since doors fit into door frames, the installation of the door frame is critical for proper operation of the door. This means that the frame must be

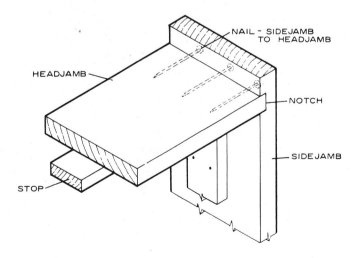

Figure 15-9 Door frame parts. (Courtesy of U.S. Department of Agriculture.)

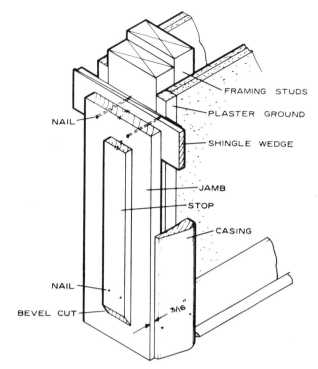

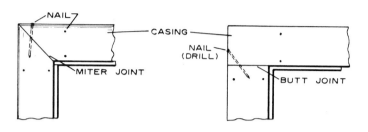

Figure 15-10   Door frame installation. (Courtesy of U.S. Department of Agriculture.)

perfectly plumb, level, and straight. If not, the door will not fit properly in the frame and may stick, bind, or warp. Door frames are nailed into the wall studs. Around the door frame on both sides of the wall is nailed a molding called a casing (Fig. 15-10). Some door frames are adjustable in width to accommodate different partition thicknesses (Fig. 15-11).

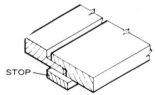

Figure 15-11   Adjustable door framing. (Courtesy of U.S. Department of Agriculture.)

The groove or recess in the door frame where the door fits when closed is called a rabbet. This rabbet acts as a stop on the door. Some frames have a rabbet on both sides, making it a double-rabbet frame. Storm doors require a double-rabbet frame.

A threshold is considered a part of a door frame and is located at the bottom of the frame or floor level. They can be of wood or nonrusting metal and are used to seal the air space under the door. They are sometimes called sills (Fig. 15-12).

Door frames can also be installed in concrete brick and block walls, called masonry (Fig. 15-13). The frame width need not relate to the wall thickness as long as the door frame is not wider than the wall thickness. A knocked-down (K.D.) frame has to be assembled on the job. Doors and frames must be handled carefully to prevent damage or denting.

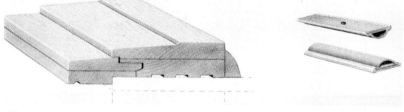

Figure 15-12   Door threshold. (Courtesy of Brockway Smith Company.)

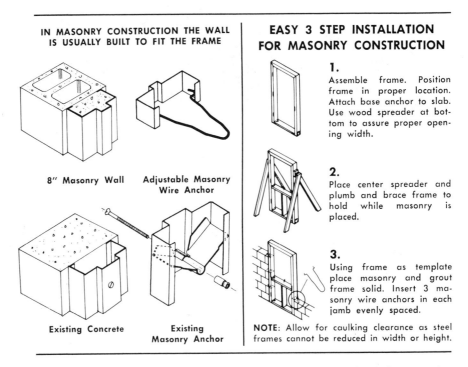

IN MASONRY CONSTRUCTION THE WALL
IS USUALLY BUILT TO FIT THE FRAME

8" Masonry Wall   Adjustable Masonry
                    Wire Anchor

Existing Concrete   Existing
                    Masonry Anchor

EASY 3 STEP INSTALLATION
FOR MASONRY CONSTRUCTION

1.
Assemble frame. Position frame in proper location. Attach base anchor to slab. Use wood spreader at bottom to assure proper opening width.

2.
Place center spreader and plumb and brace frame to hold while masonry is placed.

3.
Using frame as template place masonry and grout frame solid. Insert 3 masonry wire anchors in each jamb evenly spaced.

NOTE: Allow for caulking clearance as steel frames cannot be reduced in width or height.

Figure 15-13 Masonry construction. (Courtesy of Brockway Smith Company.)

WINDOWS

All windows are factory made in a variety of styles, materials, and sizes. Windows are generally made from wood, steel, aluminum, or vinyl. Wood windows can also be purchased covered with vinyl or aluminum. The advantage of such a covering is that the window does not have to be painted.

Regardless of size or style, all windows have parts that are common to all (see Fig. 15-14 for some of these):

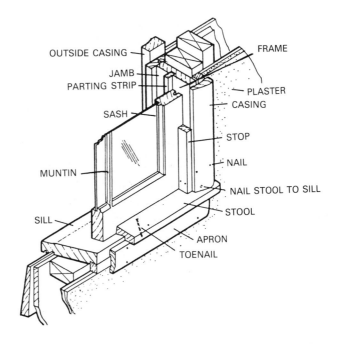

OUTSIDE CASING
JAMB
PARTING STRIP
SASH
MUNTIN
SILL
FRAME
PLASTER
CASING
STOP
NAIL
NAIL STOOL TO SILL
STOOL
APRON
TOENAIL

Figure 15-14 Window parts. (Courtesy of U.S. Department of Agriculture.)

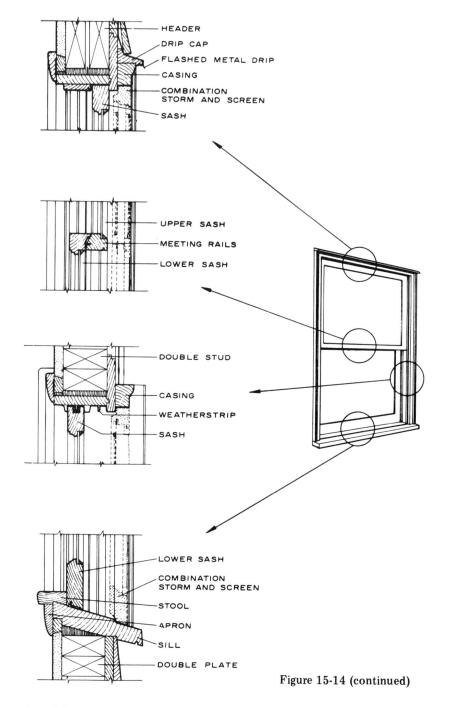

Figure 15-14 (continued)

Head: horizontal top of the window

Sill: outside horizontal bottom

Stool: inside horizontal bottom

Jamb: vertical side

Mullion: two windows assembled together as one unit

Muntin: wood or metal between the panes of glass; the spacing of the muntins will determine the size of glass

Sash: operating part of the window or the movable part

Frame: holds the sash in position

Rough opening (R.O.): stud opening dimension in the wall to receive the window

Window Types

There are three main types of windows: sliding, swinging, and fixed. Each has a specific design or means of operating (Fig. 15-15).

Double hung: vertical sliding window consisting of two sashes that slide up and down in separate channels, one behind the other. They are held in place by mechanical devices that cause a friction fit against the frame. In the same category of window is the single-hung window, which differs from the double-hung window only in that the lower sash unit operates while the upper sash unit is fixed. The appearance of the two is the same. Single-hung or double-hung windows all provide only 50% ventilation.

Sliding: two or more units sliding past each other horizontally in a common frame.

Casement: sash swings out like a door. They can be single units or several units grouped together as one. They are operated by a crank handle or a push bar. Locking is done by a latch. This type of window permits 100% opening, for ventilation. Nonoperating or fixed units are sometimes combined with operating units. This type of unit is recommended for hard-to-reach places such as over kitchen cabinets, because the crank makes it easy to operate. The swing of the window can be left or right.

Awning: swing outward or inward and are hinged top or bottom. They can be stacked or installed in rows by adding several units together as one unit. Another name for this type of window is "hopper."

Fixed: do not operate or open but are stationary. They consist of large sheets of glass installed in a frame. The term "picture window" usually means "fixed window." This window is used mostly for letting in light and for a view to the outside. Another category of fixed windows is the glass block window.

Jalousy: series of horizontal glass slots much like venetian blinds held together in a frame. The glass slats are adjustable and work simultaneously by turning a crank. This type of window is recommended only for porches and breezeways because they have little weather-tightness and should not be used in cold climates. When the glass slats are closed, each slat overlaps the one below it slightly.

Bow: gracefully curved outward, made up of casement, double-hung, or awning-type windows grouped together as one unit. Any number of units can be operating or fixed. Bow windows may require a separate roof. The windows making up the bow window are not curved; they are conventional windows installed together on a tangent to look like a continuous curve.

Bay: similar to a bow window except that it is not a curve, but a series of windows assembled at an angle, usually 30 or 45°. Each unit has three sides and any size or style of window can be selected to make up the unit.

Skylight: roof-installed window, operating or fixed. Used primarily for light and/or ventilation for an inside room without exterior walls. Recommended use is in hallways, attics, and bathrooms. They are available in a variety of sizes and in square, rectangular, or circular shapes.

Storm windows: installed over main windows to add another pane of glass, thus reducing heat loss. These are called "combination windows"

Figure 15-15 Window types: (a) bay; (b) sliding; (c) bow; (d) jalousie (clearview); (e) double hung; (f) special; (g) casement; (h) skylight; (i) awning. [(a), (c), (e), (f), (g), (i) Courtesy of Brockway Smith Company; (b) courtesy of Caradco Corp.; (d) courtesy of Clearview Corp.; (h) courtesy of Dur-Red Products.]

when they also contain screens. These units are made of wood, aluminum, or vinyl and can be hinged or fixed to the main window unit. They operate in the same way as a double-hung sash. Some units require that the screens and sash be removed with the seasons, and some units have triple tracks, permitting lowering or raising the screen or sash according to the season.

Special windows: made for application in gable ends, garages, hallways, and stairwells. They are usually fixed, provide light, and are octagonal or half-round in shape.

FLASHING

To avoid leaks, all windows and doors must be sealed with flashing (Fig. 15-16). Flashing can be a nonrusting thin-gauge metal such as aluminum, lead, or copper. A heavy, reinforced tarred or waterproof paper or plastic can also be used as flashing.

The problem areas for leakage are the top or head, and the bottom or sill. Water running down the exterior of the building will leak between the sheathing and the door or window frame top. Wind-driven rain will cause leakage at the window or door sill. Sealing the areas with flashing will avoid leakage. Flashing on top of doors and windows is called cap flashing.

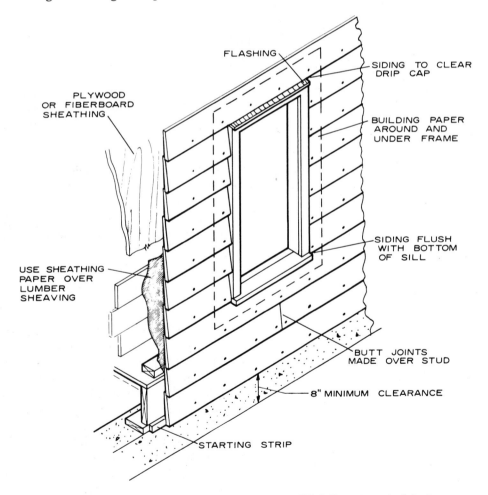

Figure 15-16 Window flashing. (Courtesy of U.S. Department of Agriculture.)

The best flashing material affordable is recommended because it is very expensive and time consuming to replace door and window flashing. The finish siding must be removed on the top or bottom of the door and window to replace flashing. Sometimes these spaces are sealed with caulking, which is only a temporary protection because sun, wind, and time will break down the caulking, causing leaks. The flashing must be installed after the door and window are in place and before the exterior siding is installed.

Flashing is attached with nails, being careful where the nails are placed. If a nail is applied to the exposed part of the flashing, leakage will occur at the nail hole, defeating the purpose of the flashing.

If the flashing is metal, nails of the same material should be used to secure the flashing; otherwise, a reaction called galvanic action will occur between the two different metals, causing corrosion to the weaker metal. The ranking of metals, called the electromotive series, is as follows, with aluminum the metal affected to the greatest degree:

1. Aluminum
2. Zinc
3. Steel
4. Tin
5. Lead
6. Brass
7. Copper
8. Bronze

Heavy, reinforced tarred or waterproof paper or plastic used as flashing is not subject to galvanic action. A typical example of galvanic corrosion is that of steel nails applied to aluminum flashing. Aluminum is more subject than steel to galvanic corrosion, and the aluminum will corrode at the spots where the steel nails have been driven. Aluminum nails should be used to apply aluminum flashing, to prevent metal breakdown through galvanic action.

The minimum thickness of aluminum flashing should be 0.019 in. Copper flashing should be 0.020 in. thick. The sides of doors and windows are flashed by installing 12.-in-wide strips of felt paper or tarred paper down the full length of the door or window frame, between the frame back and the sheathing.

GLAZING

Traditionally, glass has performed three important services: it provides light, keeps out the elements, and controls a building's climate.

Glass and windows are synonymous, and glass is a major source of heat loss within a building. The heat loss can be greatly reduced by doubling the glass within the window (Fig. 15-17). This is called insulating glass. The two panes of glass are separated by an air space or a blanket of dry air, which makes it difficult for heated or cooled air to bridge the space between the glass. Insulating glass, which is also available in triple glazing, will reduce the heating and cooling cost of the building, reduce condensation, and afford more comfort.

Glass is available in a variety of designs and colors. For a bathroom window at ground level, frosted glass can be used, which will admit light but prevent seeing through the glass. In fire-rated doors, wire is incorporated in

Figure 15-17 Insulating glass. (Courtesy of Brockway Smith Company.)

the glass to prevent the glass from shattering when broken. Tempered glass is also used for this purpose. Tempered glass has had a special heat treatment which increases its strength. Tempered glass is also used to control sound, such as in airport buildings.

Glass is available not only in different designs and colors but also in different thicknesses, from $\frac{3}{32}$ to 2 in. thick. Bullet-proof glass is 2 in. thick and is used for bank drive-up windows and other places that require security. This glass consists of several thicknesses of glass laminated together.

One-way vision glass is designed for see-through on one side only, with mirror-like reflection on the other side. Solar glass is used to absorb the sun and is used on solar panels or greenhouse-type construction.

Glass is held in place by glazing compound, which resembles putty. Glazing compound stays soft and pliable, to compensate for expansion and contraction. There is a high percentage of insulating glass failure because of poor or faulty glazing materials or techniques. A precaution to avoid failure is to have the sash or frame of proper design and strength to support the weight of the glass. Glass edges must never come in contact with the sash and framing members. The sealing of glass or the glazing used must be designed to prevent moisture from accumulating in the glazing groove or rabbet.

If glass is used on a slope of $15°$ or more, such as in a greenhouse or solar room, tempered glass should be used outside because the weight of snow and wind may break the glass. Heat-strengthened laminated glass should be used inside.

Plastic glass is also manufactured and used for safety, such as in skylights, domes, solar panels, and lighting fixtures. This is glass made from cast acrylic sheeting, which is light in weight and offers good see-through. This type of glass is also used for tub and shower enclosures. It will not shatter when broken.

The thickness of glass or plastic used is determined by the size of the pane of glass. Glass can be manufactured with a curve and can be cut to any shape, including a radius. Normally, doors and windows are preglazed at the factory. When ordering, it must be stated whether single, double, or triple glazing is desired.

Tinted glass is used to control the sun's ray. Translucent glass allows light to pass but it cannot be seen through. Environmental tinted glasses were first developed in the 1950s; more recently, reflective glass has been widely used in residential construction. Tinted glass radiates more glare, ultraviolet transmittance, and solar heat than does clear glass. Bronze-tinted, gray-tinted, and aquamarine-tinted glass are heat absorbing.

Compared to clear glass, bronze-tinted glass reduces light by about two-thirds. This has an advantage where glare is magnified by reflection from snow or water. It will also prevent fabrics from fading.

Insulating glass is made up of two pieces of $\frac{1}{8}$-, $\frac{3}{16}$-, or $\frac{1}{4}$-in. annealed or tempered glass separated by a space around the edges and hermetically sealed. The trapped air inside the two pieces of glass is at atmospheric pressure and is kept that way by a drying agent located in the spacer. The air space between the two pieces of glass is from $\frac{1}{4}$ to $\frac{1}{2}$ in.

STORM SASHES AND SCREENING

Manufacturers of windows and doors also make storm sash and storm doors to fit the units. Storm units fit into or against door and window frames and are made of wood, aluminum, or vinyl.

The screens for storm units are applied on the outside of double-hung and sliding windows. Other types of windows have the screen inside. Storm units work well with single-thickness windows to reduce the heat loss within the building.

INSTALLATION

Be sure that doors and windows will fit the rough stud opening. Check the dimension of the windows to be sure that they are the size ordered. Most wood units are factory primed with paint to protect the wood. If they are not, they should be prime-painted with good-quality paint.

Units must be handled very carefully and must be square. Rough openings are about 1 in. larger than the frame dimension, to allow for adjustment to make it plumb, level, and square during installation. Frames are shipped with diagonal, temporary braces for protection and to keep the units square. These temporary diagonal braces are not to be removed until the frames are properly secured in the stud opening provided. Door and window frames are nailed through the jambs, and under no circumstances should nails be driven through the window or door sill because they will leak through the nail hole.

Rough Openings

Door and window sizes must be preplanned before the studs are installed in the walls. This size selection will determine what the openings in the walls must be. The window and door manufacturer will recommend the rough opening to prepare, based on the door and window size. Generally, these rough openings (Fig. 15-18) are about 1 in. larger than the unit size of door and window frames. The opening top or head must have a header to support the loads above the doors or windows. The header is a beam.

The sill and jambs are double studded for wall strength. If 2 × 6 exterior wall studs are used instead of 2 × 4's, it will make a difference on the depth of the door and window frames. The sheathing must be applied before door and window frames can be installed.

Weather Stripping

To avoid air leakage around door and window frames, the space must be sealed. This is accomplished with weather stripping. Windows are shipped pre-weather stripped at the factory and generally no other attention is re-

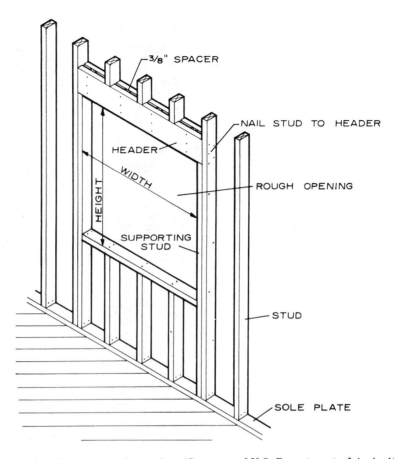

Figure 15-18 Window rough opening. (Courtesy of U.S. Department of Agriculture.)

quired. The factory weather stripping is adjustable to allow for settling or movement of door and window frames as the building moves. This adjustment allows for refitting to make the doors and windows tight. Weather stripping also helps to control noise, light, and dust.

Exterior metal doors are factory-weather stripped with a compression seal. Wood doors generally are not pre-weather stripped and must be weather stripped at the job. This can be accomplished in many ways (Fig. 15-19). The most simple and least effective is to apply a felt strip which sticks to the inside of the door frame; the felt is compressed when the door is closed. Time and use will dry out and wear down the felt strip, making it ineffective. Plastic stripping, much like the felt, is also available. The most positive wood door weather stripping is the aluminum interlocking type, which is a two-piece unit. One section is applied to the frame; the other section is applied

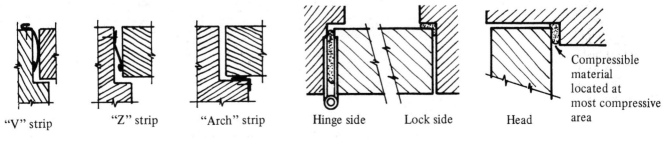

Figure 15-19 Weather stripping.

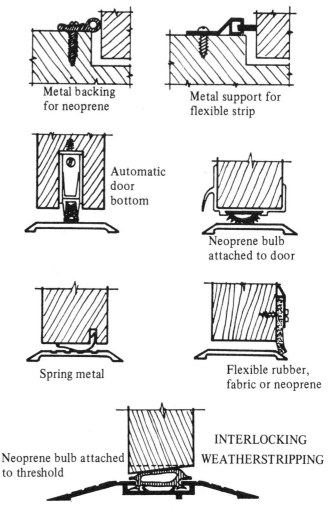

Figure 15-19 (continued)

to the door. The two pieces interlock when the door closes, causing a positive seal around the perimeter of the door and the frame. The sill has a metal threshold on the frame which interlocks with the door bottom weather stripping.

QUESTIONS

1. What is the dimension unit width of doors? _____

   _____

2. The stile of the door is which of the following?
   A. Design
   B. Type
   C. Panel
   D. None of the above

3. Define *hollow-core door*. _____

   _____

4. A fire door is a door that catches fire easily.   True or False

5. Define *pass door*. _____

_____

6. Name five types of windows.
   1. _____
   2. _____
   3. _____
   4. _____
   5. _____

7. A muntin is used to separate doors from frames.   True or False

8. What is the difference between a bay window and a bow window?

_____

9. Flashing is used to brighten up door design.   True or False

10. What is galvanic action? _____

_____

11. Glazing is the finish on doors and windows.   True or False

12. What is tempered glass? _____

_____

13. A rough opening is which of the following?
    A. Width of window
    B. Size of room
    C. Door size
    D. Stud opening

14. Why is weather stripping used? _____

_____

15. Define *interlocking weather stripping*. _____

_____

16

Exterior Wall Covering and Roof Trim

INTRODUCTION

Upon completion of the structural wall and roof framing system, the sheathing applied to the wall and the roof not only braces and reinforces the framing system, but acts as a surface on which to apply the exterior wall covering and the roof trim. The exterior wall covering acts as a skin for the framework and is designed for protection against the elements; it is also used for aesthetic reasons. If the exterior wall covering were removed from a building, the building would remain standing, indicating that the exterior wall covering has no structural value.

The selection of material for exterior wall coverings is determined by geographic location, availability of material, aesthetics, and budget. The range is from an almost no-maintenance material, to a periodic-maintenance material, to a constant-maintenance material. Personal preference by the contractor or homeowner also plays an important part in the selection of the exterior wall covering material. The cost of the material and the cost of labor in applying the material must also be considered.

The most lasting, lowest-maintenance materials are brick, concrete block, stucco, and stone. Wood products, such as plywood, shingles, and clapboards, require periodic maintenance. Aluminum or vinyl require little maintenance; man-made panel materials require more maintenance or frequent maintenance.

Since all exterior wall covering is designed in part to keep the interior dry, the skill of the tradesperson in applying the material is very important in keeping out the elements. If the building leaks through from the outside, serious damage can occur on the inside.

WOOD MATERIALS

Exterior finishes for walls in the wood family include (1) shingles/shakes, (2) clapboards, (3) vertical or horizontal siding, and (4) plywood.

There are three species of wood that are more resistant to weather and wood-boring insects than other species. These are redwood, cedar, and cyprus. That is why wood exterior wall covering is often manufactured from one of these three species. Exterior wood siding is measured in "squares"; one square equals an area 10 ft by 10 ft, or 100 ft^2.

Shingles and shakes are manufactured from red or white cedar, cyprus, and redwood. Clapboards are manufactured from redwood, vertical or horizontal siding is manufactured from cyprus, and plywood face could be made from any one of the three wood species.

Shingles/Shakes

Exterior shakes and shingles (Fig. 16-1) are manufactured from red or white cedar. The only difference between red and white cedar shingles is in the color. Shingles are sawed in wedge shape, and shakes are hand split. The thick part of the shingle is called the butt. Shingle width varies from 3 to 14 in. and shingle length varies from 16 to 32 in. The length used is determined by the exposure of the shingle, called "to the weather." The greater the exposure, the longer the shingle. The exposure is between 5 and 8 in. but not more than one-half the shingle length to be exposed. Shingles are applied over sheathing paper. All nails used to apply wood shingles are rustproof or galvanized, and they are concealed. The nails are concealed because each course covers the preceding course of shingles, or is slightly above the butt line of the course that follows. In applying shingles, a space of about ⅛ in. should be left between shingles, to allow for expansion. If shingles are applied without the space, expansion will cause them to buckle, because

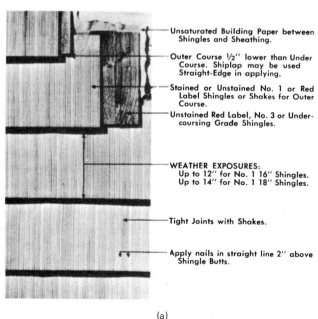

Unsaturated Building Paper between Shingles and Sheathing.

Outer Course ½" lower than Under Course. Shiplap may be used Straight-Edge in applying.

Stained or Unstained No. 1 or Red Label Shingles or Shakes for Outer Course.

Unstained Red Label, No. 3 or Undercoursing Grade Shingles.

WEATHER EXPOSURES:
Up to 12" for No. 1 16" Shingles.
Up to 14" for No. 1 18" Shingles.

Tight Joints with Shakes.

Apply nails in straight line 2" above Shingle Butts.

(a)

Figure 16-1   (a) Wood shakes.

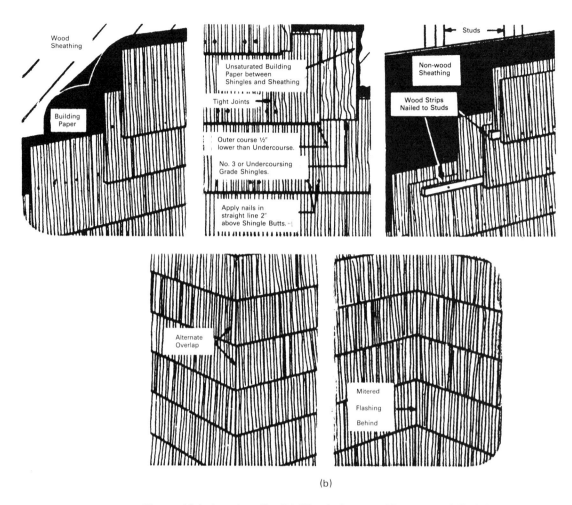

(b)

Figure 16-1 (continued) (b) Wood shingles. (Courtesy of Red Cedar Shingle and Handsplit Shake Bureau.)

they have no room to move or expand. It is not necessary to paint or stain cedar shingles because cedar requires no protection. Its natural color will change with time.

Shingles and shakes are well equipped by nature to endure without a protective finish or stain. In this natural condition, the wood will eventually weather to silver or dark gray. The speed of change and final shade will depend primarily on atmospheric and climatic conditions.

There are several ways of treating corners. Interior corners can be finished by nailing a $1\frac{1}{8} \times 1\frac{1}{8}$ finish wood strip from the first shingle course to the last shingle course. Each shingle, which has a $\frac{1}{2}$-in.-thick butt, is nailed against the finish piece (Fig. 16-2a). An alternative way of finishing the interior corner is to alternate the shingle courses to avoid a straight-line joint. This is called weaving the shingle (Fig. 16-2b).

A third way is to use a rustproof preformed metal corner from the first course to the last course (Fig. 16-2c). Exterior corners can be finished by a preformed rustproof metal, much like the interior corner (Fig. 16-2d) or by nailing a 1×4 finished wood piece on each corner and butting the shingles against this wood. This is called a corner board. This board reaches from the first shingle course to the last shingle course (Fig. 16-2e).

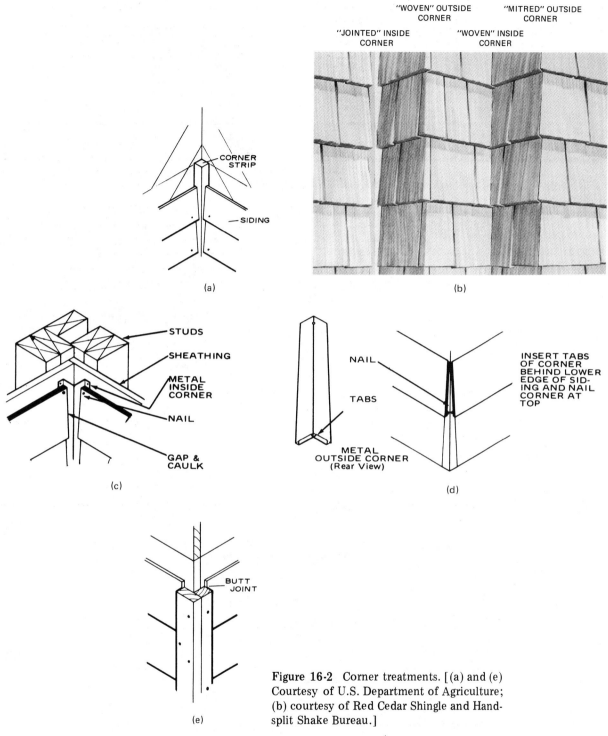

Figure 16-2 Corner treatments. [(a) and (e) Courtesy of U.S. Department of Agriculture; (b) courtesy of Red Cedar Shingle and Hand-split Shake Bureau.]

There are four grades of cedar shingles: grades 1, 2, 3, and 4. All come in lengths of 16, 18, and 24 in. (Fig. 16-3).

The most expensive and best are No. 1 shingles, which are manufactured from the heartwood of the tree and are clear of all knots and defects. No. 2 shingles are of poorer quality than No. 1, but better than No. 3. They are used for good-quality, but not top-quality, jobs. No. 3 shingles are allowed defects above the exposure part of the shingle. They are used for

GRADE	Length	Thickness (at Butt)	No. of Courses Per Bundle	Bdls/Cartons Per Square		Description
No. 1 BLUE LABEL	16″ (Fivex) 18″ (Perfections) 24″ (Royals)	.40″ .45″ .50″	20/20 18/18 13/14	4 bdls. 4 bdls. 4 bdls.		The premium grade of shingles for roofs and sidewalls. These top-grade shingles are 100% heartwood . . . 100% clear and 100% edge-grain.
No. 2 RED LABEL	16″ (Fivex) 18″ (Perfections) 24″ (Royals)	.40″ .45″ .50″	20/20 18/18 13/14	4 bdls. 4 bdls. 4 bdls.		A proper grade for some applications. Not less than 10″ clear on 16″ shingles, 11″ clear on 18″ shingles and 16″ clear on 24″ shingles. Flat grain and limited sapwood are permitted in this grade.
No. 3 BLACK LABEL	16″ (Fivex) 18″ (Perfections) 24″ (Royals)	.40″ .45″ .50″	20/20 18/18 13/14	4 bdls. 4 bdls. 4 bdls.		A utility grade for economy applications and secondary buildings. Not less than 6″ clear on 16″ and 18″ shingles, 10″ clear on 24″ shingles.
No. 4 UNDER-COURSING	16″ (Fivex) 18″ (Perfections)	.40″ .45″	14/14 or 20/20 14/14 or 18/18	2 bdls. 2 bdls. 2 bdls. 2 bdls.		A utility grade for undercoursing on double-coursed sidewall applications or for interior accent walls.
No. 1 or No. 2 REBUTTED-REJOINTED	16″ (Fivex) 18″ (Perfections) 24″ (Royals)	.40″ .45″ .50″	33/33 28/28 13/14	1 carton 1 carton 4 bdls.		Same specifications as above for No. 1 and No. 2 grades but machine trimmed for exactly parallel edges with butts sawn at precise right angles. For sidewall application where tightly fitting joints are desired. Also available with smooth sanded face.

		Maximum exposure recommended for roofs:								
PITCH		NO. 1 BLUE LABEL			NO. 2 RED LABEL			NO. 3 BLACK LABEL		
		16″	18″	24″	16″	18″	24″	16″	18″	24″
3 IN 12 TO 4 IN 12		3¾″	4¼″	5¾″	3½″	4″	5½″	3″	3½″	5″
4 IN 12 AND STEEPER		5″	5½″	7½″	4″	4½″	6½″	3½″	4″	5½″

LENGTH AND THICKNESS	Approximate coverage of one square (4 bundles) of shingles based on following weather exposures																									
	3½″	4″	4½″	5″	5½″	6″	6½″	7″	7½″	8″	8½″	9″	9½″	10″	10½″	11″	11½″	12″	12½″	13″	13½″	14″	14½″	15″	15½″	16″
16″ x 5/2″	70	80	90	100*	110	120	130	140	150‡	160	170	180	190	200	210	220	230	240†	....	....	....	....	....	....	....	....
18″ x 5/2¼″	....	72½	81½	90½	100*	109	118	127	136	145½	154½	163½	172½	181½	191	200	209	218	227	236	245½	254½	....	....	....	....
24″ x 4/2″	....	....	....	....	....	80	86½	93	100‡	106½	113	120	126½	133	140	146½	153	160	166½	173	180	186½	193	200	206½	213†

NOTES: *Maximum exposure recommended for roofs.   ‡Maximum exposure recommended for single-coursing No. 1 grades on sidewalls. Reduce exposure for No. 2 grades.
†Maximum exposure recommended for double-coursing No. 1 grades on sidewalls.

(a)

GRADE	Length and Thickness	18″ Pack**			Description
		# Courses Per Bdl.	# Bdls. Per Sq.		
No. 1 HANDSPLIT & RESAWN	15″ Starter-Finish 18″ x ½″ Mediums 18″ x ¾″ Heavies 24″ x ⅜″ 24″ x ½″ Mediums 24″ x ¾″ Heavies	9/9 9/9 9/9 9/9 9/9 9/9	5 5 5 5 5 5		These shakes have split faces and sawn backs. Cedar logs are first cut into desired lengths. Blanks or boards of proper thickness are split and then run diagonally through a bandsaw to produce two tapered shakes from each blank.
No. 1 TAPERSPLIT	24″ x ½″	9/9	5		Produced largely by hand, using a sharp-bladed steel froe and a wooden mallet. The natural shingle-like taper is achieved by reversing the block, end-for-end, with each split.
No. 1 STRAIGHT-SPLIT	18″ x ⅜″ True-Edge* 18″ x ⅜″ 24″ x ⅜″	**20″ Pack** 14 Straight 19 Straight 16 Straight	4 5 5		Produced in the same manner as tapersplit shakes except that by splitting from the same end of the block, the shakes acquire the same thickness throughout.

NOTE: * Exclusively sidewall product, with parallel edges.
** Pack used for majority of shakes.

SHAKE TYPE, LENGTH AND THICKNESS	Approximate coverage (in sq. ft.) of one square, when shakes are applied with ½″ spacing, at following weather exposures, in inches (h):						
	5½	7½	8½	10	11½	16	
18″ x ½″ Handsplit-and-Resawn Mediums (a)	55(b)	75(c)	85(d)	100	. . . .	. . . .	
18″ x ¾″ Handsplit-and-Resawn Heavies (a)	55(b)	75(c)	85(d)	100	. . . .	. . . .	
24″ x ⅜″ Handsplit	. . . .	75(e)	85	100(f)	115(d)	. . . .	
24″ x ½″ Handsplit-and-Resawn Mediums	. . . .	75(b)	85	100(c)	115(d)	. . . .	
24″ x ¾″ Handsplit-and-Resawn Heavies	. . . .	75(b)	85	100(c)	115(d)	. . . .	
24″ x ½″ Tapersplit	. . . .	75(b)	85	100(c)	115(d)	. . . .	
18″ x ⅜″ True-Edge Straight-Split	. . . .	. . . .	. . . .	. . . .	. . . .	112(g)	
18″ x ⅜″ Straight-Split	65(b)	90(c)	100(d)	. . . .	. . . .	. . . .	
24″ x ⅜″ Straight-Split	. . . .	75(b)	85	100(c)	115(d)	. . . .	
15″ Starter-Finish Course	Use supplementary with shakes applied not over 10″ weather exposure.						

(a) 5 bundles will cover 100 sq. ft. roof area when used as starter-finish course at 10″ weather exposure; 6 bundles will cover 100 sq. ft. wall area at 8½″ exposure; 7 bundles will cover 100 sq. ft. roof area at 7½″ weather exposure; see footnote (h).

(b) Maximum recommended weather exposure for 3-ply roof construction.

(c) Maximum recommended weather exposure for 2-ply roof construction.

(d) Maximum recommended weather exposure for single-coursed wall construction.

(e) Maximum recommended weather exposure for application on roof pitches between 4-in-12 and 8-in-12.

(f) Maximum recommended weather exposure for application on roof pitches of 8-in-12 and steeper.

(g) Maximum recommended weather exposure for double-coursed wall construction.

(h) All coverage based on ½″ spacing between shakes.

(b)

Figure 16-3   Cedar-shingle grading: (a) Certigrade red cedar shingles; (b) Certi-split red cedar hand-split shingles. (Courtesy of Red Cedar Shingle and Handsplit Shake Bureau.)

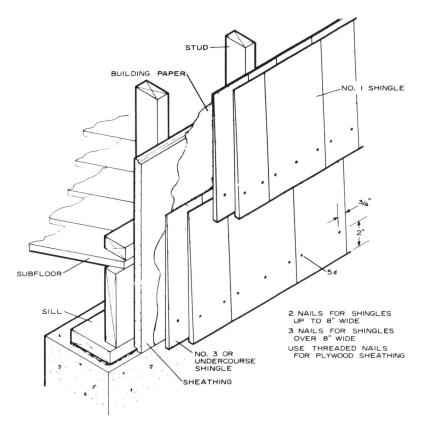

Figure 16-4 Double-course siding. (Courtesy of U.S. Department of Agriculture.)

economy or secondary buildings, such as tool sheds. No. 4 shingles are used for undercoursing, where a second layer is applied over the first. The best grade of wood shingles is cut so that the annual rings are perpendicular to the surface. They are also used for interiors where a shingle finish is desired.

Wood shingles are sometimes applied with a double course of shingles (Fig. 16-4). This is known as a shadow or underlayment course. This application of shingles give a deeper shadow-line effect on the wall.

Heartwood shingles are more decay resistant than those manufactured from sapwood. Edge-grain shingles are less likely to warp or cup. A flat-grain shingle is cut parallel to the wood grain. Thick shingles warp less than thin shingles, and narrow shingles warp less than wide shingles.

Three types of wood shakes are available: hand-split, then resawed; taper split; and straight-split. They are similar in size and width to wood shingles.

Clapboards

Clapboard, sometimes called bevel siding or lap siding, is a wedge-shaped wood siding in widths of 4 to 12 in. and random lengths (Fig. 16-5). The butt thickness is $7/16$ to $3/4$ in. thick and $3/16$ in. at the thin edge. These units are made by diagonally ripping a board the entire length. The lap is from 1 to 2 in. For example, a 6-in.-wide clapboard might have $4\frac{1}{2}$ in. to the weather. Clapboard siding is nailed close to the bottom or butt of the clapboard. Since the nails are exposed, they should be of a rustproof material such as aluminum or galvanized. If rustproof nails are not used, rust stains

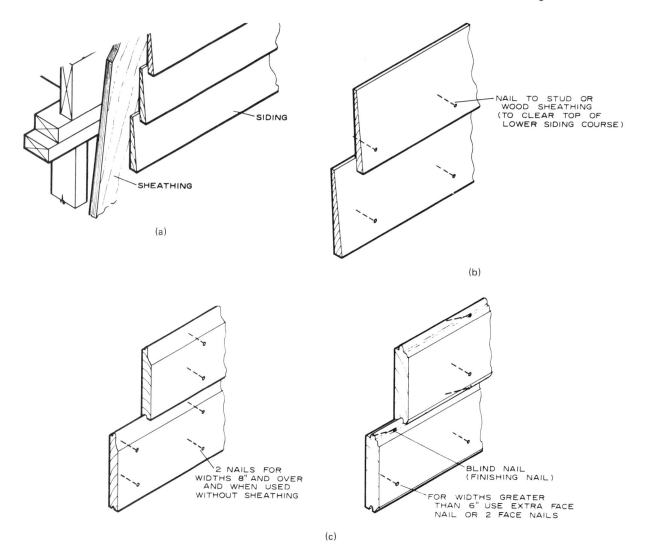

(a)

(b)

(c)

Figure 16-5 (a) Clapboard siding; (b) bevel siding; (c) drop or rabbeted siding. (Courtesy of U.S. Department of Agriculture.)

will run down the siding from the nail head because the rust will bleed through to the finish surface of the siding, including paint.

The corners of clapboards are treated similarly to shingles. The spacing or exposure of the siding may be uniform, or one wall may have more than one exposure dimension.

Vertical Siding

This type of siding is usually a solid wood member with tongue-and-groove construction. The length is random and the width is 6 and 8 in. One of the many features of this type of siding is the manufacture of the board. One side of the board is rough cut, the other side is planed or smooth. Either side can be exposed, giving a rustic rough appearance or a smooth appearance.

The boards are nailed into the tongue with rustproof nails. These nails are concealed by the groove of the next board. Care must be used in joining the length of these boards to assure a tight, waterproof joint. This is usually done with caulking or flashing. Watertightness is assured if the board is of

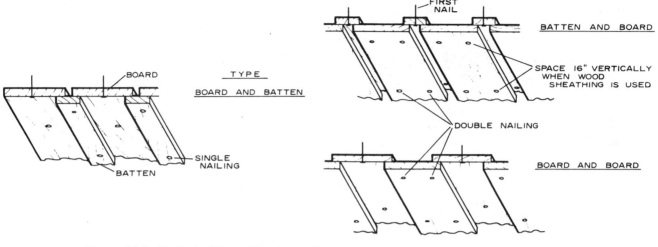

Figure 16-6 Vertical siding. (Courtesy of U.S. Department of Agriculture.)

NOTE : NAIL FOR FIRST BOARD - 8d OR 9d
NAIL FOR SECOND BOARD - 12d

one length with no joint running the full height of the wall. The sheathing on which the boards are nailed is covered with 15-lb felt paper.

Some designs offer a V joint to accentuate the vertical joining of the boards. Square-edge boards are also manufactured, which eliminate the tongue and groove. If this type of design is selected, the vertical joints must be sealed with caulking and a batten strip applied over the joint. A batten strip is a narrow piece of wood covering the entire length of the vertical joint (Fig. 16-6). The batten strip should be nailed into one board only, leaving the other board free for expansion and contraction. These units can also be installed in a diagonal pattern.

Plywood

The selection of wood finish and texture of plywood siding is almost unlimited (Fig. 16-7). It offers an attractive alternative to other sidings, but must be carefully planned and installed. Plywood sheets or panels are 4 ft wide and 8, 9, 10, and 12 ft long. The plywood is from $\frac{3}{8}$ to $\frac{5}{16}$ in. thick and is installed over sheathing with building paper between the sheathing and the plywood. All plywood siding is the exterior type, which is manufactured with waterproof glue.

(a)   (b)

Figure 16-7 Plywood siding: (a) cedar-sawn board and batten—select knotty; (b) cedar sawn reverse board and batten—premium.

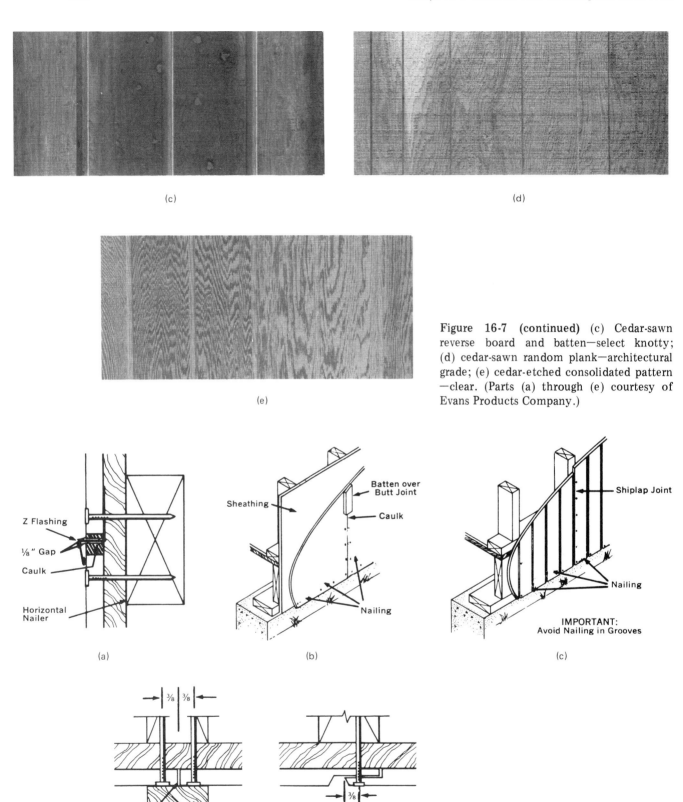

(c)

(d)

(e)

Figure 16-7 (continued) (c) Cedar-sawn reverse board and batten—select knotty; (d) cedar-sawn random plank—architectural grade; (e) cedar-etched consolidated pattern —clear. (Parts (a) through (e) courtesy of Evans Products Company.)

(a)

(b)

(c)

(d)

(e)

Figure 16-8 Plywood siding installation: (a) horizontal joint detail; (b) nailing detail over sheathing; (c) nailing detail over studs; (d) butt joint detail; (e) shiplap joint detail.

The weakest part of the plywood panel is the edge. If the panels are not applied in a weathertight joint, water will find its way along the plywood edge and will eventually break down the glue, causing the several layers or plys of wood to separate or delaminate, resulting in failure. There is no cure for this type of failure. The panels must be removed and replaced with sound panels.

The joints must be sealed with caulking or flashing and batten strips must be applied over the joints. Sometimes the plywood edge is manufactured in a lap joint construction to reduce the possibility of failure. The lap joint must also be sealed to prevent penetration of water (Fig. 16-8).

The plywood panels should cover the entire height of the wall, avoiding horizontal joints. The veneer or face sheet of plywood is usually Douglas fir, cedar, and redwood. Outside corners are finished off with corner moldings of plastic or wood. All nails used for plywood siding must be rustproof.

STUCCO

One of several exterior wall coverings that require little or no maintenance is stucco. It is a plaster-like material made of a mixture of cement, lime, sand, and water. Stucco is water and fire resistant. It is troweled onto a metal lath in three coats totaling about ¾ in. thick (Fig. 16-9). The first coat is called a brown coat and is applied to the metal lath for stiffness. The second coat is the scratch coat, building the thickness to a little less than ¾ in., and the final coat is the skim coat or finish coat.

Each coat must dry before the next one is applied. Coloring can be mixed into the last coat. If no color is added, the natural color of stucco is white. Different finish textures are available, from a smooth to a rough finish to a sandy or pebbled surface.

Exterior and interior corners of stucco are protected by a metal corner bead (Fig. 16-10). All hardware used, such as nails, lath, and corner beads, must be of a nonrusting metal; otherwise, rust will bleed through the stucco.

Wood-frame walls and masonry walls move through expansion and contraction. If stucco is applied directly onto these walls, the stucco may crack when the walls move. Stucco should be separated from these surfaces by nailing 1 × 3 wood strips to the sheathing or masonry wall and applying the metal lath to the wood strips. These wood strips are called furring. Furring strips can also be of nonrusting metal. In addition, no more than a 150-ft²

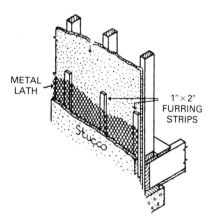

METAL
LATH

1″ × 2″
FURRING
STRIPS

Stucco

Figure 16-9   Stucco.

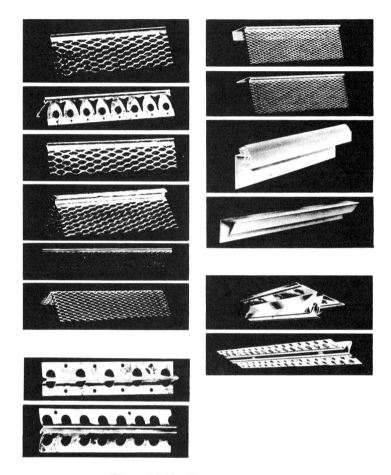

Figure 16-10   Stucco metal beads.

stucco panel should be applied, to avoid damage or cracking. A relief joint is used in internal corners to permit movement of the stucco. Control joints are to relieve stresses due to shrinkage or structural movement of the base wall or the wall on which the stucco is applied. The control joints should be spaced about 18 ft apart. A metal bead is used to terminate or end the stucco at the bottom of the wall. This is called a base screed.

VINYL AND ALUMINUM SIDING

These units are manufactured in double courses of panels in clapboard design with either 4 or 8 in. of course exposure. The panels are in lengths up to 12 ft 6 in. The color and texture varies and all panels are blind-nailed. The unit locks into the previous course and the top is nailed. The next course covers the nails of the preceding course. The units are easily cut with a power or hand backsaw or sheet metal shears. Premolded or preshaped interior and exterior corner units are manufactured (Fig. 16-11). The finish on the aluminum is baked on in a variety of colors; in time, the colors will fade and the aluminum may need painting. Aluminum siding is light in weight and easy to apply. Vinyl and aluminum siding are most popular in residing existing buildings.

If faulty bare electrical wires are in contact with the aluminum siding, the entire exterior of the house can be charged with electricity. To safeguard against this danger, the aluminum siding should be grounded with a No. 8

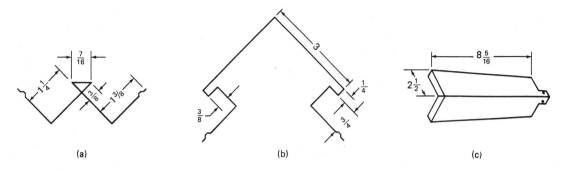

(a)   (b)   (c)

Figure 16-11 Vinyl/aluminum siding accessories: (a) inside corner post; (b) outside corner post; (c) outside corner cap.

wire or larger connected to any convenient place on the siding or to a cold water pipe or an electric-service ground. All connectors should be U.L. approved.

One of the disadvantages of aluminum siding is that it dents and scratches easily and cannot be repaired successfully. A damaged panel has to be replaced. Putting a ladder against a house that has aluminum siding is difficult without denting the siding, and any object thrown against the house can damage the siding.

STONE AND BRICK VENEER

Maintenance-free exterior sidings include stone and brick veneer, also known as masonry (Fig. 16-12). The frame of the exterior wall does not change if masonry veneer is selected. Veneer means that the masonry is not a structural

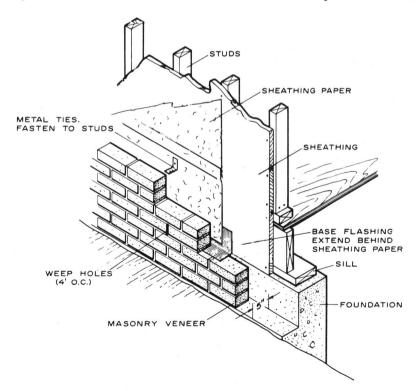

Figure 16-12 Wood-frame wall with masonry veneer. (Courtesy of U.S. Department of Agriculture.)

part of the house, merely a facing supported by the foundation and tied to the wood frame walls with corrugated metal ties. The ties are nailed into the wood frame and built into the mortar joint of the veneer. The ties are placed 24 in. apart vertically and horizontally. If the veneer were removed, the house will not be affected; it will remain standing. Masonry veneer averages 4 in. in thickness and the size and color of the veneer will vary. It differs from a solid masonry wall in that the veneer is only a facing.

Masonry veneer is also known as a single-width finish, which means that the wall is one stone or brick thick. The veneer usually starts a few inches below the finish grade and is sometimes extended to the bottom of the windows instead of the full height of the wall. The veneer above the doors and windows is supported by an L-shaped steel piece called a lintel or steel angle (Fig. 16-13). Sometimes an arch will take the place of the lintel (Fig. 16-14).

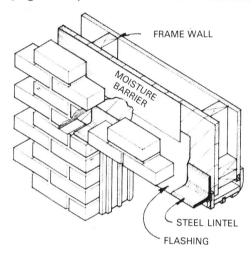

Figure 16-13 Steel lintel above brick veneer openings. (From Edward J. Muller, *Architectural Drawing*, 3rd ed., © 1985, p. 182. Reprinted by permission of Prentice-Hall, Inc., Englewood Cliffs, N.J.)

There is a 2-in. space between the back of the masonry veneer and the wood-frame sheathing. Wind-driven rain will penetrate a veneer wall and the 2-in. space is to prevent the water from damaging the wood-frame wall of the house. The water falls to the bottom of the cavity and is released through weep holes. Weep holes are voids in the joints of the masonry veneer close to the bottom of the wall (Fig. 16-12). The area at the bottom of the wall is sealed with flashing to prevent the water from damaging the wood frame. Seal or flashing is also used at the window and door sills and at the head of doors and windows. Various patterns of brick can be chosen, among them: Common bond, English bond, Flemish bond, and Stack bond. Different mortar joints can also be selected: weathered joint, struck joint, groove joint, flush joint, raked joint, bead joint, and slush joint. The brick pattern and joint selected is an aesthetic consideration that has no effect on the soundness of the veneer (Fig. 16-15).

COMPOSITION PANELS

To achieve the appearance of exterior siding, manufactured panels are available called composition building panels (Fig. 16-16). They are manufactured from cellulose fibers and lignin (lignin is a by-product of wood). These panels are 4 ft wide and 8 or 9 ft long. They are applied to sheathing in much the same manner as real siding, with similar interior and exterior corner hardware. The textures of these panels are wide and varied, as are the colors. The thickness is $7/16$ in.

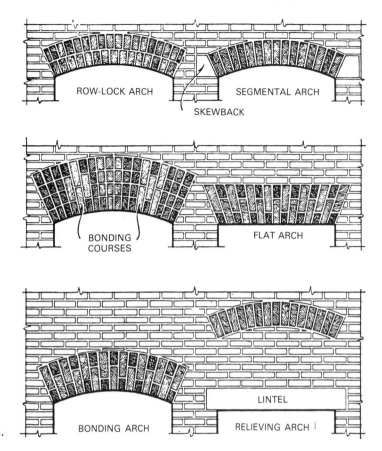

Figure 16-14 Brick arch designs.

ROW-LOCK ARCH SEGMENTAL ARCH SKEWBACK

BONDING COURSES FLAT ARCH

BONDING ARCH RELIEVING ARCH LINTEL

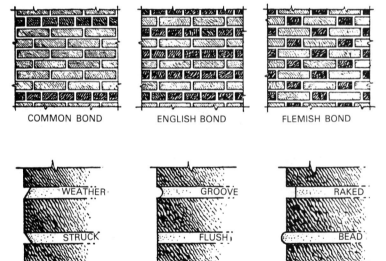

COMMON BOND   ENGLISH BOND   FLEMISH BOND

WEATHER   GROOVE   RAKED

STRUCK   FLUSH   BEAD

Figure 16-15 Brick coursing.

Figure 16-16 Composition panel. (Courtesy of Masonite Corporation.)

GUTTERS AND CONDUCTORS

Installed along the outer edge of the roof overhang, gutters collect the water that falls from the roof. The gutters direct the water to conductors or downspouts, which lead the water to the ground (Fig. 16-17). Gutters are built in or hanging (Fig. 16-18), made of wood, aluminum, fiberglass, vinyl, copper, or galvanized metal. Gutters have a slight pitch toward the conductors to allow the water to flow along the gutter into the conductor. The conductors are usually of the same material as the gutters. The size and design of gutters will vary according to the roof size and design. The water can spill from the conductors onto the ground or lead to a drywell. The gutter applied to the roof overhang is called a cornice. Gutters are sometimes called eave troughs and conductors are sometimes called leaders.

Gutters and downspouts are manufactured in several shapes, from half round, to molded, to box shape, in widths of 4 and 5 in. and in lengths of 10 to 40 ft (Fig. 16-19). The system includes accessories, such as interior and exterior corner pieces, connectors for joining lengths together, outlets to connect the gutter to the conductor, and sections for terminating as well as strips for securing the conductor to the wall. Conductors have a variety of bend accessories, called elbows, used for turning corners (Fig. 16-20). Conductors are manufactured in three shapes—round, corrugaged, and rectangular—and must be properly supported by straps to the house.

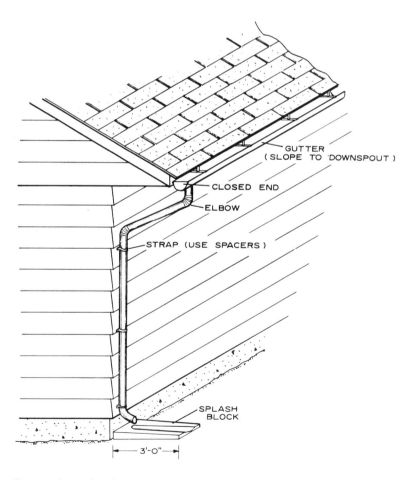

Figure 16-17   Roof gutters. (Courtesy of U.S. Department of Agriculture.)

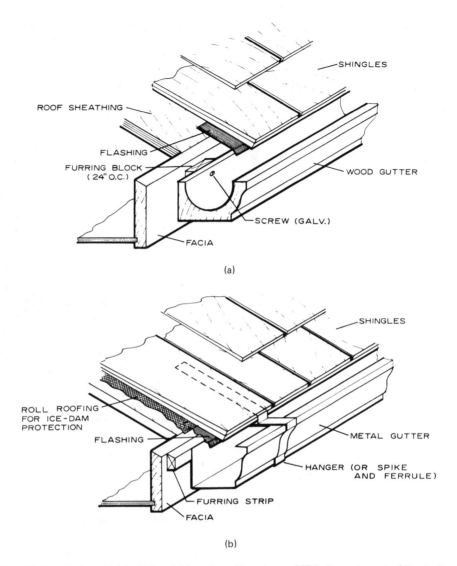

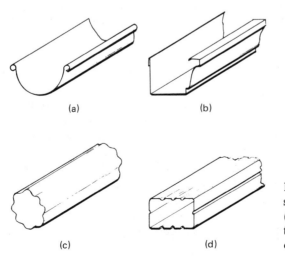

Figure 16-18 Gutters: (a) built-in; (b) hanging. (Courtesy of U.S. Department of Agriculture.)

Figure 16-19 Gutters and downspouts: (a) half-round; (b) formed; (c) round; (d) rectangular. (Courtesy of U.S. Department of Agriculture.)

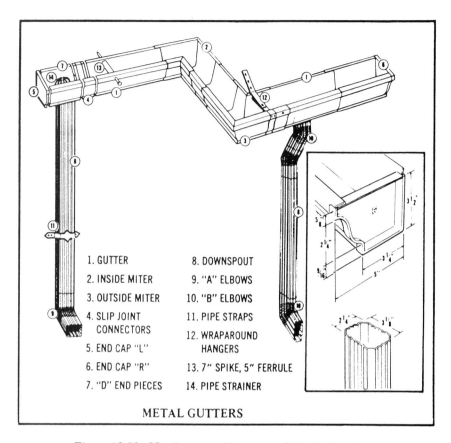

1. GUTTER	8. DOWNSPOUT
2. INSIDE MITER	9. "A" ELBOWS
3. OUTSIDE MITER	10. "B" ELBOWS
4. SLIP JOINT CONNECTORS	11. PIPE STRAPS
5. END CAP "L"	12. WRAPAROUND HANGERS
6. END CAP "R"	13. 7" SPIKE, 5" FERRULE
7. "D" END PIECES	14. PIPE STRAINER

METAL GUTTERS

Figure 16-20   Metal gutters. (Courtesy of Bird & Son, Inc.)

Gutters should be properly supported or the weight of ice and snow will cause them to fall or collapse. Gutters are pitched toward the downspouts to allow proper drainage of water falling from the roof.

The size of gutters and conductors is determined by roof area. An area of 750 ft² or less will require a 4-in. gutter. A 5-in. gutter is required for roof areas greater than 750 ft². Roof areas with 1000 ft² require a 3-in. downspout. More than 1000ft² of roof area require a 4-in. downspout.

Special care must be taken to properly seal the joining of gutter, to avoid leaks. A leaking wood gutter can cause serious decay, with the possibility of having to replace the gutter (Fig. 16-21).

CORNICES

The finished wood trim along the roof overhang is called a cornice. There are a variety of designs, which usually indicate the style of architecture. The overhang of the roof will vary according to the design. The gutter is part of the cornice. The underside of the roof overhang is called the soffit. A wide cornice or overhang will afford greater protection to the house against rain and snow and will also provide a greater amount of shade from the summer sun (Fig. 16-22). The cornice is also used to fasten and support the gutters. Not all cornices have gutters. Some designs allow the water to fall from the roof directly to the ground. The soffit is often used to ventilate the attic

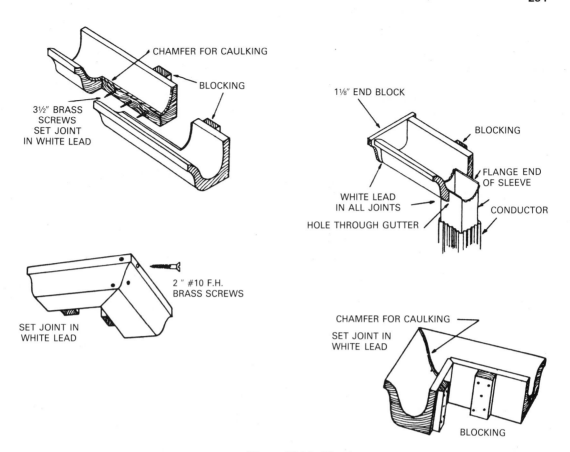

CHAMFER FOR CAULKING

BLOCKING

3½" BRASS SCREWS SET JOINT IN WHITE LEAD

1⅛" END BLOCK

BLOCKING

FLANGE END OF SLEEVE

WHITE LEAD IN ALL JOINTS

CONDUCTOR

HOLE THROUGH GUTTER

2 " #10 F.H. BRASS SCREWS

SET JOINT IN WHITE LEAD

CHAMFER FOR CAULKING

SET JOINT IN WHITE LEAD

BLOCKING

Figure 16-21 Wood gutters.

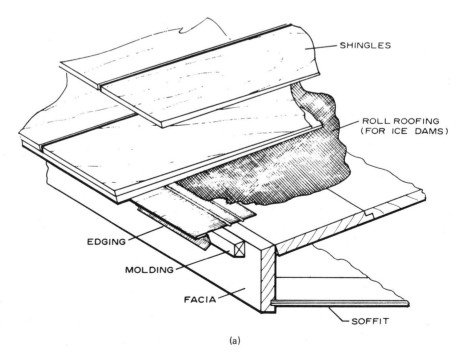

SHINGLES

ROLL ROOFING (FOR ICE DAMS)

EDGING

MOLDING

FACIA

SOFFIT

(a)

Figure 16-22 Cornices.

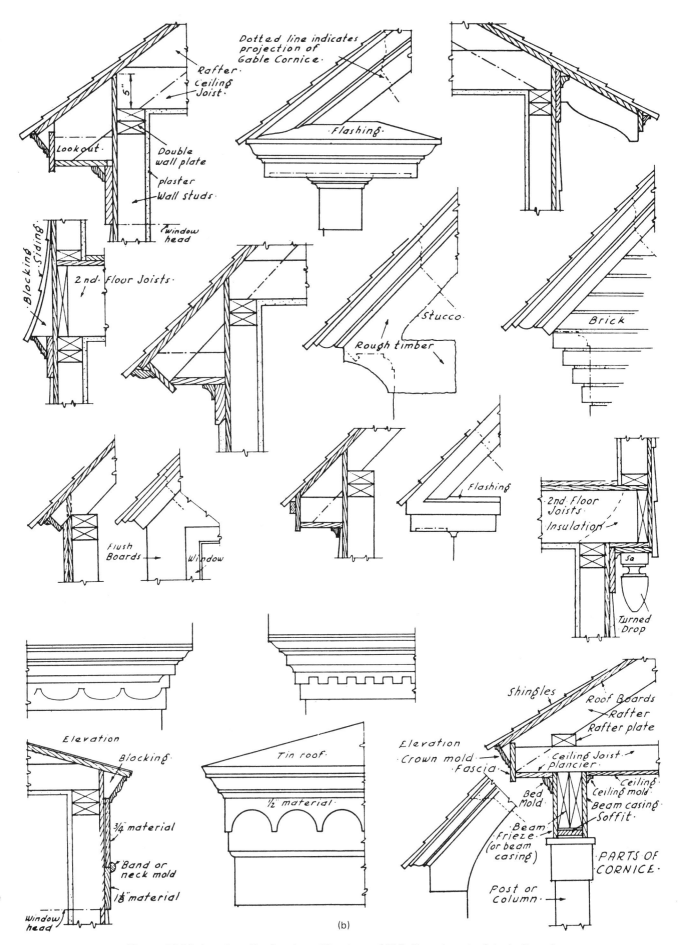

Figure 16-22 (continued) Cornices. (Courtesy of U.S. Department of Agriculture.)

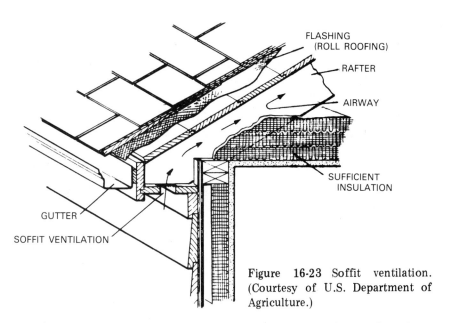

FLASHING
(ROLL ROOFING)

RAFTER

AIRWAY

SUFFICIENT
INSULATION

GUTTER

SOFFIT VENTILATION

Figure 16-23 Soffit ventilation. (Courtesy of U.S. Department of Agriculture.)

space by including several screened vents in addition to the roof vents or gable vents. A continuous screen at the soffit is sometimes used to ventilate the attic (Fig. 16-23).

QUESTIONS

1. Name four types of exterior wood sidings.
   1. _____
   2. _____
   3. _____
   4. _____

2. "To the weather" means that work cannot be performed if it is raining.
   True or False

3. Which of the following wood species is (are) resistant to weather?
   A. Pine
   B. Spruce
   C. Redwood
   D. Fir
   E. None of the above

4. Wood siding is measured in squares.   True or False

5. What is the difference between shingles and shakes? _____
   _____

6. Any type of plywood can be used on the exterior.   True or False

7. Stucco should be applied directly to which of the following?
   A. Sheathing
   B. Masonry
   C. Studs
   D. None of the above

8. Vinyl or aluminum siding is used only on new buildings.
   True or False

9. Define *veneer*. _____
   _____

10. A cornice is the exterior corner of the house.   True or False

17

Masonry

INTRODUCTION

Masonry construction is defined as brick, stone, and concrete block. Houses are sometimes constructed with solid masonry exterior walls of concrete block, brick, or stone no less than 8 in. thick. A mixture of sand, lime, cement, and water mixed together, called mortar, is used to hold masonry units together.

Chimneys and fireplaces are generally built from masonry, as are veneer walls. A veneer wall is a single thickness of brick, stone, or concrete block facing, usually 4 to 6 in. thick, with conventional wood framing behind the veneer.

Stone, concrete block, and brick are available in a variety of sizes, color, texture, and price. They have the advantage that little or no maintenance or upkeep is required on the walls.

All masonry above openings such as doors and windows are supported by steel called lintel. A seal or flashing to avoid leaks must be installed at all sills and the heads of doors and windows. Flashing is also used for chimneys built through the roof line and for roofs against masonry walls. Concrete foundations must be designed for supporting masonry walls, which differ slightly from concrete foundations without masonry.

The decision to build of masonry is dependent on budget, aesthetics, and the availability of material in particular geographical locations. In areas that have an abundance of clay from which bricks are made, bricks are more economical than in areas from which bricks must be shipped long distances.

MASONRY UNITS

There are several sizes, styles, shapes, and uses for masonry units. The units are classified as brick, block, or stone (Fig. 17-1). Brick is a molded clay product baked in a kiln and ready for use. Brick size will vary, the most

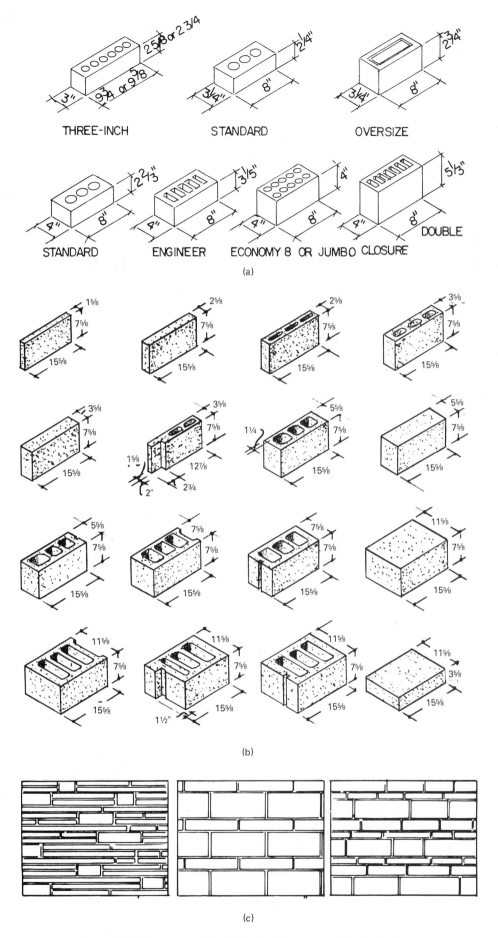

Figure 17-1 Masonry units: (a) brick; (b) concrete block; (c) stone.

popular being $2\frac{5}{8}$ in. high, $3\frac{5}{8}$ in. wide, and $7\frac{5}{8}$ in. long. The color, finish, and texture of brick offer a wide choice. Basically, there are three types of brick: face brick, common brick, and firebrick. Face brick is used for walls that are exposed or visible. Common brick is used in backup walls or as filler. This brick, which is not exposed, or if exposed, is not generally visible, can be used in closets, attics, and basements, where the finish brick surface is not important. Brick is also made of concrete. Firebrick is used to line the firebox of a fireplace. It is manufactured from a special clay called fire clay, which is designed to withstand the high temperatures generated by a fire in the fireplace. Ordinary brick would crack and fail if exposed to such high temperatures.

Block is manufactured from concrete and pumice. Pumice is a volcanic ash, light in weight, load bearing, and of high insulating value. Blocks are $7\frac{1}{2}$ in. high, $15\frac{1}{2}$ in. long, and from $1\frac{1}{2}$ to $11\frac{1}{2}$ in. wide in increments of 2 in. Blocks are sometimes sculptured on the face to offer an aesthetic choice. Block can be used as a solid wall or as a backup for other masonry or stucco. The thickness of the block used is determined by the height of the wall and the use of the block.

Stone is a natural quarried product of random size, color, texture, and shape. It is generally used as a facing with studs or concrete block backup.

All masonry units are installed in a mixture of lime, cement, sand, and water called mortar. A bond is formed by the mortar joint, which holds all the units together. Masonry units are long lasting, requiring little or no maintenance. The masonry is supported by the foundation, which is designed for this purpose.

Stucco is sometimes used in a pattern to resemble brick or stone. Color is added to the stucco, and while the stucco is still soft, it is scored or marked to imitate block or brick.

FLUES

All masonry chimneys must have a flue. This is clay pipe, 2 ft long, stacked one above the other with mortared joints. The flue is covered with masonry (Fig. 17-2). The masonry is an envelope covering the clay flue pipe. This clay flue pipe is sometimes called a flue lining. The flue pipe is square, round, or rectangular. The size of the pipe is determined by the size of unit it serves. Units that require a flue lining are: heating plants, fireplaces, stoves, incinerators, and gas-fired domestic hot water systems. Only one unit should be attached to a single flue.

Flue linings begin at the origin of the fire and extend to the chimney top. Several flues can be installed in one chimney. The main purpose of the flue lining is to make the chimney tight, to avoid leaks, and to allow the toxic gases generated by a fire to flow up the flue lining to the outdoors. This flow is a draft or sucking action generated by the flue lining.

CHIMNEYS

Whenever a fire from any fuel burns, toxic gases are released that can be harmful or fatal if inhaled. The purpose of the chimney is to release these gases to the outside. Therefore, the size will vary according to the size or

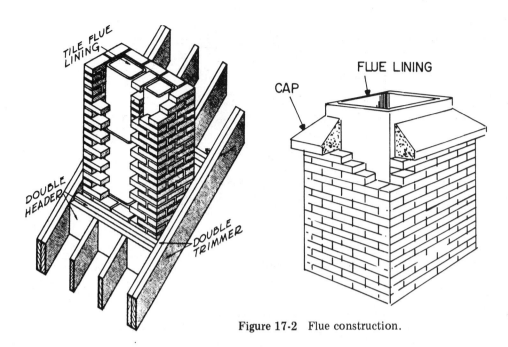

Figure 17-2   Flue construction.

type of fire. A chimney is made up of one or more flue linings. The dimensions of the flue linings are modular with the brick size, to allow brick to be built around the flue linings. There may be several flue linings in a single chimney. The brick on the chimney is an envelope covering the flue linings. A concrete cap is recommended at the top of the chimney to prevent water from getting between the brick joints, causing possible damage to the chimney by loosening the brick.

Any chimney that is 10 ft or less from the roof ridge must be extended at least 2 ft above the roof ridge to prevent a down draft in the chimney. The portion of masonry chimney not visible, such as in basements, closets, attics, and walls, can be built of a less expensive masonry, such as common brick or concrete block. The exposed portion is usually built of face brick.

If a flue lining needs to be added after the house is built, it can be installed separately, not as part of the original chimney, by using a metal chimney. Metal chimneys consist of two separate pipes with insulation between and are installed by a twist connection. Various fittings are made to turn corners and go through floors, walls, ceilings, and roofs. All sizes are available. The finish on prefab or metal chimneys is stainless steel, aluminum, or galvanized metal (Fig. 17-3).

FIREPLACES

If a fireplace is built of masonry, the firebox, which includes the floor and walls, is of fire clay brick, and mortar. This brick is designed to withstand the high temperature generated by an open fire in the firebox (Fig. 17-4). An alternative method of building a fireplace is to use a prebuilt metal firebox. Brick is not required with a metal insert (Fig. 17-5, page 260).

The hearth is an extension of the floor of the fireplace firebox, designed to hold any sparks that might shoot from a burning fire. The hearth must be built of fireproof material.

CHIMNEY TERMINATIONS

Drawings not to scale.

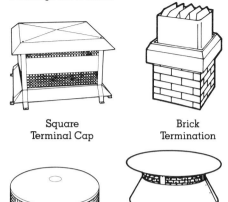

Square Terminal Cap

Brick Termination

Round Terminal Caps

CHIMNEY ASSEMBLY

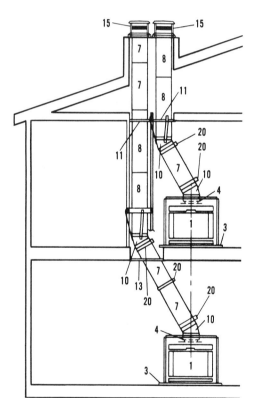

ITEM	DESCRIPTION
1	HF36A
3	Hearth Extension
4	Chimney Starter
7	36″ Air-Cooled Chimney
8	48″ Air-Cooled Chimney
10	30° Offset and Return
11	Straight Firestop Spacer
13	30° Firestop Spacer
15	Terminal Cap
20	Joint Band

FIREPLACE CHECKLIST

ITEM
1. Fireplace
2. Hearth Extension
3. Glass Doors
4. Outside Air Kit
5. Flex Duct
6. Fan Kit
7. Brass Trim
8. INSULSTACK Chimney Sections 36″
9. INSULSTACK Chimney Sections 24″
10. INSULSTACK Chimney Sections 12″
11. INSULSTACK Chimney Sections 6″
12. Air-Cooled Chimney Starter Section
13. Air-Cooled Chimney Sections 48″
14. Air-Cooled Chimney Sections 36″
15. Air-Cooled Chimney Sections 18″
16. Air-Cooled Chimney Sections 12″
17. Air-Cooled Chimney Sections 6″
18. Firestop Spacer Straight
19. Firestop Spacer 15° Oval
20. Firestop Spacer 30° Oval
21. Offset/Return 15°
22. Offset/Return 30°
23. Chimney Stabilizer
24. Chimney Bracket
25. Chimney Joint Band
26. Roof Flashing
27. Vent Shield
28. Chase Top
29. Chimney Termination

Figure 17-3 Metal insulated chimney and air-cooled chimney. (Courtesy of Heatilator.)

The chimney with the built-in security blanket.

The chimney system features a 1¼" thick layer of blanket-type insulation between double steel walls. Convenient twist-lock assembly speeds installation time. Comes in four standard lengths: 6", 12", 24" and 36". Offers slim dimensions of 8" I.D. and 10½" O.D. Provides the maximum in safety, dependability and installation ease.

Air-Cooled Chimney

Features double-wall construction—galvanized steel outside and stainless steel inside. Outside diameter is 13". Inside diameters available are 8" and 10", depending on which fireplace you choose. Chimney sections come in standard lengths: 6", 12", 36" and 48". (Also available in 18" for 8" chimney only.) The Air-Cooled chimney offers a safe, dependable system with big price advantages and ease of handling.

IMPORTANT CONSIDERATIONS

- Chimney pipe must always maintain a 2" clearance from combustible material. In a multi-chase installation, chimney pipe should be 20" apart, measured center to center.
- Joint bands must be used at any exposed chimney joints above the roof line, and at each joint between offsets and returns.
- Chimney stabilizers must be used at every 25' of vertical chimney height with INSULSTACK and every 35' of vertical chimney height with Air-Cooled chimney.
- A firestop spacer must be used whenever a ceiling, floor or sidewall is penetrated.
- Chimney sections may be offset from vertical twice, and must be returned to vertical twice. Offsets may be used directly off the top of the fireplace, or be positioned anywhere in the system.
- Never arrange two offsets to form an angle greater than 30°.

Figure 17-3 (continued)

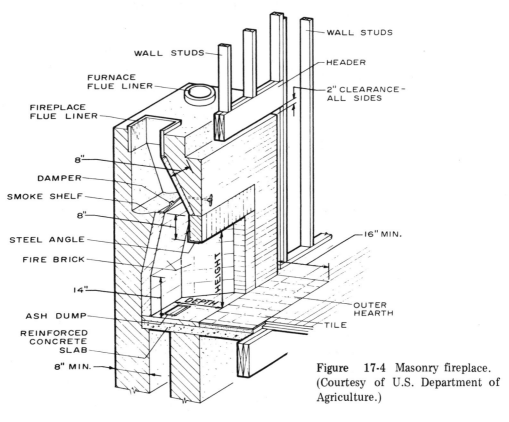

Figure 17-4 Masonry fireplace. (Courtesy of U.S. Department of Agriculture.)

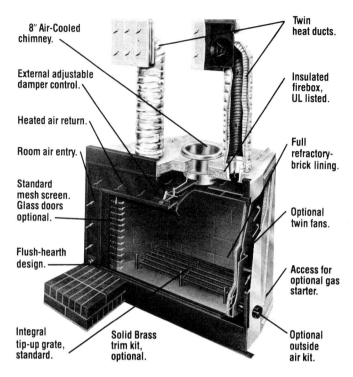

8″ Air-Cooled chimney.

External adjustable damper control.

Heated air return.

Room air entry.

Standard mesh screen. Glass doors optional.

Flush-hearth design.

Integral tip-up grate, standard.

Solid Brass trim kit, optional.

Twin heat ducts.

Insulated firebox, UL listed.

Full refractory-brick lining.

Optional twin fans.

Access for optional gas starter.

Optional outside air kit.

Figure 17-5 Metal insert fireplace. (Courtesy of Heatilator.)

A fireplace firebox must have the correct proportions; otherwise, the fire will not burn properly, which will cause smoke and gases from the fire to enter the room. When a fireplace is not in use, the chimney opening must be blocked to prevent heat in the house from escaping through the chimney. This is done with a fireplace damper, which is a cast-iron door-like unit built into the firebox top. The fireplace is part of the chimney. Inside the chimney a flue lining is built to serve the fireplace.

STOVES

Supplementary heat is often provided by coal or woodburning stoves. Care must be taken when installing stoves to prevent the building from burning. The local building code may have to be studied before installation, to ensure compliance with the laws. The floor and walls surrounding the stove must be fire-protected. The metal stove pipe must be thick enough to avoid the danger of fire burning through the metal. The gases of the stove must be exhausted by a clay or metal flue.

VENEERS

In the construction trade, a veneer is the front, face, or finish of a wall. The finish is not the same material through the wall. A coat of paint can be called a veneer. A veneer is not a load-bearing or structural part of the building. A veneer wall will not stand up by itself; it must be supported by a structural backing. Veneer walls are built of stone, block, or brick, usually about 4 in. thick, supported by the foundation. A 4-in.-thick masonry veneer wall is not self-supporting and will tend to fall forward from its own mass and weight.

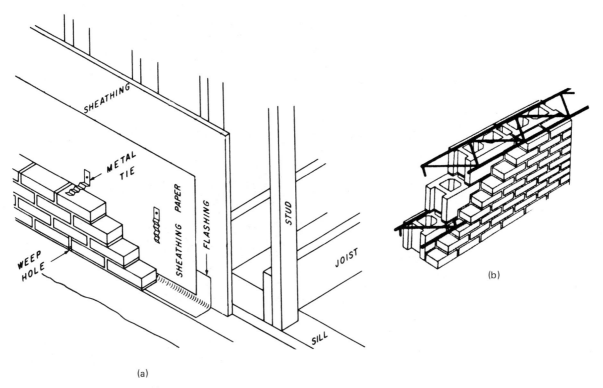

Figure 17-6 (a) Application of masonry veneer over sheathing and wood framing; (b) composite wall. [(b) Courtesy of DUR-O-WAL.]

It must be held in place by the backup wall. This is accomplished by using corrugated metal ties spaced about 24 in. apart vertically and horizontally. If the backup wall is a stud wall, these ties are nailed into the studs and locked in or built into the mortar joint of the masonry unit. If the backup wall is concrete block, the ties are built into the block mortar joints and tied into the veneer mortar joint. This is sometimes called a composite wall (Fig. 17-6).

Wind-driven rain will penetrate a masonry veneer wall. A 2-in. space is built between the backup wall and the back of the masonry veneer wall. This will separate the two walls so that the water will not come into contact with the backup wall. The water finds its way to the bottom of the 2-in. cavity and is released through weep holes built into the bottom of the masonry veneer. Weep holes are voids in the joints of the masonry units providing a space for the water to escape. Often, no mortar is used in the vertical joint of the masonry unit to form the weep hole. The space or void is at the course closest to the ground and the voids or weep holes are spaced about 4 ft apart (Fig. 16-12).

Stone Veneer

A stone wall need not be a solid stone wall. Only the face of the wall need be stone; a less expensive backup such as concrete block, brick, or wood can be used. Such face material is called stone veneer. The thickness of the veneer is usually between 4 and 6 in. and is supported by the backing. Stone veneers are often used on exterior and interior house walls. Stone veneer must be supported by a concrete foundation and never be supported by a

Figure 17-7 Ashlar stone. (Courtesy of Georgia Marble Company.)

wood foundation because of the weight of the stone and the movement of the walls will cause possible cracks and failure to the wall.

Stone masonry is divided into two types:

1. *Rubble masonry:* stone of different size, shape, and joints, installed as the mason picks them up from the pile. There is a stone wall pattern called random rubble, which is a casual jointed stone wall coursing. This is a mixture of small and large stone with small stone chips in between.

2. *Ashler:* more uniform stone, cut to square edges with uniform joints (Fig. 17-7).

Brick Veneer

Much like stone veneer, brick veneer is a brick facing one brick thick. The brick veneer is supported by the backing wall and the brick veneer is not a structural wall. The veneer can be removed without danger to the building.

The brick veneer wall must never be supported by a wood foundation because weight and movement may cause the wall to fail. Concrete foundations or masonry walls should always be used to support a brick veneer. Brick veneer used on building walls can be backed up by concrete block or wood studs (Fig. 17-6). A variety of brick coursing and joints is available to choose from (Fig. 17-8).

EFFLORESCENCE

The bleeding of soluble salt deposit in masonry joint construction causes a white stain on the wall. This is called efflorescence. It is calcium and magnesium sulfate in the mortar joint which is bleached out by water or rain. This will eventually stop streaking the wall surface, but the streak has to be cleaned by muriatic acid.

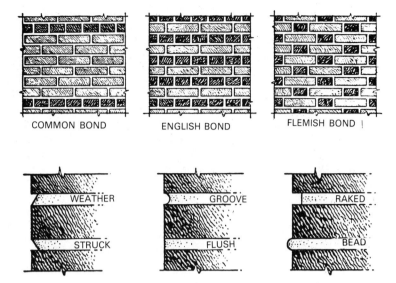

COMMON BOND ENGLISH BOND FLEMISH BOND

WEATHER GROOVE RAKED

STRUCK FLUSH BEAD

Figure 17-8 Brick coursing.

One way to prevent this staining is to use a water-repellent mortar, making the joints tight with a full bed of mortar as each unit is laid. The wall should be protected from rain and snow during construction.

In using muriatic acid for cleaning a stain, a stiff wire brush is used. After cleaning, the wall is washed with clean water to remove the acid. Great care should be exercised when using muriatic acid, following the manufacturer's recommendation for use.

REINFORCING

Earth movement caused from pressure or earthquakes will cause masonry walls to move. If precautions are not taken, the walls will fail by cracking or falling. To minimize this type of failure, it is necessary to reinforce the masonry wall by installing steel rods in the joints of the masonry (Fig. 17-9). The holes in the block are filled with concrete and reinforcing wire, or rods are installed in the concrete-filled block core or holes. This ties together the

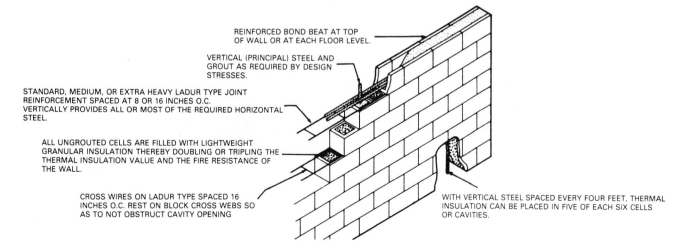

REINFORCED BOND BEAT AT TOP OF WALL OR AT EACH FLOOR LEVEL.

VERTICAL (PRINCIPAL) STEEL AND GROUT AS REQUIRED BY DESIGN STRESSES.

STANDARD, MEDIUM, OR EXTRA HEAVY LADUR TYPE JOINT REINFORCEMENT SPACED AT 8 OR 16 INCHES O.C. VERTICALLY PROVIDES ALL OR MOST OF THE REQUIRED HORIZONTAL STEEL.

ALL UNGROUTED CELLS ARE FILLED WITH LIGHTWEIGHT GRANULAR INSULATION THEREBY DOUBLING OR TRIPLING THE THERMAL INSULATION VALUE AND THE FIRE RESISTANCE OF THE WALL.

CROSS WIRES ON LADUR TYPE SPACED 16 INCHES O.C. REST ON BLOCK CROSS WEBS SO AS TO NOT OBSTRUCT CAVITY OPENING

WITH VERTICAL STEEL SPACED EVERY FOUR FEET, THERMAL INSULATION CAN BE PLACED IN FIVE OF EACH SIX CELLS OR CAVITIES.

Figure 17-9 Masonry wall reinforcing. (Courtesy of DUR-O-WAL.)

rows of block, which will act as one solid unit instead of as individual rows of blocks. In addition, reinforcing rods are placed in the mortar joints between the rows of block about every three courses. This type of reinforcing also allows the entire wall to become one solid unit, minimizing wall cracking or failure.

If block is used for a backup wall with a brick veneer face, the block and brick are tied together with steel reinforcing to give strength to the two materials. There is a module size between brick and block to allow the horizontal joints to line up. One block course high is equal to three brick courses high.

LINTELS

Whenever there is an opening for a door or a window in a masonry wall (such as brick, block, or stone), something must support the masonry wall above the opening. A door or window cannot be used to support masonry. Steel must be used, and this steel is called a lintel. The lintel is an L-shaped steel piece. The lintel is supported by the side walls of the opening and the brick, stone, or block above is supported by the steel (Fig. 17-4). The steel lintel can take other forms, shapes, and sizes. Sometimes a reinforced concrete beam is used as a lintel. In addition, stone may be used for a lintel. If an arch were built above the opening, no lintel is required because the curve in the arch will carry the load above (Fig. 17-10). The greater the loads to be supported by the lintel, the stronger the lintel must be. The number of angles

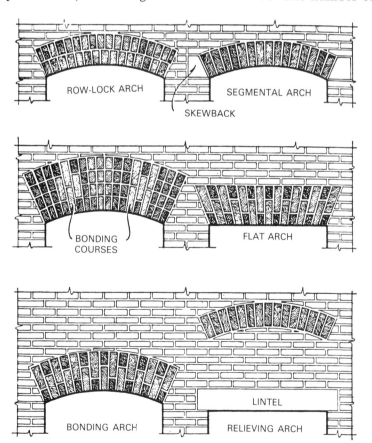

Figure 17-10 Brick arch designs.

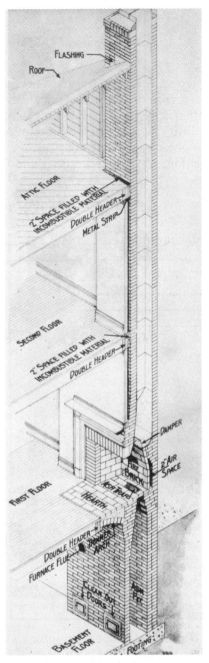

Figure 17-11 Chimney flashing.

will depend on the thickness of the brick, block, or stone—usually, one angle for every 4-in. thickness of brick or stone. The size and thickness of this steel angle will depend on the width of the opening and the amount of height of wall above the opening.

FLASHING

Wherever chimneys, pipe, skylights, or dormers are built through a roof, the opening must be sealed to prevent the roof from leaking. This is done by flashing. The material used for flashing can be any nonrusting metal, such as copper, sheet lead, aluminum, zinc, terne metal, or heavy reinforced tarred paper or copper-backed paper. In addition, the top of all wall openings in masonry walls must be flashed to prevent water running down the wall from entering through the wall at the top of the opening. This seal is accomplished by installing flashing at the top of the opening (Fig. 17-11). The flashing is built into the mortar joint of the masonry and installed into the roof covering.

Another type of seal used in masonry is caulking. Caulking is a mastic-like seal released from a tool called a caulking gun. Caulking does not provide a long-lasting seal. At best it is only temporary. The sun beating down on caulking will dry it out, crack it, and loosen its holding power. When this happens it must be cleaned out and the area recaulked. Caulking is not used to replace flashing, but is used with flashing, especially around door and window frames.

QUESTIONS

1. Define *masonry units.* _____

   _____

2. Name three types of brick:
   1. _____
   2. _____
   3. _____

3. The length of a concrete block is which of the following?
   A. 12 in.
   B. 16 in.
   C. 24 in.
   D. 14 in.
   E. None of the above

4. Stone is used as one of several ingredients in mortar.   True or False

5. A flue is which of the following?
   A. Chute for masonry
   B. Escape for water
   C. Seal for brick
   D. None of the above

6. Which of the following is the minimum height for a chimney above the roof?
   A. 10 in.
   B. 48 in.
   C. 16 in.
   D. 24 in.

7. What type of brick is used for building a fireplace firebox? _____

   _____

8. A metal chimney should never be installed to take the place of a masonry chimney.   True or False

9. Define *veneer.* _____

   _____

10. Name two types of stone masonry:
    1. _____
    2. _____

11. Efflorescence is caused by the effluent in the wall.   True or False

12. Why is reinforcing used in masonry walls? _____

    _____

13. Define *lintel.* _____

    _____

14. Flashing is the due point in brick manufacture to prevent a flash or spark.   True or False

15. Why is caulking used? _____

    _____

18

Mechanical Systems

Whenever reference is made to a mechanical system of a building, it means plumbing, heating, electrical, air conditioning, and ventilation.

To compute the size of the heating system of a house, it is necessary to know the amount of glass, the area of the outside wall, the height of the ceiling, the amount of insulation, and the building material used in the floor, walls, ceiling, and roof. From this information, the size of the heating plant is designed in units of Btu, the British thermal unit, which is the amount of heat required to raise 1 pound of water 1 degree Fahrenheit. Once the heating system size is determined, it must be decided if the building will be heated with water or air, and what fuel will be used to generate the heat.

A plumbing system is divided into two main categories: water and waste. The house must have hot and cold water and waste pipes connected to the sewer to drain all the waste and water from the house. The type and size of piping must be chosen.

The electrical system is designed in amperes (amp), which is the amount of electricity coming into the house. The minimum amperage for houses is 100 amp without electric heat and 200 amp for houses with electric heat.

Air conditioning can be designed with an air heating system, using the same ducts for cooling and heating. This is called a central system. The alternative to a central air-conditioning system is one or more window units.

A central air-conditioning system with any other type of heat except air heat requires a separate system of ducts to supply the cold air throughout the house. Air conditioning works on a similar principle to that of a refrigerator. A condensor extracts the warm air from the house and replaces it with cooler air.

Ventilation is not a problem in house construction. It is simply a mechanical or natural way of changing the stale air in the house. This can be accomplished by exhaust fans, most often found in the bathroom and kitchen. The air change is also natural, by leakage of air around the cracks of doors and windows. This is called infiltration. Opening and closing the exterior doors will also cause a change of air in the house.

HEATING

Heat is transferred from warm to cold surfaces by three methods: radiation, convection, and conduction.

An open fire in a fireplace is an example of radiation. The fire heats the brick in the firebox and the brick radiates the heat into the room.

Convection heat is caused by a warm surface heating the air around it. Hot air registers are an example of convection. The heat from the register causes the hot air to heat the air in the room from the heat coming in through the register.

Conduction moves through a solid material. A hot frying pan is an example. The heat from the stove is transmitted to the pan.

Two types of heat are available: (1) wet heat, such as hot water or steam, and (2) dry heat, such as hot air, electric, or solar. Insulation plays a very important part in heating. Its purpose is to reduce the heat from within the house that will escape through the walls, floors, and ceilings. The purpose of a heating system is to replace this heat loss and to maintain a constant temperature within the building.

Temperature Differences

Heat flows from an area of high temperature to an area of low temperature. Warm objects lose heat to cold objects. In a heated house, the inside warmer air is being pulled to the cold air outside the building through the walls, floors, and ceilings, and that loss must be replaced by the heating system.

The outside walls of a house serve as a barrier between the warm inside air and the cold outside air, and the amount of heat loss depends on the material used to build the wall and the amount and type of insulation.

There is no heat loss between adjacent walls if each room is heated to the same temperature. Wall effectiveness is the ability of a certain building material to resist the flow of heat loss through the wall. All building materials have a heat-loss factor. Good insulation will reduce the heat loss. Heat-loss factors are known as heat-transmission coefficients (Table 18-1).

Degree-day temperature is the difference between the inside room temperature, expressed as the Fahrenheit temperature $70°F$, and the coldest temperatures likely to occur in a given area. The size of the heating system must be designed to maintain $70°F$ inside.

Infiltration

Another factor to consider in designing a heating system is infiltration, which is the amount of heat lost through doors and window cracks and fireplaces. Even with doors and windows closed, heat finds its way between the door and window frames and the wall frame. This space must be properly packed with insulation.

The top of the fireplace firebox has a door-like unit called a damper which is used to control the fire. Even with the damper closed, heat will escape through the fireplace, up the chimney, and out.

TABLE 18-1

Building Material Heat-Transmission Coefficients, U (Btu per Hour per Square Foot per Degree)

Walls

Wood siding, plastered interior, no insulation	0.26
Wood siding, plastered interior, 2" insulation	0.10
Brick veneer, plastered interior, no insulation	0.26
Brick veneer, plastered interior, 2" insulation	0.10
8" solid brick, no interior finish	0.50
8" solid brick, furred and plastered interior	0.31
12" solid brick, no interior finish	0.36
12" solid brick, furred and plastered interior	0.24
10" cavity brick, no interior finish	0.34
10" cavity brick, furred and plastered interior	0.24

Partitions

Wood frame, plastered, no insulation	0.34
4" solid brick, no finish	0.60
4" solid brick, plastered one side	0.51
4" solid brick, plastered both sides	0.44
6" solid brick, no finish	0.53
8" solid brick, no finish	0.48

Ceilings and Floors

Frame, plastered ceiling, no flooring, no insulation	0.61
Frame, plastered ceiling, no flooring, 2" insulation	0.12
Frame, plastered ceiling, no flooring, 4" insulation	0.06
Frame, no ceiling, wood flooring, no insulation	0.34
Frame, no ceiling, wood flooring, 2" insulation	0.09
Frame, no ceiling, wood flooring, 4" insulation	0.06

Ceilings and Floors (continued)

Frame, plastered ceiling, wood flooring, no insulation	0.28
Frame, plastered ceiling, wood flooring, 2" insulation	0.09
Frame, plastered ceiling, wood flooring, 4" insulation	0.06
3" bare concrete slab	0.68
3" concrete slab, parquet flooring	0.45
3" concrete slab, wood flooring on sleepers	0.25

Roofs

Asphalt shingled piched roof, no ceiling, no insulation	0.52
Asphalt shingled pitched roof, no ceiling, 2" insulation	0.11
Asphalt shingled pitched roof, plastered ceiling, no insulation	0.31
Asphalt shingled pitched roof, plastered ceiling, 2" insulation	0.10
Built-up flat roof, no ceiling, no insulation	0.49
Built-up roof, no ceiling, 2" board insulation	0.12
Built-up flat roof, plastered ceiling, no insulation	0.31
Built-up flat roof, plastered ceiling, 2" board insulation	0.11

Windows and Doors

Single glazed windows	1.13
Double glazed windows	0.45
Triple glazed windows	0.28
Glass blocks (8" x 8" x 4")	0.56
1 3/4" solid wood doors	0.44
1 3/4" solid wood door with storm door	0.27

HUMIDITY

Humidity is the amount of moisture mixed with heat. Warm temperatures hold more moisture. A comfortable level of humidity is 50% when the temperature is about 72°F. During cold weather, the moisture content is low. If there is not sufficient moisture in the air, the throat and skin will be irritated and furniture joints will dry, shrink, and crack. In the summer, too much moisture is also a problem. Wood will expand, furniture, drawers and doors will not operate properly, and water is likely to condense.

Unless replaced through circulation, air will become stale, stagnant, and unhealthy. Provision must be made to circulate fresh air throughout the house, and the air should be filtered against dust and foreign particles.

HEATING SYSTEMS

Hot Water Heat

Another name for hot water heat is "hydronic." Hot water heat consists of a boiler for heating water between 200 and 240°F. This heated water is then pumped through a series of pipes which carry the heat to various rooms throughout the house. The heat is distributed through radiators, convectors, or baseboards. As the heat from the water is extracted into the room, the cooled water is returned to the boiler, reheated, and recirculated. The cycle repeats over and over (Fig. 18-1).

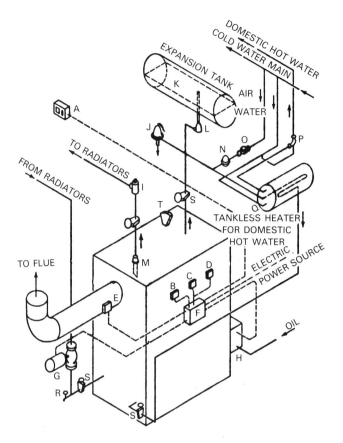

Figure 18-1 Hot water heating system. (Adapted from *ASHRAE Systems Handbook.*)

A	House thermostat	K	Expansion tank
B	Low-limit control	L, M	Tank and boiler air control
C	High-limit control		fittings
D	Reverse-acting control	N	Pressure-reducing valve
E	Stack-temperature control	O	Check valve
F	Junction box and relays	P	Tempering valve
G	Circulating pump	Q	Tankless heater
H	Oil burner	R	Drain
I	Flow-control valve	S	Gate valve
J	Pressure relief valve	T	Temperature and pressure gauge

There are two piping designs for hot water heat: one-pipe and two-pipe systems (Fig. 18-2). In a one-pipe system, the cool water is returned to the boiler through the same pipe as the hot water. In a two-pipe system, the cool water is returned to the boiler in a separate piping system from the hot water. A two-pipe system is more efficient and more expensive. Generally, the piping used for a hot water heating system is copper. Any hot water system is slow in heating the elements, but they cool off more slowly when the heat is turned off.

Radiant Heat

Another type of hydronic or hot water heat is radiant heat. It is similar to hot water heat, except there are no radiators. A serpentine endless line or coil of copper is concealed in the floor or ceiling. Hot water passes through these lines, heating the entire floor or ceiling (Fig. 18-3).

Radiant heat does not depend on air movement; it passes directly to the object or person in the room, making it the most comfortable type of

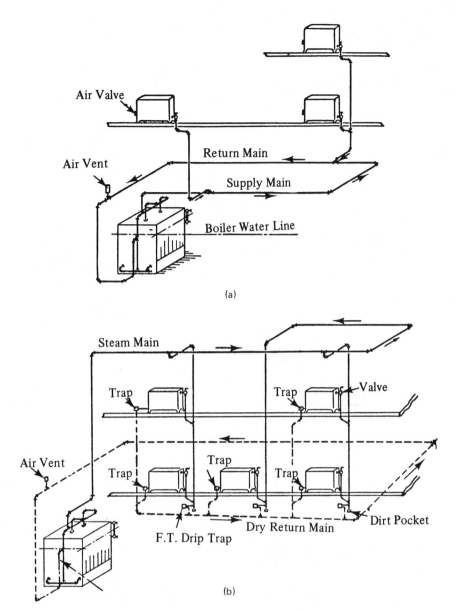

(a)

(b)

Figure 18-2 Piping designs: (a) up-feed gravity one-pipe air-vent system; (b) down-feed two-pipe system. (Adapted from *ASHRAE Systems Handbook*.)

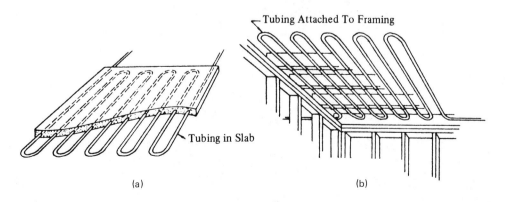

(a)   (b)

Figure 18-3 Radiant heat: (a) floor panel; (b) ceiling panel. (From Ernest R. Weidhaas, *Architectural Drafting and Construction*, 2nd ed. Copyright © 1981 by Allyn and Bacon, Inc. Reprinted with permission.)

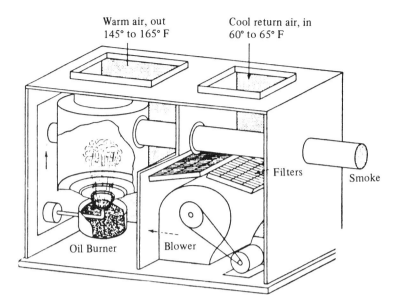

Figure 18-4 Mechanical warm air heating furnace. (Adapted from *ASHRAE Systems Handbook.*)

heating design. Should a leak develop in the line, the ceiling or floor will need to be removed to make repairs. The system must be thoroughly tested before any surface is finished. Radiant heat acts as one large radiator on the ceiling or in the floor.

Warm Air Heat

In a warm air heating system, air is heated in a furnace (Fig. 18-4) and forced to all parts of the house through ducts called supply ducts (Fig. 18-5) and by a fan or blower. Air is returned through the return ducts back to the furnace, where it is filtered, humidified, and reheated, and the same process is repeated. The heated air provides a quick source of heat. There are three types of warm air heating units: a standard up-flow furnace, designed for basement installation with ducts overhead; a counterflow furnace, designed for basementless buildings or main floor installation with ducts below the

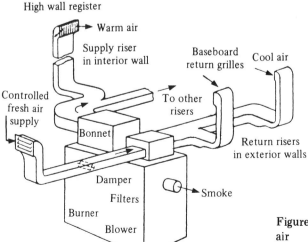

Figure 18-5 Duct system for warm air heating. (Adapted from *ASHRAE Systems Handbook.*)

floor, such as crawl spaces; and a horizontal furnace, which can be suspended in a crawl space or attic. The ducts are designed to fit between the joists and studs. There should be a supply duct and a return duct in all rooms except the kitchen and bath. These rooms need only a supply, to prevent odors from being pulled into the rest of the house. The main and largest duct is called a trunk line, and smaller ducts are branched off from the trunk to various rooms in the house. The farther away the furnace is, the smaller the duct size, because the amount of air it is required to move is less. Ducts can be rectangular or round. The ends of ducts terminate in the room at a grille or register. The registers are adjustable to control the flow of heat in balancing the system. Sometimes baseboard registers are used to distribute the heat over a wider area. Warm air heating (not in conjunction with air conditioning) requires the registers to be located close to the floor. If the system is designed for air conditioning as well as heating, the supply registers are close to the floor and the return registers are close to the ceiling. The theory is that hot air rises and is drawn into the return register for conditioning and recycling.

Where warm air supply outlets are installed low on exterior walls, room air temperatures are largely unaffected by the location of the return-air intakes. However, returns placed above the occupied space, either high in the inside wall or in the ceiling, are preferred because air motion (drafts) in the occupied zone is then less noticeable. For year-round air conditioning, high returns also reduce stratification of cool air by drawing off the warm air.

Underfloor plenum systems are similar to perimeter duct systems with respect to arrangement and location of heating unit and floor supply registers, but with the omission of the connecting ductwork, the entire crawl space is maintained at furnace air temperatures. Thus duct costs are reduced somewhat and the entire floor is kept warm, but heat loss by transmission and leakage is increased substantially and musty odors may develop unless the crawl space is moisture-proofed.

Perimeter system ducts are usually embedded in concrete. By being embedded, heat is transmitted from the ducts directly to the concrete, thereby warming the cold concrete floor slab. The ducts may also be installed in a crawl space or in a basement, thereby warming the space under the floor for greater comfort.

Perimeter systems should not be installed in slabs-on-ground located in swales or flat, low-lying areas, where there is a possibility of (1) flooding, (2) high groundwater after rains, and (3) subsurface springs or excessive moisture in the ground (poor drainage). Drain tiles installed outside the house at the footings will help to alleviate some of these moisture problems provided that there is a good outfall or a reliable automatic sump pump system.

Solar Heat

Heat generated from the sun is measured in Btu per hour and is partially lost through the atmosphere. A portion is scattered by contact with air, smoke, moisture, and dust and absorbed by water vapor, carbon dioxide, and ozone. The remainder of energy striking the earth is called direct solar radiation. When this radiation strikes a surface, part of it is absorbed and part is transmitted through the material or surface. This surface will also radiate heat to the atmosphere. Thus the energy used for heating comes from the sun, but only 40% of this energy is efficient; 60% is lost as described.

The sun is the most practical energy source. It is constant, nonpolluting, and there is no cost. Its life span is infinite and in every 24 hours the amount of energy reaching the earth from the sun is 5000 more than the sum of all energy sources on earth. Solar energy, which is sometimes intermittent, reaches us in two forms: direct and diffused. Direct radiation casts a shadow from the sun. Diffused radiation is dispersed or reflected and does not cast a shadow. The average intensity of solar energy will deliver about 100 to 200 Btu for every square foot of ground. The entire nation's energy needs can be filled by the sun.

Solar energy could reduce air pollution by 430,000 tons and solid waste by 20,000,000 tons annually. The simplest form of solar heating, called direct or passive, converts sunlight into thermal energy within the space to be heated. The technique is to install large south-facing windows that trap direct solar radiation during the winter daylight hours and store it in the walls, giving it back into the room when the sun sets. The other form of solar heating is the indirect system, converting sunlight into thermal energy outside the building. This system requires a means of collecting and storing the heat until it is to be distributed. The heart of the indirect system consists of the solar collection panels (Fig. 18-6), which gather the solar radiation and intensify it to heat water or air, which is piped to a conventional system.

There are two types of collectors in the indirect system: concentration and flat plate. The concentration collector consists of a highly reflective curved surface which focuses sunlight onto a radiation absorbing area. The collectors can reach temperatures of 250°F. They are dish-shaped with a tracking system that follows the sun's rays. Flat-plate collectors are more popular because they absorb both diffuse and direct sunlight. In simple terms, these collectors are large flat trays or panels of water or air, covered with glass or plastic to create a concentration of heat, which in turn heats the water or air. The surface of these panels is coated with an absorbent material to soak up the rays of the sun. The panels are about 4 ft by 8 ft in size and are mounted on a roof or on the ground tilted to capture the most direct radiation. The back side of the panels is insulated. The heated water is carried through the collectors into a storage tank large enough to hold a

Figure 18-6   Solar panel. (Courtesy of Acorn Structures Inc.)

2-day supply of heat. The heat is transferred to the rooms by convection, circulating the heated water in the storage tank through the conventional heating system or through water coils in a warm air ducting system.

Heat from the air system is stored in large bins of stone. Domestic hot water is preheated by cold water passing through the storage tank and being heated up to 145°F. In addition to domestic hot water, the system is capable of heating water in swimming pools and whirlpools.

Solar heat is not new; it was the first type of heat experienced by man. Solar heating will generally provide the most heat in the spring and fall, when the heating load is light and the sun is brightest. Conventional heating systems which are designed to heat a house to 70°F when the outside temperature is 0°F work at only about one-third capacity during a 10-month heating season. In some parts of the country, a solar system designed for a smaller capacity than a conventional system will take the heating load for a large percentage of the heating period. The number of Btu of heating falling per hour from the sun on 1 square foot of surface is called insolation.

Electric Heat

The least expensive heating system to install is electric heat. It requires no space for boilers or furnaces, nor is a chimney necessary. It has individual room control, it is clean, but it may not be the least expensive to operate. Proper insulation is the key to an efficient electric heating system. Basically, there are three types of electric heat. One is the electric resistance cable, consisting of covered wire cables heated by electricity and concealed in the floor or ceiling. The wires are made in the exact length to provide the necessary wattage. The finish ceiling or floor conceals this system. The second system is by electric panels. These are prefabricated finished ceiling panels that cover the entire ceiling. They can be painted, plastered, or papered. The third type is baseboard. These are convector heaters consisting of heating elements enclosed in a metal baseboard. The top and bottom are slotted to allow air to circulate. The value of electricity converted to heat loss is: 1 watt of electricity equals 3.41 Btu.

Latent Heat

As winter heat is lost through a building, so summer heat enters by transmission through floors, walls, glass, and ceilings, in addition to cracks around doors and windows. Latent heat must also be considered. This is heat within the house generated by cooking, which generates about 1200 Btu/hr, and people, who produce about 300 Btu/hr. Motors from refrigerators, dish washers, and so on, also generate heat. Lights contribute about 3.5 Btu/hr for each watt of electricity.

HEAT PUMPS

A dual system of heating and cooling is produced by a heat pump. Basically, this is a refrigeration unit which pumps natural heat, or water to be heated, from the outside air. Heat pumps work on the principle that outside air contains heat which is pumped into the house by electricity for heating, and in summer, heat is pumped out for cooling. A heat pump may not be practical for cold climates because when the outside temperature drops below 30°F, the efficiency of the system drops. This necessitates a supplementary heating system. A heat pump does not require a chimney to operate. The system is more efficient for cooling than for heating. Heat pumps employ a system of water to water and air to air. If the water system is used, an economical source of uniform temperature must be available for the heat exchanger. Heated water is distributed through a conventional hot water piping system. In the air-to-air system, air is distributed similar to a warm air heating system utilizing metal ducts.

The heat pump is a packaged unit which can be located outdoors, or it may have two cabinets, called a remote unit, with one inside and one outside. The operation of the heat pump draws outside air or water into the unit, the refrigerant in the evaporator absorbs the heat, and a compressor pumps the refrigerant to a high temperature and pressure and the condenser gives off the heat to the outside air, creating a heating cycle.

Steam Heat

In a steam heating system, water is heated to make steam by means of a boiler. The steam is carried through radiators, convectors, or baseboards, through pipes that give off heat. The steam condenses into water, which returns to the boiler and is again converted into steam. The boiler must be located below the level of the rooms being heated. Valves on radiators control heat and air vents allow air to escape from the radiators while retaining the steam. The steam changes into water in the radiators and gives off heat. All piping must be sloped back toward the boiler to allow the water to return to the boiler. The boiler should be located as near as possible to the center of the house to avoid long runs of piping. Steel and wrought-iron pipes with threaded joints are generally used in steam heating.

A one-pipe system carries steam to the radiators, and water or condensate back to the boiler in the same pipe. This is the more economical system. A two-pipe system has a separate pipe for condensate or water returning to the system.

FUELS

One of many fuels can be used to heat air in a furnace or water in a boiler. Electricity, solar, oil, gas, and diesel are called fossil fuels. Coal and wood are called solid fuels. Cost and availability are the deciding factors.

Some fuels, such as gas, solar, and electricity, are clean burning, with no after-cleaning. Coal and wood require removal of ashes, which can track dirt and dust.

Solar, gas, and electricity require no storage space for storing fuel. Oil, wood, and coal require a storage tank or space with periodic fuel delivery. Solar, gas, and electricity require no delivery service because they are built into the building by installing pipes or wires.

Gas Piping

Since gas is highly dangerous, all joints must be leakproof. Gas is supplied by the public utility company or stored in tanks on the site. The utility company is responsible for the piping to the building, including the gas meter. From that point it becomes the responsibility of the owner to run the gas piping into the building to the appliance or fixture. If gas is supplied at high pressure, a pressure-regulating valve is furnished and installed by the utility company. A shutoff valve is placed on the main line to shut off the entire system, in addition to each fixture having a valve.

Gas piping should be of best-quality standard, black wrought-iron or steel pipe, The fittings should be of galvanized, malleable iron with cocks and valves of brass. A certain amount of moisture is contained in gas, so all pipes should be straight without sags and pitched back so that condensation will flow back into the service pipe, or the piping should have a drop connection. Gas piping should not be bent; change in directions are made with screw couplings and changes in pipe size with reducing fittings. Connections at fixtures should be made with flexible pipe to allow for positioning of fixtures and appliances.

AIR CONDITIONING

The process of air conditioning is simply a matter of drawing heat from the air and replacing it with cooler air (Fig. 18-7). Human comfort is a matter of both temperature and humidity; the two are inseparable. If the air is dry (low humidity), perspiration easily evaporates and cools the skin. Therefore, dehumidification is necessary for comfort in air conditioning. This is what the air-conditioning machinery does. A summer temperature of 75°F at a relative humidity of 60% is comfortable. Indoor temperatures in the summer should not be more than 15°F below the outdoor temperature, to avoid an unpleasant chill upon entering the building or the feeling of intense heat when leaving the building.

Ventilation, humidity, and temperature are all important to human comfort. For satisfactory results, air should move about 25 ft/min. Air conditioners are continually changing the air by introducing fresh air from outdoors and exhausting stale air containing carbon dioxide, reduced oxygen, and unpleasant odors. This stale air is not recirculated in the house but is discharged directly to the outside. A complete air change every 15 minutes is desirable. Infiltration in homes, in most cases, provides a satisfactory amount of fresh air to make the change. This air needs to be filtered to remove impurities; the dry-type filter is the most commonly used.

Warm air heating is most adaptable for central air conditioning, using the same ducts for heating and cooling. Supply ducts must be insulated because of condensation forming on the surface of the metal and the loss

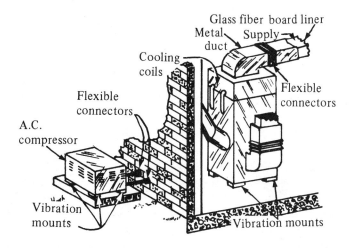

Figure 18-7   Central air conditioner. (Adapted from *ASHRAE Systems Handbook.*)

of cooled air. If a separate air-conditioning system is installed, that is, one that is not part of the heating system, all the equipment that is part of a warm air heating system will need to be installed, in addition to other equipment.

A hot water or steam heating system can also be employed as air conditioning by circulating chilled water through the piping system with a water chiller. In this case, blowers are installed on the convectors to circulate the warm air over the chilled air coils.

Cooling units are rated by tons of refrigeration. The measurement used is the amount of refrigeration produced by melting 1 ton of ice in 24 hours. A ton is equivalent to 12,000 Btu/hr. An average-size house will require a 2- or 3-ton unit, a larger house, a 4- to 6-ton unit. One horsepower of electricity is required for each ton of air conditioning.

The mechanical makeup of an air-conditioning system consists of two units. One is the evaporator, which absorbs heat and vaporizes the refrigerant. This unit must be placed in the house, and if part of the warm air heating system, is contained in the plenum, connected directly to the furnace. The other unit is the condenser, which gives off the heat and must be placed outdoors. It may be installed inside but must be on an outside wall, discharging the heat outdoors.

WATER LINES

Public Water

The cost of installation of a public water supply is less than the cost of installation of a private water supply. In the case of a public water supply, the town or city hall will have a record of the water facilities, including the size of the water main, depth below the surface, and the pressure of the water. All that is required is to run a $3/4$-in. or larger water main from the public supply to the house, deep enough to protect the pipe from the frost. This pipe is usually copper. The utility company will make the connection from the street to a shutoff at the property line. From that point into the house is the responsibility of the homeowner. When the line is brought into the house, the utility company will install a water meter and from the water meter, the water is distributed throughout the house. When building the foundation, a chase or opening is left to receive the water pipe.

Private Water

If a public water supply is not available, a private water system must be planned. In nature, water is seldom free of impurities. The pure vapor in the atmosphere may collect airborne bacteria. In percolating through the earth, it filters the water, losing most of these bacteria, but picking up salts or gases. Some are harmful and some are not. In some parts of the Central states, methane gas is present in groundwater. Calcium and magnesium in the form of sulfates or carbonates as well as iron are common. Earth strata, as well as minerals, vary from one community to another.

Water containing large amounts of calcium and magnesium salts is called hard water, and sudsing from soaps is difficult. Rainwater is soft and suds easily. A glass of water that looks clear may contain millions of dangerous organisms. Contaminated water can cause typhoid fever, dysentery, diarrhea, and intestinal disorders, as well as several varieties of intestinal worms. Sand, soft sandstone, or sand and gravel substrata as a rule will yield safe water.

The important requirement is to keep at least 100 ft away from any private sewage system and preferably to locate the well on high ground (check the local code). All well water should be analyzed for chemical content and purity. This will dictate which type of treatment to use. As a rule, this analysis will be done by local health officials. New wells must be disinfected and kept sealed. If a water softener is necessary, there are several complete packages on the market. The most satisfactory method is to pass the water through zeolite, which is a special kind of sand. Another product for filtering water is charcoal. There is no way to determine the amount of water a well will yield, but there are certain minimum requirements which are necessary. The minimum amount of water should be 50 gal/day per person for domestic use only. If water is used for other purposes, such as firefighting, more water will be required. In addition to the well, a water pump is necessary (Fig. 18-8). These fall into five categories: (1) plunger or reciprocating type, (2) turbine, (3) centrifugal, (4) rotary, and (5) ejector. The pumps not only push or pull the water from the well into the house, but also provide pressure to allow the water to flow through the pipes within the house. In most cases, a storage water tank is included in the package, and these tanks can cause a problem with condensation. One solution is to set

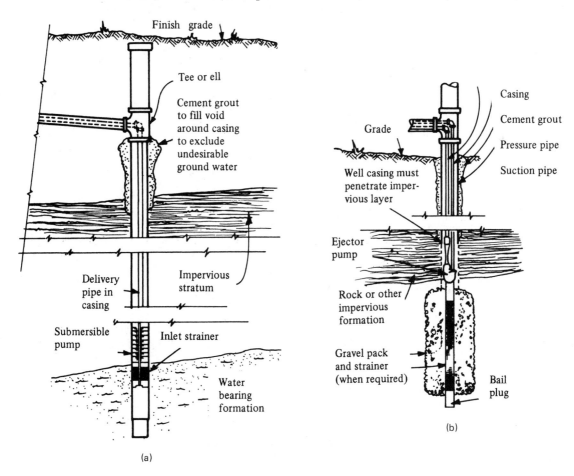

Figure 18-8 Water supply system deep well installation: (a) submersible-type pump; (b) ejector-type pump. (Courtesy of U.S. Department of Housing and Urban Development.)

the tank over a sand bed to collect the condensation. A hand pump over the well can be very convenient when electric power is lost. If a hand pump is installed, it should be the completely enclosed type.

Water Valves

Control of water through pipes is accomplished with gate valves, check valves, and globe valves. Some valves have a small wheel on the side of the handle, which will release any water trapped in the pipe. Gate valves are used to shut off the water supply completely. Globe valves are used to throttle the flow of water, and check valves are used to prevent water from flowing in the opposite direction and also when there is a possibility of flowing in reverse because of back pressure. Other valves are cock, bibb, and faucet. Faucets are used in plumbing fixtures, such as sinks, lavatories, and tubs. Valves for connecting to garden hose are called hose bibbs or sill cocks.

When the source of water supply is brought into the house, a water main valve must be installed to shut off the water supply within the house to make pipe repairs. From the main water line, a branch is connected to the domestic hot water tank if the water is not heated as an integral part of the hot water heating system. This tank should be large enough to hold at least a 1-hour supply of hot water at the rate of 8 gal/hr per person. All hot water tanks should have a pressure relief valve to prevent excessive pressure due to overheated water throwing off steam inside the tank.

From the main water line, the cold water is carried through piping to all plumbing fixtures requiring cold water, and from the hot water source the piping is carried to all plumbing fixtures requiring hot water. All hot and cold water lines should have a valve or water shutoff at all fixtures to make repairs at the fixture without shutting the water off from the entire house (Fig. 18-9).

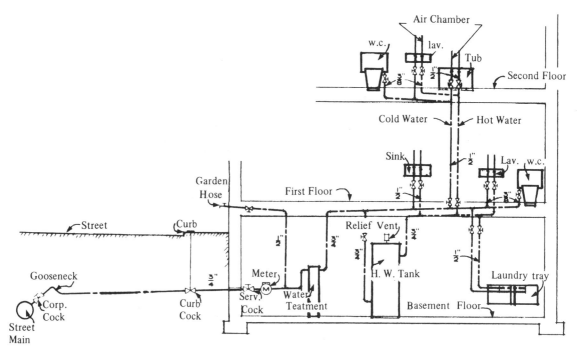

Figure 18-9 Hot and cold water lines. (From Ernest R. Weidhaas, *Architectural Drafting and Construction*, 2nd ed. Copyright © 1981 by Allyn and Bacon, Inc. Reprinted with permission.)

Water Piping

Pipings used for water are: galvanized iron, wrought iron, brass, and copper. Hard water will deposit a coating of lime and gypsum on the inside of the pipe and a water softener should be used. Copper is available in three types: K, L, and M, which are designations for the thickness of the pipe wall. K is designed for underground service and where corrosion conditions are severe, L is designed for general plumbing purposes, and Type M is for use with soldered joints and fittings and is generally used for residential plumbing. Types K and L come in hard or soft tempers; type M is hard only and requires fittings at all turns. Soft copper comes in coils and can be shaped to turn corners but is also easily punctured and damaged.

Cold water lines will condense, causing water to drip from the surface of the pipe, which may cause damage to the ceiling. To avoid this, the pipe should be covered with insulation. Hot water pipes should also be insulated, but for a different reason: to avoid rapid cooling of water, which will need to be reheated, causing an extra demand on energy.

All piping should be properly supported with pipe hangers. These are brackets attached directly to wood, holding the pipe in position. Hangers should be spaced about 10 ft apart.

Water Piping Installation

To trace the route of a water supply from the street to the house, the local water utility authority, upon request, will excavate the street to open or expose the water main and install a tap or connection to the property line. A gooseneck type of fitting is installed to allow for settlement of the pipe. Two valves, a corporation cock and a curb cock, are located on the line. The curb cock has a long stem reaching up to the level of the ground so that water can be disconnected without entering the home or without excavation. This completes the work of the utility authority; from here on the owner is responsible. From the curb cock $3/4$-in. copper tubing is installed below the frostline in a trench to the building, and immediately inside the building a service cock or valve is installed, which is used to shut off the water throughout the entire building. Following the service valve is a water meter, which measures the amount of water consumed. Following the meter is a drain valve for removing or draining all the water in the piping within the house. If water softeners are used, hose bibbs can be connected without going through the water softener; otherwise, the water softener is connected next in line and from there to the source of hot water supply. A $3/4$-in. cold water line is installed in the basement ceiling and $1/2$-in. lines are connected directly to the fixtures. Manufacturers' catalogs of plumbing fixtures state the spacing and height above the floor for all water lines.

Each pipe or riser is installed 2 ft higher than the fixture, with the ends capped to provide an air chamber, to reduce knocking or hammering of water lines. Valves are installed under each riser so that repairs can be made without shutting off the water to the entire house (Fig. 18-9).

The hot water system has a $3/4$-in. pipe installed in the basement ceiling and $1/2$-in. lines connected directly to the fixtures. (Hot water tanks will collect sediment which rusts the bottom. The water needs to be drained at least once a year.) Cold water enters the tank, and the water leaves at about $130°$ F. There is a setting on the tank to adjust the water temperature.

If the water is from a private source, the corporation cock, curb cock, and water meter are not required. All else remains the same. At least 6 in.

must be spread between hot and cold water piping so that the temperature in either pipe is not affected by the other. When installing the riser to the fixtures, the cold water line is always on the right-hand side.

WASTE LINES

Plumbing waste pipe depends on gravity for carrying waste to the sewer. The pitch of the pipe must be at least $\frac{1}{8}$ in./ft. If air is not circulated into the plumbing waste line, the waste will not flow, and it will decompose in the pipe. This will emit a poisonous gas and cause the pipe to corrode. The air in the pipe is accomplished by extending the waste pipe above the roof. This is called a vent pipe or vent stack. In addition to introducing air into the system, it discharges dangerous gases to the outside (Fig. 18-10).

The main soil or waste pipe in residential construction is 4 in. in diameter, and the branch waste lines and vents are usually $1\frac{1}{2}$ or 2 in. in diameter. All pipe joints must be gas- and water-tight. In addition to cast iron piping, vitrified clay pipe, wrought iron pipe, and polyvinyl chloride (PVC) piping are used. All exposed waste piping is chrome-coated brass. Water and waste lines have many shapes and sizes (Fig. 18-11).

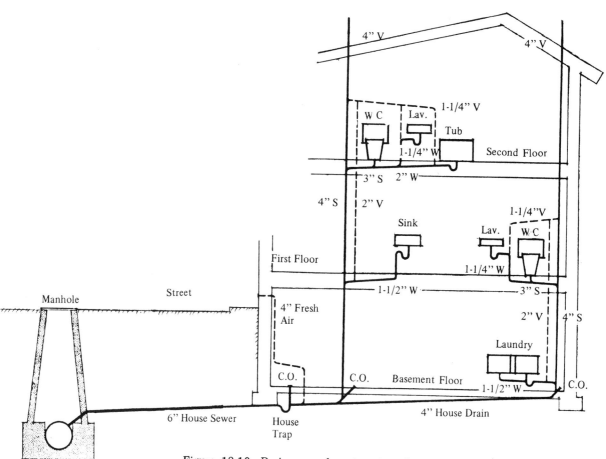

Figure 18-10 Drainage and vent system for a single-family dwelling. (From Ernest R. Weidhaas, *Architectural Drafting and Construction*, 2nd ed. Copyright © 1981 by Allyn and Bacon, Inc. Reprinted with permission.)

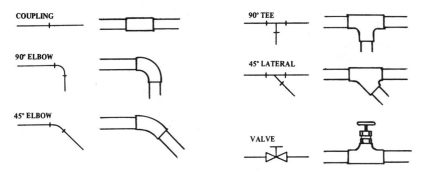

Figure 18-11 Pipe connections.

CLEANOUTS

Sometimes the plumbing waste lines become clogged or blocked. It becomes necessary to free the blockage from the pipe. This is done through a clean-out, which is a section of pipe with a removable threaded connection to gain access into the pipe for cleaning. Cleanouts are required by plumbing or building codes (Fig. 18-12).

TRAPS

Sewer or waste lines produce offensive and harmful gases which would permeate the entire house coming in through the plumbing fixtures unless a trap were installed. A trap is a pipe similar to a "U" in shape and is installed under the plumbing fixture which is part of the waste piping. Water is held in the trap forming a seal against poisonous gases coming into the house from the waste pipe. All plumbing fixtures must have a trap (Fig. 18-13).

PRIVATE SEWER DISPOSAL SYSTEMS

Where public sewers are not available, a private system must be built. It consists of a septic tank and a leach field. A concrete or fiberglass septic tank is buried outside and collects all the waste from the house (Fig. 18-14). The

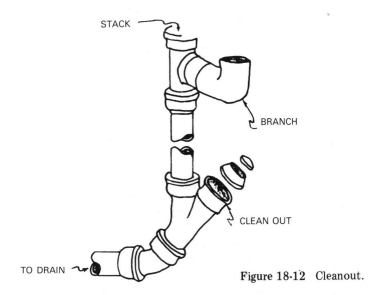

Figure 18-12 Cleanout.

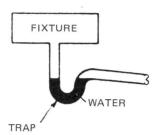

Figure 18-13 Plumbing trap.

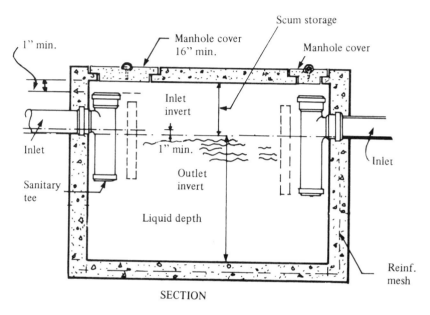

Figure 18-14 Septic tank. (Courtesy of U.S. Department of Housing and Urban Development.)

collected waste in the septic tank breaks down the solids into liquid through bacterial action. From the septic tank, the liquefied waste is led to, and distributed into the ground through a series of buried piping with open joints called a leach system (Fig. 18-15). In addition to the ground absorbing the waste, the sun helps through evaporation of the liquid. The design of the system is based on the condition of the ground and the number of people using the system. The condition of the ground is determined by a percolation test which determines how much water the ground will support. This percolation test is sometimes called a "perc test."

ELECTRICITY

In planning an electrical system, safety is the prime concern. Electricity passes through wires, creating heat. If undersized wires are used, not only is the system inefficient, but the electricity passing through the wire will overload the service, resulting in a breakdown, and melting the protective coating or insulation covering the wires, creating the hazard of a possible fire. Minimum requirements will be found in local codes and the National Electrical Code®.

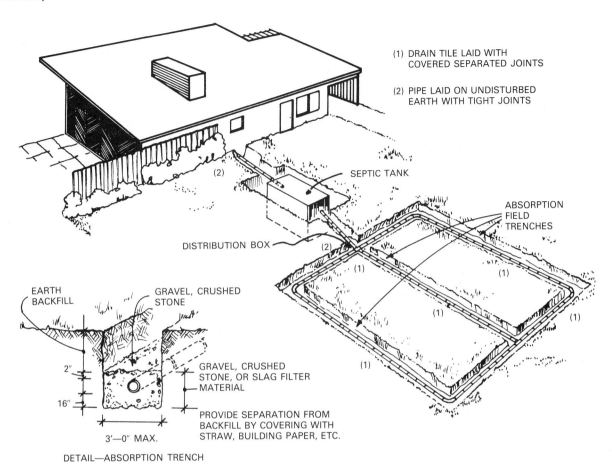

(1) DRAIN TILE LAID WITH
COVERED SEPARATED JOINTS

(2) PIPE LAID ON UNDISTURBED
EARTH WITH TIGHT JOINTS

SEPTIC TANK

ABSORPTION
FIELD
TRENCHES

DISTRIBUTION BOX

EARTH
BACKFILL

GRAVEL, CRUSHED
STONE

GRAVEL, CRUSHED
STONE, OR SLAG FILTER
MATERIAL

2"

16"

PROVIDE SEPARATION FROM
BACKFILL BY COVERING WITH
STRAW, BUILDING PAPER, ETC.

3'—0" MAX.

DETAIL—ABSORPTION TRENCH

Figure 18-15 Plumbing waste distribution field. (Courtesy of U.S. Department of Housing and Urban Development.)

Terms

Ampere: unit of current to measure the amount of electricity passing through wire

Circuit: two or more wires from a source of electrical supply to one or more outlets and return

Circuit breaker: switch that shuts off the flow of electricity at the source of supply

Conductor: wire that carries electricity

Ground: connection between electricity and earth, minimizing the danger of electric shock and damage from an electrical storm

Horsepower: unit of measuring work, such as electric motors (1 hp = 745 watts)

Outlet: electric plug, switch, or light

Receptacle: electric plug

Service entrance: electric wires from outside building (utility company) to building distribution or electric panel

Service panel: steel box containing main electric service, which distributes electricity through the house, and a fuse or circuit breaker system

Short circuit: incorrect wiring connection

Volt: measure or push of electric current

Fuse: safety device, at the source of electrical supply, which melts, cutting off the flow of electricity

Watt: measure of electric power used by appliance

Kilowatt: 1000 watts

Kilowatthour: 1000 watts per hour (utilities charge by kilowatthour)

Electrical Systems

The heart of an electrical system is the distribution panel, which is made of metal, attached to the wall or built in, and contains a number of fuses or circuit breakers (Fig. 18-16). All electricity must be grounded by running a wire from the panel to a water pipe or a ground terminal. At the point on the house where the wires are attached is an electric meter. From the meter, the wires are attached to the panel inside the house. The wires can be copper or aluminum, overhead or underground. The minimum service required should be 100 amp.

Wires are furnished to the home by the local electric company. These wires supply 240 and 120 volt, single phase, 60 cycles of alternating current, and should be at least 10 ft above the ground at the point of house attachment. The size of the distribution panel is determined by the total electrical load in the house plus any planned future loads. From the electrical distribution box, branch circuits are extended to various parts of the house, all of which are fused either through a circuit breaker or a fuse-type panel.

Figure 18-16   Electric distribution panel.

Figure 18-17 Electrical wire: (a) metal-armored cable (BX); (b) non-metallic sheath cable (ROMAX).

Branch circuits carry different electrical loads, depending on the work required to be done, ranging from 15 to 50 amp. The wires used from the distribution panel to the branch circuits are sized according to the service performed. A single cable consists of two or three insulated wires all wrapped into one. These wires have numbers stamped on the wrapping which indicate the number of wires in the cable and the diameter of the wire. 12/2 indicates two wires of No. 12 gauge. The larger the wire, the smaller the number. The minimum size wire for residential work is No. 14 gauge. Two types of wire covering are available: nonmetallic sheath cable (Romax), which is a flexible cable covering of plastic or fabric, and metal armored cable (BX), which is a steel spiral covering not recommended in damp places (Fig. 18-17).

Having all electric outlets in a single circuit in the same room is not recommended. The circuits should be separated to provide some lighting should the fuse blow or the circuit breaker trip. Generally, one circuit should take care of about 375 ft^2 of floor space using No. 12 gauge wire carrying a minimum of 2400 watts, not exceeding 75 ft in length. A longer run will require a heavier wire.

It is recommended that a separate outlet be installed for the following equipment:

Electric range	Air conditioner
Dishwasher	Refrigerator
Clothes washer	Garbage disposer
Dryer	Freezer
Furnace or boiler	Motors
Water heater	

Wall switches are used to control the flow of electricity to outlet, usually a light. The principle is simple. Electricity is running from the distribution panel to the switch, called a toggle switch. Within the switch are contacts that break or stop the flow of electricity to the light when the switch is in the off position. When the switch is on, contact is made, allowing electricity to flow to the light, turning it on. Switches are placed 48 in. above the floor in a convenient location on the wall. If one switch operates one or more lights, it is called a two-way switch. If two switches operate the same lights, it is called a three-way switch. Dimmer switches may also be installed to adjust the brightness of a light.

ELECTRICAL BOXES

All outlets, such as lights, switches, and plugs, must be installed in an electrical box. There are three types of electrical boxes: square, hexagon, and outlet (Fig. 18-18). The outlet box is used for switches and plugs which are attached directly to the wall studs flush with the finish wall material. The hexagon box is generally used for hanging electrical fixtures which are at-

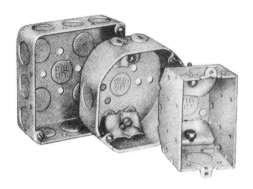

Figure 18-18 Electric outlet boxes.

tached directly to the studs or ceiling joists, again protruding from the joist or stud the thickness of the finish. The square box and the hexagon box are used to splice wires together. Under no circumstances should electrical wire be spliced with tape and left exposed. They must be placed into a square or hexagon junction box. The two wires to be spliced are held together with a wire nut, which locks and twists the two wires together. All wiring is brought into any of these three boxes, and the switches, plugs, or lighting fixture is connected at or to the box. Plastic boxes are also available.

Outlet Location

Thought should be given to the location of electric outlets. Each room should have a minimum of three outlets or plugs spaced about 10 ft apart, except the kitchen, where outlets should be spaced about every 4 ft apart. The height of the plugs should be about 18 in. above the floor except in the kitchen, where the plugs should be placed between the countertop and the underside of the upper cabinets. All outdoor outlets should be of the water-proof type. The boxes for all outlets should be secured in place first and then the wire brought to the box from the distribution panel or fed from another outlet box. All wiring is concealed in the floor, wall, or ceiling. The same outlet boxes are used for fluorescent and incandescent lighting fixtures.

Fluorescent Lighting

Fluorescent lighting fixtures require less electricity to operate for a given watt. One foot of fluorescent-tube length = 10 watts of electricity. Light is measured in footcandles, which is the amount of light given off by 1 candle on a square foot of surface 1 ft away.

Lighting Types

There are five types of lighting:

1. *Direct:* ceiling light shining down only
2. *Indirect:* partially concealed
3. *Semidirect:* lamp shining up and down
4. *Semidirect:* ceiling light shining up and down
5. *Diffused:* spread evenly in all directions, such as a hanging globe type of fixture

Recommended footcandle levels for various applications are as follows:

TV viewing	5
Storage	10
Stairway	20

Footcandles (continued)

Dining	20
Bedroom	20
Bath	30
Living	30
Den	30
Reading	50
Sewing	50
Kitchen	50
Shop	70

Low-Voltage Systems

Another type of electrical system for residential use is called low voltage. This is a 24-volt system that controls switches through a relay. Bell wire can be used for low-voltage wiring and there is no danger of electrical shock. All outlets can be controlled from a central station. Lights can be controlled from one or more stations.

BURGLAR, SMOKE, AND FIRE ALARMS

According to the National Fire Protection Association, 75% of dwelling fires start as slow, smoldering fires. Toxic fumes and carbon monoxide—not flames—are the real danger to human life. A smoke-activated fire warning device can alert residents well before the heat level reaches the 135° F needed to activate most heat sensors. Two types of smoke detectors which can provide this kind of advanced warning are available: ionization and photoelectric detectors. The ionization type contains a small amount of radioactive material, usually americium 241, which transforms the air inside the detector chamber into a conductor of electric current. If smoke particles enter the chamber, they mix with the ionized air, slow the ionization process, reduce the current flow, and set off an alarm. The photoelectric detector has a light-sensitive cell as the key component. If smoke enters the chamber, the smoke particles reflect this light beam on the sensitive cell, setting off the alarm. The ionization detector is somewhat faster to detect flaming fires, which may produce little or no visible smoke. The photoelectric detector responds to smoldering fires more quickly.

Do not confuse fire detectors with smoke detectors. A smoke detector will give off a visual or audio alarm only if set off by smoke; a fire alarm will signal only the heat of a fire, not smoke. There are two means of powering detectors: batteries and common house electricity. The ionization detector requires very little current, so can be run effectively by batteries. The batteries need to be monitored, which will require some maintenance, but it must also be understood that the electric current type will not work during power failure. Either type of detector can be designed to operate on house power and to switch automatically to an internal battery for power if there is a power failure. All units can be interconnected so that when any detector senses smoke, the others in the home also sound an alarm. All battery-operated models sound a warning, an intermittent signal, when the batteries run low.

Burglar alarms can be activated by sound or movement and are powered by batteries or house current.

QUESTIONS

1. Name three methods of transferring heat.
   1. _____
   2. _____
   3. _____
2. Two types of heat are wet heat and dry heat.   True or False
3. Warm air is attracted to cold air.   True or False
4. Infiltration is which of the following?
   A. Filtering heat
   B. Introducing outside air
   C. Maintaining a constant temperature
   D. None of the above
5. Name two types of hot water heat.
   1. _____
   2. _____
6. Radiant heat is the least comfortable type of heat.   True or False
7. Warm air heat is delivered by which of the following?
   A. Wires
   B. Pipe
   C. Ducts
   D. All of the above
8. Solar heat has a limited fuel supply.   True or False
9. Electric heat is the least expensive to install.   True or False
10. Name three types of fuel used for heat.
    1. _____
    2. _____
    3. _____
11. Moisture is contained in gas piping.   True or False
12. Hot water heating systems can also be used for air conditioning.
       True or False
13. What is an evaporator? _____

    _____
14. A heat pump can be used for heating and cooling.   True or False
15. What is the difference between steam heat and hot water heat?

    _____
16. Water can be hard or soft.   True or False
17. Name the types of piping material used for water installation.

    _____
18. What is a cleanout? _____

    _____
19. Define *percolation test.* _____

    _____
20. Define the following:
    (a) Watt _____
    (b) Volt _____
    (c) Ampere _____
    (d) Kilowatt _____

19

Interior Finish

The impression that a person receives when walking into a house for the first time is set by the appearance of the floors, walls, and ceilings. These areas thus require special attention to detail because they are visible to all who enter a building.

The choice of material selected for the interior finish is usually a personal choice made by the owner or contractor. The budget also plays an important part in the selection of materials. It generally follows that the longer-lasting materials, those that require little or no maintenance, may not be the best choice because it may limit or restrict a later change in decoration.

Interior finish is sometimes referred to as "cosmetics," and any material selected may have a variety of qualities. Interior finish generally refers to the finish on the floor, walls, ceilings, kitchen cabinets, moldings, doors, fireplace mantel, stairs, built-ins such as shelves, counters, and cabinets, and hardware.

Often, prebuilt units are selected, which means they have been built in a shop, delivered to the house ready for installation. Prebuilt units are called stock units. Any unit built specially by predesign, not selected from stock, is tailored and built for that job only.

WALLS

Prefinished Plywood

One of the richest-looking and most attractive interior wall finishes is prefinished plywood (Fig. 19-1). The plywood panels are $3/16$ and $1/4$ in. thick with a width of 4 ft and lengths of 7 or 8 ft. This material is available in nut-

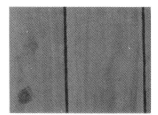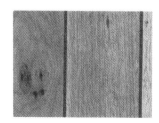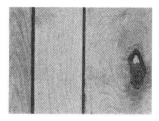

Figure 19-1 Prefinish plywood. (Courtesy of Georgia-Pacific.)

meg, oak, birch, elm, pecan, pine, cherry, hickory, cedar, cypress, cottonwood, teak, rosewood, butternut, redwood, chestnut, mahogany, and other
finishes.

Patterns can be had in random width, grooved, V-grooved, channel-
grooved, random scoring, and pegged. Finishes range from antique to shad-
ows, plank, tonings, and embossed. The way a log is cut determines the
finish surface of the panel: plain sliced will give a subdued grain appearance
whereas a rotary cut will accentuate the grain, with a finer-grain appearance.
The material can be applied either by nailing or with ready-to-use adhesive.
The wall surface on which these panels are applied must be solid.

Plywood is manufactured in flat panels or sheets of wood glued under pressure with the grain alternating. This cross-bonding produces great
strength in both directions, the wood is split-proof and puncture-proof, and
is, by weight, one of the strongest building materials made.

Factory-finished or prefinished paneling is a plywood or processed
wood fiber product with an almost limitless variety of face treatments. Many
paneling faces are hardwood or softwood veneers finished to enhance their
visual appearance. Other faces are printed to simulate wood grain. Plywood
wall paneling is manufactured with a face core and a back veneer. The face
and back veneer wood grain run vertically, with the core running horizontally. This gives dimensional strength and stability to the panel. Some natural
wood-faced panels may be embossed, antiqued, or color-toned. They may
receive other wood-grain embellishments to achieve a distinctive aesthetic
appeal. Processed wood fiber (particleboard, hardboard) wall panels are
available with grain-printed vinyl or paper overlays or printed face surface.
Most panels are random grooved, falling on 16-in. centers for nailing over
studs. Grooves are cut or embossed into the panel in V-grooves or channel
grooves. Other panels have striped grooves on the surface (Fig. 19-2).

Composition Paneling

Hardboard is a man-made wood product, also known as pressed wood board,
composition board, fiberboard, flakeboard, and by other descriptive or
brand names. Basically this material is made from wood residue—fiber, chips,

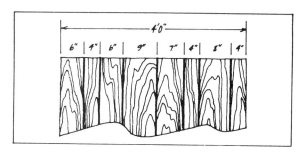

Figure 19-2 Grooved panels.

flakes, particles, and shavings—to produce a usable by-product from waste or leftover material in the processing or manufacturing of lumber and plywood. Hardboard is a smooth panel without knots or grain, yet is made almost entirely of natural wood cellulose for strength. The fibers are rearranged to provide special properties of hardness and density. Hardboard will not crack or splinter, check, craze, or flake, and is impact resistant. The panels are available in sizes up to 4 ft wide and 8 ft long, in thicknesses from $\frac{1}{8}$ to $\frac{1}{4}$ in., surfaced smooth on one or both sides. There are three basic types of hardboard: service type, used for storage areas, closet liners, shelving cabinet backs, and drawer bottoms; standard type, for interior paneling, underlayment, screens and wardrobe doors, storage areas, garage liners (perforated), and special prefinished decorative panels used in a variety of patterns and textures; and tempered type, manufactured by a process that introduces oil into the board and is permanently set with a heat process, giving the board greater strength and moisture resistance.

Particleboard is another engineered wood product consisting of wood residues from lumber and plywood manufacturing operations, mainly planer shavings and veneer clippings, processed and bonded by adding synthetic resins and a wax emulsion for moisture resistance. The result is a highly uniform product noted for its smooth surface and strong bond. It has excellent screw- and nail-holding properties and dimensional stability. Particleboard may be used for shelving, drawers, bookcases, cabinets, countertops, and the like; it will accept stain, varnish, paint, and lacquer. To minimize warping, both sides should be finished.

Particleboard is worked like natural lumber and although denser, may require carbide-tipped blades for extensive cutting. Screws are recommended for holding, instead of nails.

Wood-Fiber Substrate Paneling

Processed wood fiber (particleboard, hardboard) wall panels are available with grain-printed vinyl or paper overlays or printed face surface. These prefinished panels are rigid, aesthetically appealing, and economical. Thicknesses range from $\frac{1}{8}$ to $\frac{1}{4}$ in.

Groove Treatments

Most vertical wall panelings are "random-grooved," with grooves falling on 16-in. centers so that nailing over studs will be consistent (Fig. 19-2). Other groove treatments include uniform spacing (4, 8, and 16 in.) and cross-scored grooves randomly spaced to give a "planked effect." Grooves are generally striped darker than the panel surface. Grooves are cut or embossed into the panel in V-grooves or channel grooves. Less expensive panels sometimes have a groove just "striped" on the surface.

Simulated Panels

Simulated panels are 4 ft × 8 ft simulating brick, stone, and wood, made of fiberglass (Fig. 19-3). Panels are fingered for joining, pretrimmed, and precut ready for installation, with no cutting or sawing except for closing. The seams or joints are on the mortar line, which is filled with a special compound to match panels. Panels are applied with a special adhesive backing pressed into place and nailed at the mortar joints about 12 in. apart along every other joint line.

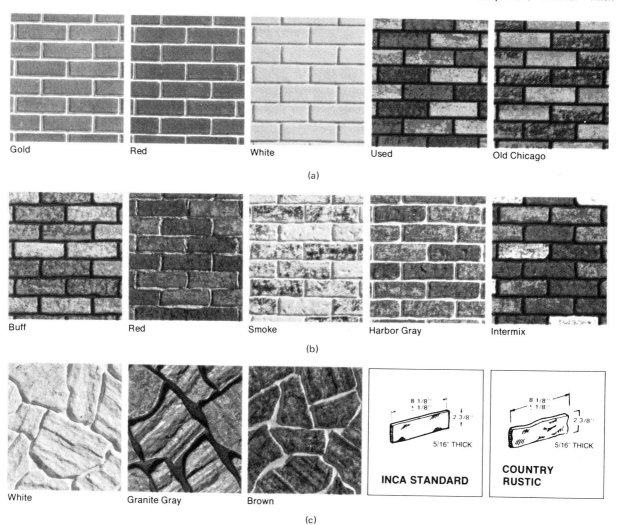

Figure 19-3 Simulated panels: (a) straight cut, square corners, slightly rounded edges; (b) irregular profile and surface contours, slightly rounded edges; (c) varied shapes and dimensions, individual pieces. (Courtesy of Z-Brick.)

Laminated Plastic

Laminated plastic (Fig. 19-4) is made by several companies in all colors and patterns (it is sometimes called Formica, which is a manufacturer's registered trademark). It is a paper product consisting of several layers of kraft paper impregnated together with resins fused together in a press at a temperature of 250°F. Patterns are printed and protected with a plastic coating. This product is manufactured in four different types. Type I is used for counters and tables, type II is used for tabletops and sink tops, type III is used for furniture and walls, and type IV is used for paneling and doors. Sheet sizes are 4 ft, 8 ft, and larger.

Laminated plastic must be applied to a solid backing, preferably plywood, with a special adhesive brushed on the back side of the panel. Adhesive must also be applied to the plywood backing. Sometimes a composition paneling is used for a backing. Metal moldings are used for corners.

Figure 19-4 Laminated plastic. (Courtesy of Formica Corporation.)

Factory-Vinyl-Surfaced Plasterboard

This is a wall-covering plasterboard with vinyl surfacing preapplied at the factory in sizes of ½ in. thick and 8-, 9-, and 10-ft lengths (Fig. 19-5). Wood-grain patterns are square edged; others are beveled edged. There are two basic methods of applying this material over a solid backing: nailing and adhesive. Nailing is done with color-coded nail heads to match the fabric and is nailed along the entire perimeter of the panel on about 12-in. spacing. Adhesive is applied with a caulking gun, including nailing at the top and bottom of the panel. The adhesive is special, as recommended by the manufacturer. The colors and patterns are as varied as the sheet-rolled vinyl, the only difference being that it is factory applied to a plasterboard backing. Trim accessories include matching color metal molding used at exterior corners and for trimming around doors and windows, and top and bottom moldings (Fig. 19-6).

Figure 19-5 Vinyl-faced plasterboard. (Courtesy of Gold Bond Building Products.)

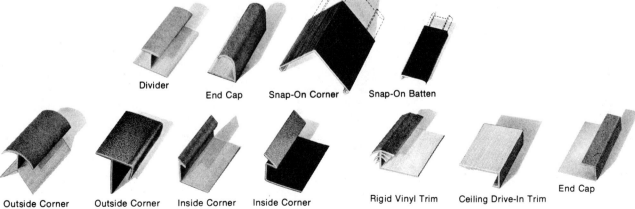

Divider   End Cap   Snap-On Corner   Snap-On Batten

Outside Corner   Outside Corner   Inside Corner   Inside Corner   Rigid Vinyl Trim   Ceiling Drive-In Trim   End Cap

Figure 19-6 Metal moldings. (Courtesy of United States Gypsum.)

Vinyl Wall Covering and Paper

This is a chemical product made into a wall covering, with designs ranging from plain to prints and embossings. In texture it goes from relatively smooth to deep three-dimensional effects. There are three qualities of vinyl wall covering, classified as type I, light duty, having a minimum of 7 oz/yd^2, for use in areas exposed to normal wear; type II, medium duty, having a minimum weight of 13 oz/yd^2, used for walls, with better wearing quality and deeper and more attractive embossing; and type III, heavy duty, with a minimum of 22 oz/yd^2, used for walls with heavy traffic, such as corridors. Vinyl wall covering generally comes in rolls of 54-in. width.

Vinyl wall covering must be applied on a smooth-surfaced wall such as plaster or drywall in sound condition. Masonry block or concrete walls can be used if filled with plaster or cement rubbed smooth. If applying on a painted surface, all loose paint and scale must be removed. If application is over a new plaster or drywall surface, a coat of sizing will be necessary to fill the pores of the wall, thus affording the paste greater holding power. If sizing is not applied, the paste may be absorbed by the open pores of the new wall surface.

Architectural Paneling

Architectural paneling (Fig. 19-7) is a genuine solid wood veneer cut paper thin in widths up to 24 in. and lengths up to 22 ft. It is available in the following wood species: afromosia, ash, avodire, benge, red birch, white birch, African brownwood, butternut, camphor burl, cherry, wormey chestnut, teak, ebony, elm, red gum, koa, korina, lacewood, laurel mahogany, makori, maple, narra, oak, palado, pecan, pine, vera, redwood, sapeli, satinwood, tigerwood, walnut, and zebrawood. This product is a wall covering applied similar to vinyl wall covering. The wood finish is raw and requires finishing after installation.

Figure 19-7 Architectural paneling. (Courtesy of Flexible Materials, Inc.)

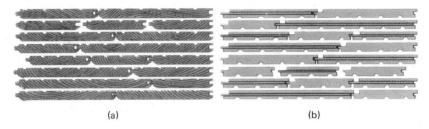

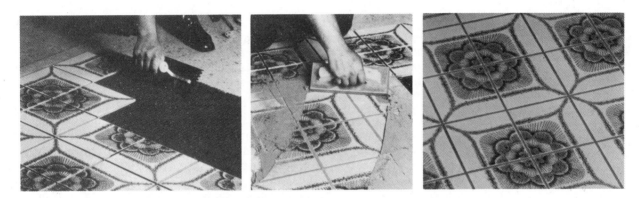

Figure 19-8 Interior planking: (a) V-groove; (b) square groove. (Courtesy of Potlatch Corporation.)

Figure 19-9 Ceramic tile. (Courtesy of Bostik Construction Products, UPCo Division.)

Interior Planking

Interior planking (Fig. 19-8) is solid wood ½ and ¾ in. thick, 4 to 12 in. wide in random widths, V-groove, square edge, channel rustic, spaced boards, and finger-jointed, applied vertically or horizontally in prefinished or unfinished redwood, walnut, oak, ash, cypress, butternut, cottonwood, pecan, cherry, and pine. It may be applied directly over studs for new work and over existing wall surfaces in remodeling, with no preparation of the existing wall. Planking is tongue-and-grooved, and nailing into the joints will conceal the nails.

Ceramic Tile

Ceramic tile (Fig. 19-9) is a clay product in thicknesses of ¼, 5/16, ½, and 7/16 in. Ceramic tile has a variety of finishes, including glazed, unglazed, slip-proof, and mat. Ceramic tile has only a light coating finish, whereas ceramic mosaic tile has the finish through the total thickness of the tile. It is made with a fine-grained body impervious to water, stains, dents, and frost. Mosaics are mounted on a prespaced backing sheet in sizes of 12 in. by 12 in., ready for application. The size of the tile is 1 in. by 1 in., 2 in. by 1 in., and 2 in. by 2 in. Ceramic tile, on the other hand, is larger and may or may not be mounted on a backing sheet, depending on the tile size. In that only the surface is colored, these tiles can break or chip easily. The colors and patterns are unlimited in both, including murals. Special pieces are available to match the color for trimming around doors, windows, interior and exterior corners, and wainscot caps (Fig. 19-10). This product can be used in any room and is easy to maintain.

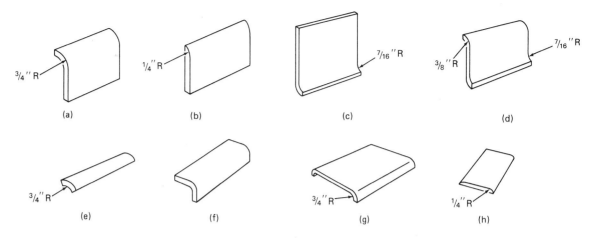

Figure 19-10 Ceramic tile trim pieces: (a) bullnose for conventional mortar installation; (b) bullnose for thin-setting bed installation; (c) cove for conventional mortar installation; (d) round-top base; (e) bead; (f) counter trim; (g) curb tile; (h) surface curb. (Courtesy of American Olean Tile.)

A solid wall backing is necessary for the application of ceramic tile. A ready-to-use adhesive is applied to the wall with a notched trowel. Cutting for fitting is done with a special cutting tool. After the adhesive has set, about 24 hours, a premixed grout, which requires only water mixed to a working consistency, is applied with a sponge trowel. The entire wall surface is covered and the grout is worked into the joints of the tile.

Drywall

Plaster sandwiched between two layers of heavy paper, also known as plasterboard, sheetrock, or gypsum board, is a construction technique known as drywall. The panels are available in thicknesses of $\frac{1}{4}$, $\frac{3}{8}$, $\frac{1}{2}$, and $\frac{5}{8}$ in. and is 4 ft in width. Lengths are 8, 10, 12, and 14 ft, recommended for the following use:

$\frac{5}{8}$-in. drywall: provides resistance to fire and sound transmission
$\frac{1}{2}$-in. drywall: for single-layer application in residential construction
$\frac{3}{8}$-in. drywall: applied principally over wood framing and in repair and remodeling work
$\frac{1}{4}$-in. drywall: used over old walls and ceiling surfaces
Imperial board: used for a thin coat of plaster applied over the board
Cement composition board: cement-based product used for ceramic tile finish applied over the board

Gypsum board is an engineered building panel consisting of gypsum (hydrated calcium sulfate, a mineral), fibers, and other ingredients, finished on both sides with special paper to provide smooth surfaces and panel reinforcement. Actually a low-density rock, gypsum is noncombustible and nontoxic. The properties that make gypsum board an important part of nearly every building are gypsum's inherent resistance to fire and to the transmission of sound. Gypsum board products are readily available and relatively easy to apply. They are the least expensive wall surfacing materials available which offer a structurally sound, fire-resistant interior finish.

Gypsum-board panels were designed primarily to reduce cost and time in construction. They take the place of wet plaster, and if properly installed, are very functional and effective. The secret of success in the installation of these panels is the taping of the joints to conceal them, making one homogeneous unbroken continuous wall surface for papering or painting. All panels have a tapered edge along the length on both edges designed to receive the paper product tape to conceal the joining of the panels (Fig. 19-11). These panels are screwed to the studs with the head slightly countersunk below the surface of the panel. Once the panel is screwed to the studs, a premixed plaster compound is applied to the recessed area, and reinforcing tape is applied to the compound. The compound is then applied in several thin coats to build the panel recess up to board thickness. Each coat is allowed to dry before applying the next coat (Fig. 19-12). When completed, the joint compound is sanded smooth. The same compound is used to conceal the

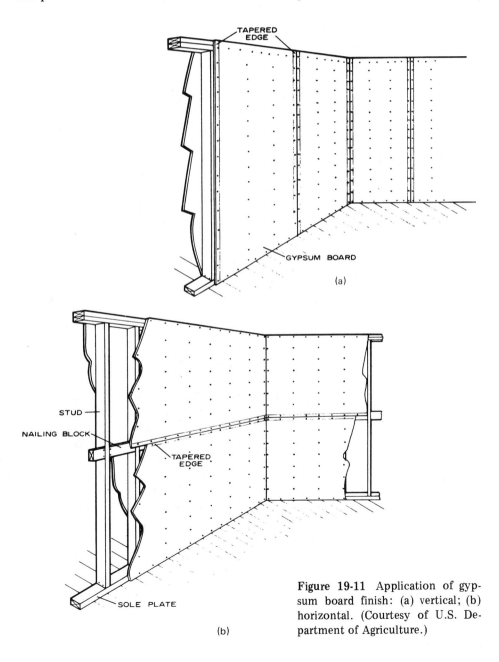

Figure 19-11 Application of gypsum board finish: (a) vertical; (b) horizontal. (Courtesy of U.S. Department of Agriculture.)

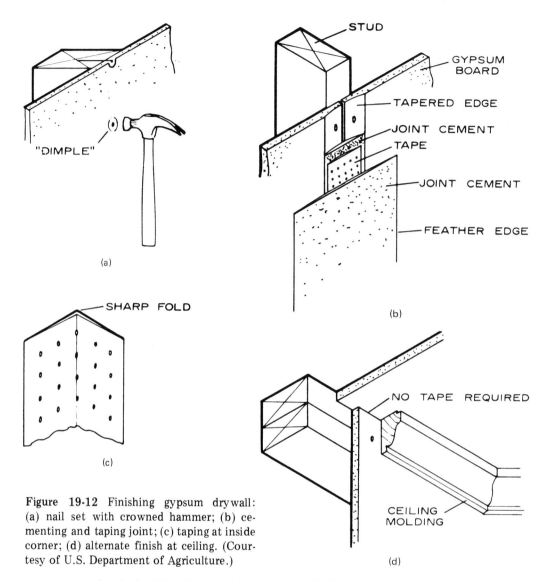

Figure 19-12 Finishing gypsum drywall: (a) nail set with crowned hammer; (b) cementing and taping joint; (c) taping at inside corner; (d) alternate finish at ceiling. (Courtesy of U.S. Department of Agriculture.)

screwheads holding the panel at each stud. The same tape is used for interior corners. The buildup must be gradual, by applying several thin coats. If the compound is applied too heavily, it will crack and shrink.

The properties that make gypsum an important building product are its resistance to fire and sound transmission. When gypsum is exposed to fire, the water of crystallization is slowly released as steam, which retards heat transfer. Exterior corners of drywall construction need metal beads to protect the corners from breaking. This bead is applied over the panel and is sealed with the same filler as that used in taping. If drywall is applied to a masonry or concrete wall, the wall needs to be furred.

Plaster

Many finishes are available in plaster work, including acoustical plaster for soundproofing. Where reduction in noise level is desirable, an acoustical plaster may be used instead of the conventional hard plaster material. A plastered surface is an extremely effective fire barrier. The application of either acoustical or conventional plaster is similar, differing only in mix and ingredients.

Two systems are available (Fig. 19-13): plaster over rock lath or metal lath, and gypsum lath. The rock lath application is a two-coat system and the wire or metal lath is a three-coat system. Gypsum lath is a factory-constructed plaster core with layers of paper on both sides. It is available in $\frac{3}{8}$- or $\frac{1}{2}$-in. thicknesses and in a sheet size 16 in. by 48 in.; the $\frac{3}{8}$-in. thickness is usually applied directly to the studs, with metal beads at the interior and exterior corners, forming a base for plastering with an additional thickness of $\frac{3}{8}$ in. in two coats, making a total finish thickness of $\frac{3}{4}$ in. The first coat is called the brown coat and the second coat is the finish coat.

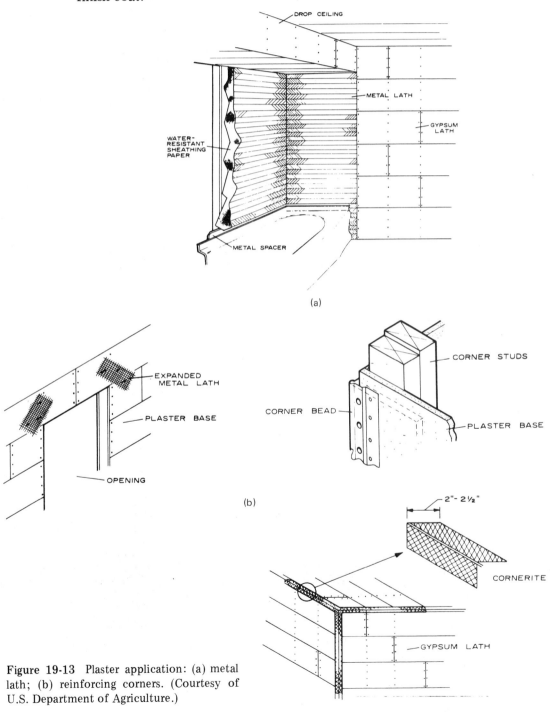

Figure 19-13 Plaster application: (a) metal lath; (b) reinforcing corners. (Courtesy of U.S. Department of Agriculture.)

The metal lath application is similar to that of stucco, requiring three coats: scratch coat, brown coat, and finish coat. To ensure uniform plaster thickness, grounds are installed. These are narrow strips of wood or metal placed around the edges of surfaces and openings. Insulated gypsum lath will add to energy savings if used on interior of exterior walls.

Plaster is available premixed, requiring only water to make it of a working consistency. A very light finish coat of plaster can be sprayed over drywall construction, making an attractive, inexpensive plaster-finished surface. Many finishes can be achieved with plaster, from smooth to scrolled. If ornamental work is desired, plaster is the best material because it will conform to any shape in finish.

Metal Wire Lath. Several shapes, designs, and sizes are available in metal wire lath, which is a base for applying plaster:

$3/8$-*in. Rib lath:* used as a combination form and reinforcing for floor slabs over steel joists and plaster base for ceilings below them. The sheet size of 27 in. by 96 in. permits faster lathing with fewer laps. The small $1/8$-in. reverse rib at the outer edge simplifies lapping. It is available in painted steel, copper alloy steel, and galvanized steel. Standard weights are 3.4 and 4.0 lb/yd^2.

Small diamond mesh lath (Fig. 19-14a): used as a plaster base and reinforcing on almost all types of walls and ceilings. It is used over wood or steel framing. It is excellent for flat or curved surfaces. Expanded sheets contain over 11,000 meshes per square yard, which reinforce the plaster. Sheets are square and lie perfectly flat against supports. It is furnished in painted, copper alloy steel and galvanized steel. Standard weights are 2.5 and 3.4 lb/yd^2.

$1/8$-*in. Flat rib lath* (Fig. 19-14b): designed to meet the demand for a more rigid expanded metal lath. It is widely used as a plaster base in all types of walls and ceilings.

Gypsum Lath. Another base for applying plaster is gypsum lath, which is a plaster form sandwiched between two sheets of special paper. This is available in a variety of manufactured shapes, sizes, and uses.

Perforated gypsum lath (Fig. 19-15a): has $3/4$-in.-diameter holes punched through the lath spaced 16 in. apart. This permits high fire protection by providing a double plaster bond. The sheet size is 16 in. by 48 in. and is $3/8$ in. thick.

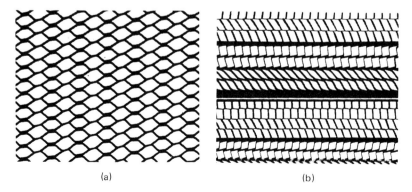

(a)   (b)

Figure 19-14 (a) Diamond mesh lath; (b) rib lath. (Courtesy of Gold Bond Building Products.)

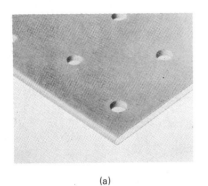
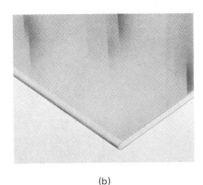

(a)   (b)   (c)

Figure 19-15 Gypsum lath: (a) perforated; (b) foil back; (c) plain. (Courtesy of Gold Bond Building Products.)

Insulating gypsum lath (Fig. 19-15b): plain gypsum lath with aluminum foil laminated to the back face. It serves as a plaster base, and the foil acts as an insulation and vapor barrier. These units are 16 in. by 48 in. and are $\frac{3}{8}$ in. thick.

Plain gypsum lath (Fig. 19-15c): standard gypsum plaster base for application to wood or steel framing. May also be applied to furring with clips. The size is 16 in. by 48 in. in thicknesses of $\frac{3}{8}$ or $\frac{1}{2}$ in. and 16 in. by 96 in. with a thickness of $\frac{3}{8}$ in.

CEILINGS

Acoustical Tile

Sound control is the purpose of acoustical tile. There are basically three construction methods of applying acoustical tile: (1) cemented to a solid sound surface, (2) applied to 1 × 3 wood furring strips spaced 12 in. apart, and (3) suspended or lay-in panels fastened in a metal suspension system with tees (Fig. 19-16). The selection of texture and color (Fig. 19-17), and

(a)   (b)

Figure 19-16 Acoustical tile installation: (a) cement; (b) wood furring; (c) suspended. (Courtesy of Armstrong World Industries, Inc.)

(c)

Figure 19-17 Acoustical tile designs. (Courtesy of Armstrong World Industries, Inc.)

tile size varies: 12 in. by 12 in., 12 in. by 24 in., and 24 in. by 48 in. The thicknesses are ½ and ⅝ in., and the tiles are made of mineral fiber, asbestos, or fiberglass. The size of the grid is 24 in. by 24 in. or 24 in. by 48 in. The metal suspension system must be installed by establishing a ceiling height. The minimum working space required when suspending a ceiling below another ceiling or framing members is 3 in. A sheet metal angle is nailed along the wall. The main suspension beams are put into place by hanging wire from the structure above with the ends of the suspended beams resting on the wall angle. These main carrying beams or tees are 12 ft long and should span the short dimension of the room. These main suspension beams are placed 4 ft apart. The metal cross tees are snapped into the spacing of the main suspension beams and are spaced 2 ft apart. This completes the 2 ft by 4 ft grid and the ceiling panels are placed into the grid (Fig. 19-18).

In addition to the acoustical tile panel drop-in, there is a choice of clear plastic unit with fluorescent lighting above the plastic, which will illuminate the entire ceiling, or a plastic egg-crate shaped unit with a ½-in. square grid used in the same fashion as the plastic grid. In either case, a very inexpensive industrial-type fluorescent lighting fixture without the shield or lens can be used above the suspension system because the fixtures are not directly visible. The lighting fixtures must be installed before the suspension system.

Some acoustical ceiling materials are more abuse-resistant than others. It is not good practice to locate acoustical tile or panels on low wall or ceiling surfaces where they might be damaged. Most acoustical ceilings are good thermal insulators. In relatively cold climates where the problem is one of preventing condensation on the underside of a cold roof surface, it is best to locate vapor-sealed insulation on top of the suspension system.

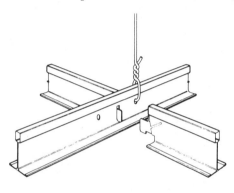

Figure 19-18 Acoustical tile grid suspension. (Courtesy of National Rolling Mills Company.)

Exposed Wood Planks

Unlike most conventional ceilings in wood construction, there is a system of construction called plank and beam (Fig. 19-19). The wood plank is a structural part of the framing system and is exposed as a finish ceiling. With

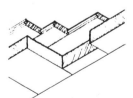

Squared edges with finish flooring at right angles.

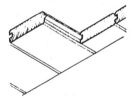

Tongued-and-grooved.

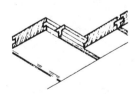

Grooved plank with splined insert moulding.

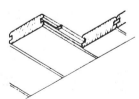

Grooved plank with spline and V-joint.

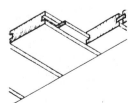

Grooved plank with exposed spline.

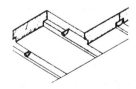

Rabbeted plank with batten insert.

Figure 19-19 Wood plank joints.

TABLE 19-1

Parquet Flooring

	PRODUCT DESCRIPTION AND PATTERN	PANEL SIZE	GRADE	SPECIES
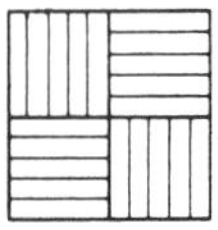	STANDARD Pattern Unfinished—Paper-Faced	5/16" x 19" x 19" 16 equal alternating squares 5/16" x 12" x 12" 4 equal alternating squares	Premium Select Rustic	Cherry—Maple Red Oak—White Oak—Cedar—Pecan—Walnut Rhodesian Teak Angelique (Guiana Teak) Panga-Panga
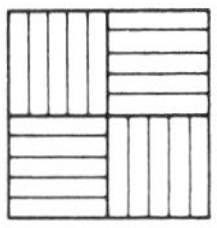	STANDARD Pattern Unfinished—WebBack or Mesh-Back	5/16" x 19" x 19" 16 equal alternating squares 5/16" x 11" x 11" 4 equal alternating squares	Premium Select Rustic Select & Better (Par & Better) Rustic	Red Oak—White Oak Pecan Red and White Oak
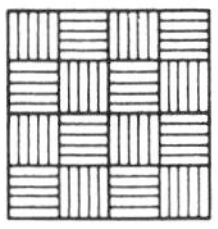	STANDARD Pattern Unfinished—WebBack (For Industrial Use)	5/16" x 19" x 19" 16 equal alternating squares 9/16" x 19" x 19" 16 equal alternating squares	Select & Better (Par & Better) Select Rustic & Better Rustic	Maple—Red Oak White Oak Pecan
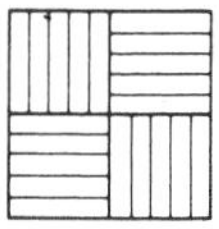	STANDARD Pattern Unfinished WebBack (For Industrial Use)	11/16" x 11" x 11" 4 equal alternating squares ¾" x 12-11/16" x 12-11/16" 4 equal alternating squares	Select & Better (Par & Better) Industrial & Better (Rustic & Better)	Red Oak—Maple
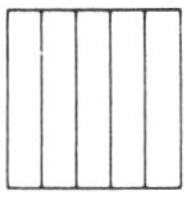	STANDARD Pattern Factory-Finished (Available in various colors)	5/16" x 6⅜" x 6⅜" 5/16" x 6½" x 6½" individual unit	Choice Natural & Better Natural Cabin	Oak—Walnut Pecan—Maple
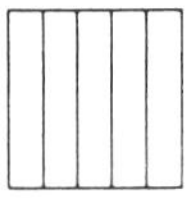	STANDARD Pattern Factory-Finished Foam-Back Tile	5/16" x 6½" x 6½" individual units . . . ⅛" foam, 2 lb. density	Natural & Better Natural Cabin	Oak—Pecan Maple
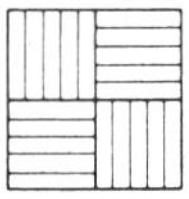	ANTIQUE TEXTURED (Factory-finished and Unfinished)—Kerfsawn Various colors available	5/16" x 6⅜" x 6⅜" individual squares 5/16" x 6½" x 6½" individual squares 5/16" x 11" x 11" 4 equal alternating squares	Select Natural & Better Select & Better (Par & Better)	Red Oak & White Oak Red Oak & White Oak
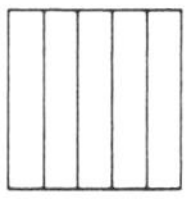	ANTIQUE TEXTURED (Factory-finished and Unfinished)—Wire brushed Various colors available	5/16" x 6⅜" x 6⅜" 5/16" x 6½" x 6½" individual squares	Natural & Better	Oak
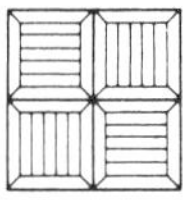	MONTICELLO Pattern Unfinished—Paper-Faced	5/16" x 13¼" x 13¼" 4 equal alternating squares	Select & Better (Par & Better)	Angelique (Guiana Teak) Red Oak—White Oak Panga-Panga—Black Walnut
	HADDON HALL Pattern Unfinished—Paper-Faced	5/16" x 13¼" x 13¼" 4 equal squares	Select & Better (Par & Better)	Angelique (Guiana Teak) Red Oak—White Oak Panga-Panga—Black Walnut
	HERRINGBONE Pattern Unfinished—Paper-Faced	5/16" x 14⅛" x 18⅛" (Approximate overall) 2 - "V" shape courses wide and 11 slats long	Select & Better (Par & Better)	Angelique (Guiana Teak) Red Oak—White Oak Panga-Panga—Black Walnut
	SAXONY Pattern Unfinished—Paper-Faced	5/16" x 19" x 19" 4 equal squares on diagonal and 8 equal half squares	Select & Better (Par & Better)	Angelique (Guiana Teak) Red Oak—White Oak Panga-Panga—Black Walnut
	CANTERBURY Pattern Unfinished—Paper-Faced	5/16" x 13¼" x 13¼" 4 equal alternating squares with diagonal center slats	Select & Better (Par & Better)	Angelique (Guiana Teak) Red Oak—White Oak Panga-Panga—Black Walnut
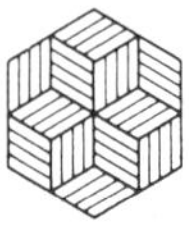	RHOMBS Pattern Unfinished—Paper-Faced	Hexagonal Shape 5/16" x 15⅛" x 15⅛" 12 equal Rhomboids	Select & Better (Par & Better)	Red Oak & White Oak

TABLE 19-1 (continued)

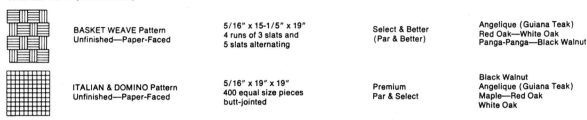

	BASKET WEAVE Pattern Unfinished—Paper-Faced	5/16″ x 15-1/5″ x 19″ 4 runs of 3 slats and 5 slats alternating	Select & Better (Par & Better)	Angelique (Guiana Teak) Red Oak—White Oak Panga-Panga—Black Walnut
	ITALIAN & DOMINO Pattern Unfinished—Paper-Faced	5/16″ x 19″ x 19″ 400 equal size pieces butt-jointed	Premium Par & Select	Black Walnut Angelique (Guiana Teak) Maple—Red Oak White Oak

Source: Harris Manufacturing Co.

this type of construction, no further finish is required on the wood. This system is protected inside the building, and any stain finish will do nothing more than change the color of the wood.

Gypsum Board, Plaster, and Drywall

See the discussion of these materials under "Walls."

FLOORS

Wood Parquet or Blocks

This type of floor is a hardwood factory-finished flooring applied over concrete or wood with a ready-to-use mastic. This floor offers a wide variety of wood species and patterns to choose from (Table 19-1), with ease of maintenance. The units or panels are completely unitized for fast and simple installation. The wood species available are white oak, red oak, pecan, black walnut, hard maple, cherry, cedar, teak, and others.

Planks or Strips

This is wood flooring that must be laid one piece at a time. The sizes vary from 2 to 8 in. wide and ³⁄₈ and ³⁄₄ in. thick. The length is from 1 to 5 ft. These units are blind-nailed (Fig. 19-20), keyed, pegged or screwed, and prefinished or unfinished, with beveled edges, in oak, maple, beech, birch, pecan, teak, walnut, and other exotic woods. This flooring can be applied over a wood or concrete base.

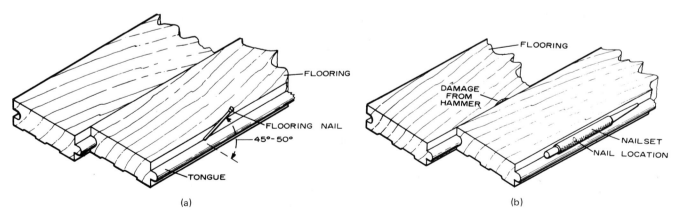

Figure 19-20 Nailing flooring: (a) nail angle; (b) setting the nail. (Courtesy of U.S. Department of Agriculture.)

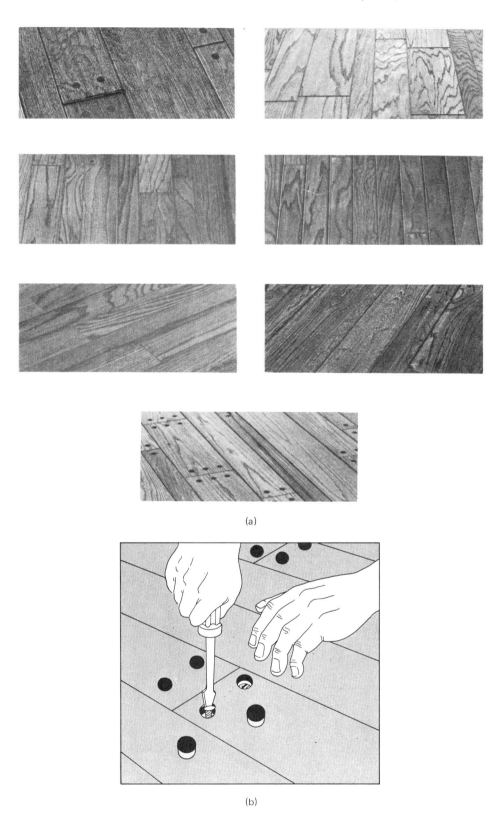

(a)

(b)

Figure 19-21   (a) Wood plank flooring; (b) countersunk screws covered with plugs.
(Courtesy of Bruce Hardwood Floors.)

The pegged flooring is predrilled with countersunk holes on top of the units. The flooring is screwed through the countersunk holes into the sub-floor and the holes are plugged with prefitted wood plugs (Fig. 19-21).

Cracking

It is natural for wood floors to expand and contract with the seasons. To minimize this condition, the following precautions should be followed:

1. Assure that the dealer has properly protected the stock while it was in the yard.
2. Do not allow the floor to be delivered on a rainy day.
3. Make sure that the plaster or masonry walls are dry before the floor is delivered.
4. Discard all badly crooked boards or use them in inconspicuous places. Cutting boards into shorter lengths helps lessen the crook in each piece.
5. Prevent moisture absorption by the flooring after it is delivered to the house.

Air humidity can be lowered and flooring kept dry by maintaining some heat in the house from the time workers leave until they return the next day, even during warm summer weather. Whenever possible, the heating plant should be installed before the interior trim is applied or the finish floor. It is good practice to open the bundles and spread the flooring out so that all surfaces are exposed to the air for at least 4 days. This allows time for the flooring to reach a moisture equilibrium with the air in the heated house before it is installed. The temperature inside the house should be about 70°F.

After the flooring receives its protective coat of finish, temperatures should be kept approximately the same as they will be when the house is occupied. Another reason for keeping down moisture is that a better and smoother floor is obtained with mechanical sanders when the floor and the atmosphere are dry.

In any building, the floor receives the greatest wear. It must be of such quality that replacement or general repair is not necessary. Floors should remain serviceable throughout the life of the building.

Wood flooring is graded for quality and appearance as follows (see Fig. 19-22):

Clear. The face must be practically clear, admitting an average of $^3/_8$ in. of sap. The question of color is not considered. Bundles to be $1^1/_4$ ft and up, average length to be $3^3/_4$ ft.

Select. The face may contain sap, small streaks, pinworm holes, burls, slight imperfections in working, and small tight knots which do not average more than one to every 3 ft. Bundles to be $1^1/_4$ ft and up, average length to be $3^1/_4$ ft.

No. 1 common. Of such a nature that it will provide a good residential floor and may contain varying wood characteristics, such as flags, heavy streaks and checks, worm holes, knots, and minor imperfections in working. Bundles to be $1^1/_4$ ft and up, average length to be $2^3/_4$ ft.

A brief grade description, for comparison only, flooring is bundled by averaging the lengths. A bundle may include pieces from 6 inches under to 6 inches over the nominal length of the bundle. No piece shorter than

9 inches admitted. The percentages under 4 ft. referred to apply on total footage in any one shipment of the item. ¾ inch added to face length when measuring length of each piece.

Figure 19-22 Guide to hardwood flooring grades. (Courtesy of Oak Flooring Institute, affiliate of National Oak Flooring Manufacturer's Association.)

No. 2 common. May contain sound natural variations of the forest product and manufacturing imperfections. The purpose of this grade is to furnish an economical floor suitable for homes for general utility use or where character marks and contrasting appearances are desired. Bundles to be $1\frac{1}{4}$ ft and up, average length to be $2\frac{1}{2}$ ft.

Wood Floors Over Concrete

Wood flooring may be installed over concrete using $\frac{3}{4}$-in. plywood as a nailing surface. The plywood is installed over a 4-mil polyethylene vapor barrier. The plywood is fastened to the slab with power-actuated fasteners spaced 12 in. apart, starting $2\frac{1}{2}$ to 3 in. from the edges of the plywood.

An alternative method in wide use and still considered satisfactory is to use sleepers (Fig. 19-23). Sleepers, sometimes called screeds, should be of a lumber grade equivalent to No. 1 Common or No. 2 Common and impregnated with an approved wood preservative and termite repellent. They should not be treated with creosote or other preservative material that might bleed through nail holes and stain the finish floor. If laid in mastic they shall be 2 × 4's, 2 × 3's, or two 1 × 4's. If embedded in the concrete or affixed to it by means of clips or anchors, they shall be 2 × 4's, 2 × 3's, or 2 × 2's.

Sleepers are embedded in the concrete or attached to it by means of clips or anchors designed so that the sleepers will never loosen. Sleepers are spaced 16 in. on centers and laid at right angles to the intended direction of the finish flooring. They are wedged up to level after being nailed to the anchors. In the sleeper-type installation, a moisture barrier should be placed over the fill before the concrete slab is poured.

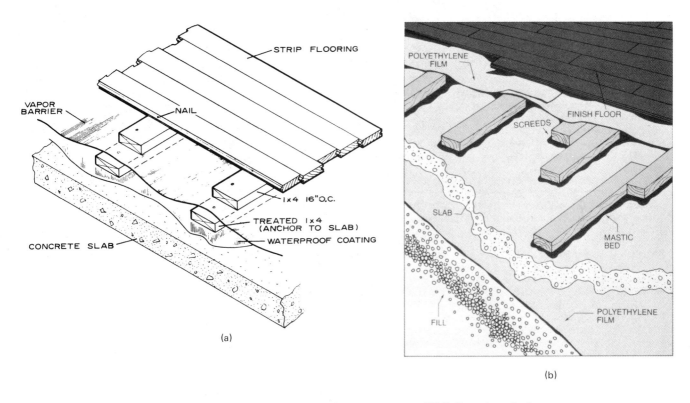

(a)

(b)

Figure 19-23 Sleepers or screeds. ((a) Courtesy of U.S. Department of Agriculture; (b) courtesy of Oak Flooring Institute, affiliate of National Oak Flooring Manufacturer's Association.)

Resilient Flooring

This type of flooring includes sheet vinyl, vinyl asbestos, and vinyl composition (Fig. 19-24). Sheet vinyls are among the most popular flooring materials today. The vinyl content allows them to be extra colorful and adds to their

Figure 19-24 Resilient flooring installation. (Courtesy of Armstrong World Industries, Inc.)

ability to resist wear, grease, alkalis, stains, and scratches, and allows for easy cleaning. Rolls come in 6- and 12-ft widths, in thicknesses of 0.160, 0.090, 0.080, 0.075, 0.070, and 0.065, and can be used for both below- and above-ground installations.

Subfloor

An important part of the success of any floor covering installation and its finished appearance is the subfloor over which it is installed. Subfloors that are rough or uneven will telegraph every irregularity through to the finished flooring installation once the adhesive sets up. The finished flooring installation can look no better than the subfloor over which it is installed.

The wood underfloor must be solid and free from movement. The subfloor must be clean, dry, smooth, and free of wax, grease, or other foreign materials, or the adhesive will not properly bond to the subfloor.

The most common type of wooden subfloor is one of the underlayment types. The three most commonly used underlayments are: plywood, hardboard, and particleboard (also referred to as chipboard or flakeboard).

The preferred underlayment is $\frac{1}{4}$-in. plywood. Any sanded exterior-grade plywood may also be used. In areas that are subject to surface moisture, plywood bonded with exterior glue is recommended. Masonite brand underlayment board installed smooth side down may also be used (minimum thickness, $\frac{1}{4}$ in.).

Carpet

Carpet is made by inserting face yarn or tufts through premanufactured backing by the use of needles, similar in principle to a sewing machine. Yarns are held in place by coating the back with latex, and a secondary back is applied to add body and stability. A variety of textures is possible (Fig. 19-25).

A woven carpet will be one of three styles: velvet, Axminster, or Wilton. The face and back are formed by the interweaving of the warp and weft yarns. The warp yarns run lengthwise and usually consists of chain, stuffer, and pile yarns. The weft yarns or "shot" run across the width. The weft yarns bind in the pile and weave in the stuffer and chain yarns which form the carpet back.

The simplest of all carpet weaves, pile, is formed as the loom loops the warp yarns over wires inserted across the loom. The pile height is determined by the height of wire inserted. Velvets are traditionally known for smooth-cut pile plush or loop pile textures, but can also create hi–lo or cut–uncut textures.

The Wilton loom operates in basically the same way as the velvet loom, with up to six colors or frames. Because only one color is being utilized in the surface at a time, the other yarns remain buried in the body of the carpet until utilized. Wilton looms can produce cut-pile, level-loop, multilevel, or carved textures.

The Axminster loom is highly specialized and nearly as versatile as hand weaving. Color combinations and designs are limited only by the number of tufts in the carpet. Almost all the yarn appears on the surface, and characteristic of this weave is a heavy ribbed back, allowing the carpet to be rolled lengthwise only. Axminsters produce single-level cut-pile textures. The process produces a complete carpet by embedding pile yarns and adhering backing to a viscous vinyl paste, which hardens after the carpet is cured. It has

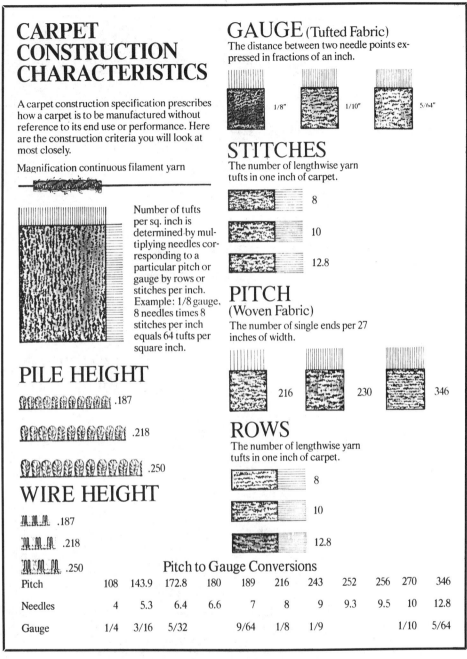

CARPET CONSTRUCTION CHARACTERISTICS

A carpet construction specification prescribes how a carpet is to be manufactured without reference to its end use or performance. Here are the construction criteria you will look at most closely.

Magnification continuous filament yarn

Number of tufts per sq. inch is determined by multiplying needles corresponding to a particular pitch or gauge by rows or stitches per inch. Example: 1/8 gauge, 8 needles times 8 stitches per inch equals 64 tufts per square inch.

PILE HEIGHT

.187
.218
.250

WIRE HEIGHT

.187
.218
.250

GAUGE (Tufted Fabric)

The distance between two needle points expressed in fractions of an inch.

1/8"   1/10"   5/64"

STITCHES

The number of lengthwise yarn tufts in one inch of carpet.

8
10
12.8

PITCH (Woven Fabric)

The number of single ends per 27 inches of width.

216   230   346

ROWS

The number of lengthwise yarn tufts in one inch of carpet.

8
10
12.8

Pitch to Gauge Conversions

Pitch	108	143.9	172.8	180	189	216	243	252	256	270	346
Needles	4	5.3	6.4	6.6	7	8	9	9.3	9.5	10	12.8
Gauge	1/4	3/16	5/32		9/64	1/8	1/9			1/10	5/64

(a)

Figure 19-25 (a) Carpet construction.

a superior tuft bind and practically eliminates backing delamination. Over 90% of yarn is in the face. A fusion bonded process produces very dense cut-pile or level-loop fabrics in solid or moresque colors.

The knitted process resembles weaving in that the face and back are made simultaneously. Backing and pile yarns are looped together with a stitching yarn on machines with three sets of needles. Knitted carpets are usually solid or tweed in color, with a level loop pile texture.

In tufted carpet, gauge is the spacing of needles across the width of the tufting machine expressed in fractions of an inch: $\frac{1}{8}$ gauge = 8 ends or needles/in.

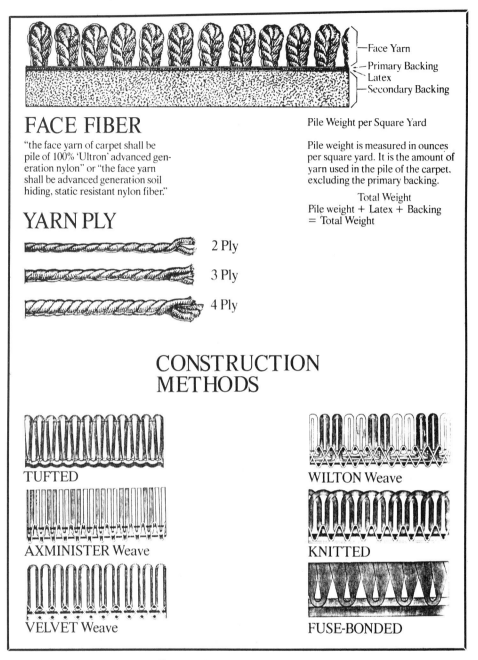

FACE FIBER

"the face yarn of carpet shall be pile of 100% 'Ultron' advanced generation nylon" or "the face yarn shall be advanced generation soil hiding, static resistant nylon fiber."

YARN PLY

2 Ply

3 Ply

4 Ply

Pile Weight per Square Yard

Pile weight is measured in ounces per square yard. It is the amount of yarn used in the pile of the carpet, excluding the primary backing.

Total Weight
Pile weight + Latex + Backing = Total Weight

CONSTRUCTION METHODS

TUFTED

WILTON Weave

AXMINISTER Weave

KNITTED

VELVET Weave

FUSE-BONDED

Figure 19-25 (a) (continued)

Secondary backing is an extra layer of material—usually, latex, jute, foam, sponge rubber, or vinyl—laminated to the underside of a carpet for additional dimensional stability and body (Fig. 19-25).

Proper carpet installation is of prime importance in ensuring maximum wear and appearance. A faulty installation can result in rippling, bubbling, split and open seams, buckling, creasing or folding, and baseboard climbing. There are two principal methods of installing carpet: the tackless strip method and the direct glue-down method (Fig. 19-25).

The tackless strip method should have a detached cushion or backing underneath. A tackless strip is a wood strip with two or more rows of rust-resistance pins embedded, pointed up at an angle. These strips are nailed to the floor a carpet thickness away from the walls around the entire perimeter

Figure 19-25 (continued) (b) Carpet cushion: secondary backing, glue-down method; (c) carpet cushion: separate backing, tackless strip method.

of the room with the pins angled toward the walls. The carpet is stretched in all directions and locked or hooked onto the pins, then forced down between the strip and the wall. The direct glue-down method involves gluing the carpet directly to the floor with adhesive.

Any carpet, glue-down or tackless strip, will not have the same wear life as that of the same carpet installed over a pad. Carpets that have a cushion bonded directly to the backing are usually installed by the glue-down method.

Sun will fade carpets, especially dyed fibers. The carpet industry has a standard for lightfastness in dyed carpets rated by continuous exposure of 80 hours of xenon lamp. Carpets in low humidity or inside air-conditioned buildings can build up static electricity—at best, a nuisance, at worst, a hazard. The level of human sensitivity to static electricity is 2.5 to 3 kilovolts.

Density: weight of fiber per unit of volume. It varies with the denier of the yarn and the closeness of tufts and inversely with the pile height. The heavier the traffic, the higher the density should be.

Construction: high-traffic areas call for low pile. In a low-traffic area, a high pile will not jeopardize carpet performance.

Color: should vary according to the nature of soiling: beige in a sandy area, gray or blue where there is industrial soot, red or tan where the soil is predominantly clay. In that way, carpets will hide dirt better and reduce maintenance cost.

Maintenance of a carpet plays an important part in its wear. The best and least expensive method of caring is preventive maintenance. Frequent vacuuming will make routine maintenance and cleaning easier and more effective. The grit below the surface of the pile causes an abrasive effect, wearing down the fibers. These are removed by frequent vacuuming. The single and most difficult problem in carpet maintenance is that of spilling and stains. Immediate action following a spill can work wonders on stains. If allowed to dry, it may become difficult or impossible to remove a stain completely. If the carpet cannot be removed for cleaning, good results can be obtained through rotary shampooing, steam extraction, or dry foam cleaning.

In selecting carpet cushion or backing, a choice of soft or firm is available. A soft cushion is squashed by each foot step, stretching the carpet until it breaks. A firm cushion is best for long carpet life. Cushion is the reason for long life. Tests have shown that a carpet will last 20% longer with a cushion or backing. The secret is to select a cushion or backing with enough give to absorb impact shock and with enough firmness to keep supporting the carpet back to its resting position.

Tile

Under the heading of tile are included ceramic mosaic tile (Fig. 19-26), slate, blue stone, flagstone, quarry tile, and terrazzo. Terrazzo is a concrete mix with marble chips mixed in. After setting, the entire floor is ground with a grinding machine for a smooth, even, colorful finish. Quarry tile is installed the same as ceramic tile (see "Ceramic Tile" under "Walls"); slate, bluestone, and flagstone must be prefitted before installation over a concrete base.

INTERIOR TRIM

Installing interior trim requires great care and accuracy in mating the parts together. This phase of construction can greatly enhance or detract from an overall project.

Stair Construction

Stairs should be designed for ease, comfort, and safety. Stock stair parts for complete staircases of excellence can be selected from manufacturers' catalogs or purchased from lumber dealers (Figs. 19-27 and 19-28).

Figure 19-26 Ceramic floor tile. (Courtesy of American Olean Tile.)

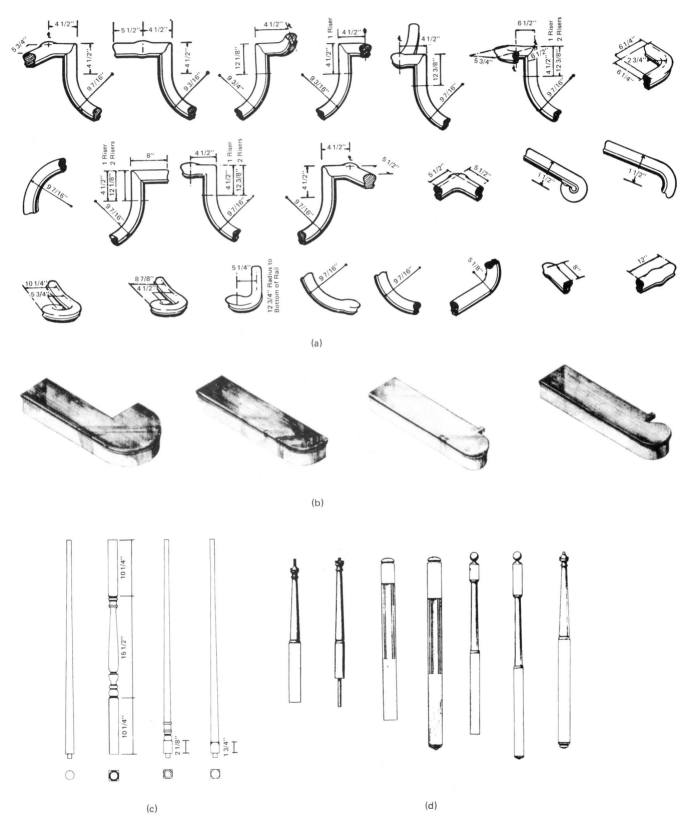

Figure 19-27 Stair parts: (a) stair rails; (b) starting steps; (c) balusters; (d) newel posts. (Courtesy of Brockway Smith Company.)

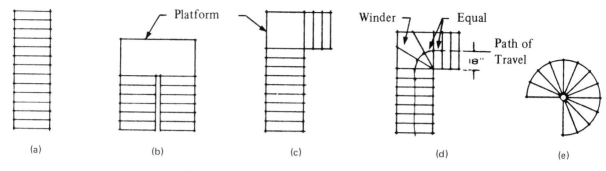

Figure 19-28 Stair types: (a) straight run; (b) U-type; (c) L-type with platform; (d) L-type with winders; (e) spiral.

The criteria for stair design are the vertical distance from finish floor to finish floor and the width of the stairs. Minimum width should be 3 ft 6 in. from finish wall to finish wall (Fig. 19-29). Terms used in stair construction may be defined as follows:

Rise: total height from floor to floor

Run: total length of stairs

Riser: vertical height of one step

Tread: width of horizontal step

Nosing: projection of tread beyond face of riser

Carriage or stringer: rough lumber supporting risers and treads

Newel: main post of railing at start of stairs

Railing: projection of open stair or wall for hand grasping

Baluster: vertical member of railing supporting hand rail

Winders: radiating or turns at stairs

Landing: floor at top or bottom between stair endings of runs or flights

Platform: intermediate landings between two parts of stairs

Bullnose: the first step which extends out forming a semicircle after receiving the newel post

The dimensions of treads and risers were established during the planning stage in order to prepare the rough stair opening. The total distance

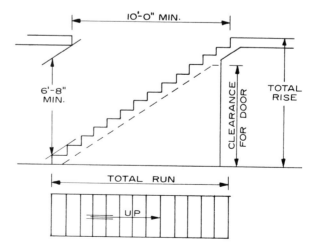

Figure 19-29 Stair clearances. (Courtesy of U.S. Department of Agriculture.)

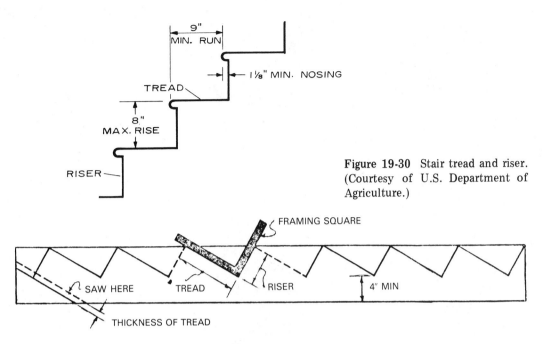

Figure 19-30 Stair tread and riser. (Courtesy of U.S. Department of Agriculture.)

Figure 19-31 Stringer layout.

from floor to floor is divided by the number of risers to reach that distance. Risers should not exceed 8 in. in height. Between 7 and 8 in. is a comfortable height. The stair treads should not be less than 9 in. nor more than 12 in. The total number of treads multiplied by the width or dimension of the tread will equal the stair run (Fig. 19-30).

Stairs are made up of stringers cut from 2 × 12's with one on each side or wall and one in the center (Fig. 19-31). Careful planning and cutting are necessary. If the risers are too high, the climb will strain the muscles and heart; if too low, the discomfort will be just as severe because of the multiple repetition of movement. If the tread is too short, the stair will be too steep, and if too long will result in fatigue and waste of space. Experience has proven that a riser between 7 and 7½ in. high offers the best comfort. A good stair ratio can be provided by using one of the following formulas: One tread plus two risers equals 24 or 25. One riser and one tread equals 17 or 18. One tread multiplied by one riser equals 70 to 75. The natural path or line of travel in climbing stairs that have a hand rail is taken at a distance of 1 ft 8 in. to 2 ft from the rail. The minimum head room required at any point or part of an overhead structure is 6 ft 6 in. measured vertically from the face of the riser.

Handrail and Railing Details

Handrails should be placed on the right side of stairs, descending. The horizontal dimension of the handrail (grip) should not exceed 2⅝ in. Handrails should return to the wall or floor, or terminate in a post, scroll, or loop. Mounting height for stoops and porches should be at least 30 in. (Fig. 19-32).

Kitchen Cabinets

Three types of cabinets are available for kitchens: built on the job, custom-built in a shop, and stock or mass-produced cabinets, selected to fit the allocated space (Fig. 19-33).

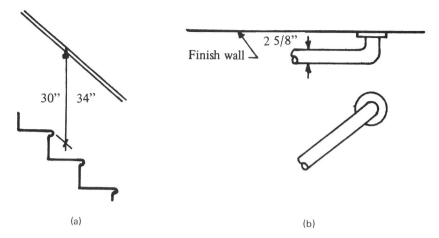

Figure 19-32 Stair handrails: (a) height; (b) wall flange.

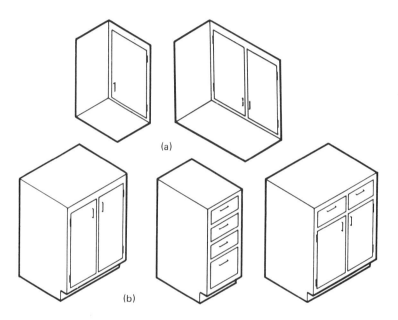

Figure 19-33 Kitchen cabinets: (a) wall; (b) base. (Courtesy of U.S. Department of Agriculture.)

All dimensions are standard, with the base unit being 36 in. high and 24 in. deep, 15 to 18 in. from countertop to under side of upper cabinets, upper shelves 12 in. deep; the distance from the floor to the uppermost cabinet should be door height, usually 6 ft 8 in. above the floor. The lower or base cabinet has a toe space 2 in. deep and 4 in. high. The toe space is necessary because without it, working at the counter will be very uncomfortable. One's feet could not get close enough to the counter for working comfort (Fig. 19-34).

Built-on-the-job parts are built from ¾-in. lumber core plywood with a choice of veneer. The parts are cut, sanded, and assembled, or built to the wall piece by piece, attached to the wall and floor. The vertical members are called stiles and the horizontal members are called rails.

Baseboard

This stock molding is attached to the wall at floor level before the finish floor is installed. It is one of the last pieces of trim installed. Baseboards run around the entire perimeter of the room and stop against the door casing (Fig. 19-35).

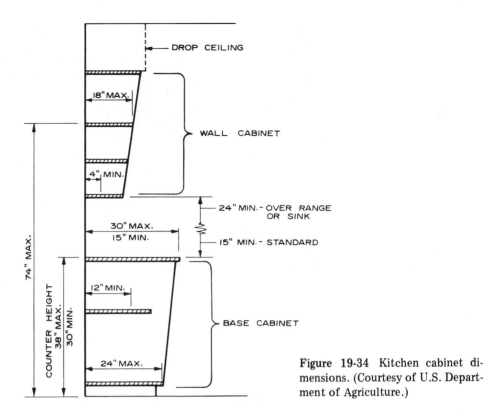

Figure 19-34 Kitchen cabinet dimensions. (Courtesy of U.S. Department of Agriculture.)

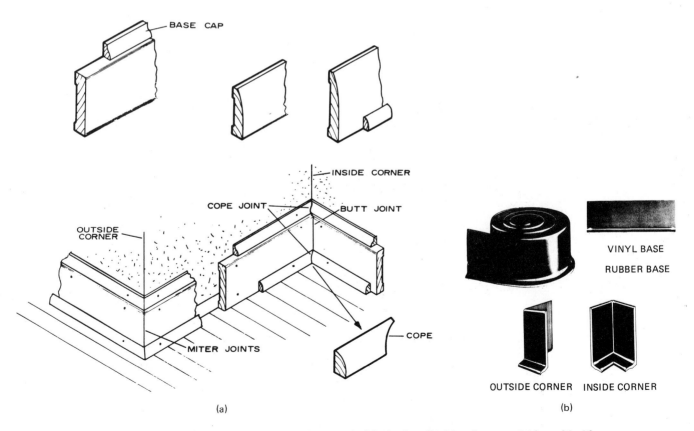

(a)

(b)

Figure 19-35 Baseboard: (a) wood; (b) vinyl and rubber bases, outside and inside corners. (Courtesy of U.S. Department of Agriculture.)

Moldings

Wood and plastics are used to form moldings for the final step before painting. Examples are shown in Fig. 19-36. These are precision building products manufactured to national standards as trim material. To "trim out" a house means to install and finish the moldings. Literally, moldings are strips of wood or plastic up to 16 ft long and milled into about 30 different stock patterns, or profiles, continuous throughout their length. Each profile is designed for a primary use, and some have a large number of secondary uses as well.

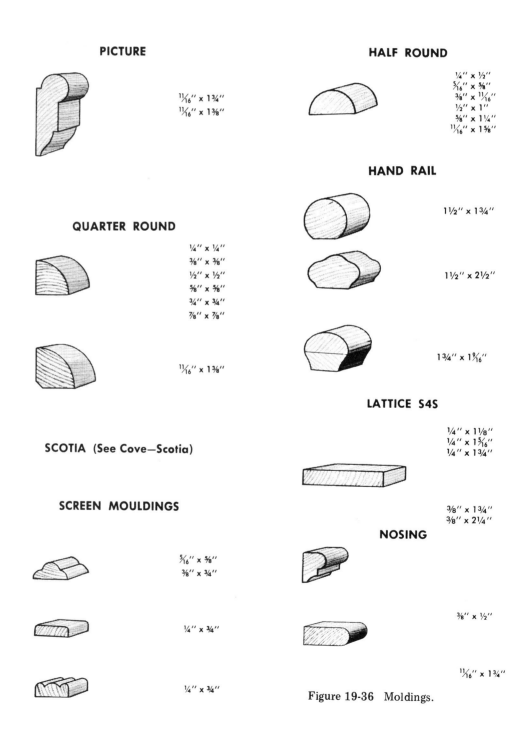

Figure 19-36 Moldings.

SUB SILL

$1\frac{1}{16}'' \times 4\frac{1}{4}''$

WALL

$\frac{5}{8}'' \times \frac{7}{8}''$

STOPS SETS FOR DOOR TRIM

$\frac{3}{8}'' \times 1\frac{5}{16}''$

$\frac{3}{8}'' \times 1\frac{5}{16}''$

STOPS

$\frac{3}{8}'' \times 1\frac{5}{8}''$
$\frac{3}{8}'' \times 1\frac{5}{16}''$
$\frac{3}{8}'' \times \frac{11}{16}''$
$\frac{3}{8}'' \times \frac{7}{8}''$
$\frac{3}{8}'' \times 1\frac{3}{4}''$
$\frac{3}{8}'' \times 3\frac{5}{8}''$

$\frac{3}{8}'' \times 2\frac{1}{2}''$
$\frac{3}{8}'' \times 4\frac{1}{4}''$
$\frac{3}{8}'' \times 3\frac{5}{8}''$
$\frac{3}{8}'' \times 1\frac{5}{8}''$
$\frac{3}{8}'' \times 1\frac{5}{16}''$

$\frac{3}{8}'' \times 1\frac{5}{8}''$

$\frac{3}{8}'' \times 1\frac{5}{16}''$
$\frac{3}{8}'' \times 1\frac{5}{8}''$
$\frac{3}{8}'' \times \frac{7}{8}''$
$\frac{3}{8}'' \times \frac{11}{16}''$

CASING (TRANSOM)

$\frac{1}{2}'' \times 1\frac{1}{4}''$

PANEL STOCK S4S

$\frac{7}{16}'' \times 2\frac{1}{2}''$
$\frac{7}{16}'' \times 3\frac{1}{2}''$
$\frac{7}{16}'' \times 4\frac{1}{2}''$
$\frac{7}{16}'' \times 5\frac{1}{2}''$
$\frac{7}{16}'' \times 7\frac{1}{2}''$

PANEL, WALLBOARD, AND TILEBOARD

$\frac{11}{16}'' \times \frac{7}{8}''$

$\frac{3}{8}'' \times 1\frac{3}{4}''$
$\frac{5}{8}'' \times 2\frac{1}{4}''$

$\frac{3}{8}'' \times 1''$

$\frac{7}{16}'' \times 1\frac{1}{8}''$

$\frac{1}{2}'' \times \frac{9}{16}''$

STOOL CAP

$\frac{11}{16}'' \times 3\frac{1}{4}''$

$\frac{3}{4}'' \times 4\frac{1}{4}''$

$\frac{11}{16}'' \times 3\frac{1}{2}''$

$\frac{11}{16}'' \times 2\frac{1}{4}''$

$1\frac{1}{16}'' \times 4\frac{1}{4}''$

$1\frac{1}{16}'' \times 3\frac{1}{4}''$

ASTRAGAL

$\frac{11}{16}'' \times 1\frac{3}{4}''$

Figure 19-36 Moldings (continued).

APRON

$\frac{5}{8}'' \times 3\frac{1}{2}''$

$\frac{9}{16}'' \times 2\frac{1}{2}''$

$\frac{5}{8}'' \times 2''$

$\frac{5}{8}'' \times 2\frac{1}{2}''$

PARTING BEAD

$\frac{1}{2}'' \times \frac{3}{4}''$
$\frac{3}{8}'' \times \frac{3}{4}''$

OFFSET PARTING BEAD

$\frac{1}{2}'' \times \frac{13}{16}''$

SCREEN STOCK

$\frac{11}{16}'' \times 1\frac{3}{4}''$
$1\frac{1}{16}'' \times 1\frac{3}{4}''$

$\frac{11}{16}'' \times 1\frac{3}{4}''$

CLOSET POLE

$1\frac{1}{8}''$
$1\frac{1}{16}''$
$1\frac{5}{16}''$
$1\frac{5}{8}''$

SHELF CLEAT

$\frac{11}{16}'' \times 1\frac{1}{2}''$

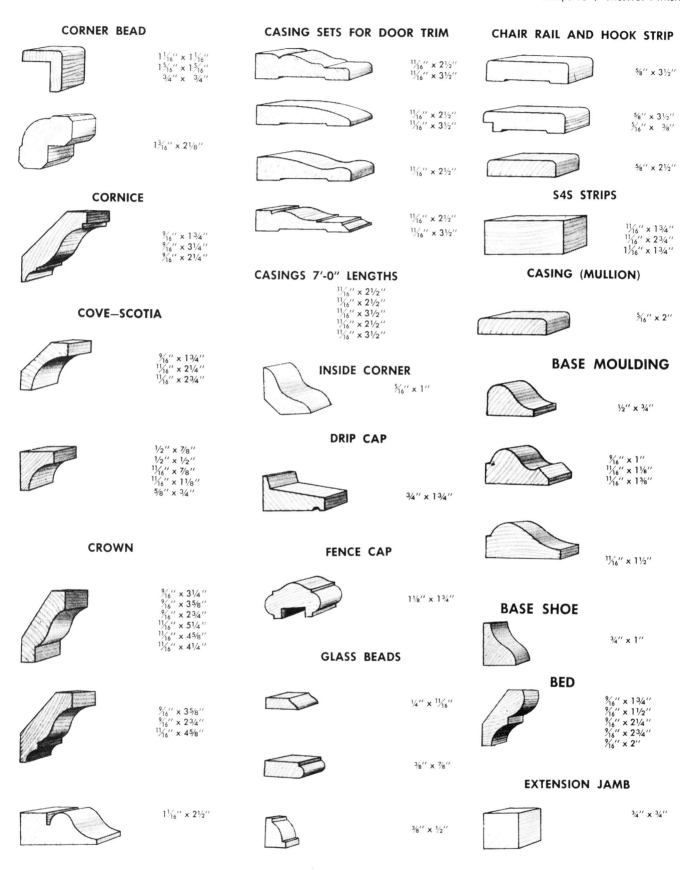

CORNER BEAD

$1\frac{1}{16}'' \times 1\frac{1}{16}''$
$1\frac{5}{16}'' \times 1\frac{5}{16}''$
$\frac{3}{4}'' \times \frac{3}{4}''$

$1\frac{3}{16}'' \times 2\frac{1}{8}''$

CORNICE

$\frac{9}{16}'' \times 1\frac{3}{4}''$
$\frac{9}{16}'' \times 3\frac{1}{4}''$
$\frac{9}{16}'' \times 2\frac{1}{4}''$

COVE—SCOTIA

$\frac{9}{16}'' \times 1\frac{3}{4}''$
$\frac{11}{16}'' \times 2\frac{1}{4}''$
$\frac{11}{16}'' \times 2\frac{3}{4}''$

$\frac{1}{2}'' \times \frac{7}{8}''$
$\frac{1}{2}'' \times \frac{1}{2}''$
$\frac{11}{16}'' \times \frac{7}{8}''$
$\frac{11}{16}'' \times 1\frac{1}{8}''$
$\frac{5}{8}'' \times \frac{3}{4}''$

CROWN

$\frac{9}{16}'' \times 3\frac{1}{4}''$
$\frac{9}{16}'' \times 3\frac{5}{8}''$
$\frac{9}{16}'' \times 2\frac{3}{4}''$
$\frac{11}{16}'' \times 5\frac{1}{4}''$
$\frac{11}{16}'' \times 4\frac{5}{8}''$
$\frac{11}{16}'' \times 4\frac{1}{4}''$

$\frac{9}{16}'' \times 3\frac{5}{8}''$
$\frac{9}{16}'' \times 2\frac{3}{4}''$
$\frac{11}{16}'' \times 4\frac{5}{8}''$

$1\frac{1}{16}'' \times 2\frac{1}{2}''$

CASING SETS FOR DOOR TRIM

$\frac{11}{16}'' \times 2\frac{1}{2}''$
$\frac{11}{16}'' \times 3\frac{1}{2}''$

$\frac{11}{16}'' \times 2\frac{1}{2}''$
$\frac{11}{16}'' \times 3\frac{1}{2}''$

$\frac{11}{16}'' \times 2\frac{1}{2}''$

$\frac{11}{16}'' \times 2\frac{1}{2}''$
$\frac{11}{16}'' \times 3\frac{1}{2}''$

CASINGS 7'-0" LENGTHS

$\frac{11}{16}'' \times 2\frac{1}{2}''$
$\frac{11}{16}'' \times 2\frac{1}{2}''$
$\frac{11}{16}'' \times 3\frac{1}{2}''$
$\frac{11}{16}'' \times 2\frac{1}{2}''$
$\frac{11}{16}'' \times 3\frac{1}{2}''$

INSIDE CORNER

$\frac{5}{16}'' \times 1''$

DRIP CAP

$\frac{3}{4}'' \times 1\frac{3}{4}''$

FENCE CAP

$1\frac{1}{8}'' \times 1\frac{3}{4}''$

GLASS BEADS

$\frac{1}{4}'' \times \frac{11}{16}''$

$\frac{3}{8}'' \times \frac{7}{8}''$

$\frac{3}{8}'' \times \frac{1}{2}''$

CHAIR RAIL AND HOOK STRIP

$\frac{5}{8}'' \times 3\frac{1}{2}''$

$\frac{5}{8}'' \times 3\frac{1}{2}''$
$\frac{5}{16}'' \times \frac{3}{8}''$

$\frac{5}{8}'' \times 2\frac{1}{2}''$

S4S STRIPS

$\frac{11}{16}'' \times 1\frac{3}{4}''$
$\frac{11}{16}'' \times 2\frac{3}{4}''$
$1\frac{1}{16}'' \times 1\frac{3}{4}''$

CASING (MULLION)

$\frac{5}{16}'' \times 2''$

BASE MOULDING

$\frac{1}{2}'' \times \frac{3}{4}''$

$\frac{9}{16}'' \times 1''$
$\frac{11}{16}'' \times 1\frac{1}{8}''$
$\frac{11}{16}'' \times 1\frac{3}{8}''$

$\frac{11}{16}'' \times 1\frac{1}{2}''$

BASE SHOE

$\frac{3}{4}'' \times 1''$

BED

$\frac{9}{16}'' \times 1\frac{3}{4}''$
$\frac{9}{16}'' \times 1\frac{1}{2}''$
$\frac{9}{16}'' \times 2\frac{1}{4}''$
$\frac{9}{16}'' \times 2\frac{3}{4}''$
$\frac{9}{16}'' \times 2''$

EXTENSION JAMB

$\frac{3}{4}'' \times \frac{3}{4}''$

Figure 19-36 Moldings (continued).

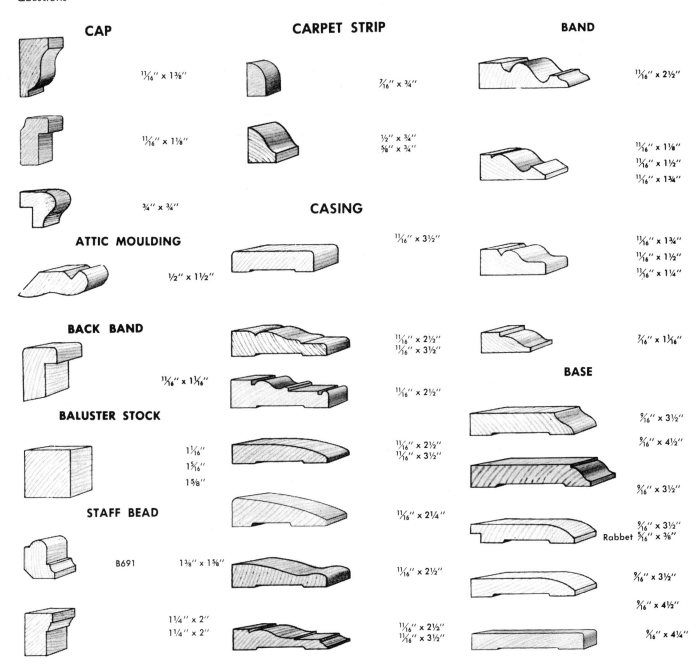

Figure 19-36   Moldings (continued). (Courtesy of Brockway Smith Company.)

QUESTIONS

1. Define *composition paneling*. _____

_____

2. All prefinished paneling is plywood.   True or False
3. Laminated plastic is used for floor covering.   True or False

4. Which of the following plaster board is known as drywall?
   A. Sheetrock
   B. Gypsum board
   C. Drywall
   D. None of the above
5. Plaster can be applied over studs.   True or False
6. Define *wire lath* or *metal lath.* _____

   _____

7. Wood flooring is manufactured from which of the following?
   A. Oak
   B. Maple
   C. Beech
   D. Birch
   E. All of the above
8. Moisture will not affect hardwood flooring.   True or False
9. Define *sleeper.* _____

   _____

10. Which of the following is resilient flooring?
    A. Sheet vinyl
    B. Carpet
    C. Vinyl asbestos
    D. Wood
11. There is only one way to manufacture carpet.   True or False
12. Define *stair riser.* _____

    _____

13. Stairs that radiate at turns are called circular stairs.   True or False
14. Stair handrails should be mounted at what height above the stairs?
    A. 36 in.
    B. 28 in.
    C. 30 in.
    D. 34 in.
15. What does *trim out* mean? _____

    _____

20

Hardware

INTRODUCTION

Hardware used for buildings is grouped into two categories: rough hardware, which includes nails, screws, anchor bolts, hangers, and straps, and finish hardware, including hinges, butts, locks, drawer pulls, cabinet door closers, magnetic catches, and closet poles, hangers, and racks.

Rough hardware is manufactured from steel, copper, zinc, brass, yellow metal, and aluminum. Finish hardware is manufactured from brass, copper, aluminum, stainless steel, and plastics. The finish is available in smooth, hammered, highly polished, matt finish, and rough finish. Finish hardware can be applied flush, recessed, semirecessed, or concealed.

NAILS

No matter what building material is selected for construction, special nails for that material have been designed (Fig. 20-1). Nails are the most popular way of holding wood members together. When a nail is driven into a piece of wood, the fibers of the wood grip onto the nail shank, giving it its holding power.

The two main headings of nails are cut nails and wire nails. Cut nails are stamped or sheared from a steel plate with tempered edges and blunt points. Wire nails are manufactured from steel wire of various gauges and thicknesses. Copper and aluminum wire is also used for wire nails, giving them rust-resistance qualities. The heads of nails vary with the design and use. Nails used for finish work have narrow heads to prevent the wood from splitting. They are often driven below the wood surface with a nail set, and

Common and box nails:

16d for general framing.
8d and 10d for toenailing.
6d and 8d for subfloor, wall sheathing and roof sheathing.
Size depends on thickness of plywood sheathing.

Scaffold nails:

8d and 10d most common, for scaffolds, bracing, and any temporary fastening that must be later removed.

Siding nails:

Nonstaining nails of size specified for siding thickness (usually 6d and 8d).

Casing and finish nails:

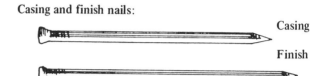

Figure 20-1 Nails commonly used for residential construction.

the hole is filled with a filler such as putty or plastic wood. Nails used for framing have a wide head, for more holding power. These are called common nails. The shank on some nails is grooved to give the nail greater holding power.

The points of nails are designed for specific purposes. Diamond-pointed nails are the ordinary type, and it is easy to begin nailing or driving the nail with only a light tap to hold it in position for more forceful blows, to drive it completely. The diamond point paves the way for the nail as it is driven firm. Winged-point nails are used for common nails without fear of wood splitting. Nail heads also vary in design. They include flat, conical, and spherical, all of which are designed to be countersunk below the surface of the wood. Others have countersunk heads for holding the nail set in position to drive the nail below the wood surface. Without the countersunk head the nail set may slip, damaging the wood. Double-headed nails are used for temporary nailing. The first head is for holding power, and the second head is for gripping the nail with hammer claws for removal. These nails are used mostly for form work and staggings.

Nail shanks also have a variety of designs, including barbed, knurled, grooved, fluted, twisted, and threaded. The twisted and threaded nails have greater holding power (Fig. 20-2). Nail sizes are indicated by "penny." The larger the penny number, the larger the nail. High-carbon-steel nails are very hard and are used for driving nails into concrete and masonry without bending.

BOLTS AND SCREWS

As with nails, a variety of construction projects require bolts or screws (Fig. 20-3). These have a special head and shape for each specific purpose. The most common are flat head, used mostly for countersinking or setting

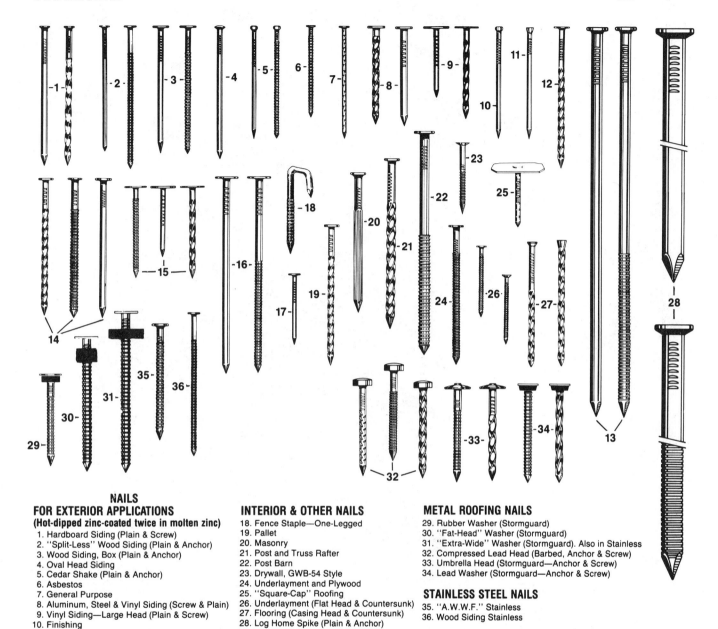

Figure 20-2 Twisted and threaded nails. (Courtesy of Maze Nail Co.)

NAILS
FOR EXTERIOR APPLICATIONS
(Hot-dipped zinc-coated twice in molten zinc)
1. Hardboard Siding (Plain & Screw)
2. "Split-Less" Wood Siding (Plain & Anchor)
3. Wood Siding, Box (Plain & Anchor)
4. Oval Head Siding
5. Cedar Shake (Plain & Anchor)
6. Asbestos
7. General Purpose
8. Aluminum, Steel & Vinyl Siding (Screw & Plain)
9. Vinyl Siding—Large Head (Plain & Screw)
10. Finishing
11. Casing
12. Cribber
13. Gutter Spike (Plain & Anchor)
14. Pressure Treated Lumber (Screw, Anchor & Plain)
15. Asphalt Shingle (Anchor, Plain & Screw)
16. Insulation Roof Deck (Plain & Anchor)
17. Cedar Shingle

INTERIOR & OTHER NAILS
18. Fence Staple—One-Legged
19. Pallet
20. Masonry
21. Post and Truss Rafter
22. Post Barn
23. Drywall, GWB-54 Style
24. Underlayment and Plywood
25. "Square-Cap" Roofing
26. Underlayment (Flat Head & Countersunk)
27. Flooring (Casing Head & Countersunk)
28. Log Home Spike (Plain & Anchor)

METAL ROOFING NAILS
29. Rubber Washer (Stormguard)
30. "Fat-Head" Washer (Stormguard)
31. "Extra-Wide" Washer (Stormguard). Also in Stainless
32. Compressed Lead Head (Barbed, Anchor & Screw)
33. Umbrella Head (Stormguard—Anchor & Screw)
34. Lead Washer (Stormguard—Anchor & Screw)

STAINLESS STEEL NAILS
35. "A.W.W.F." Stainless
36. Wood Siding Stainless

flush with the surface. The round head is used for surface hardware. The oval head is used where periodic removal is anticipated.

Expansion bolts (Fig. 20-4) are used for fastening into concrete or masonry. Holes must be predrilled slightly larger than the hardware and the unit is forced into the predrilled hole. As the screw portion is inserted and turned, the tapered screw forces the hardware open, wedging it against the drilled hole's walls.

Screws are made from brass, steel, aluminum, and stainless steel, and some may be plated for special purposes. Screws are from ¼ to 5 in. long. They are turned with a Phillips screwdriver or a standard screwdriver. Lag

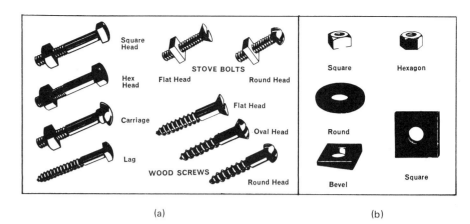

(a)   (b)

Figure 20-3   (a) Bolts and screws; (b) nuts and washers. (Courtesy of Heckman Building Products, Inc.)

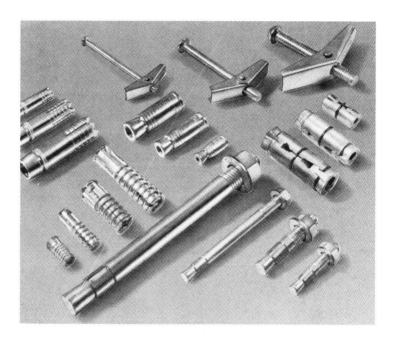

Figure 20-4   Expansion bolts. (Courtesy of U.S.E. Diamond, Inc.)

screws are turned with a wrench and are used for fastening heavy timbers or steel structural members to wood.

Bolts have two threaded designs, standard thread and machine thread. Machine threads have more grooves per inch for more holding power. Holes must be predrilled to receive lag bolts, and the two members are held together by a washer and a nut.

FINISH HARDWARE

One of the last projects to be done on a construction project is to install the finish hardware. This hardware is visible when installed and the aesthetic design of hardware is wide and varied, to complement any building design or style. Finish hardware falls under the category of butts, hinges, door closers, locks, latches, pulls, lifts, and miscellaneous hardware.

A hinge consists of two metal straps rotating on a pin (Fig. 20-5). These units are screwed to the surface of the door without any cutout or recess. The term "hinge" is mostly used for cabinet hardware.

A butt, sometimes called a hinge, is similar in design except that it is cut into or mortised into the door and frame (Fig. 20-6). The round central

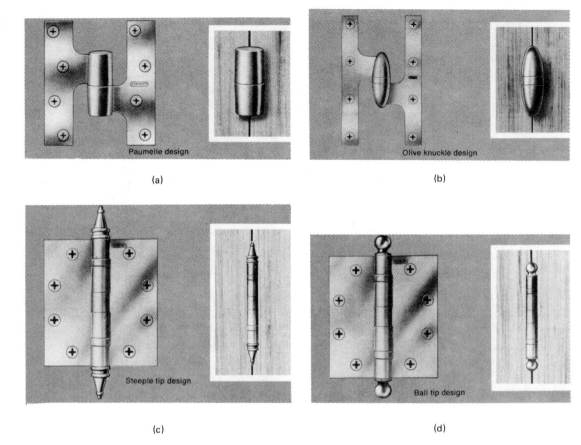

(a)   (b)

(c)   (d)

Figure 20-5 Hinges: (a) Paumelle; (b) olive knuckle; (c) steeple tip; (d) ball tip. (Courtesy of Stanley Hardware.)

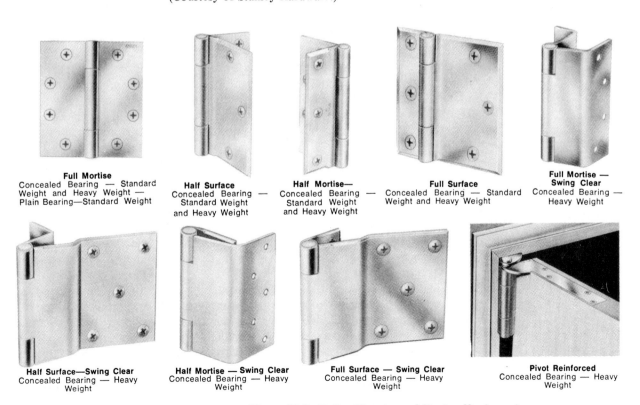

Full Mortise
Concealed Bearing — Standard Weight and Heavy Weight — Plain Bearing—Standard Weight

Half Surface
Concealed Bearing — Standard Weight and Heavy Weight

Half Mortise—
Concealed Bearing — Standard Weight and Heavy Weight

Full Surface
Concealed Bearing — Standard Weight and Heavy Weight

Full Mortise — Swing Clear
Concealed Bearing — Heavy Weight

Half Surface—Swing Clear
Concealed Bearing — Heavy Weight

Half Mortise — Swing Clear
Concealed Bearing — Heavy Weight

Full Surface — Swing Clear
Concealed Bearing — Heavy Weight

Pivot Reinforced
Concealed Bearing — Heavy Weight

Figure 20-6 Butts. (Courtesy of Stanley Hardware.)

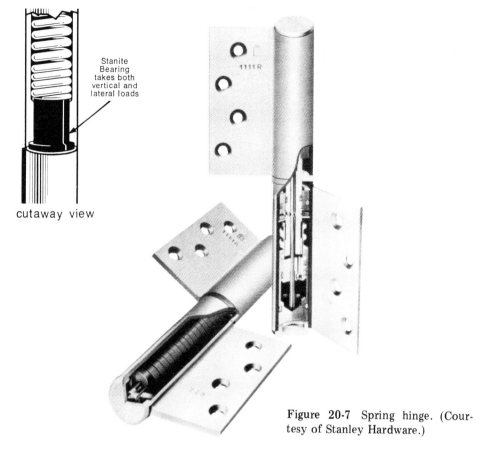

Stanite Bearing takes both vertical and lateral loads

cutaway view

Figure 20-7 Spring hinge. (Courtesy of Stanley Hardware.)

part of the butt, the part the pin slides into, is called a knuckle, and the flat part is called a flap or leaves. Some pins which hold the leaves together are removable. These are called loose pins. A nonremovable pin is called a fast pin. There are also loose self-locking pins to prevent tampering with the door when the door is closed. Some pins have built-in springs to self-close the door (Fig. 20-7). There are also invisible hinges or butts, which are completely recessed and cannot be seen when the door is closed (Fig. 20-8). Double-acting hinges or butts allow the door to open in both directions. As a rule, double-acting hardware is mounted on the floor and the bottom of the door (Fig. 20-9).

DOOR CLOSERS

Door closers, sometimes called door checks, are devices that close the door automatically without slamming. These can be surface mounted, recessed, or semirecessed (Fig. 20-10). They are installed in the floor under the door or on top of the door.

Two types of door closers are available: liquid or hydraulic type and pneumatic type. Large doors require the liquid type, and small doors require the pneumatic type. Door closers can be adjusted to control the action of the door closing, based on door weight. There are also electric door openers and closers, such as those used on overhead garage doors. These are controlled by a pushbutton or a radio-controlled remote box. This type of door works on a chain-drive system.

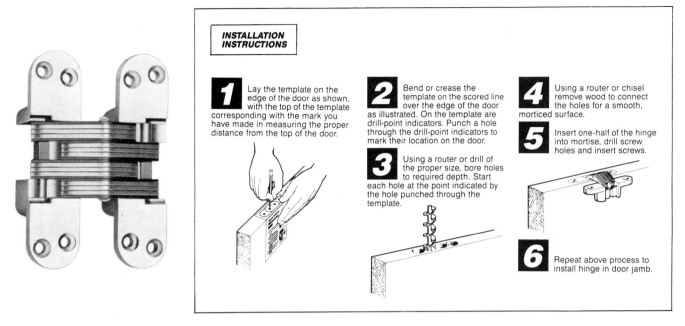

Figure 20-8 Invisible hinge. (Courtesy of Soss Manufacturing Co.)

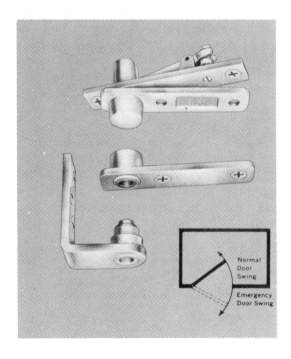

Figure 20-9 Double-acting door pivot. (Courtesy of Stanley Hardware.)

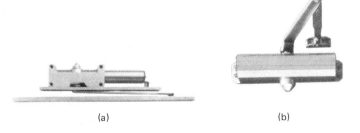

(a)   (b)

Figure 20-10 Door closers: (a) concealed; (b) surface. (Courtesy of Norton Door Controls.)

LOCKS AND LATCHES

Hardware used to hold doors closed are called locks and latches. Sometimes the lock or latch is a single unit which is called a lock. There are many types of locks: mortise lock, cylinder lock, dead bolt lock, unit lock, rim lock, and so on, all of which serve a specific function.

Mortise lock: concealed into the door except for the face plate and door knob (Fig. 20-11).

Cylinder lock: has pins in a barrel which mate with grooves on a key; can be opened from the outside only with a key (Fig. 20-12).

Dead bolt lock: sliding bolt activated only by a key (Fig. 20-13).

Unit lock: factory-made assembly that fits into a prepared recess in the door; similar to a mortise lock except that the lock cylinder has a knob (Fig. 20-14).

Rim lock: jimmy-proof; for extra security.

Padlock: portable and requires a lasp for attaching (Fig. 20-15).

Key-operated locks work on the principle of free-moving pins and key which when combined form a combination of freeing the cylinder to unlock the lock. Five or more pins generally form the lock combination. The key fits into a slot in the cylinder and the grooves in the key set the positions of all pins to afford the cylinder to turn opening the lock (Fig. 20-16). Combination locks work on a preset system of numbers which when matched in sequence, release the mechanism to open the lock. Some combination locks require a key to complete the combination (Fig. 20-17).

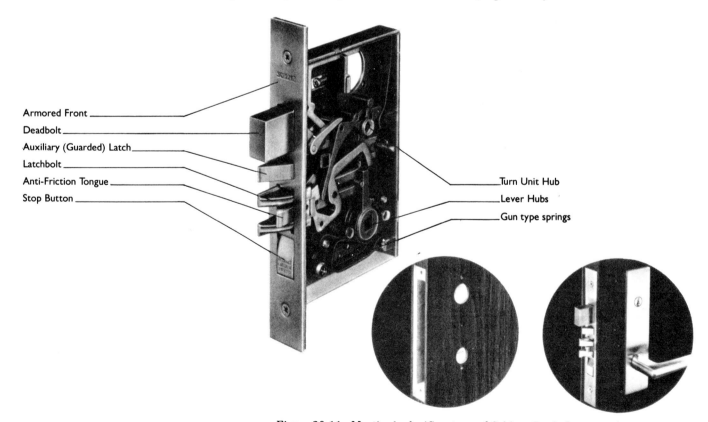

Armored Front
Deadbolt
Auxiliary (Guarded) Latch
Latchbolt
Anti-Friction Tongue
Stop Button

Turn Unit Hub
Lever Hubs
Gun type springs

Figure 20-11 Mortise lock. (Courtesy of Schlage Lock Company.)

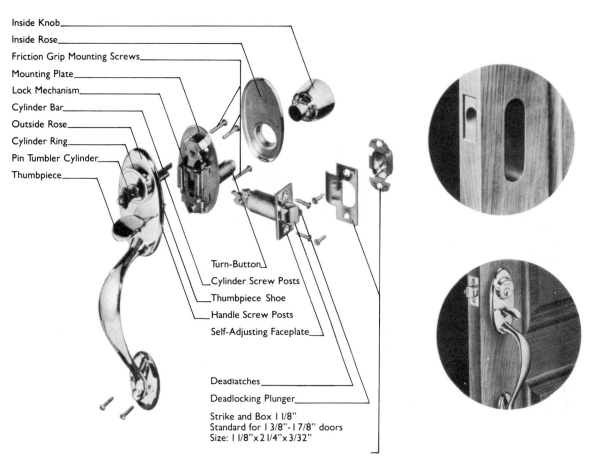

Inside Knob

Inside Rose

Friction Grip Mounting Screws

Mounting Plate

Lock Mechanism

Cylinder Bar

Outside Rose

Cylinder Ring

Pin Tumbler Cylinder

Thumbpiece

Turn-Button

Cylinder Screw Posts

Thumbpiece Shoe

Handle Screw Posts

Self-Adjusting Faceplate

Deadlatches

Deadlocking Plunger

Strike and Box 1 1/8"
Standard for 1 3/8"-1 7/8" doors
Size: 1 1/8" x 2 1/4" x 3/32"

Figure 20-12 Cylinder lock. (Courtesy of Schlage Lock Company.)

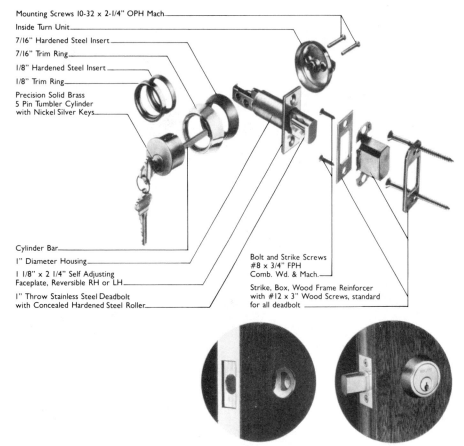

Mounting Screws 10-32 x 2-1/4" OPH Mach

Inside Turn Unit

7/16" Hardened Steel Insert

7/16" Trim Ring

1/8" Hardened Steel Insert

1/8" Trim Ring

Precision Solid Brass
5 Pin Tumbler Cylinder
with Nickel Silver Keys

Cylinder Bar

1" Diameter Housing

1 1/8" x 2 1/4" Self Adjusting
Faceplate, Reversible RH or LH

1" Throw Stainless Steel Deadbolt
with Concealed Hardened Steel Roller

Bolt and Strike Screws
#8 x 3/4" FPH
Comb. Wd. & Mach.

Strike, Box, Wood Frame Reinforcer
with #12 x 3" Wood Screws, standard
for all deadbolt

Figure 20-13 Deadbolt lock. (Courtesy of Schlage Lock Company.)

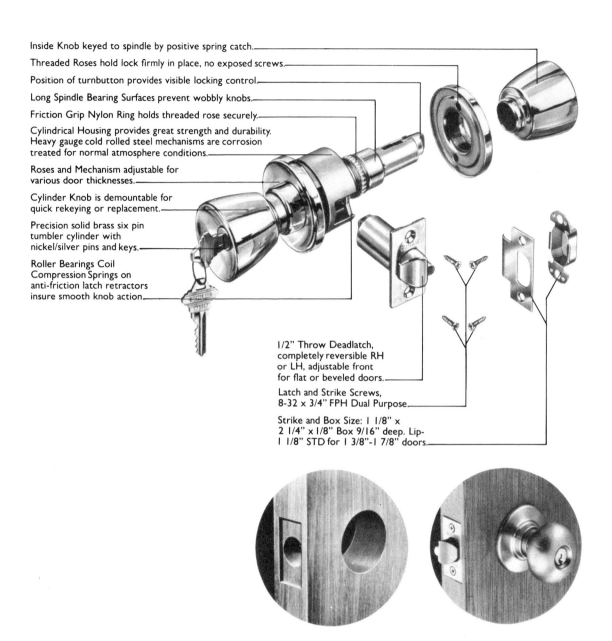

Inside Knob keyed to spindle by positive spring catch.

Threaded Roses hold lock firmly in place, no exposed screws.

Position of turnbutton provides visible locking control.

Long Spindle Bearing Surfaces prevent wobbly knobs.

Friction Grip Nylon Ring holds threaded rose securely.

Cylindrical Housing provides great strength and durability. Heavy gauge cold rolled steel mechanisms are corrosion treated for normal atmosphere conditions.

Roses and Mechanism adjustable for various door thicknesses.

Cylinder Knob is demountable for quick rekeying or replacement.

Precision solid brass six pin tumbler cylinder with nickel/silver pins and keys.

Roller Bearings Coil Compression Springs on anti-friction latch retractors insure smooth knob action.

1/2" Throw Deadlatch, completely reversible RH or LH, adjustable front for flat or beveled doors.

Latch and Strike Screws, 8-32 x 3/4" FPH Dual Purpose.

Strike and Box Size: 1 1/8" x 2 1/4" x 1/8" Box 9/16" deep. Lip-1 1/8" STD for 1 3/8"-1 7/8" doors.

Figure 20-14   Unit lock. (Courtesy of Schlage Lock Company.)

Figure 20-15 Padlock. (Courtesy of Schlage Lock Company.)

MISCELLANEOUS HARDWARE

Many small items of hardware, such as window pulls, cabinet door pulls, magnetic door holders, tracks for sliding doors, hangers, drawer pulls, door stops, closet hardware such as hat racks and coat racks, shoe racks, supports for adjustable shelves, and many more are called miscellaneous hardware.

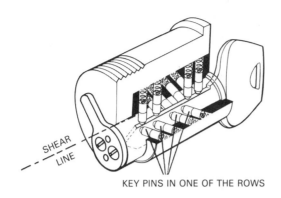

Figure 20-16 Key-operated lock. (Courtesy of Sargent Manufacturing.)

KEY PINS IN ONE OF THE ROWS

SHEAR LINE

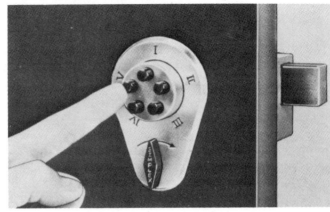

(a)   (b)

Figure 20-17 Combination lock: (a) key type; (b) keyless type. (Courtesy of Simplex Security Systems, Inc.)

QUESTIONS

1. What is the most common way of holding wood members together?

2. Which of the following is the part of the wood that grips the nail for holding power?
   A. Moisture
   B. Grain
   C. Molecules
   D. Fibers

3. Name two nail headings.
   1. _____
   2. _____

4. Nails are purchased by the pound.   True or False

5. The size of nails is measured in inches.   True or False

6. All nails have sharp-pointed tips.   True or False

7. Name three types of screws.
   1. _____
   2. _____
   3. _____

8. Screws are made from which of the following?
   A. Plastic
   B. Brass
   C. Aluminum
   D. Copper
   E. None of the above
   F. All of the above

9. Bolts can be screwed into wood.   True or False

10. Define *finish hardware*. _____

_____

11. What is a butt? _____

_____

12. Door hardware hinges and butts have loose pins and fast pins.
    True or False

13. Door closers work only on friction.   True or False

14. Define *cylinder lock*. _____

_____

15. Miscellaneous hardware is which of the following?
    A. Screws
    B. Bright finish
    C. Window pulls
    D. Combination lock
    E. None of the above
    F. All of the above

21

Plank and Beam Framing

INTRODUCTION

The plank-and-beam method for framing floors and roofs has been used for many years in building heavy timber-type houses. Whereas conventional framing utilizes joists, rafters, and studs spaced 16 to 24 in. apart, the plank-and-beam method requires fewer and larger pieces spaced farther apart.

In plank-and-beam framing, lumber 2 in. or more thick is used to support floors and roofs using beams spaced up to 8 ft apart. The ends of the beams are supported on posts or piers. Wall spaces between the posts are provided with supplementary framing to the extent required for attachment of exterior and interior finishes. This supplementary framing and its covering also serve to provide lateral bracing for the building.

A combination of conventional framing and plank-and-beam framing is sometimes used. Where the two adjoin each other side by side, it presents no particular problem. Where a plank-and-beam floor or roof is supported on a stud wall, a post should be placed under the end of the beam to carry the concentrated load. When conventional roof framing is used with plank-and-beam construction, a header should be installed to carry the load from the rafters to the posts.

LIMITATIONS

There are limitations on the use of the plank-and-beam system, but these can be resolved by careful study and planning. When this is done, the parts of the house fit together very quickly and easily.

Plank floors are designed for moderate uniform loads and are not intended to carry heavy concentrated loads. Where such loads occur, as those for bearing partitions, bathtubs, refrigerators, and so on, additional framing is needed beneath the planks to transmit the loads to the beams.

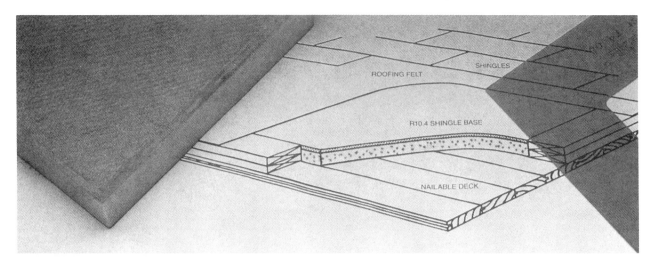

Figure 21-1 Rigid roof insulation. (Courtesy of International Permalite, Inc.)

In moderate climates, the insulation provided by the 2-in.-thick plank is usually adequate. In colder climates additional insulation is often added to satisfy local conditions. Insulation may be applied on top of the planks under the roof shingles. The insulation used is the rigid type (Fig. 21-1). A vapor barrier between the wood plank and the insulation is recommended.

Location of the electrical cable may present a problem in concealing the wiring because there is no space for running the service. This problem is usually solved by making the beams of several pieces of 2-in. lumber separated by blocking to accommodate the electric wiring and pipes (Fig. 21-2). Solid beams may be used to run the electric wiring by covering them with molding. When stud walls are used, wiring presents no problem.

CONSTRUCTION DETAILS

The plank-and-beam system is essentially a skeleton framework. Planks are designed to support a moderate load, uniformly distributed. This is carried to the beams, which in turn transmit their loads to posts which are supported on the foundation. Where heavy concentrated loads occur in places other than over main beams or posts, supplementary beams are needed to carry such loads (Fig. 21-3).

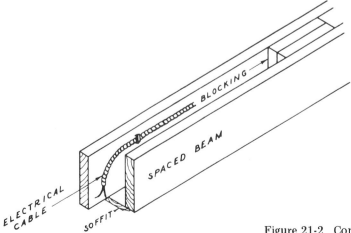

Figure 21-2 Concealed electric wiring.

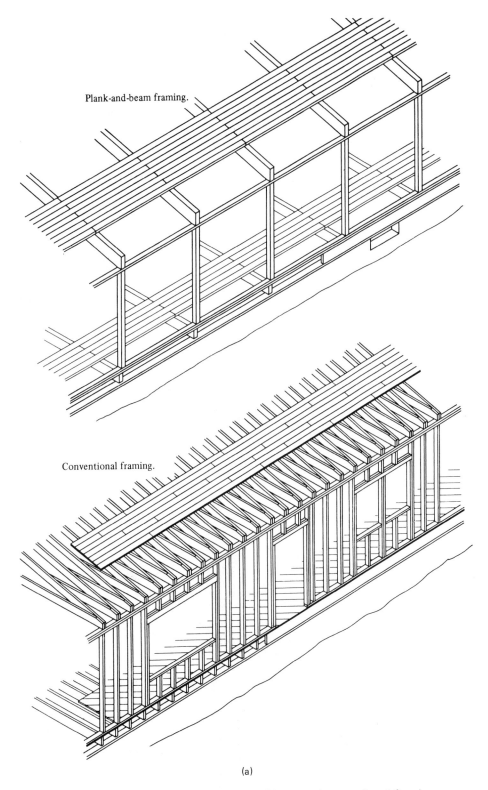

Plank-and-beam framing.

Conventional framing.

(a)

Figure 21-3   (a) Comparison of plank-and-beam and conventional framing.

Foundations for plank-and-beam framing may be continuous walls or piers, supported on adequate footings. With posts spaced up to 8 ft apart in exterior walls, this system is well adapted to pier foundations for houses without basements.

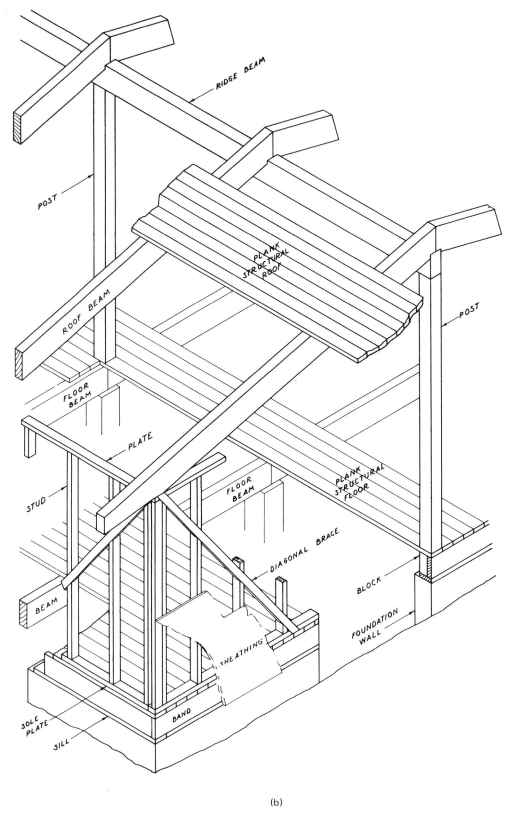

(b)

Figure 21-3 (continued) (b) Plank-and-beam framing for a one-story house.

Posts should be of adequate size to carry the load and large enough to provide full bearing for the ends of beams. In general, posts should be at least 4 X 4 in., nominal. The posts may be solid or made up of several pieces of 2-in. lumber well spiked together.

The size of beams will vary with the span and spacing. Beams may be solid or glued laminated pieces (Fig. 21-4) or may be built up of several thinner pieces securely nailed to each other or to spacer blocks between them. They may also be hand hewn (Fig. 21-5). When built-up beams are used, a cover plate attached to the underside provides the appearance of a solid piece. Fastening of beams to posts is accomplished by framing anchors or angle clips.

Since the 2-in. plank floor or roof frequently serves as the finish ceiling for the room below, appearance as well as structural requirements of the plank should be considered (Fig. 21-6). For the purpose of distributing load, tongued-and-grooved or grooved-for-spline lumber is recommended. Methods

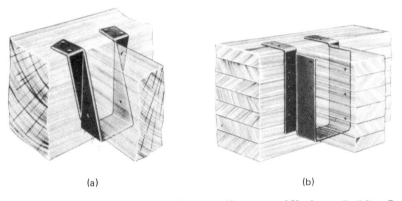

(a)   (b)

Figure 21-4   (a) Solid and (b) laminated beams. (Courtesy of Heckman Building Products.)

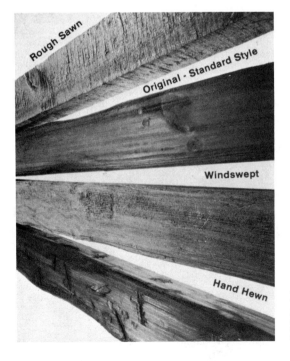

Rough Sawn

Original - Standard Style

Windswept

Hand Hewn

Figure 21-5 Hand-hewn beams. (Courtesy of Rusticated Beams, Inc., Norman LeBlanc, Pres., West Warwick, R.I.)

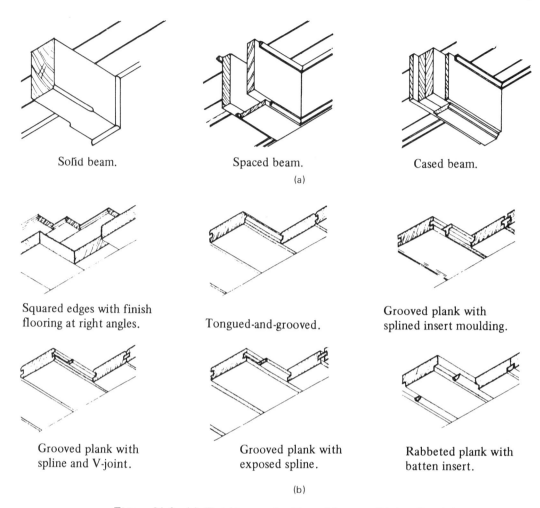

Solid beam.   Spaced beam.   Cased beam.

(a)

Squared edges with finish   Tongued-and-grooved.   Grooved plank with
flooring at right angles.   splined insert moulding.

Grooved plank with   Grooved plank with   Rabbeted plank with
spline and V-joint.   exposed spline.   batten insert.

(b)

Figure 21-6 (a) Finishing undersides of beams; (b) treating joints in
exposed-beam ceilings.

of making the joint to provide various architectural effects provide a pleasing
appearance. A reasonably good grade of lumber should be selected, and it
should be seasoned to meet the requirements of service conditions so as to
avoid large cracks at the joints.

In laying the plank, greater advantage can be taken of the strength and
stiffness of the material by making the planks continuous over more than
one span (Fig. 21-7). For example, using the same span and uniform load
in each case, a plank that is continuous over two spans is nearly two and one-
half times as stiff as a plank that extends over a single span. Planks should
be nailed to each support with two 16d nails (Fig. 21-8). Where standard
lengths of lumber are used, such as 12, 14 or 16 ft, beam spacings of 6, 7 or
8 ft are indicated, and this has a bearing on the overall dimensions of the
house. Where end joints in the plank are allowed to occur between supports,
random-length planks may be used and the beam spacing adjusted to fit the
dimensions of the house.

The finish floor should be laid at right angles to the plank subfloor,
using the same procedure as that followed in conventional construction.
Where the underside of the plank is to serve as a ceiling, care is needed to
make sure that the flooring nails do not penetrate through the plank.

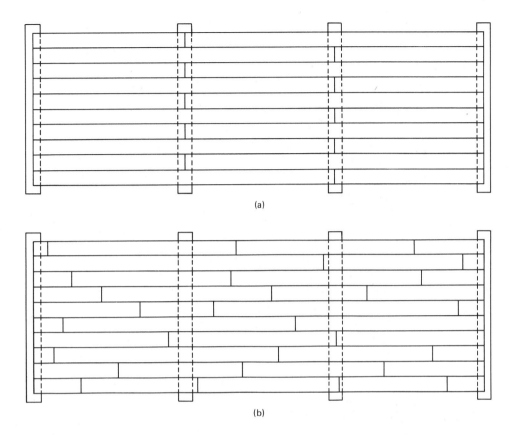

Figure 21-7   (a) Butt-jointed decking; (b) random-length decking.

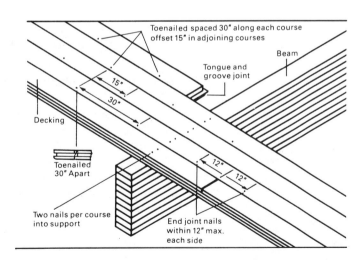

Figure 21-8   Roof plank nailing. (Courtesy of Potlatch Corporation.)

Partitions in the plank-and-beam system usually will be nonbearing (Fig. 21-9). Where bearing partitions occur, they should be placed over beams and the beams enlarged to carry the added load. If this is not possible, supplementary beams must be placed in the floor framing arrangement. Nonbearing partitions, which are parallel to the planks, should have support to carry this load to the beams. This may be accomplished by using two 2 × 4's set on edge as the sole plate. Where openings occur in the partition, the two

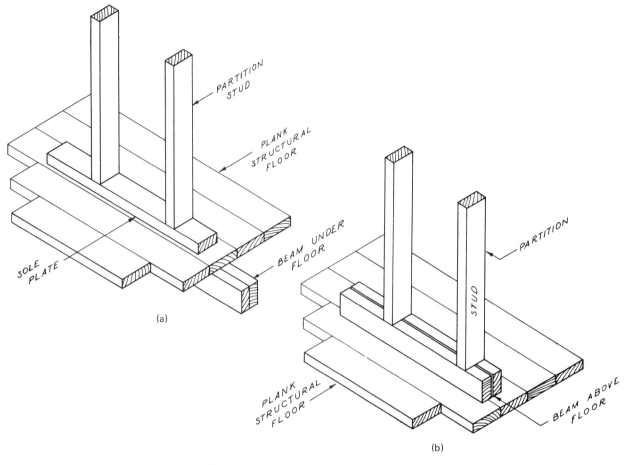

Figure 21-9 Support for nonbearing partition parallel to plank: (a) beam under the floor; (b) beam above the floor.

2 X 4's may be placed under the plank floor and supported on the beams by framing anchors. Where the nonbearing partition is at right angles to the planks, no supplementary framing is needed since the partition load will be distributed across a number of planks.

As in conventional framing, lateral bracing is required in the exterior walls to provide resistance against wind forces. In plank-and-beam framing, this is accomplished by installing solid panels at appropriate intervals, with the supplementary wall framing and the posts tied together by diagonal bracing or suitable sheathing.

STRUCTURAL REQUIREMENTS

Good design requires that all members be properly fastened together in order that the house will act as a unit in resisting external forces (Fig. 21-10). With fewer pieces than in conventional framing, particular care must be given to connections where beams abut each other and where beams join the posts. Where gable roofs are used, provision must be made to absorb the horizontal thrust produced by sloping roof beams.

In most cases, the structural design of a plank-and-beam house will be controlled by the local building code to the extent of specifying design leading requirements. A live load of 40 lb/ft^2 is commonly specified for floors. For roofs, some codes specify 20 lb/ft^2 and others 30 lb/ft^2.

The convenience, economy, and appearance of timber floor and roof decking are advantages long recognized by architects, engineers, and builders. Although nominal 2-in. standard-length decking is generally available, some waste results where end trimming is necessary to conform with a standard arrangement of framing.

Where random-length plank floors are continuous over three or more spans, such decks provide 30% more stiffness under uniform load than do decks composed of short planks laid in a series of single spans.

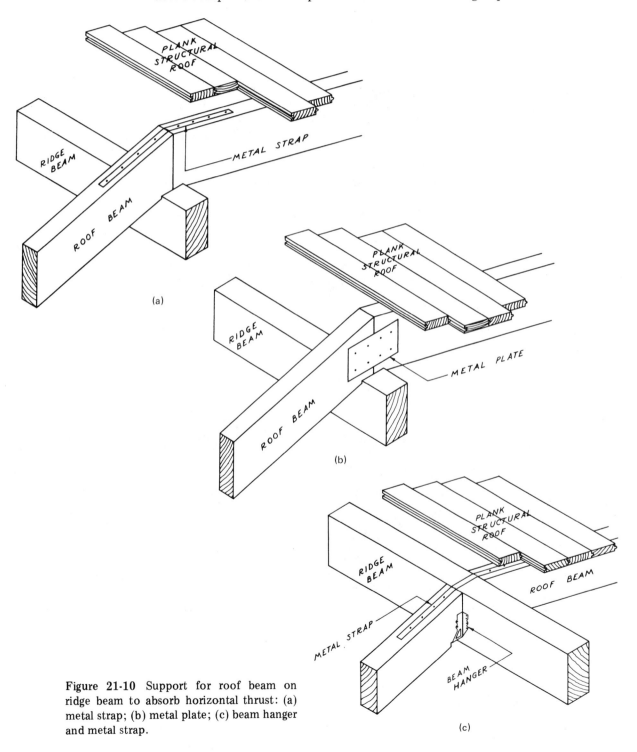

Figure 21-10 Support for roof beam on ridge beam to absorb horizontal thrust: (a) metal strap; (b) metal plate; (c) beam hanger and metal strap.

When this type of decking is used as a structural floor, it is recommended that nominal-1-in. strip flooring be applied at right angles to the planks to distribute the loads over the floor system.

End-matched planks may not always be readily available. Square-end planks may be used with the effect of end matching, provided by grooving the ends of the planks for metal splines to extend ¾ in. into the ends of pieces. Such splines will transfer loads as well as provide conventional end matching.

ADVANTAGES

There are many advantages to be gained through the use of the plank-and-beam system of framing. Perhaps the most outstanding is the distinctive architectural effect provided by the exposed plank-and-beam ceiling (Fig. 21-11). In many houses, the roof plank serves as the ceiling, thereby providing added height to living areas with no increase in cost. Where planks are selected for appearance, no further ceiling treatment is needed except the application of a stain, sealer, or paint, and this results in quite a saving in cost.

Well-planned plank-and-beam framing permits substantial savings in labor. The pieces are larger and there are fewer of them than in conventional framing. Cross-bridging of joists is eliminated entirely. Larger and fewer nails are required. All of this adds up to labor saving at the job site.

In plank-and-beam framing, the ceiling height is measured to the underside of the plank, whereas in conventional construction, it is measured to the underside of the joists. The difference between the thickness of the plank and the depth of the joist results in a reduction in the volume of the building. It also reduces the height of the exterior walls (Fig. 21-12).

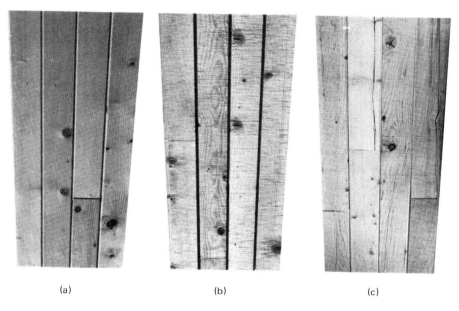

(a)   (b)   (c)

Figure 21-11 Plank grades: (a) premium; (b) architectural; (c) California rustic.

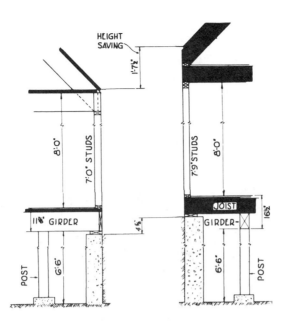

Figure 21-12 Comparison of height of conventionally framed house (right) and plank-and-beam house (left).

QUESTIONS

1. Define *plank-and-beam framing*. _____

2. Which of the following is the usual spacing of beams in plank-and-beam construction?
   A. 6 ft
   B. 3 ft
   C. 8 ft
   D. 4 ft

3. Roof insulation is placed under the ceiling when using plank roofing.
   True or False

4. How is electrical wiring installed in the ceiling of plank roofing?
   _____

5. The underside of the roof plank must be finished with plaster.
   True or False

6. There are many grades of finish of roof planks.   True or False

7. Plank-and-beam construction interior partitions are which of the following?
   A. Bearing
   B. Nonbearing
   C. Curtain wall
   D. None of the above

8. What are the advantages of plank-and-beam framing? _____

9. With plank-and-beam framing, is the cubic-feet control increased or decreased? _____

10. Planks are blind-nailed.   True or False

22

Remodeling and Alterations

INTRODUCTION

No home can be successful unless it combines four basic essentials: good design, an efficient plan, the right material, and sound construction. A home may be large or small, elaborate or inexpensive, it may boast of every modern convenience and laborsaving device, yet without all four of these essentials it can never be a permanent, substantial, and satisfactory home.

Saving a few nails at the cost of squeaking floors, or saving a little labor and material at the expense of excessive fuel bills and repair costs, are expensive economies. The chief breeder of shoddy structures, unwarranted repair bills, and short-lived houses is the lack of appreciation of the value of proper construction in house building, remodeling, and alterations.

There are economies that can and should be practiced in house building. The history of a house is written not only in the original purchase price but also on future costs for maintenance, additions, and alterations.

FOUNDATIONS

The purpose of the foundation is to support the house. This statement may seem superfluous, perhaps ridiculous, yet there are many houses in which defects are traceable to foundations that have failed to perform their full duty. It is still true that a house is no stronger than its foundation.

Concrete is not a synonym for permanency. There is good concrete and there is bad concrete. The strength of concrete for foundations is dependent on the use of well-washed sand and gravel, mixed in proper proportions with cement and water. It is important that concrete be prepared and applied to do its job. There may be a tendency to cheapen foundation walls by making them thinner than they should be.

The proper thickness of foundation walls is a matter usually governed by local building codes. These codes, and good practice, require walls at least 12 in. thick and in the case of stone, brick, or block walls, 12 or 16 in. thick.

FOOTINGS

Foundation walls are enlarged at their base to furnish a larger bearing surface against the soil beneath. This enlarged base is termed a footing.

Footings are an important part of the foundation, and particular attention should be paid to their size and shape. In a house where cheapness is practiced, the footings are often omitted. The footings, which must bear most of the weight of the structure, should be carried down to firm ground and below the frostline. Placing them on frozen ground will cause no end of problems. Poor footings cause uneven settling of the foundation walls. This in turn is transmitted to the whole house, throwing it out of plumb. The damage is visible inside the house in the form of cracked basement walls (Fig. 22-1), cracked walls on the upper floors, binding doors and windows, and sagging floors. Joints in the woodwork will be forced open both inside and outside the house. The pitch of the gutters may be altered, causing water to back up instead of flowing off. This water will overflow the gutters and may back up under the roofing, ruining and staining interior finishes. Consid-

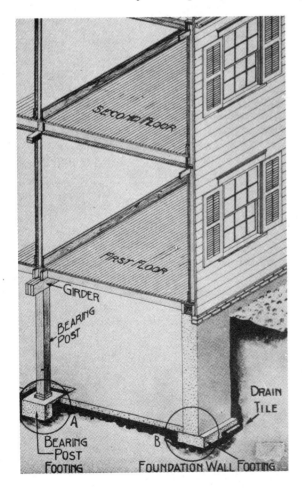

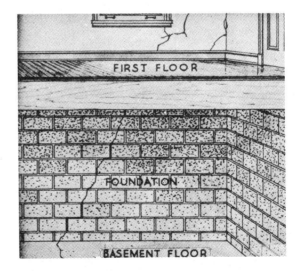

Figure 22-1 Footings.

erable expense may be involved in redecorating. This problem will continue with every thaw or heavy rain until the gutters are repaired or rebuilt. Proper precautions will forestall such weaknesses and provide a firm base for the superstructure.

Often, footings that are correct in every way are undermined to permit the entrance of service connections. This weakens the footings at this spot and may result in some of the ills just mentioned. At places where it is necessary to undermine footings, they should either be enlarged or, better still, reinforced with steel rods. The importance of the footings under the foundation wall and bearing posts is apparent. To support the weight of the structure above, all footings should rest on firm ground.

With so many sizes and weights of houses and with such a disparity in the bearing power of various soils, it stands to reason that one size of footing is not suitable for all conditions. However, it has been found that for the small house with average soil conditions the foundation wall footings should extend at least 4 in. beyond the wall on both sides and should be at least 8 in. deep. It is a good rule to make the bearing post footings from 8 to 12 in. deep and from 18 to 24 in. square, depending on the load to be carried and soil conditions.

When the foundation is built in damp soil, the site should be drained with 4-in. drain tile around the outside of the footings. This should be connected with the sewer or other drainage system. In excessively damp soil, if a dry basement is to be assured, it is well to waterproof the outside of the foundation wall.

Sagging porches are the result of insufficient support, again a matter of improper footing. Sometimes very good porch piers settle when service connection trenches are dug too close to them and are not properly refilled. The condition is by no means uncommon. It can easily be avoided by proper attention to footings at the time a house is being altered or added to. In a completed house, it is difficult and expensive to remedy. To avoid the heaving action of frost, porch foundations should be well footed and should run down below the frostline.

As a business proposition, it is cheaper to build a good house than a poor one. The slight additional cost of building a house right is made up many times over by lower repair costs and higher resale value.

Bearing Post Footings

The foundation supports the outside walls and the weight of about half of the floor area. The remainder of the weight of the house is dependent on the bearing posts for support. The bearing post footings should therefore not be neglected.

When bearing posts settle unduly, the effect is apparent throughout the house. Cracks appear on the inside walls, doors and windows become balky, and floors settle at the inner walls. The annoyances that result from uneven floors are familiar to everybody.

FRAMING

The framework of the house has aptly been termed its skeleton, and its purpose obviously is to give strength and rigidity to the structure. There are many types of house framing in use in various sections of the country, but for practical purposes, they may be grouped into four classes: (1) braced timber frame, (2) modern braced frame, (3) balloon frame, and (4) platform frame.

Braced Timber Frames

The braced timber frame is the oldest type and originated in New England. The early colonists brought with them a tradition of heavy, European half-timber construction, and this was nourished by the abundance of standing timber directly at hand. Nails had to be made by hand; therefore, the early craftsmen used them sparingly, devising methods of fastening that consisted of mortises and tenons held together by wooden dowel pins.

The principal framing members of the old New England houses were often hewn out of the trees nearest at hand and were ordinarily of much larger dimensions than were required to give the necessary strength. The time required in those days to prepare the timbers necessary for the building of a house, as well as the time required for its building, permitted the timbers and framing members to dry out thoroughly before the building was completed, and under these conditions the old braced timber frame resulted in a practically faultless house, of which hundreds of old houses still standing in the Eastern states today bear evidence.

Modern Braced Frames

In those sections of the country where many of the old braced timber frame houses still stand, a modern adaptation of the old braced timber frame has been developed. This type of frame is sometimes called the "combination frame." Corner posts and girts built up of two or three pieces of 2-in. lumber take the place of the solid timbers formerly used. Nails largely replace mortises, tenons, and dowel pins for fastening. With the elimination of the heavy timber girts the intermediate posts formerly required to support them have been done away with, and the studs, in addition to furnishing bearing surfaces for the inside and outside walls, are utilized for support. However, the corner bracing is retained as in most cases. This modern braced frame is in every way adaptable to modern building needs, yet to be thoroughly efficient should not be slighted in its construction.

Balloon Frames

The balloon frame is another modern and accepted type of framing applicable to the building of substantial houses in all parts of the country. As in the case of the modern braced frame, it is built almost entirely of 2-in lumber. Nails are also used for fastening, instead of mortises and tenons. The distinguishing feature of the balloon frame, however, is that the wall studs are made to extend up two stories high, with the ends of the second-floor joists spiked to their sides and resting on a false girt or ribbon board which is notched into them on the inside. A box sill is ordinarily used with this type of framing. The elimination of the girts in the walls has required the fitting of firestops between the studs to prevent the circulation of air throughout the walls. The bearing partition studs rest on the girders. Corner bracing is also required. Figure 22-2 shows an example of improper construction.

The balloon frame offers the advantages of speed and economy. It also possesses excellent rigidity. Properly constructed, it is in every way to be recommended.

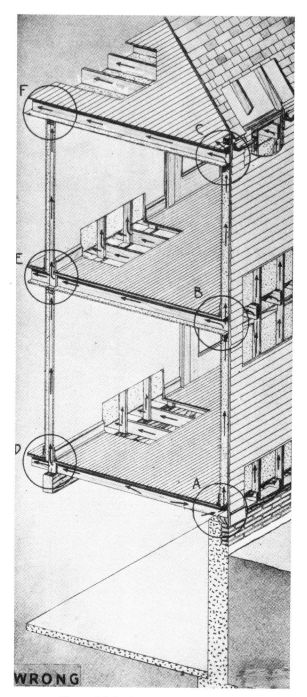

Figure 22-2 Improper construction.

Arrows indicate the free circulation of air. Letters A to F indicate points where firestopping should have been used.

Platform Frames

This type of framing is unquestionably the fastest and safest form of good construction. Interior and exterior walls are framed exactly alike, thereby assuring balanced shrinkage or settling. Each floor is framed separately, with the subfloor in place before the wall and partition studs are raised. All studding may be the same length. This permits the specification and use of precision manufactured, exact-length, ready-to-use lumber products, with consequent labor and waste saving on the job. Braced with let-in bracing, the platform frame is adequately rigid to withstand severe windstorm conditions.

SUPPORTING TIMBERS

The function of the supporting timbers is not merely to prevent the house from tumbling down. Many a house is cheapened by the use of undersized or too few supporting timbers, and yet has strength enough to support any ordinary load. But the floors of these houses lack stiffness, and stiffness is vital to a satisfactory house.

Posts and Girders

The outer ends of the joists that support the first floor rest directly on the foundation wall, or on a sill which, in turn, rests on the foundation wall. The inner ends of these joists rest on girders which are supported by bearing posts. These girders and bearing posts support the main bearing partitions as well as a part of the weight of the floors and the contents of the house. They should be of a size sufficient to support this weight.

Sills

The sill furnishes a means of securing the superstructure to the foundation and provides a nailing surface for the joists. There are several types of sills in use.

If a house is to be firmly anchored to the foundation, the sill must be more than merely set on the foundation. The solid or timber sill should be anchored by means of bolts. When a solid sill or a combination sill is used, the joint between it and the foundation should be sealed by placing the sill on a bed of mortar.

In the hurry-up kind of construction, this anchoring and sealing is often neglected or done in such a haphazard manner as to be of little value. Good workmanship in such places as this costs no more.

Joists

The joists furnish the support for the floors. Joist sizes, like girder sizes, are dependent on the length of the span they bridge and on the load they are required to carry. Failure to use joists of sufficient size is sometimes the cause of sagging, squeaking floors that seem insecure under foot, rattling light fixtures, and cracked plaster in the ceilings underneath (Fig. 22-3).

Bridging Floor Joists

By bridging is meant those small braces that extend crosswise from the top of one joist to the bottom of the next in a straight, continuous line the length of the house. It may be difficult to realize the value of these small braces, but their importance can hardly be overemphasized.

The purpose of bridging is to distribute to all the joists any exceptionally heavy, concentrated loads or sudden jolts that may be applied directly above one or two of them. Tests have shown that it requires three times as much weight to cause a certain amount of deflection in a bridged beam as it does to cause the same deflection in one that is not bridged. Bridging is just as necessary between the second-floor joists. It is difficult to remedy defects due to poor bridging, or lack of bridging, once the house is built.

SECOND FLOOR JOIST

Figure 22-3 Sagging floor and cracked ceiling as a result of using joists of insufficient depth.

FLOORS

Despite the fact that precautions are employed to assure proper floor support, attention must also be given to correct methods of laying the subfloor and finish floor. The subfloor is the rough underfloor which is nailed to the joists and over which the finish floor is laid.

The importance of properly nailing the floors can hardly be overstated. Many people are surprised to learn that it is the working up and down of the nails in their sockets that causes the annoying creaking and squeaking of floors when they are walked over. Bulging, humpy floors are also often the result of too few nails or of improper nailing.

SHRINKAGE

Shrinkage is the natural result of the drying of wood. Although certain difficulties in many houses are directly traceable to it, it does not follow that these defects need to be a part of the wood house. Shrinkage may be minimized by the use of seasoned lumber and a few simple construction methods.

Water exists in wood in two conditions, as free water contained within the cell cavities, and as water absorbed in the cell walls. Removal of the free water merely reduces the weight of the wood. Shrinkage begins with the removal of the absorbed water, and the amount of shrinkage that will take place in a piece of wood is directly proportionate to the amount of moisture that the cell walls have absorbed.

Therefore, since lumber with a moisture content of 25 to 30% will shrink more than lumber with a moisture content of 15%, the wisdom of using seasoned lumber in the framework of a house is immediately clear. The development of modern dry kilns at all of the reputable mills makes it possible in most places to buy correctly seasoned framing lumber at no greater cost than that of green, unseasoned lumber.

Shrinkage of wood, like the expansion and contraction of steel, cannot be entirely eliminated. Just as steel expands under heat and contracts when cold, so lumber, unprotected by paint, takes on and gives off moisture according to the variations in the humidity of the surrounding atmosphere. As a house ages, the lumber in its framework dries to a moisture content as low as 6 to 8%. It is not practical to use framing lumber in the building of a house with as low a moisture content as this, since even though the lumber was dried to this state in the beginning, it would absorb enough atmospheric moisture to bring it back to air-dry condition.

This additional shrinkage must be taken care of in the manner in which the house is built. This is easy because of the fact that, in drying, lumber shrinks mostly across the grain and only infinitesimally lengthwise.

In the properly designed house frame, the horizontal framing members in the outside walls and bearing partitions are minimized and equalized as far as it is possible without sacrificing the strength and rigidity of the structure.

WALL AND PARTITION FRAMING

The first essentials of wall framing are strength and rigidity, since the walls of the house must resist pressure from occasional high winds. Wall and partition framing consists of 2 × 4's or 2 × 6's, top and bottom plates, and the necessary bracing and firestopping. Careful cutting, fitting, nailing, bracing, and workmanship are all essential to sound substantial walls and partitions.

There are two types of walls and partitions, bearing and nonbearing. A bearing partition or wall is one that runs at right angles to and supports the ends of the joists or rafters. In other words, it is a wall that supports a load from above. A nonbearing wall or partition acts only to divide space.

Nonbearing partitions should be supported by double joists. The studs that support the framing around stairways should also be doubled. Bearing partitions require special support when these partitions do not occur directly over the partition below. In such cases the studs in the bearing partition below should be reinforced with two rows of bridging.

When a partition supports more than the weight of the roof and two floors of a two-story house, the studs should not be less than 2 × 6 or 2 × 4. In all cases, bearing partitions should have double top plates and should be braced with solid bridging not less than 2 in. thick and not less than the full width of the studs.

WINDOW AND DOOR OPENINGS

It becomes necessary in the alterations of a house to cut away part of the framing in the outside wall for door and window openings in addition to the inside walls. This weakens the framework and the strength lost must be regained by reinforcing the framework around these openings (Fig. 22-4).

Figure 22-4   Right and wrong door openings.

CHIMNEYS

No structural member is to be supported by the chimney. It is to be absolutely independent of the house framing. Figure 22-5 shows two examples of improper chimney construction. Soil conditions govern the size of the chimney footing, but they should never be less than 12 in. deep and should always extend at least 6 in. beyond each face of the chimney. The thickness of the walls of a chimney that has flue linings should be not less than 8 in. thick. All framing members should be at least 2 in. from chimney walls. The space between should be filled with mortar, mineral wool, or other noncombustible material. If the chimney walls are to be finished, they should be studded, setting the studs 2 in. free of the chimney and on these the wall

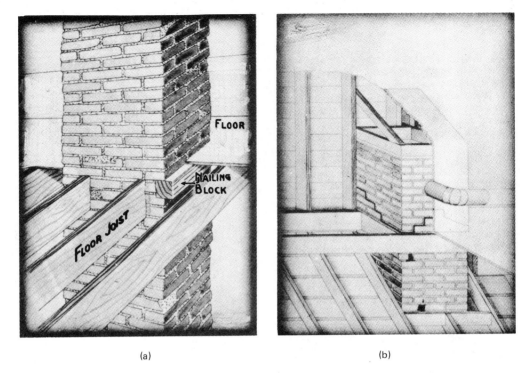

(a)   (b)

Figure 22-5 Improper chimney construction.

In part (a), floor joists, boards, and nailing blocks built into chimney.
In part (b), chimney set on a bracket attached to a wall, rafters and
floor joists framed tight against chimney, which has only a 4-in. wall
without flue lining.

covering can be applied. The chimney should be capped on top with stone,
concrete or preformed chimney cap and should extend at least 3 ft above
the roof or 2 ft above the roof ridge. This will assure a good draft for the
heating plant, fireplace, or stove.

ROOFS

Insufficient roof pitch causes more trouble than any other single factor,
especially in climates where there is snow (Fig. 22-6). It is difficult to build
a tight roof of low pitch in these areas. Simple straight roof design works
best in this case.

Rafters

The framing members of the roof must be of sufficient size and strength to
support the weight of the roof plus the snow load and wind load without
sagging. If the rafters are undersized or spaced too far apart, they will sag,
causing the roof to split, loosening the shingles, and causing leaks.

WALLS

If the joints around doors and windows are not tight, leakage will occur,
creating serious problems of rotting the frame. Humidifying systems in
homes increase the vapor pressure, forcing water vapor through the wall

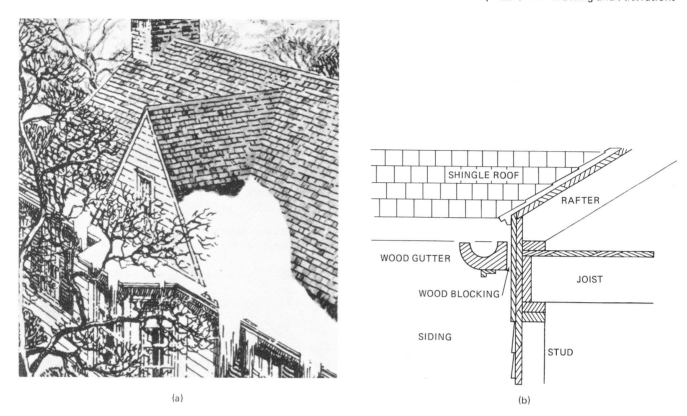

(a)   (b)

Figure 22-6 (a) Moisture infiltration due to improper gutter installation; (b) proper installation.

covering and into the wall construction. If the wall is insulated but has no barrier against the passage of this vapor, the inside surface of the sheathing will be below the dew point temperature. The moisture will condense on the inside of the sheathing, forming ice in very cold weather and when thawing will penetrate the sheathing and framing, causing paint failure and eventual rotting of the framework. Sheathing permits the wall to breathe. The cell structure of the wood permits taking and giving moisture. With vaporproof sealing inside, the sheathing is safe and dry and a breathing wall is created.

Interior Wall Coverings

Plaster or plasterboard is not elastic and regardless of the type used, it will crack if there is any movement in the framing that holds it (Fig. 22-7). The framework of the house must be rigid. Cutting and notching of walls for passage of pipes must be properly reinforced (Fig. 22-8). Large jagged cracks will form above wall openings and will cause a crevice at the ceiling. The casing will open at the joints and the entire opening will sag. The floor and partition above will also sag, causing cracks in the partition on both sides. The headers should be doubled and the plate should be doubled. If the span is too great for the double headers, a truss should be used which will give the proper strength and rigidity to the wall.

Stiffeners around window framing will eliminate one cause of window binding. All framing around door and window openings should be doubled. The wall should be braced by let-in bracing, which is accomplished by notch-

Figure 22-7 Interior finish problems due to settling.

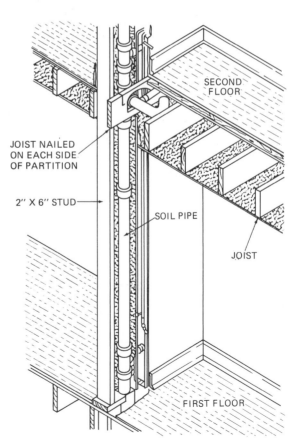

SECOND FLOOR

JOIST NAILED ON EACH SIDE OF PARTITION

2″ X 6″ STUD

SOIL PIPE

JOIST

FIRST FLOOR

Figure 22-8 Wall reinforcing for pipes.

ing the studs to receive a continuous 1 × 4 or 2 × 4 securely nailed to each stud. Another system of bracing consists of 2 × 4 members carefully cut and fitted between the studs. All bracing must be done before the sheathing is installed.

INTERIOR FINISHING

The pleasing appearance of interior woodwork and the satisfaction of having it stay in place is dependent on its treatment and application. It should be well and tightly joined and properly finished. Interior trim, which includes baseboard, picture mold, doors, windows, and casing, is seasoned and kiln dried before it leaves the factory and should be protected from water and moisture until it is in place and sealed. It should not be allowed to stand in the open after delivery to the house. If it is allowed to absorb moisture, it will swell and warp, and if nailed in place when wet, unsightly cracks will develop as it dries.

The care of doors before they are installed is just as important as the trim. Troublesome doors can be avoided if the top and bottom edge of each door is sealed with paint to prevent the absorption of moisture, which will otherwise cause the door to swell and bind.

EXTERIOR FINISHING

The construction of the framework is the same regardless of the siding used. Lumber is available in the form of siding cut to various patterns, thicknesses, and widths. In applying exterior siding, all joints around doors and windows should be carefully fitted (Fig. 22-9). Siding should be sealed with paint or a preservative as soon as it is installed. If it becomes wet, it should be permitted to dry before sealing.

Figure 22-9 Dirt infiltration around poorly installed window.

QUESTIONS

1. What are the four essentials of a successful house?
    1. _____
    2. _____
    3. _____
    4. _____

2. Improper foundation thickness is not the cause of foundation failure. True or False

3. What is a footing? _____
   _____

4. In average soil conditions, footings are not required.   True or False

5. Sagging porches are the result of which of the following?
    A. Improper footings
    B. No footings
    C. Frostline
    D. None of the above

6. Name two types of house framing.
    1. _____
    2. _____

7. The foundation sill provides which of the following?
    A. Stability to the framework
    B. Means of securing bridging
    C. Nailing surface
    D. None of the above

8. The use of bridging is to keep the floor rigid.   True or False

9. Name two types of bracing.
    1. _____
    2. _____

10. A chimney may be used as a supporting member of framing. True or False

Scaffolding and Ladders

23

INTRODUCTION

In modern construction, substantial heights must be reached by the work force in completing a building. This is accomplished by the use of ladders, scaffolding, and stagings. Although these are temporary platforms, they must be designed for safety and convenience. Some of these platforms are free standing and some are attached temporarily to the building. They may be owned or leased.

There are more accidents in construction work than in any other occupation because of the use of sharp tools, heavy building materials, and scaffoldings, stagings, and platforms. Safety precautions must be followed.

SCAFFOLDING

The simplest form of scaffolding is called a trestle (Fig. 23-1). It is a platform without rails and is supported on both ends by sawhorses. Planks are supported by a trestle and the planks must be at least 2 in. thick and 10 or 12 in. wide with ends at least 6 in. beyond the supports, but not more than 12 in. beyond the supports. There are also extension planks (Fig. 23-2).

If more than one plank is used, they must be held together by nailing a temporary cleat on the underside of the planks, spacing them about 4 ft apart. The supports must be straight and level with a solid supporting base. For safety reasons it should not extend beyond 4 ft in height without a rail.

Scaffolds can also be of single-pole type (Fig. 23-3) or double-pole type (Fig. 23-4). The single-pole type is composed of two 2 × 4's or one 4 × 4 upright, cross-braced, secured to a building wall, and properly braced. Cross members are used to support a platform. The double-pole type is free-standing, cross-braced with rails on both sides.

Another type of scaffold is called swinging (Fig. 23-5). This type is

Figure 23-1 Adjustable folding trestle.

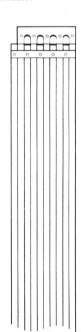

Figure 23-2 Extension planks.

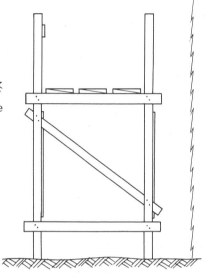

Figure 23-3 Single-pole scaffold.

Figure 23-4 Double-pole scaffold.

Figure 23-5 Swinging scaffold. (Courtesy of Safway Steel Products.)

generally used by painters. It is supported by heavy lines attached to a block and tackle. These are supported in turn by brackets locked and secured to the roof of the house (Fig. 23-6).

Scaffolding is manufactured from metal and can be stacked to almost any height. Scaffolding is tubular; one section fits onto another section as sections are added to reach the desired height (Fig. 22-7). The assembly of sections is cross-braced, which also acts as a rail. The legs are adjustable to make the scaffold level and straight on even ground. Some models have casters for easy moving. There is great flexibility of height and length in tubular scaffolding, and it is easily assembled and disassembled.

Figure 23-6   Swinging scaffold brackets. (Courtesy of Sky Climber, Inc.)

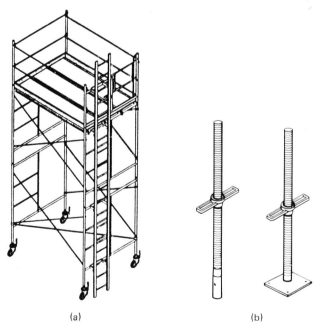

(a)   (b)

Figure 23-7   (a) Sectional scaffold; (b) screw jacks. (Courtesy of Safway Steel Products.)

All scaffolding requires the following safety considerations:

1. All lumber should be straight grained and free from defects.
2. Bracing should be in a triangular shape.
3. Splicing of uprights should be done with no less than 4-ft-long members secured on both sides of the joint.
4. Floor planking should be of uniform thickness and extend at least 6 in. beyond the support.
5. Hand rails should be 42 in. high, and 5½-in. toe boards should be installed.
6. Wire screening should be installed between the toe board and the hand rails.
7. If work is being done above scaffolding, overhead protection—light lumber, heavy canvas, or wire mesh—should be used.
8. Scaffoldings should not be in use during storms or high winds.
9. All scaffolding should be cleaned at the end of each day's work.
10. A safe means of access, such as ladders or stairs, should be used between scaffolding sections.
11. Trucks should be warned against striking, or dumping material against, scaffolding.

Sidewall Brackets

Another type of scaffold is a triangular-shaped metal scaffold attached to a wall (Fig. 23-8). Planks, which span from one bracket to another, are used as a platform. They require little space and are convenient to install and remove.

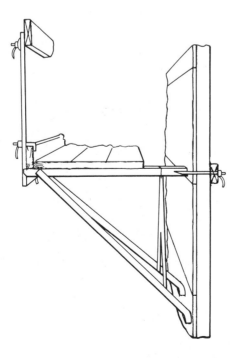

Figure 23-8 Sidewall bracket scaffold.

Pump Jack Scaffolds

Wood posts made of 4 × 4's are used as a standing column for the pump jack scaffold. They are operated by a foot lever (Fig. 23-9) which lowers or raises the attached bracket to any convenient height. A wedge-type action locks the pump jack to the wood post to hold its position and avoid slippage. These scaffolds are single-pole type.

Ladder Jacks

A ladder is required to support a ladder jack scaffold. The ladder jack is held onto the ladder by brackets that fit around the ladder rails (Fig. 23-10). The brackets are adjustable in height, limited to the height of the ladder. More than one ladder jack and ladder is needed to support a platform of planks.

Roof Brackets

This type of scaffold (Fig. 23-11) is used on roofs. They are held in place by temporary nailing into the roof sheathing. The brackets are adjustable to the roof pitch. More than one is required to support a plank spanning the brackets. This type of bracket is useful for working on roofs with steep pitches.

LADDERS

A variety of ladders are manufactured from wood or aluminum: straight ladders, stepladders, extension ladders, trestle ladders, and safety rolling ladders.

Straight ladders, sometimes called single ladders (Fig. 23-12) are up to 40 ft in length and require a wall for support. The proper angle of the ladder against the wall is important to prevent injury caused by ladder slippage. The ladder must rest firmly and levelly on the ground. A straight ladder has rungs for climbing. Stand-off brackets are used to keep the ladder away from the wall or windows (Fig. 23-13).

Stepladders are self-supporting and are sometimes called folding ladders (Fig. 23-14). They have flat steps instead of rungs and are manufactured in heights up to 20 ft. These ladders must be on a level surface for safety and support.

Extension ladders (Fig. 23-15) are telescopic in shape and require a wall for support. They have two sliding sections which are used to adjust the ladder height. The two sections lock in position to prevent slippage. When the two sections are locked into position, the rungs are in alignment. These ladders can be extended to lengths of 60 ft.

A trestle ladder is a folding ladder with an adjustable vertical ladder between the fold (Fig. 23-16). The height is limited on this type of ladder.

Safety ladders have wheels for easy positioning of the ladder. The wheels lock in place to prevent the ladder from moving. Safety rolling ladders are usually limited to two or three steps in height (Fig. 23-17). Ladders and scaffolding are potential danger areas and should be inspected frequently for proper nailing or bolting.

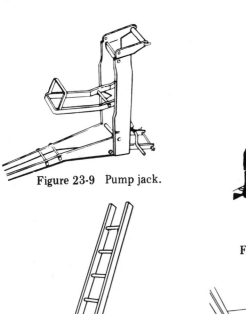

Figure 23-9 Pump jack.

Figure 23-10 Ladderjack.

Figure 23-11 Adjustable roofing bracket.

Figure 23-12 Single ladder

Figure 23-13 Stand-off bracket and ladder stabilizer.

Figure 23-14 Step ladder.

Figure 23-15 Extension ladder.

Figure 23-16 Extension trestles.

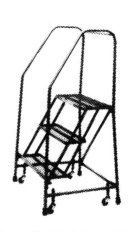

Figure 23-17 Safety ladder.

Figure 23-18   Ladder safety feet.

Ladders and rungs, as well as ladder rails, should be inspected for soundness. All ladders should have safety feet (Fig. 23-18).

Do not use a ladder as a scaffold or as a horizontal working platform. To erect a ladder, place the lower end against a solid object such as a wall so that it will not slide while placing it in position, or have someone stand and hold the lower end. Raise the top end and walk toward the bottom end while raising the ladder one rung at a time as you walk. When the ladder is vertical, carefully place it against the wall at an angle so that the distance on the lower end is at least one-fourth the ladder length away from the wall. Be sure that both rails rest on solid footing before climbing the ladder.

QUESTIONS

1. Name three types of scaffolding.
    1. _____
    2. _____
    3. _____
2. What are sidewall bracket scaffolds? _____
    _____
3. A trestle type of scaffold is used only for bridge work.
    True or False
4. Describe a pump jack scaffold. _____
    _____
5. Name three different ladder types.
    1. _____
    2. _____
    3. _____
6. Ladders can be used as scaffolding.   True or False
7. Name three safety considerations regarding scaffold use.
    1. _____
    2. _____
    3. _____
8. Not all ladders require safety feet.   True or False
9. What is the proper angle for a ladder against a wall? _____
    _____

24

Factory Housing

INTRODUCTION

The original mass construction technique was post-and-beam framing. Large timbers were hand-cut from the forest and were fitted and joined together by skilled workers in the form of custom or tailored houses.

Before the invention of the mechanized sawmill, this was the only way to construct houses. The frame of a house was so well designed and constructed that it was able to withstand almost anything without fear of failure. The house served as shelter and provided security.

Soon after the introduction of the sawmill, post-and-beam construction was replaced by conventional framing, called light construction. This type of construction was easy for the semiskilled worker because fitting of large members was not necessary. A large number of these popular houses have been built. With the recent fast-paced increase in technology has come the beginning of the precut, prebuilt, prefabricated building industry.

PREBUILT SECTIONS

Sections or panels are built in the shop and delivered to the building site for assembly. As in conventional construction, all local and state building and zoning laws must be followed.

The foundation generally is not part of the package and must be built separately and ready for assembly of the prebuilt sections on the foundation (Fig. 24-1). The total house package varies with the manufacturer. Some manufacturers supply only the framework, while others may include the entire house except for the mechanical systems: plumbing, heating, and electrical. The size of the prebuilt panels is limited only by road transportation. Basic construction techniques are followed, much as those used for a conventional field-built house, with minor changes (Fig. 24-2).

371

(a)   (b)

Figure 24-1 (a) Prebuilt foundation; (b) beginning construction of a manufactured house. (Courtesy of Berger Homes, Kingston Kottage Div.)

Figure 24-2 Assembly of manufactured homes. (Courtesy of Berger Homes, Kingston Kottage Div.)

PRECUT PACKAGES

A house that is precut follows conventional construction methods. All the framing members are cut to proper length in the shop, delivered to the building site, and erected. Shop cutting has an advantage over field cutting because production in the shop continues regardless of the weather, whereas work may have to be postponed in the field during inclement weather.

Precut packages may or may not include windows, doors, and trim, depending on the terms of agreement between the buyer and the manufacturer. An entire house, ready to move in, can also be purchased. If the package is not a complete package, arrangements will need to be made for completion after the precut members are assembled.

PREFABRICATED SECTIONS

There is little difference between prebuilt and prefabricated sections. Both are prepared in the shop using conventional framing methods. Panels are assembled into sections, sometimes consisting of as much as half the house. Generally, the mechanical systems are included in the package, but not the foundation. This means that the plumbing fixtures are in place, and the floors, walls, and ceilings are complete. These units are also available in post-and-beam construction and in log houses.

As with other types of prefabricated houses, the foundation may have to be built separately before delivery of the house. Tolerance in foundation building is limited to about $\frac{1}{2}$ in. There is limited design choice in a pre-built house because the designs are set by the manufacturer's shop and designers. Some modifications can be made before actual production begins (Fig. 24-3). There may be an added cost if any changes are made from the stock design.

PRODUCTION

Manufactured houses are constructed under controlled conditions with specialized equipment (Fig. 24-4). Prefabrication in modern plants is accomplished with large production equipment, which reduces the time usually required for field or conventional construction.

High-production-rate saws are used to cut members to exact length, and jigs with automatic nailing machines are used to assemble the parts. As the completed units move along a conveyor belt, wall surface materials are placed in position and gang-nailed. Power tables turn the panels over for

Figure 24-3 Planning. (Courtesy of Berger Homes, Kingston Kottage Div.)

Figure 24-4 Production plant. (Courtesy of Berger Homes, Kingston Kottage Div.)

Figure 24-5 Inspected parts. (Courtesy of Berger Homes, Kingston Kottage Div.)

Figure 24-6 Ready for delivery. (Courtesy of Berger Homes, Kingston Kottage Div.)

Figure 24-7   Completed home. (Courtesy of Berger Homes, Kingston Kottage Div.)

completing work on the other side. All the necessary parts, including insulation, wiring, and piping, are included. As the panels reach the end of the assembly line, they are inspected and numbered for easy assembly (Fig. 24-5). When all is completed, the panels are loaded on a truck, ready for delivery (Fig. 24-6). Some sections may require a crane for handling. An entire house can be assembled by an experienced crew in a matter of days (Fig. 24-7).

QUESTIONS

1. What is the name of the original mass construction technique?

   _____

2. Name three types of shop-manufactured housing.
   1. _____
   2. _____
   3. _____

3. The foundation is generally part of a prebuilt package.
       True or False

4. Prebuilt homes include which of the following?
   A. Plumbing
   B. Electrical
   C. Foundation
   D. Frame
   E. Some of the above
   F. All of the above

5. The size of factory-built houses is limited to _____ .

6. Factory construction is different from field construction.
       True or False

7. Name three advantages of factory-built houses.
   1. _____
   2. _____
   3. _____

8. All factory-built houses include doors, windows, and trim.
   True or False, may or may not

9. What is the difference between prebuilt and prefabricated? _____
   _____

10. Which of the following is the accuracy or tolerance in building foundations for a premanufactured house?
    A. 1 in.
    B. ¼ in.
    C. ½ in.
    D. 2 in.
    E. 1½ in.

Appendix

This appendix consists of additional useful information used in the construction industry. This information is grouped together to avoid time-consuming research into other publications for answers or solutions to frequent questions or problems. It is information that is constantly used by both students and professionals.

BRICK AND BLOCK COURSES

BLOCK NO. OF COURSES	BRICK NO. OF COURSES	HEIGHT OF COURSE	BLOCK NO. OF COURSES	BRICK NO. OF COURSES	HEIGHT OF COURSE
	1	0' – 2 5/8"		37	8' – 2 5/8"
	2	0' – 5 3/8"		38	8' – 5 3/8"
1	3	0' – 8"	13	39	8' – 8"
	4	0' – 10 5/8"		40	8' – 10 5/8"
	5	1' – 1 3/8"		41	9' – 1 3/8"
2	6	1' – 4"	14	42	9' – 4"
	7	1' – 6 5/8"		43	9' – 6 5/8"
	8	1' – 9 3/8"		44	9' – 9 3/8"
3	9	2' – 0"	15	45	10' – 0"
	10	2' – 2 5/8"		46	10' – 2 5/8"
	11	2' – 5 3/8"		47	10' – 5 3/8"
4	12	2' – 8"	16	48	10' – 8"
	13	2' – 10 5/8"		49	10' – 10 3/8"
	14	3' – 1 3/8"		50	11' – 1 3/8"
5	15	3' – 4"	17	51	11' – 4"
	16	3' – 6 5/8"		52	11' – 6 5/8"
	17	3' – 9 3/8"		53	11' – 9 3/8"
6	18	4' – 0"	18	54	12' – 0"
	19	4' – 2 5/8"		55	12' – 2 5/8"
	20	4' – 5 3/8"		56	12' – 5 3/8"
7	21	4' – 8"	19	57	12' – 8"
	22	4' – 10 5/8"		58	12' – 10 5/8"
	23	5' – 1 3/8"		59	13' – 1 3/8"
8	24	5' – 4"	20	60	13' – 4"
	25	5' – 6 5/8"		61	13' – 6 5/8"
	26	5' – 9 3/8"		62	13' – 9 3/8"
9	27	6' – 0"	21	63	14' – 0"
	28	6' – 2 5/8"		64	14' – 2 5/8"
	29	6' – 5 3/8"		65	14' – 5 3/8"
10	30	6' – 8"	22	66	14' – 8"
	31	6' – 10 5/8"		67	14' – 10 5/8"
	32	7' – 1 3/8"		68	15' – 1 3/8"
11	33	7' – 4"	23	69	15' – 4"
	34	7' – 6 5/8"		70	15' – 6 5/8"
	35	7' – 9 3/8"		71	15' – 9 3/8"
12	36	8' – 0"	24	72	16' – 0"

MORTAR JOINT IS 3/8"

BOARD FEET CONTENT

LENGTH IN FEET

Size in Inches	8	10	12	14	16	18	20	22	24
1 x 2	1-1/3	1-2/3	2	2-1/3	2-2/3	3	3-1/3	3-2/3	4
1 x 3	2	2-1/2	3	3-1/2	4	4-1/2	5	5-1/2	6
1 x 4	2-2/3	3-1/3	4	4-2/3	5-1/3	6	6-2/3	7-1/3	8
1 x 5	3-1/3	4-1/6	5	5-5/6	6-2/3	7-1/2	8-1/3	9-1/6	10
1 x 6	4	5	6	7	8	9	10	11	12
1 x 8	5-1/3	6-2/3	8	9-1/3	10-2/3	12	13-1/3	14-2/3	16
1 x 10	6-2/3	8-1/3	10	11-2/3	13-1/3	15	16-2/3	18-1/3	20
1 x 12	8	10	12	14	16	18	20	22	24
1 x 14	9-1/3	11-2/3	14	16-1/3	18-2/3	21	23-1/3	25-2/3	28
1 x 16	10-2/3	13-1/3	16	18-2/3	21-1/3	24	26-2/3	29-1/3	32
5/4 x 4	3-1/3	4-1/6	5	5-5/6	6-2/3	7-1/2	8-1/3	9-1/6	10
5/4 x 6	5	6-1/4	7-1/2	8-3/4	10	11-1/4	12-1/2	13-3/4	15
5/4 x 8	6-2/3	8-1/3	10	11-2/3	13-1/3	15	16-2/3	18-1/3	20
5/4 x 10	8-1/3	10-5/12	12-1/2	14-7/12	16-2/3	18-3/4	20-5/6	22-11/13	25
5/4 x 12	10	12-1/2	15	17-1/2	20	22-1/2	25	27-1/2	30
6/4 x 4	4	5	6	7	8	9	10	11	12
6/4 x 6	6	7-1/2	9	10-1/2	12	13-1/2	15	16-1/2	18
6/4 x 8	8	10	12	14	16	18	20	22	24
6/4 x 10	10	12-1/2	15	17-1/2	20	22-1/2	25	27-1/2	30
6/4 x 12	12	15	18	21	24	27	30	33	36
2 x 4	5-1/3	6-2/3	8	9-1/3	10-2/3	12	13-1/3	14-2/3	16
2 x 6	8	10	12	14	16	18	20	22	24
2 x 8	10-2/3	13-1/3	16	18-2/3	21-1/3	24	26-2/3	29-1/3	32
2 x 10	13-1/3	16-2/3	20	23-1/3	26-2/3	30	33-1/3	36-2/3	40
2 x 12	16	20	24	28	32	36	40	44	48
2 x 14	18-2/3	23-1/3	28	32-2/3	37-1/3	42	46-2/3	51-2/3	56
2 x 16	21-1/3	26-2/3	32	37-1/3	42-2/3	48	53-1/3	58-2/3	64
3 x 4	8	10	12	14	16	18	20	22	24
3 x 6	12	15	18	21	24	27	30	33	36
3 x 8	16	20	24	28	32	36	40	44	48
3 x 10	20	25	30	35	40	45	50	55	60
3 x 12	24	30	36	42	48	54	60	66	72
3 x 14	28	35	42	49	56	63	70	77	84
3 x 16	32	40	48	56	64	72	80	88	96
4 x 4	10-2/3	13-1/3	16	18-2/3	21-1/3	24	26-2/3	29-1/3	32
4 x 6	16	20	24	28	32	36	40	44	48
4 x 8	21-1/3	26-2/3	32	37-1/3	42-2/3	48	53-1/3	58-2/3	64
4 x 10	26-2/3	33-1/3	40	46-2/3	53-1/3	60	66-2/3	73-1/3	80
4 x 12	32	40	48	56	64	72	80	88	96
4 x 14	37-1/3	46-2/3	56	65-1/3	74-2/3	84	93-1/3	102-2/3	112
4 x 16	42-2/3	53-1/3	64	74-2/3	85-1/3	96	106-2/3	117-1/3	128
6 x 6	24	30	36	42	48	54	60	66	72
6 x 8	32	40	48	56	64	72	80	88	96
6 x 10	40	50	60	70	80	90	100	110	120
6 x 12	48	60	72	84	96	108	120	132	144
6 x 14	56	70	84	98	112	126	140	154	168
6 x 16	64	80	96	112	128	144	160	176	192
8 x 8	42-2/3	53-1/3	64	74-2/3	85-1/3	96	106-2/3	117-1/3	128
8 x 10	53-1/3	66-2/3	80	93-1/3	106-2/3	120	133-1/3	146-2/3	160
8 x 12	64	80	96	112	128	144	160	176	192

WEIGHTS OF BUILDING MATERIALS

MATERIAL	WEIGHT
CONCRETE	
With stone reinforced	150 pcf
With stone plain	144 pcf
With cinders, reinforced	110 pcf
Light concrete (Aerocrete)	65 pcf
(Perlite)	45 pcf
(Vermiculite)	40 pcf
METAL AND PLASTER	
Masonry mortar	116 pcf
Gypsum and sand plaster	112 pcf
BRICK AND BLOCK MASONRY (INCLUDING MORTAR)	
4" brick wall	35 psf
8" brick wall	74 psf
8" concrete block wall	100 psf
12" concrete block wall	150 psf
4" brick veneer over 4" concrete block	65 psf
WOOD CONSTRUCTION	
Frame wall, lath and plaster	20 psf
Frame wall, 1/2" gypsum board	12 psf
Floor, 1/2" subfloor + 3/4" finished	6 psf
Floor, 1/2" subfloor and ceramic tile	16 psf
Roof, joist and 1/2" sheathing	3 psf
Roof, 2" plank and beam	5 psf
Roof, built-up	7 psf

MATERIAL	WEIGHT
WOOD CONSTRUCTION (CONTINUED)	
Ceiling, joist and plaster	10 psf
Ceiling, joist and 1/2" gypsum board	7 psf
Ceiling, joist and acoustic tile	5 psf
Wood shingles	3 psf
Spanish tile	15 psf
Copper sheet	2 psf
Tar and gravel	6 psf
STONE	
Sandstone	147 pcf
Slate	175 pcf
Limestone	165 pcf
Granite	175 pcf
Marble	165 pcf
GLASS	
1/4" plate glass	3.28 psf
1/8" double strength	1.63 psf
1/8" insulating glass with air space	3.25 psf
4" block glass	20.00 psf
INSULATION	
Cork board 1" thick	.58 psf
Rigid foam insulation 2" thick	.3 psf
Blanket or bat 2" thick	.1 psf

SIZES AND DIMENSIONS FOR REINFORCING BARS

WEIGHT LB. PER FT.	NOMINAL DIAMETER INCHES	SIZE	NUMBER	NOMINAL CROSS SECT. AREA SQ. IN.	NOMINAL PERIMETER
.376	.375	3/8	3	.11	1.178
.668	.500	1/2	4	.20	1.571
1.043	.625	5/8	5	.31	1.963
1.502	.750	3/4	6	.44	2.356
2.044	.875	7/8	7	.60	2.749
2.670	1.000	1	8	.79	3.142
3.400	1.128	1*	9	1.00	3.544
4.303	1.270	1-1/8*	10	1.27	3.990
5.313	1.410	1-1/4*	11	1.56	4.430
7.650	1.693	1-1/2*	14	2.25	5.320
13.600	2.257	2*	18	4.00	7.090

*These sizes rolled in rounds equivalent to square cross section area.

RECOMMENDED STYLES OF WELDED WIRE FABRIC
REINFORCEMENT FOR CONCRETE

TYPE OF CONSTRUCTION	RECOMMENDED STYLE	REMARKS
Barbecue Foundation Slab	6x6-8/8 to 4x4-6/6	Use heavier style fabric for heavy, massive fireplaces or barbecue pits.
Basement Floors	6x6-10/10, 6x6-8/8 or 6x6-6/6	For small areas (15-foot maximum side dimension) use 6x6-10/10. As a rule of thumb, the larger the area or the poorer the sub-soil, the heavier the gauge.
Driveways	6x6-6/6	Continuous reinforcement between 25- to 30-foot contraction joints.
Foundation Slabs (Residential only)	6x6-10/10	Use heavier gauge over poorly drained sub-soil, or when maximum dimension is greater than 15 feet.
Garage Floors	6x6-6/6	Position at midpoint of 5- or 6-inch thick slab.
Patios and Terraces	6x6-10/10	Use 6x6-8/8 if sub-soil is poorly drained.

Porch Floor
  a. 6-inch thick slab up to 6-foot span
  b. 6-inch thick slab up to 8-foot span
	6x6-6/6	Position 1 inch from bottom form to resist tensile stresses.

Sidewalks	6x6-10/10 6x6-8/8	Use heavier gauge over poorly drained sub-soil. Construct 25- to 30-foot slabs as for driveways.
Steps (Free span)	6x6-6/6	Use heavier style if more than five risers. Position fabric 1 inch from bottom form.
Steps (On ground)	6x6-8/8	Use 6x6-6/6 for unstable sub-soil.

metric

Unit	Current U.S. term (multiply factor)	Conversion Factor	SI term (divide factor)	SI Symbol
Length	inch	25.400	millimeter	mm
	foot	0.305	meter	m
	yard	0.914	meter	m
	mile	1.609	kilometer	km
Area	square inch	645.2	square millimeter	mm2
	square foot	0.093	square meter	m2
	square yard	0.836	square meter	m2
	square mile	2.590	square kilometer	km2
	acre	0.405	hectare	ha
Mass (weight)	ounce	28.350	gram	g
	pound	0.454	kilogram	kg
	ton (2000 pounds)	0.907	metric ton	t
Volume	fluid ounce	29.574	milliliter	ml
	pint	0.473	liter	L
	quart	0.946	liter	L
	gallon	3.785	liter	L
	cubic foot	0.028	cubic meter	m3
	cubic yard	0.765	cubic meter	m3
	barrel (petroleum)	0.159	cubic meter	m3
Force Pressure and Stress	pound force	4.448	newton	N
	psi (pounds per square inch)	6.895	kilopascal	kPa
	psf (pounds per square foot)	.048	kilopascal	kPa
	ton per square foot	95.760	kilopascal	kPa
Electric Current	ampere	no conversion	ampere	A
Light	lumen	no conversion	lumen	lm
	candela	no conversion	candela	cd
	foot candle	10.76	lux	lx
Heat, work or energy	Foot pound	1.356	joule	J
	kilowatt hour	3.600	megajoule	MJ
	BTU	1.055	kilojoule	kJ
Power	foot pound per second	1.355	watt	W
	BTU/hour	0.293	watt	W
	horse power	0.746	kilowatt	kW
	tons (refrigeration)	3.517	kilowatt	kW
Heat factors	U value	5.679	metric U value	undecided
	K value	1.730	metric K value	undecided
Temperature	degree Fahrenheit		degree Celcius	°C
	degree Fahrenheit		Kelvin	K

Conversion Factors

Linear Measure

10 millimeters	= 1 centimeter		
10 centimeters	= 1 decimeter		
10 decimeters	= 1 meter		
10 meters	= 1 decameter		
10 decameters	= 1 hectometer		
10 hectometers	= 1 kilometer		

1 inch	=		= 2.54 centimeters
1 foot	= 12 inches		= 0.3048 meter
1 yard	= 3 feet		= 0.9144 meter
1 rod	= 5½ yards or 16½ feet		= 5.029 meters
1 furlong	= 40 rods		= 201.17 meters
1 mile (statute)	= 5280 feet or 1760 yards		= 1609.3 meters
1 league (land)	= 3 miles		= 4.83 kilometers

Square Measure

100 sq. millimeters	= 1 sq. centimeter		
100 sq. centimeters	= 1 sq. decimeter		
100 sq. decimeters	= 1 sq. meter		
100 sq. meters	= 1 sq. decameter		
100 sq. decameters	= 1 sq. hectometer		
100 sq. hectometers	= 1 sq. kilometer		

1 sq. inch	=	= 6.452 sq. centimeters
1 sq. foot	= 144 sq. inches	= 929 sq. centimeters
1 sq. yard	= 9 sq. feet	= 0.8361 sq. meter
1 sq. rod	= 30¼ sq. yards	= 25.29 sq. meters
1 acre	= 43,560 sq. feet or 160 sq. yards	= 0.4047 hectare
1 sq. mile	= 640 acres	= 259 hectares or 2.59 sq. kilometers

Cubic Measure

1000 cu. millimeters	= 1 cu. centimeter
1000 cu. centimeters	= 1 cu. decimeter
1000 cu. decimeters	= 1 cu. meter

1 cu. inch	=	= 16.387 cu. centimeters
1 cu. foot	= 1728 cu. inches	= 0.0283 cu. meter
1 cu. yard	= 27 cu. feet	= 0.7646 cu. meter

Weights

10 milligrams	= 1 centigram
10 centigrams	= 1 decigram
10 decigrams	= 1 gram
10 grams	= 1 decagram
10 decagrams	= 1 hectogram
10 hectograms	= 1 kilogram
100 kilograms	= 1 quintal
10 quintals	= 1 ton

Liquid Measure

10 milliliters	= 1 centiliter
10 centiliters	= 1 deciliter
10 deciliters	= 1 liter
10 liters	= 1 decaliter
10 decaliters	= 1 hectoliter
10 hectoliters	= 1 kiloliter

Angular and Circular Measure

1 minute	= 60 seconds
1 degree	= 60 minutes
1 right angle	= 90 degrees
1 straight angle	= 180 degrees
1 circle	= 360 degrees

DECIMAL EQUIVALENTS

DECIMAL OF A FOOT						DECIMAL OF AN INCH	
FRACTION	DECIMAL	FRACTION	DECIMAL	FRACTION	DECIMAL	FRACTION	DECIMAL
1/16	0.0052	4-1/16	0.3385	8-1/16	0.6719	1/64	0.015625
1/8	0.0104	4-1/8	0.3438	8-1/8	0.6771	1/32	0.03125
3/16	0.0156	4-3/16	0.3490	8-3/16	0.6823	3/64	0.046875
1/4	0.0208	4-1/4	0.3542	8-1/4	0.6875	1/16	0.0625
5/16	0.0260	4-5/16	0.3594	8-5/16	0.6927	5/64	0.078125
3/8	0.0313	4-3/8	0.3646	8-3/8	0.6979	3/32	0.09375
7/16	0.0365	4-7/16	0.3698	8-7/16	0.7031	7/64	0.109375
1/2	0.0417	4-1/2	0.3750	8-1/2	0.7083	1/8	0.125
9/16	0.0459	4-9/16	0.3802	8-9/16	0.7135	9/64	0.140625
5/8	0.0521	4-5/8	0.3854	8-5/8	0.7188	5/32	0.15625
11/16	0.0573	4-11/16	0.3906	8-11/16	0.7240	11/64	0.171875
3/4	0.0625	4-3/4	0.3958	8-3/4	0.7292	3/16	0.1875
13/16	0.0677	4-13/16	0.4010	8-13/16	0.7344	13/64	0.203125
7/8	0.0729	4-7/8	0.4063	8-7/8	0.7396	7/32	0.21875
15/16	0.0781	4-15/16	0.4115	8-15/16	0.7448	15/64	0.234375
1-	0.0833	5-	0.4167	9-	0.7500	1/4	0.250
1-1/16	0.0885	5-1/16	0.4219	9-1/16	0.7552	17/64	0.265625
1-1/8	0.0938	5-1/8	0.4271	9-1/8	0.7604	9/32	0.28125
1-3/16	0.0990	5-3/16	0.4323	9-3/16	0.7656	19/64	0.296875
1-1/4	0.1042	5-1/4	0.4375	9-1/4	0.7708	5/16	0.3125
1-5/16	0.1094	5-5/16	0.4427	9-5/16	0.7760	21/64	0.328125
1-3/8	0.1146	5-3/8	0.4479	9-3/8	0.7813	11/32	0.34375
1-7/16	0.1198	5-7/16	0.4531	9-7/16	0.7865	23/64	0.359375
1-1/2	0.1250	5-1/2	0.4583	9-1/2	0.7917	3/8	0.375
1-9/16	0.1302	5-9/16	0.4635	9-9/16	0.7969	25/64	0.390625
1-5/8	0.1354	5-5/8	0.4688	9-5/8	0.8021	13/64	0.40625
1-11/16	0.1406	5-11/16	0.4740	9-11/16	0.8073	27/64	0.421875
1-3/4	0.1458	5-3/4	0.4792	9-3/4	0.8125	7/16	0.4375
1-13/16	0.1510	5-13/16	0.4844	9-13/16	0.8177	29/64	0.453125
1-7/8	0.1563	5-7/8	0.4896	9-7/8	0.8229	15/32	0.46875
1-15/16	0.1615	5-15/16	0.4948	9-15/16	0.8281	31/64	0.484375
2-	0.1667	6-	0.5000	10-	0.8333	1/2	0.500
2-1/16	0.1719	6-1/16	0.5052	10-1/16	0.8385	33/64	0.515625
2-1/8	0.1771	6-1/8	0.5104	10-1/8	0.8438	17/32	0.53125
2-3/16	0.1823	6-3/16	0.5156	10-3/16	0.8490	35/64	0.546875
2-1/4	0.1875	6-1/4	0.5208	10-1/4	0.8542	9/16	0.5625
2-5/16	0.1927	6-5/16	0.5260	10-5/16	0.8594	37/64	0.578125
2-3/8	0.1979	6-3/8	0.5313	10-3/8	0.8646	19/32	0.59375
2-7/16	0.2031	6-7/16	0.5365	10-7/16	0.8698	39/64	0.609375
2-1/2	0.2083	6-1/2	0.5417	10-1/2	0.8750	5/8	0.625
2-9/16	0.2135	6-9/16	0.5469	10-9/16	0.8802	41/64	0.640625
2-5/8	0.2188	6-5/8	0.5521	10-5/8	0.8854	21/32	0.65625
2-11/16	0.2240	6-11/16	0.5573	10-11/16	0.8906	43/64	0.671875
2-3/4	0.2292	6-3/4	0.5625	10-3/4	0.8958	11/16	0.6875
2-13/16	0.2344	6-13/16	0.5677	10-13/16	0.9010	45/64	0.703125
2-7/8	0.2396	6-7/8	0.5729	10-7/8	0.9063	23/32	0.71875
2-15/16	0.2448	6-15/16	0.5781	10-15/16	0.9115	47/64	0.734375
3-	0.2500	7-	0.5833	11-	0.9167	3/4	0.750
3-1/16	0.2552	7-1/16	0.5885	11-1/16	0.9219	49/64	0.765625
3-1/8	0.2604	7-1/8	0.5938	11-1/8	0.9271	25/32	0.78125
3-3/16	0.2656	7-3/16	0.5990	11-3/16	0.9323	51/64	0.796875
3-1/4	0.2708	7-1/4	0.6042	11-1/4	0.9375	13/16	0.8125
3-5/16	0.2760	7-5/16	0.6094	11-5/16	0.9427	53/64	0.828125
3-3/8	0.2813	7-3/8	0.6146	11-3/8	0.9479	27/32	0.84375
3-7/16	0.2865	7-7/16	0.6198	11-7/16	0.9531	55/64	0.859375
3-1/2	0.2917	7-1/2	0.6250	11-1/2	0.9583	7/8	0.875
3-9/16	0.2969	7-9/16	0.6302	11-9/16	0.9635	57/64	0.890625
3-5/8	0.3021	7-5/8	0.6354	11-5/8	0.9688	29/32	0.90625
3-11/16	0.3073	7-11/16	0.6406	11-11/16	0.9740	59/64	0.921875
3-3/4	0.3125	7-3/4	0.6458	11-3/4	0.9792	15/16	0.9375
3-13/16	0.3177	7-13/16	0.6510	11-13/16	0.9844	61/64	0.953125
3-7/8	0.3229	7-7/8	0.6563	11-7/8	0.9896	31/32	0.96875
3-15/16	0.3281	7-15/16	0.6615	11-15/16	0.9948	63/64	0.984375
4-	0.3333	8-	0.6667	12-	1.0000	1-	1.000

SAFE LOADS IN LBS. PER SQUARE FOOT ON DIFFERENT TYPES OF SOIL	
MATERIAL	Safe Load Lbs. Sq. Ft.
Soft, wet clay or soft clay and wet sand mixed	2,000
Sand and clay—Firm clay or wet sand	4,000
Dry solid clay or firm dry sand	5,000
Hard clay—Firm coarse sand—Gravel	8,000
Firm coarse sand and gravel mixed	12,000
Hard Pan	20,000

NOISE CONTROL

A variety of techniques can be used to control traffic noise in residential developments.

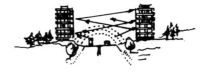

Buildings located in open areas are less noisy than in congested areas.

Traffic arteries between tall buildings are quite noisy.

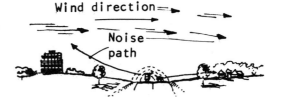

Hollows or depressions are generally noisier than flat open land.

Upwind building locations are less noisy than downwind locations.

NOISE CONTROL

Buildings located at intersections
of major traffic arteries are
extremely noisy due to accelerat-
ing, decelerating, and braking

Buildings located on the crests
of hilly traffic arteries are
very noisy due to low gear
acceleration noise.

Glossary

ABUT . . . . Joining the end of building material
ACCELERATION . . . A mixture to booster setting of concrete or plaster
ACOUSTICAL . . . . Sound absorbing material
ACRE . . . . 43,560 square feet of land area
ADHESIVE . . . . Substance used to hold materials together
AGGREGATE . . . . Material used to make concrete such as stone
ALCOVE . . . . Recessed space off a larger room
ALKYD RESIN . . . . Material used to make paint and stain
ANCHOR BOLT . Threaded rod inserted in wall to anchor sill plate
ANGLE IRON . . . Steel L shaped bar used for supporting brick or block
APRON . . . . Trim under window stool
ARCH . . . . Building material used to form a curve
AREAWAY . Open recessed space in basement window for light and ventilation
ASBESTOS . . . . Fireproof building material
ASH PIT . . . . Area below fireplace to collect ashes
ASPHALT . . . . Insoluble waterproofing material
ASTRAGAL Small moulding or bead used on one of a pair of doors
ATRIUM . . . . Interior outdoor court
ATTIC . . . . Space between roof and ceiling
AWNING WINDOW . . . Outswinging window horizontally hinged
BACKFILL . . . . Earth used to fill around foundation
BALLON FRAME . Type of building with studs extending from sill to top of wall uninterrupted
BALLUSTER . . Small vertical member between stairs and top rail
BANNISTER . . . . Stair rail
BASEBOARD . . . . Wall covering at intersection of floor and wall
BASECOAT . . . . First coat of plaster
BATTEN . . . . Strip of wood covering joint
BATTER BOARD . . . Horizontal boards used to lay out building
BAY WINDOW . . . . Outward from wall projecting window
BEAD . . . . Narrow rounded moulding
BEAM . . . . . Horizontal structural member supporting loads
BEARING PARTITION . . . . Wall for supporting loads
BEARING PLATE . . Support member used to distribute load over wide area
BENCH MARK . . . . Permanent mark on ground used in surveying
BEVEL SIDING . . . Exterior finish thicker at bottom than at top

BIBB . . . . Threaded hose connection
BIRD'S MOUTH-OR HEEL . . . . . . End of rafter resting on plate
BLIND NAILING . . . . Concealed nails
BLOCKING . . . . Wood Filler
BOARD FOOT . . . Unit for measuring lumber 1" thick, 12" wide and 12" long
BOND . . . . . Arrangement of masonry units in a wall to lock wall
BRICK VENEER . . . . Brick facing
BRIDGING . . . . Cross bracing between joists and studs
BROWN COAT . . . . Second coat of plaster
BTU . . . . British Thermal Unit used to measure heat
BUILT-UP BEAM Beam constructed of small members put together
BUILT-UP ROOF . . . . Several layers of felt and asphalt
BULKHEAD . . . . Entrance from basement floor
BUTT . . . . Door hinge
CANT . . . . . . Angular roof board to eliminate sharp right angles
CANTILEVER . . . . . A beam fixed on one end free of the other
CASEMENT WINDOW . . . . . . Window opening similar to door
CASING . . . . Frame around door or window opening
CATCH BASIN . . . . Receptacle for collecting water underground
CAULKING . . . . . Waterproof material to seal joints and cracks
CEMENT PLASTER . . . . . . Plaster containing portland cement
CENTER TO CENTER . . . Measurement center of one member to center of another
CHAIR RAIL . . Rail along wall to prevent chair from marring wall
CHASE . . Vertical space containing mechanical piping and wiring
CHORD . . . . . . Horizontal member of truss connecting corners
CIRCUIT . . . . Path for electrical current
CIRCUIT BREAKER . . . . Opening and closing a circuit
CLAPBOARD . . . . Exterior siding thicker at one edge
CLEAT . . . . Wood strip holding two units together
COLLAR BEAM . . Horizontal member tieing two opposite rafters together
COMMON NAILS . . . . Large headed nails
CONDUCTOR . . . . Pipe to lead water from roof
CONDUIT . . . . Pipe carrying electric wires
CONVECTOR . . . . Heat transfer surface
COPE . . . . Cut end of moulded wood same contour as face
CORBEL . . . . To extend outward to carry superincumbent load
CORNER BEAD . . . . Metal bead at external corners

387

CORNICE . . . . Roof projection beyond wall
COUNTER FLASHING . . . . Flashing under exposed flashing
COUNTERSUNK . . . . Recessed head of nail or screw
COVE . . . . Inside curve (concave) shape to mate with right angle moulding
CRAWL SPACE . . . . . . Shallow space between ground and floor
CRICKET . . . . Pitched roof behind chimney to divert water
CROSS BRACING . . . . Diagonal boards
CROWN MOULDING . . . Decorative moulding used at ceiling and under roof overhang
CUPOLA . Small structure on top of roof usually holding weather-vane
CURTAIN WALL . Wall used for separation only non-load bearing
DADO . . . . Groove across grain of board
DAMPER . . . . Movable steel plate to regulate draft
DARBY . . . . Flat tool used for plastering
DEAD LOAD . . . . Motionless load such as wind, snow, etc.
DECIBEL . . . . Measurement of sound
DIAMOND MESH . . . . Metal lath
DIMENSION . . . . Lumber framing 2" thick
DOOR CASING . . . . Trim around door opening
DOOR FRAME . . . . Enclosure for supporting door
DOOR JAMB . . . . Vertical pieces of door frame
DOOR SILL . . . . Bottom of door frame (threshold)
DOOR STOP . . . . Wood strip stopping door at frame
DORMER . . . . Structure projecting from roof
DOUBLE HEADER . Two pieces of framing lumber nailed together
DOUBLE HUNG . . . . Window moving up and down
DOVETAIL JOINT . . . . Wedge shaped wood joint
DOWN SPOUT . . . . . Vertical pipe carrying rain water from roof
DRAIN . . . . Pipe carrying waste water
DRIP CAP Metal used to prevent water from running down window or door
DRY ROT . . . . Wood decay
DRY WALL . . . Interior use of paper covered plaster in large sheets
DRY WELL . . . . Shallow well for rain water disposal
DUCT . . . . Sheet metal shaft for air distribution
DUPLEX OUTLET . . . . Electrical plug
DUTCHMAN . . . . Wood piece to cover error
EAVE . . . . Lower portion of roof extended beyond wall
EFFLORESCENSE . . White fleecy surface deposit found on brick wall
ELBOW . . . . L shaped pipe fitting
ELEVATION . . . . Vertical side projection
ESCUTCHEON Decorative plate around door lock and pipe passing through floor or wall
EXCAVATION . . . . Hole formed by removing earth
EXPANDED METAL . . . . Diamond shaped slit sheet metal
EXPANSION JOINT . Bituminous filler used to prevent crakcing of floor and wall through expansion due to temperature change
FACADE . . . . Front or face of building
FACE BRICK . . . . Finish brick
FACE NAIL . . . . Nail driven through face of material
FASCIA . . . . Horizontal member on edge of roof
FELT PAPER . . . Thin sheet paper used for roofing and sheathing
FENESTRATION . . . . Windows and doors
FIBERBOARD . . . . Building board of fiberous material
FILL . . . . Raise subgrade
FIRE BRICK . . . . Brick to withstand high temperatures
FIRE DOOR . . . . Door to resist fire
FIRE STOP . . . . Obstruction of passage to prevent spread of fire
FIRE WALL . . . . Resist spread of fire
FLASHING . . . . Seal to prevent leaks
FLOAT . . . . Tool used for finishing concrete or plaster
FLUE . . . . Chimney passage for smoke and gases
FLUE LINING . . . . Terra-cotta or clay flue in chimney
FOOTING . . . . Foundation base of concrete
FRIEZE . . . . Wall directly under roof overhang
FURRING . . . . Wood strips fastened to wall or ceiling
FUSE . . . . Electric current cut-off
GABLE . . . . Triangular portion at end of roof
GALVANIZED . . . . Zinc coated metal
GAMBREL . . . . Two plained roof surface or slope
GIRDER . . . . Horizontal structural member
GLAZING . . . . Placing glass in windows or frame
GRADE . . . . Level of ground
GRAIN . . . . Arrangement of wood fibers
GRAVEL STOP . . . . Metal strip around edge of roof

GROUND . . . . Wood plaster stop
GROUT . . . . Plaster like material to seal joints
GUTTER . . . . Trough to carry water from roof
GYPSUM BOARD . . . . . . Plaster sandwich with paper covering
HALF TIMBER . . . Boards geometrically placed-space filled with stucco or masonry
HANGER . . . . Iron strap to support joists
HEADER . . . . Small beam
HEARTH . . . . Fireproof front of fireplace
HEARTWOOD . . . . Between pitch and sapwood of tree
HIP RAFTER . . . . Rafter from plate to ridge intersecting roof pitch
HIP ROOF . . . . Pitched on all sides
HOSE BIBB . . . . Threaded water pipe connection for hose
I BEAM . . . . steel beam I shaped
INCANDESCENT LAMP . . Bulb with filament wire used for light from electricity
INTERIOR TRIM . . . . All inside finish
JACK RAFTER . . . . Short rafter between wall and ridge
JALOUSIE . . . . Long narrow glass slats in windows
JAMB . . . . Vertical frame of door or window
JOIST . . . . Member supporting floor or ceiling
JOURNEYMAN . . . . Skilled tradesman
KALAMEIN . . . . . Metal covered wood door used for fire door
KD . . . . Knocked down must be assembled
KILN . . . . Oven for drying lumber
KIP . . . . 1,000 lbs
KNEE WALL . . . . Low wall on 1½ story house
KNOT . . . . Cross section of tree branch
LAG SCREW . . . . Square headed wood screw
LALLY COLUMN . . . . Steel column to support beam
LAMINATE . . . . Several layers of material bonded together
LATH . . . . Base used for plaster
LAVATORY . . . . Wash basin
LEADER . . . . Vertical pipe carrying rain water
LEDGER . . . . Wood strip for joist bearing
LINEAL FOOT . . . . Measure on straight line
LINTEL . . . . Horizontal wall opening supporting load
LIVE LOAD . . . . . .Movable articles such as furniture, people, etc.
LOAD BEARING WALL . . . . Wall carrying load
LOOKOUT . . . . Short lumber supporting projected cornice
M . . . . 1,000 Units
MAIN RUNNERS . . . . Heaviest supporting member of suspended ceiling
MANHOLE . . . . Sewer cover
MANSARD . . . . Two planed roof
MANTEL . . . . Fireplace shelf
MASTIC . . . . Waterproofing material to seal cracks
MATCHED LUMBER . . . . . . Tongue and grooved edge lumber
MECHANICAL EQUIPMENT . Plumbing, heating, ventilating, air-conditioning and electrical
MEETING RAIL . . . . . . Horizontal rail of double hung window
MEMBRANE . . . . Waterproofing
MESH . . . . Crossing of parallel wires forming a grid
METAL LATH . . . . Plaster base
MILLWORK . . . . Finish wood products
MITRE . . . . Beveled cut
MODULAR . . . . Fixed repeated divisional units
MONOLITHIC . . . . Concrete cast in one unit
MORTAR . . . . Mixture of sand cement and water
MORTISE . . . . Recessed cut into surface
MOSAIC . . . . Small colored glass or tile
MOTIF . . . . Design theme
MOULDING . . . . Finish trim
MULLION . . . Vertical bar section separating two or more doors or windows
MUNTIN . . . . Bar separating or dividing glass
NAIL SET . . . . Small tool used to recess nails
NEWEL . . . . Main post of stair rail
NOMINAL . . . . Lumber size before drying
NON-BEARING PARTITION . . . . Divider wall non-load bearing
NOSING . . . . Projected stair tread edge
ON CENTER-O.C. . Center to center measurement of one member to another
OUTLET . . . . Electrical wire connections
OVERHANG . . . . Projection beyond wall or roof
PALLETS . . . . Portable
PANEL . . . . Flat surface framed by thicker material

PANELBOARD . . . . Electric circuit control center
PARAPET . . . . Wall projecting above roof
PARGE . . . . To coat surface with plaster or mortar
PARQUET . . . . Patterned wood flooring
PARTICLE BOARD . . . . . Flat composition board of wood chips
PARTITION . . . . Dividing wall
PENNY . . . . A term used for length and weight of nails
PERSPECTIVE . . . . Pictorial drawing
PICTURE MOULD . . . . Moulding to hang pictures
PILASTER . . . . Built in column against wall
PILE . . . . Heavy structural column forced into earth
PITCH . . . . Roof slope
PLAIN SAWED . . . . . . Lumber cut on a tangent to growth rings
PLANCHER . . . . Underside of cornice
PLANK . . . . Lumber 2" thick or more
PLATE . . . . . Horizontal member for supporting floor or roof
PLENUM . Forced chamber of air connected to distribution ducts
PLINTH . . . . Projecting band at bottom of casing
PLUMB . . . . Level vertically
PLYWOOD . . . Three or more layers of flat sheets of wood joined
together
POINTING . . . . Filling joints in masonry wall
PORTLAND CEMENT . . . Powdered rock used to make concrete
POST & BEAM . . . . Type of construction using column and beam
PRE-CAST . . . Concrete units made in shop delivered for erection
PRE-FABRICATED . . . . Built in sections
PRIME COAT . . . . First coat of paint
PUMICE . . . . Crushed volcanic lava used for polishing
PURLIN . . . . Structural member
QUARTER ROUND . . . . Small moulding
QUARTER SAWED . . . . Lumber cut 90° to annual rings
QUARTER TILE . . . . Unglazed floor tile
QUOINS . . . . Wall projection at corners
RABBET . . . . Grooved edge to receive another piece
RADIANT HEAT . . . . Concealed in floor or ceiling
RAFTER . . . . Roof supporting member
RAKE . . . . Trim parallel to roof slope
READY MIX CONCRETE . . . . Pre-mixed at plant
REFLECTIVE INSULATION . . . . . Surfaced to reduce heat loss
REINFORCED CONCRETE . . Concrete embedded with steel rods
RESILIENT . . . . . Ability of material to withstand original shape
RETAINING WALL . . . . Lateral pressure support for earth
RETARDER . . . . Reduce evaporation rate
REVEAL . . . . Visible part of door or window jamb
RIBBON . . . . Narrow wood strip to support joists
RIDGE . . . . Top edge of roof
RIP RAP . . . . Stone placed to reduce erosion
RISER . . . . Vertical part of step
ROCK LATH . . . . Plaster base
ROLL ROOFING . . . . Roof covering material
ROOF SHEATHING . . . . Covering of roof rafters
ROTARY CUT . . . . Shaving log on lathe
ROUGH OPENING . . . . Unfinished opening
RUN . . . . Horizontal distance of stairs
SADDLE . . . . Small pitched roof behind chimney to divert water
SASH . . . . A frame for holding panes of glass in a window
SASH CORD . . . . Rope to counterbalance double hung sash
SCAFFOLD . . . . Temporary platform
SCRATCH COAT . . . . First coat plaster
SCRIBE . . . . Fitting to an irregular surface
SCUTTLE . . . . Opening in roof for access
SEASONING . . . . Removing moisture from wood
SEPTIC TANK . . . . Sewage settling tank
SHAKE . . . . Hand split shingles
SHEATHING . . . . Covering over studs or rafters
SHED ROOF . . . . Single pitched roof
SHIM . . . . Wedge

SHINGLE . . . . Exterior wall or roof covering
SHIPLAP . . . . Joint between two wood pieces
SHOE MOULD . . . . . Small moulding against baseboard at floor
SHORING . . . . Bracing to support structure during construction
SIDING . . . . Finished outside surface
SILL . . . . . . Wood member on top of foundation-wood member
across window or door bottom
SKIM COAT . . . . Finish coat usually plaster
SLEEPER . . . . . Wood piece on or in concrete to nail wood floor
SOFFIT . . . . Underside of overhang
SOFT WOOD . . . . From tree having needles
SOIL STACK . . . . Vertical plumbing waste discharge pipe
SOLE . . . . Horizontal member under studs
SOLID BRIDGING . . Full size members placed between framing
SPACKLE . . . . Plaster used to cover wall board joints
SPECIFICATIONS . . . . Written detail of building products
SPLASH BLOCK Masonry block to spread water from roof drain at
ground
STAGGER . . . . Alternate intervals
STAKE . . . . Wedge shaped stick driven in ground
STILE . . . . Vertical member of door
STIRRUP . . . . Heavy metal strap to support framing
STOOL . . . . Shelf on bottom of window inside
STOOP . . . . Small platform
STOP BEAD . . . . Moulding used to stop door in frame
STORY POLE . . . . Rod or stick used for measuring units
STRAIGHT EDGE . . . . True edge piece used for accuracy
STRETCHER . . . . Long side of brick exposed
STRINGER . . . . Stair supports
STUCCO . . . . Outside finish plaster
STUDS . . . . Vertical wall framing members
SUB FLOOR . . . . Rough floor under finish floor
SUSPENDED CEILING . . . . Hanging ceiling
TAIL BEAM . . . . Short framing member
TEE BEAM . . . . Frame member
TENSILE STRENGTH . . . . Strength of building material to
support load
TERMITE SHIELD . . . . Metal used to prevent termite damage to
building
TERRA COTTA . . . . Sand and clay baked building material
TERRAZZO . Marble chips and conc. surface ground smooth floor
THRESHOLD . . . . Sill on bottom of door frame
THROAT . . . . Smoke passage above fireplace
TOE NAIL . . . . Nail driven at angle
TOE SPACE . . . . Recessed space at floor under counter
TONGUE . . . . Projection bead of board
TRANSOM . . . . Panel opening above door
TRAP . . . . U-shaped pipe below plumbing fixture
TREAD . . . . Horizontal part of stairs
TRIM . . . . Finish wood work
TROWEL . . . . Tool used for finishing plaster or concrete
TRUSS . . . . No column roof support
UNDERLAYMENT . . . . Material under floor
UPRIGHT . . . . Timber support rafters
VALLEY . . . . Trough formed at roof intersecting slopes
VALLEY RAFTER . . . . . Diagonal rafter intersecting roof slopes
VALVE . . . . Fluid or liquid flow regulator
VAPOR BARRIER Water tight material to prevent passage of vapor
VENEER . . . . Thin faced covering
VENT . . . . Vertical pipe used to ventilate plumbing
WAINSCOT . . . . Lower part of two part wall
WATERTABLE Extend around building at bottom of exterior wall
WEATHERSTRIP . . . . Sealing of doors and windows
WEEP HOLE . . . . Opening at bottom of wall for water drainage
WELL OPENING . . . . Floor opening for stairs
WINDER . . . . Turning of stairs
WIRE GLASS . . . . Wire mesh in glass
WYTHE . . . . Single width of masonry wall

Abbreviations

Acoustic	ACST	Between	BET
Acoustical Plaster	ACST PL	Bevel	BEV
Addition	ADD	Blocking	BLKG
Adhesive	.ADH	Board	BD
Aggregate	AGGR	Board Feet	BD FT
Air Conditioning	AIR COND. OR A.C	Board Measure	BM
Alternate	ALT	Book Shelves	BK SH
Alternating Current	AC	Bottom	BOT
Aluminum	ALUM	Boulevard	BLVD
American Institute of Architects	A.I.A.	Bracket	BRKT
American Institute of Steel Construction	A.I.S.C.	Brass	BR
American Society of Heating, Ventilating Engineers	A.S.H.V.E.	British Thermal Unit	BTU
American Society of Testing Materials	A.S.T.M.	Bronze	BRZ
American Wire Gauge	AWG	Broom Closet	BC
Amount	AMT	Building	BLDG
Ampere	AMP	Building Line	BL
Anchor Bolt	AB	Built In	BLT IN
Angle	L	Bulkhead	BLKHD
Apartment	APT	Bulletin Board	BB
Approval	APP	Buzzer	BZ
Approximate	APPROX	By	2"x4" (example)
Architect	ARCH	Cabinet	CAB
Architectural Terra Cotta	ATC	Candlepower	CP
Area	A	Carpenter	CARP
Asbestos	ASB	Casing	CSG
Asphalt	ASPH	Cast Iron	CI
Asphalt Tile	AT	Catch Basin	CB
Assemble	ASSEM	Caulking	CLKG
Assembly	ASSBY	Ceiling	CLG
Associate	ASSOC	Cellar	CEL
At	@	Cement	CEM
Automatic Pressure	ATM PRESS	Cement Mortar	CEMT ' MR
Automobile	AUTO	Cement Plastic	CMT ' PL
Avenue	AVE.	Center to Center	CC or OC or C
Average	AVG	Ceramic Tile	CT
Balcony	BLCNY	Cesspool	CP
Basement	BSMT	Channel	C
Bathroom	B	Circuit	CIR
Beam	BM	Circuit Breaker	CKT' BR
Bedroom	BR	Cleanout	CO
Bench Mark	BM	Closet	CLO
		Clothes Dryer	CL'D

Coefficient	COEF
Cold Water	CW
Combination	COMB
Composition	COMP
Concrete	CONC
Concrete Block	CB
Concrete Floor	CON FL
Concrete Masonry Unit	CMU
Construction	CONST
Construction Specification Institute	C.S.I.
Contractor	CONTR
Copper	CPR
Counter	CNTR
Countersunk	CSNK
Courses	C
Cover	COV
Cross Section	X SECT
Cubic	CU
Cubic Feet	CU FT
Cubic Feet Minute	CFM
Cubic Inch	CU IN
Cubic Yard	CU YD
Damper	DMPR
Dampproofing	DMPRF
Decibel	DB
Decorative	DEC
Degree Fahrenheit	0° F
Detail	DET
Diagram	DIA
Diameter	DIA. OR Ø
Dimension	DIM
Dining Room	DR
Direct Current	D. C.
Dishwasher	DW
Distance	DIST
Ditto	DO
Divide	DIV
Door	DR
Double Hung Window	DH W
Double Strength Glass Grade A	DSA
Double Strength Glass Grade B	DSB
Dowel	DWL
Down	DN
Downspout	DS
Drain	DR
Drainboard	DB
Drawing	DWG
Dressed and Matched Four Sides	D&M4S
Drinking Fountain	DF
Dryer	D
Drywall	DW
Dry Well	DW
Each	EA
East	E
Edge Grain	EG
Elbow	ELL
Electric	ELEC
Elevator	ELEV
Emergency	EMERGCY
Enclosure	ENCL
Engineer	ENG
Entrance	ENT
Equipment	EQUIP
Estimate	EST
Excavate	EXC
Expansion Joint	EX JT
Extension	EXT
Exterior	EXT
Extra Heavy	XH
Fabricate	FAB
Face to Face	F to F
Facing Tile	FT
Fahrenheit	F
Family Room	FAM R
Federal Housing Administration	FHA
Feet	FT
Feet Per Minute	FPM
Feet Per Second	FPS
Figure	FIG
Finish	FIN
Finish Floor	FIN FL
Fire Brick	FB
Fire Extinguisher	FX
Fire Hose	FH
Fireproof	FP
Fitting	FITG
Fixture	FIXT
Flange	FLG
Flashing	FL
Floor	FL
Floor Drain	FD
Fluorescent	FLUOR
Foot Board Measure	FBM
Footing	FTG
Foundation	FDN
Frame	FR
Fresh Air Intake	FAI
Front	FR
Full Size	FS
Furred Ceiling	F CLG
Gallon	GAL
Galvanized	GALV
Gauge	GA
Glass Block	GL BL
Government	GOVT
Grade	GR
Granite	GR
Grating	GRTG
Grease Trap	GT
Gypsum	GYP
Hall	H
Hardware	HDW
Hardwood	HDWD
Head	HD
Heater	HTR
Height	HT
Hexagon	HEX
Hollow Metal	HM
Horizontal	HORIZ
Horse Power	HP
Hose Bibb	HB
Hot Water	HW
Hour	HR
House	HSE
Hundred	C
I Beam	I
Inches	" OR IN
Information	INFO
Inside Diameter	ID
Insulation	INSUL
Interior	INT
Joint	JT
Joist	JST
Kalamein	KAL
Kiln Dried	KD
Kilowatt	KW
Kitchen	KIT
Kitchen Cabinet	KIT CAB
Kitchen Sink	KIT S
Knocked Down	KD
Laboratory	LAB
Ladder	LAD
Laminated	LAM
Landing	L
Latitude	LAT
Laundry	L
Laundry Chute	LC
Lavatory	LAV
Leader	LDR
Left	L
Length	LGTH
Level	LEV
Library	LIB
Light	LT

Light Weight Concrete	LWC
Limestone	LS
Lineal Feet	LF
Linen Closet	L CL
Lining	LNG
Linoleum	LINO
Living Room	LR
Long	LG
Louver	LVR
Lumber	LBR
Machine	MACH
Manufacturer	MFG
Marble	MBL
Mark	MK
Masonry Opening	MO
Material	MAT
Maximum	MAX
Mechanical	MECH
Medicine Cabinet	MED C
Medium	MED
Metal	MET
Millemeter	m
Minimum	MIN
Miscellaneous	MISC
Model	MOD
Modular	MOD
Moulding	MLDG
National	NAT
National Board of Fire Underwriters	N.B.F.U.
National Electrical Code	N.E.C.
National Lumber Manufacturers Association	N.L.M.A.
Nominal	NOM
North	N
Not In Contract	N.I.C.
Number	NO. OR #
Octogan	OCT
Office	OFF
On Center	OC
Opening	OPNG
Opposite	OPP
Ornament	ORN
Ounce	OZ
Outside Diameter	OD
Overhead	OVHD
Page	PG
Painted	PTD
Pair	PR
Panel	PNL
Parallel	PAR
Partition	PTN
Passage	PASS
Pedestal	PED
Penny	d
Percent	%
Perforated	PERF
Perpendicular	PERP
Piece	PC
Plaster	PLAS
Plate	P
Plate Glass	P GL
Platform	PLTFM
Plumbing	PLMB
Point	P
Polish	POL
Polyvinyl Chloride	PVC
Position	POS
Pounds	LB OR #
Poured Concrete	P/C
Precast	PRCST
Prefabricate	PREFAB
Property	PROP
Push Button	PB
Quantity	QTY
Quart	QT
Radiator	RAD
Radius	R
Random length and width	RL&W
Rang	R

Receptacle	RECP
Recessed	REC
Rectangle	RECT
Redwood	RDWD
Reference	REF
Refrigerator	REFG
Register	REG
Reinforced Concrete	REINF
Required	REQ
Return	RET
Revision	REV
Revolution Per Minute	RPM
Right	R
Right Hand	RH
Riser	R
Road	RD
Roof	RF
Roof Drain	RD
Roofing	RFG
Room	RM
Rough	RGH
Round	RD
Rubber	R
Saddle	S
Schedule	SCH
Screen	SCR
Second	SEC
Section	SECT
Self Closing	SC
Service	SERV
Sewer	SEW
Sheathing	SHTNG
Sheet Metal	SM
Shelves	SH
Shower	SH
Siding	SDG
Sill Cock	SC
Single Strength Grade A Glass	SAS
Single Strength Grade B Glass	SBS
Sink	S
Slop Sink	SS
Socket	SOC
Soil Pipe	SP
South	S
Specifications	SPEC
Square Feet	SQ FT OR ⊡
Stairs	ST
Standard	STD
Stand Pipe	STP
Station	STA
Steel	ST
Steel Plate	SP
Stirrup	STIR
Stock	STK
Stone	ST
Street	ST
String	STR
Structural	STR
Substitute	SUB
Supersede	SUPSD
Supplement	SUPP
Supply	SUP
Surface	SUR
Surface 2 Sides	S2S
Surface 4 sides	S4S
Suspended Ceiling	SUS CLG
Switch	SW
Symbol	SYM
System	SYS
Tar & Gravel	T & G
Technical	TECH
Tee	T
Telephone	TEL
Television	TV
Temperature	TEMP
Terra-Cotta	TC
Terrazzo	TER
Thermostat	THERMO

Thickness	THK	Water	W
Thousand	M	Water Closet	WC
Thread	THD	Waterproof	WP
Tongue and Groove	T & G	Watts	W
Tread	T	Weatherstrip	WS
Typical	TYP	Weephole	WH
Ultimate	ULT	Weight	WT
Unfinished	UNFIN	West	W
United States Gauge	USG	Wide Flange Beam	WF
Urinal	UR	Width	WTH
Vanity	VAN	Window	WDH
Vent	V	Wire Glass	W GL
Vertical	VERT	With	W/
Vestibule	VEST	Without	WO/
Volts	V	Wood	WD
Volume	VOL	Wrought Iron	WI
Wall Cabinet	W/CAB	Yards	YD
Wall Vent	WV	Zinc	Z OR ZN

Index